本书为国家重点研发计划课题"长江流域文明进程研究"（课题编号 2020YFC1521603）和"中华文明起源进程中的生业、资源与技术研究"（课题编号 2020YFC1521606）及国家文物局"考古中国"重大项目"长江下游区域文明模式研究"的阶段性成果

This report is the phased objective of National Key R&D Program of China "Study on the Yangtze River Civilization" (Grant NO.2020YFC1521603) and "Study of Subsistence, Resources and Technology in the Origin of Chinese Civilization" (Grant NO. 2020YFC1521606), and "the Yangtze River Downstream Regional Civilization", the major projects of "Archaeology China" of National Cultural Heritage Administration.

本书出版得到浙江省委宣传部"良渚考古系列图书出版"项目经费的资助

The publication of this book is funded by "Liangzhu Archaeological Books Publication Project" by Publicity Department of Zhejiang Provincial Party Committee.

浙江省文物考古研究所田野考古报告　第 49 号

Field Archaeological Report N0. 49

Zhejiang Provincial Institute of Cultural Relics and Archaeology

# YAOSHAN

Zhejiang Provincial Institute of Cultural Relics and Archaeology

Cultural Relics Press

Beijing · 2022

图书在版编目（CIP）数据

瑶山 = YAOSHAN：英文 / 浙江省文物考古研究所编译. -- 北京：文物出版社, 2022.10
ISBN 978-7-5010-7441-9

Ⅰ.①瑶… Ⅱ.①浙… Ⅲ.①良渚文化—墓葬（考古）—发掘报告—杭州—英文 Ⅳ.①K878.85

中国版本图书馆CIP数据核字（2022）第065274号


审图号：GS（2022）0182号


浙江省文物考古研究所田野考古报告　　第49号

# YAOSHAN

编　　译：浙江省文物考古研究所

责任编辑：黄　曲　崔叶舟
责任印制：张　丽
出版发行：文物出版社
装帧设计：雅昌设计中心
社　　址：北京市东城区东直门内北小街2号楼
邮　　编：100007
网　　址：http://www.wenwu.com
经　　销：新华书店
印　　刷：北京雅昌艺术印刷有限公司
开　　本：889mm×1194mm　1/16
印　　张：24.5
版　　次：2022年10月第1版
印　　次：2022年10月第1次印刷
书　　号：ISBN 978-7-5010-7441-9
定　　价：480.00元

# INTRODUCTION

On July 6, 2019, the Liangzhu City site passed the deliberation on the 43rd World Heritage Conference and was listed on the World Heritage List. During the application process of Liangzhu City, Hangzhou Liangzhu Archaeological Site Administrative District Management Committee once organized the translation of the English versions of *Yaoshan* and *Fanshan*. In March 2019, I proposed to publish two books in English, which was supported by Liu Bin, director of Zhejiang Provincial Institute of Cultural Relics and Archaeology, and agreed by Wang Mingda, director of *Fanshan* report, and Rui Guoyao, director of *Yaoshan* report. In order to continue to do a solid job in the archaeological and propaganda work of Liangzhu City and Liangzhu culture, in 2020, with the strong support of the Publicity Department of Zhejiang Provincial Party Committee, the English versions of *Yaoshan*, *Fanshan* and other important archaeological reports were officially listed in the "Liangzhu Archaeological Books Publication Project".

Reports *Yaoshan* and *Fanshan* compiled by Zhejiang Provincial Institute of Cultural Relics and Archaeology were published by Cultural Relics Press in 2003 and 2005 respectively as the first and second archaeological reports of Liangzhu Site Cluster. When organizing the translation of the English versions of two books, we decided to revise the reports because it involved the re-collation of the original Chinese versions of the two reports and also considered that the original reports were almost out of print. The English versions of *Yaoshan* and *Fanshan* have been supplemented and adjusted according to the latest revised Chinese version.

Thanks to Mr. Li Xinwei's promise, his article *Returning to Nature – Post-reading of first of the Archaeological Reports of Liangzhu Site Cluster: Yaoshan* is included in the revised version, as the substitute of the preface.

I am responsible for the revision of *Yaoshan* and *Fanshan*, with great assistance from Mr. Chen Minghui and Ms. Zhu Yefei of Zhejiang Provincial Institute of Cultural Relics and Archaeology and Mr. Xia Yong of Liangzhu Museum.

The original English translation of *Yaoshan* was commissioned to a translation company by the Hangzhou Liangzhu Archaeological Site Administrative District Management Committee. Zhu Xiaoyu and Gao Rui, teachers of the Institute of Translation studies, Zhejiang University, Feng Yitian, Wang Yanni, Ma Qingquan, He Peifan, Ruan Yishuai and Liu Meijun, students from Zhu Kezhen College, and Gao Jie from the Hangzhou Liangzhu Archaeological Site Administrative District Management Committee made preliminary proofreading. Chen Minghui and Zhu Yefei from Zhejiang Provincial Institute of Cultural Relics and Archaeology completed the final proofreading.

    Thanks to Huang Qu and Cui Yezhou, responsible editors of Cultural Relics Press for their support and hard work.

    Thanks again to the predecessors and colleagues who worked hard for the Fanshan and Yaoshan archaeological work.

*Fang Xiangming*
January 31, 2022

The Substitute of the Preface

# RETURNING TO NATURE

– Post-reading of first of the Archaeological Reports of Liangzhu Site Cluster: Yaoshan

Li Xinwei

Liangzhu culture was the star of Chinese prehistoric archaeology in the last decade of the 20th century. In January 1988, the first issue of *Cultural Relics* published brief reports on the excavation of the two sites of Fanshan and Yaoshan. Liangzhu culture, which had just passed its fiftieth birthday in a lonely state, came on the stage again, shining with jewels. *Cong*, *huang* semi-circular pendant, *bi* disc, *yue* axe, high altar and elite tombs, shook the whole Chinese archaeology, attracting many scholars. Unprecedentedly heated discussion followed, and the jade artifacts had the right to become the focus of attention, which greatly promoted the understanding of the social nature of Liangzhu culture and its unique development path, and triggered in-depth thinking on the diversified development pattern of Chinese prehistoric society. However, the dilemma also follows, the lack of basic archaeological materials and excessive enthusiasm for jade made the research of Liangzhu culture gradually immersed in a flashy atmosphere, and it was difficult to make a breakthrough. Although the 60th birthday of Liangzhu culture was glamorous, but it was silent after the publication of the collection of celebrating papers, and "Liangzhu" is no longer a keyword that can be seen everywhere in various periodicals. At the symposium on the origin of Chinese civilization held in Beijing in 2001, scholars in Liangzhu's hometown were silent little words. I heard that they were doing solid excavation and data sorting, then thought, this place had many talents, their comeback day would not be too far.

In January this year, when I finally saw the excellent printed report of *Yaoshan*, I was very excited. Everyone who cares deeply about Liangzhu culture will feel the same way. The cover was not satisfactory, the overall tone was light, the layout was a bit chaotic, if more solemn might be better, but the content was pleasantly surprised. Yan Wenming said in his article *Talk on the Compilation of Archaeological Reports*, "Any archaeological report should be a faithful record and concentrated expression of field archaeological work." "Still holding a lute and half covering the face" is a taboo in archaeological reports. What makes "Lovers of Liangzhu" feel most gratified was the comprehensive and truthful presentation of the materials, which brings back a fresh air of nature and dissipates the diffuse vanity.

The introduction of annual excavation process is well presented. The discovery of the central altar and tombs in 1987 revealed the core of the site;  In 1996, the western No.2 and northern No. 2 stone revetments were discovered, and it was realized that the scale of the site was far beyond the original imagination.  In the first half of 1997, the southern No. 1, southern No. 2, western No. 3, western No. 4 stone revetments and M14 were discovered, and the accumulation process of the central part of the site was basically revealed.  In the second half of 1997, western No. 5 and western No. 6 stone revetments were discovered, which gave us a further understanding of the layout of the whole site.  In 1998, supplementary excavations were carried out in the northeast, northwest and south of the site, "basically reveal the layout of the Yaoshan site and the accumulation and construction process of the main part".  Although the overall layout of Yaoshan site is still confusing due to the restriction of later destruction and "protective excavation", there is no doubt that there has been significant progress compared with the understanding in 1987. The authors clearly describe the academic objectives and methods of each field work.  Readers can deeply feel that it is impossible to comprehensively understand such high-level sites as Yaoshan in one move, but requires solid field work guided by a broad academic vision. Of particular note are the large number of images that provide a wealth of visual information.  There are nine profile maps at the center of the site alone, providing maximum stratigraphic information.  Therefore, the readers who are hard to experience the excavation process have the feeling of watching the live broadcast, and can basically stand on an equal footing with the digger and conduct research according to the real objective data rather than the information "revealed" by the digger according to their own subjective will, so as to form their own understanding. There is a "risk" in doing so – flaws in fieldwork and data analysis are more likely to be exposed, and the author's ideas more likely to be challenged by readers.  For example, some readers may be inclined to think that grey-earthen ditch and tombs are not necessarily belonging to the latest period, based on the stratigraphic relationships provided by the author.  But I believe that the returning to nature style of *Yaoshan* commands more visceral respect than an archeological report that is impeccable because it makes it difficult for the reader to acquire complete material.

*Yaoshan*'s comprehensive and detailed introduction of all the tombs will win more than respect – "Lovers of Liangzhu", who are especially sensitive, will surely say good. The text and color maps of *Yaoshan* are arranged according to tomb numbers, making it very easy to retrieve. Previous published reports, *Zhaobaogou* and *Danangou*, adopted a similar structure and were well received. Thus, we can feel a quiet change: more attention is being paid to the coexistence relationship or unearthed context of the remains than to the shape of the remains. In the 1950s and 1960s, the research orientation of "seeing things and seeing people" was strongly called for. Now it has tended to flow and has naturally guided the practice of most scholars. For these tombs of great significance in Yaoshan, it is the highest courtesy to publish data without omission in accordance with the coexistence relationship. The details of the information published by the authors exceeded my expectation: each jade particle, only a few millimeters long and wide, was given the opportunity to be displayed, with plans and profiles; M10:97 comprise 201 pieces of jade tubes, each of which is illustrated and covers an entire page. Will no one accuse of pettiness? For purely typological studies, a few typical specimens are indeed sufficient. However, it is essential to study the jade production and system of using jade artifacts. When we feel that archaeological data are "useless", it is often because we have not found a way to extract valuable information from them.

The maps of tombs are even more praiseworthy. There are three characteristics. First, in addition to the panoramic view of the tomb, there are local close-up pictures, which describe in detail the unearthed background of important burial objects. Second, it shows the morphological characteristics of important artifacts in an all-round way. Most artifacts have plans, overhead views and side views, and many artifacts have back views, expansion drawings and rubbings. Such as M9:1-2 cylindrical jade object with three expansion drawings of side view and rubbings show the carved sacred animal face which are roughly the same but with differences in the details; M9:2 three-pronged jade object is fully displayed by six line drawings including front, back, profile, side view, overhead and upward views, and four rubbings of the front, back, upper, and lower sides, and two color maps of front and back sides. Third, special attention is paid to the performance of traces of jade production and using. The drilling holes of jades are very accurately represented, and the cutting marks left on the tiny jade tubes are carefully depicted. Readers who do not have the opportunity to touch precious artifacts with their own hands should stand in awe of the drawings, which showed the drawer's academic knowledge and sincerity.

The few pages about research and knowledge are economic in comparison to the plentiful description. Without the whimsical ideas common in previous studies of the Liangzhu culture, discussions on the differences between the burial objects of the tombs in the north line and the south line, and the use of the crown-shaped object were all carefully inferred from the basic materials. There are some obvious parts that could be "played", such as hierarchy differences between tombs, that the authors do not touch on. The intention of getting rid of flash and returning to nature was fully reflected.

The more we receive, the more we want. Although *Yaoshan* is so wonderful, it is still a pity. As noted in the postscript of the report, the absence of jade identification is a major shortcoming of the report. We expect a report on the proposed multidisciplinary study of jade to be published as soon as possible, and also as a "painstaking" work, detailing the texture of each piece of jade and stone artifacts. The distribution of jade artifacts in individual tombs can provide important information about the control and distribution of jade resources (see research by American scholars on prehistoric flint manufacturing in Central America. For example, K. V. Flannery, *The Early Mesoamerican Village,* New York, Academic Press, 1976). Multidisciplinary studies should also include the identification of earth, and many readers will be curious to know where the major types of piled-up earth, especially red and grey earth, came from. The strata are well described and illustrated, but it would have been better to have a plan of the distribution of the major piled-up earth. Furthermore, it would be nice if the English abstract could be longer and more detailed. The recently published report *Zengpiyan in Guilin* is a good example.

In the face of such a hard-working and sincere report as *Yaoshan*, every true lover of Liangzhu culture will have a common expectation – return to the nature of liangzhu culture research.

(Originally published in *China Cultural Relics News* on 31 March, 2004)

# CONTENTS

**Chapter IV**   **Artifacts Collected and Unearthed from the Stratum / 197**

**Chapter V**   **Research and Knowledge / 228**

**Postscript / 237**

# Figures Contents

# Pictures Contents

# *Chapter I*
# Introduction

## Section 1 The Historical Development of Yuhang and Liangzhu Site Cluster

### 1. Historical Development

As an original suburban county of Hangzhou, Zhejiang Province, Yuhang enjoys quite a long history of establishment as a county. After the unification of ancient China by Qin Shi Huang (259–210 B.C.), two counties named Qiantang and Yuhang were established (both under the jurisdiction of Kuaiji Prefecture) within the area that is now under the jurisdiction of Yuhang, and this was the first time for Yuhang to be set as a county. Later, after several changes, the original two counties of Hangxian and Yuhang were combined to become today's Yuhang. Prior to the era of the Republic of China (1912–1949), Hangxian County occupied the area of Qiantang County and Renhe County, and Qiantang County comprised today's Hangzhou. So, historically, Hangzhou and Qiantang were under the same jurisdiction. In 1927, six districts of the Hangxian County were singled out to form Hangzhou, hence the separation of Hangzhou and Qiantang since then. In May 1994, Yuhang was retitled from a county to a city in the administrative system. In March 2001, Yuhang was removed of its county-level city title and became a district under Hangzhou's jurisdiction. In 2021, Yuhang district was divided into Yuhang District in the west and Linping District in the east.

Yuhang District is located in the north of Zhejiang Province, at the northern bank of Qiantang River, within the transition zone from Hangjiahu Plain to western mountains and hills. The main natural river within the territory is the East Tiaoxi River, which originates from Majiangang hill of East Tianmu Mountain in Zhejiang Province and flows east through Lin'an, Yuhang and Deqing to Huzhou, where it meets the West Tiaoxi River. The East Tiaoxi River and the West Tiaoxi River are collectively called Tiaoxi River, the only river in Zhejiang Province that flows north into Taihu Lake. Drawing a line along the East Tiaoxi River, Yuhang can roughly be divided into two parts. On the west side of the East Tiaoxi River is the mountainous and hilly area with higher terrain. Yaotou Mountain, which adjoins Lin'an City with an altitude of 1,095 meters above the sea level, is the main peak on the east end of Tianmu Mountain Range. On the east side of the East Tiaoxi River is the extended alluvial plain with flat terrain, which forms the western edge of Hangjiahu Plain. Liangzhu Site Cluster is located along the banks of the East Tiaoxi River on the border between the mountains and hills and the alluvial plain in the middle of Yuhang (Fig. 1).

### 2. Liangzhu Site Cluster

Located in western Zhejiang, Tianmu Mountain Range is the watershed between the Yangtze River and the Qiantang River, winding eastwards till the three towns of Yuhang, namely, Pingyao, Anxi and Liangzhu. It splits into northern and southern branches at Penggong Town of Yuhang, spreading out into a fan-shaped area when it flows downward. In particular, high mountains in the southern part include Mount Kaolao (127.88 m above the sea level), Mount Daguan, Mount Tianfu (76 m) and Mount Zhutou (67 m), and higher mountains in the northern part include Mount Tamu, Mount Ursong (202.20 m),

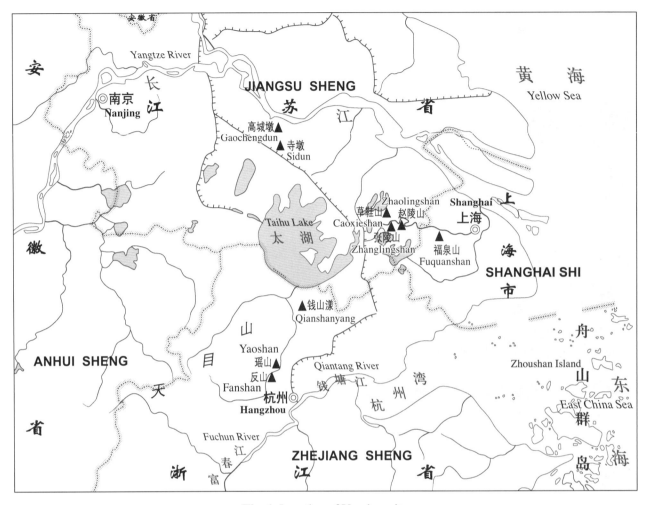

**Fig. 1.** Location of Yaoshan site

Mount Baimu (196.70 m) and East Mount (174 m). The two plier-shaped branches of the mountain range closely surround the plain area of Pingyao, Anxi and Liangzhu, which features densely interwoven water networks, fertile earth and low-lying landform with only a few hills.

The archaeological work was first conducted in this area in the 1930s. In 1936, Shi Xingeng, a fellow researcher of the former West Lake Museum of Zhejiang (today's Zhejiang Provincial Museum) found more than ten sites around Liangzhu and Changmingqiao. He excavated some sites around Liangzhu and found relics left from the Neolithic Age, which were represented by polished stone artifacts and black pottery. Later, he published *Liangzhu, a Preliminary Report on Black Pottery Culture Sites in Area II, Hangxian County*. Liangzhu then became the place where the Liangzhu culture was found for the

first time and named after.[1]

During the following six decades, through the hard efforts of several generations of archaeologists, over 100 Neolithic sites were found, and most of them belong to the Liangzhu culture. The "Liangzhu Site Cluster" we are now referring to is the collection of the Liangzhu culture sites found within the area of Pingyao, Anxi and Liangzhu. According to mapping institutes, the preservation area of Liangzhu Site Cluster has a scale of nearly 34 square kilometers, and the East Tiaoxi River flows past the western and northern parts of the Cluster. There is also a small canal flowing from west to east at the south end of the area, which is called "Liangzhugang River" by the local people, yet it is unknown as to when

---

[1] Xia Nai formally proposed the naming of "Liangzhu culture" in the *Archaeological Issues in the Yangtze River Delta*. *See* the second issue of *Archaeology*, 1960.

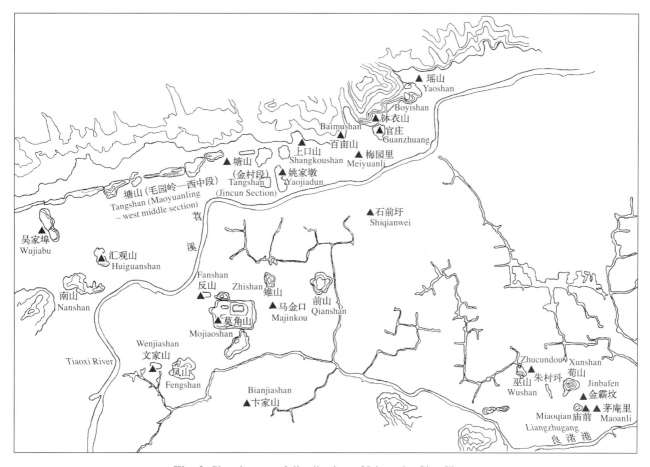

**Fig. 2.** Sketch map of distribution of Liangzhu Site Cluster

the canal was dug. Since the 1980s, a series of important sites were excavated one after another, such as those in Fanshan, Yaoshan, Huiguanshan and Mojiaoshan. Hence the "Liangzhu Site Cluster" became one of the important regions for exploring China's early civilizations (Fig. 2).

Within the area of Liangzhu Site Cluster, the lower stratum of some sites date back to the Majiabang culture and Songze culture. In the lower stratums of Wujiabu Site[1], Xunshandongpo Site[2], Meiyuanli Site[3] and Miaoqian Site[4], stratums of the late

period of Majiabang culture and no Songze culture were found.

Geographically, the East Tiaoxi River divides Liangzhu Site Cluster into the southern part and northern part. Over the years, cultural heritage authorities of Zhejiang Province and Yuhang District have excavated over 100 Liangzhu culture sites or remains of the Liangzhu culture, which can be roughly divided into three areas: (1) The east–west facing strip between the northern bank of the East Tiaoxi River and the neighboring mountain in the north. (2) The neighboring area of Xunshan Hill at Liangzhu Town in the southeast. (3) The area with Mojiaoshan Site as the center in the west. In the large area between Mojiaoshan and Xunshan Hill, no sites of the Liangzhu culture were found yet. Drilling results showed that this area was formed by deposits of low-lying marshland. Yaoshan is located exactly on the east end of the first area mentioned above.

[1] Zhejiang Provincial Institute of Cultural Relics and Archaeology, *Yuhang Wujiabu Site of Neolithic Age*, *Journal of Zhejiang Provincial Institute of Cultural Relics and Archaeology*, Science Press, 1993.

[2] Yuhang County Liangzhu Xunshan Site of Neolithic Age, *China Archaeology Yearbook* (1986), Cultural Relics Press, 1988.

[3] Excavation data provided by Zhejiang Provincial Institute of Cultural Relics and Archaeology.

[4] Ding Pin, Main Findings in the Excavation of Miaoqian Site, Liangzhu, Yuhang, *Journal of Zhejiang Provincial Institute of Cultural Relics and Archaeology*, Science Press, 1993.

## Section 2 Discovery Process

### 1. Geographic Location of Yaoshan

Yaoshan Hill is located on the northeastern corner of Liangzhu Site Cluster, with geographic coordinates of 120°00′56″N, 30°25′37″E. In terms of administrative division, it belongs to Xiaxiwan Village of Anxi Town (originally Anxi Village). In the southeast of the Yaoshan Hill, the East Tiaoxi River flows by, and in the north and northeast, there are small valleys surrounded by mountains. Originally, there was a stream flowing from the northwest into the East Tiaoxi River, yet now it has been blocked and dried up.

Yaoshan is a low-lying hill stretching eastward from the Fenghuang Mountain (with an altitude of 114.70 m), an offshoot of the Tianmu Mountain Range. Prior to excavation, cedar and tea trees were growing on the mountain. Mining was carried out over the years. By the time of excavation, the altitude of the highest eastern part was 38.20 m. Excluding the surface sediment, the actual altitude was 36 m (Figs. 3, 4; Picture 1).

There is a small hill lying in the south of Yaoshan Hill, which is called "Mantoushan Hill" by the local people, with an altitude of 37.30 m. In 1998 during the excavation of Yaoshan site, we conducted drilling survey and trial excavation on the hill. It was found that under the surface earth there were natural rock mass without any Liangzhu culture deposits. However, we did find some Liangzhu culture artifacts in the surface earth. Pottery shards and burnt earth were found widely in the southwest of Mantoushan Hill, which indicates the possible existence of a kiln of the Han dynasty (202 B.C.–220 A.D.). Southwest to Yaoshan Hill is the Fenghuangshannanpo site, and further to the west is Boyishan site. East to Yaoshan

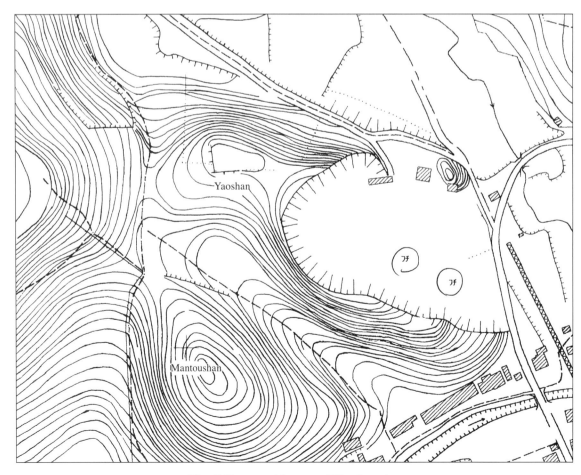

**Fig. 3.** Topographic map of Yaoshan site

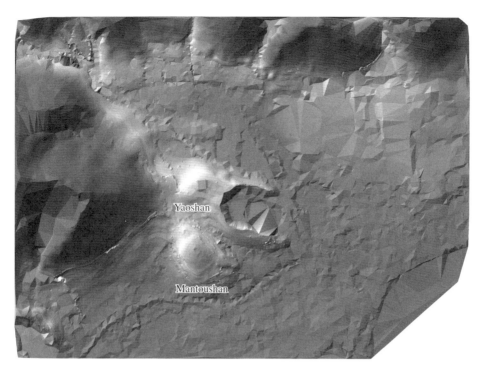

**Fig. 4.** The Digital Elevation Model of Yaoshan site

Hill is Xiaozhushan site[1] from which the jade *bi* of the Liangzhu culture was once discovered.

## 2. Discovery of Yaoshan site

On May 1, 1987, some local villagers robbed tombs on the northwestern slope of Yaoshan Hill (later becoming the official excavation area) and the southern slope of Yangweibashan Hill at the border between Yuhang County and Deqing County, and dug out a large number of jade artifacts of the Liangzhu culture. Ma Zhushan, a technician of Zhejiang Provincial Institute of Cultural Relics and Archaeology who was then spending his holidays in his hometown Houhe Village of Anxi Town, heard the news and reported to Yan Yunquan, head of the cultural station of Anxi Town, the next day. Then they rushed to Yaoshan Hill and Yangweibashan and timely stopped the robbery behavior of the local villagers. Yan Yunquan then immediately reported to the superior authority in cultural relics management. On the same day, relevant personnel of cultural relics management departments of Hangzhou City and Yuhang County came to the

site, who, together with the personnel sent by the government of Anxi Town and Yuhang cultural relics management department assisted the police to confiscate the robbed artifacts. Meanwhile, the site has been protected by the local government.

On the afternoon of May 3, cultural heritage authorities of Zhejiang Province, Hangzhou City and Yuhang County and the police department sent personnel to the site to combat the robbery and confiscate the robbed artifacts. Meanwhile, Zhejiang Provincial Institute of Cultural Relics and Archaeology set up an excavation team to carry out rescue excavation immediately. On May 4, Zhejiang Provincial Institute of Cultural Relics and Archaeology filed an application to the State Administration of Cultural Relics for rescue excavation, and set up an archaeological excavation team headed by Mu Yongkang and Wang Mingda. The actual excavation activity was organized by the No. 2 Research Department of Zhejiang Provincial Institute of Cultural Relics and Archaeology. The Hangzhou Institute of Cultural Relics and Archaeology and the Yuhang Committee of Cultural Relics Management also sent personnel to participate in the excavation. The excavation of ten-odd years in Yaoshan was begun since then.

[1] Boyishan Liangzhu Culture Site, Yuhang County, *China Archaeology Yearbook* (1990), Cultural Relics Press, 1991.

# Chapter II
# Excavation Process

## Section 1 Excavation in 1987

On May 5, 1987, Mu Yongkang and Rui Guoyao from Zhejiang Provincial Institute of Cultural Relics and Archaeology, Wang Yunlu from the Yuhang Committee of Cultural Relics Management, and Sang Jianxin from the Hangzhou Institute of Cultural Relics and Archaeology, came to the site to conduct preparation work for the excavation, which officially began on May 7 and ended on June 4. Mu Yongkang (team leader), Rui Guoyao (on-site director), Shen Yueming and Chen Huanle from Zhejiang Provincial Institute of Cultural Relics and Archaeology, and Sang Jianxin participated in the excavation throughout the entire process. Liu Bin and Fei Guoping from Zhejiang Provincial Institute of Cultural Relics and Archaeology also participated the excavation, and Qiang Chaomei from the Technical Department of Zhejiang Provincial Institute of Cultural Relics and Archaeology handled the work of on-site video recording and photo taking. During the excavation, Wang Yunlu and Yan Yunquan from the government of Anxi Town assisted with a great deal of the administrative and logistics work, which ensured the smooth progress of the excavation.

1. According to the current situation of the tomb robbery, an excavation area at a size of around 400 square meters was first defined. Within this area, four east–west facing test trenches were laid parallel with each other from the north to the south, with a distance of two meters between one another. In particular, trenches T1–T3 have an east–west length of 25 m and a north–south width of 2 m. Trench T4 has an east–west length of 15 m and a north–south width of 2 m. After the Liangzhu culture relics were found, trenches T1–T3 were extended 5 m westward and T4 was

extended 10 m westward and 3 m southward. Trench T5 was located 2 m north of trench T1, with an east–west length of 20 m and a north–south width of 3 m. During the excavation, part of the baulk between the test trenches was removed to fully reveal the relics. So the actual excavation area was nearly 600 square meters (Figs. 5, 6).

One of the significant findings of the excavation is the Liangzhu culture altar (Picture 3). The altar has a square-shaped plan, consisting of three tiers of earth with different colors from inside to outside. The innermost tier of earth is in the eastern part, forming a roughly square shaped "red-earthen mound" with an altitude of 34.80 m, laying basically in a due north–south direction. The eastern edge of the mound has a length of 7.60 m, its northern edge 5.90 m, its western edge 7.70 m, and its southern edge has a residual length of 6.20 m as both ends of the edge were disrupted by several tombs. The "red-earthen mound" has a basically flat surface. Some of the red earth is mixed up with a small number of gravels, and yet no other relics are found. As for the walls of the pit which disrupted the "red-earthen mound", no sign of ramming was shown. The second tier of earth is in gray color surrounding the "red-earthen mound", with its plan in a 回-shape (Two homocentric squares). The section of the 回-shaped ditch is square-cornered, with a straight wall and a flat bottom, with a depth of 0.65–0.85 m, and a width of 1.70–2.10 m. The earth filled in the ditch is quite loose and no artifacts are found. On the western, northern and southern sides of the second-tier gray-earthen ditch is an earthen mound built with yellowish-brown mottled earth. Gravels of various

**Fig. 5.** Plan of the excavation in 1987

sizes scattered on the mound, so it is reckoned that the mound might originally had a gravel surface. On the east side of the gray-earthen ditch was the natural earth of mountains, while on the southern side the "mound surface" has been disturbed due to years of cultivation, with only an earthen mound left with a height of around 0.20 m.

On the western and northern edges of the gravel yellow-earthen mound, there is respectively a stone revetment formed by gravels overlapping each other. The gravels are stacked up in good order, forming a slope outward from the earthen mound. During later excavation, for the convenience of recording, we named the stone revetment on the western side as the western No. 1 stone revetment (Picture 4), and named the stone revetment on the northern side as the northern No. 1 stone revetment (Picture 8). The top of the western No. 1 stone revetment has a length

of 11.30 m, and the top of the northern No. 1 stone revetment has a length of 10.60 m. The surfaces of the two stone revetments are linked together basically in a right angle, with the vertical height of 0.90 m at the corner. The top has an altitude of 34.30 m, slightly lower than the surface of the "red-earthen mound". On the outer side of the stone revetment piled up tough brown mottled earth, of which no ramming traces are found.

The other main finding of the excavation is 11 Liangzhu culture tombs, which have been numbered Yuyao tombs M1–M11. The tombs are concentrated in the southern half part of the altar, arrayed in east–west direction and divided into a north line and a south line. The north line has 5 tombs, also named as tombs M1, M4, M5, M11 and M6 respectively from west to east; and the south line has 6 tombs, with the name of tombs M3, M10, M9, M7, M2 and M8 from west to east.

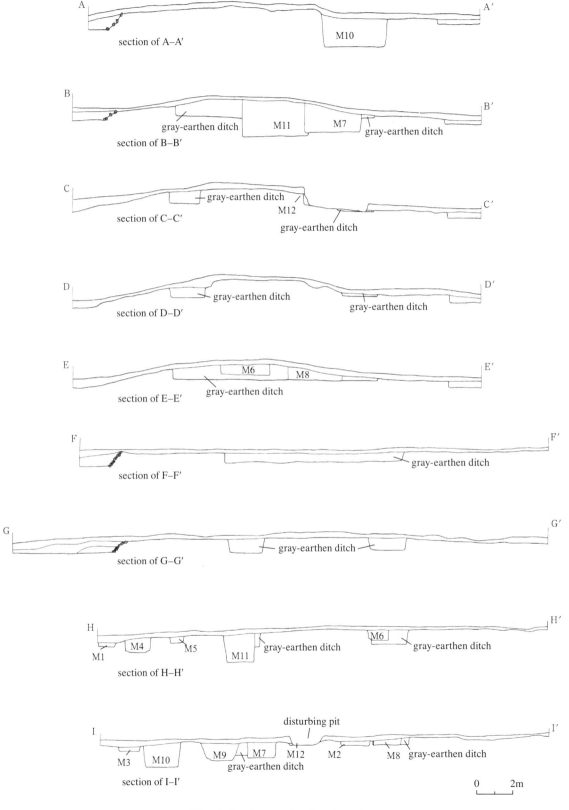

**Fig. 6.** Sections of the Yaoshan site

There is originally a tomb between tombs M7 and M2, but it was destroyed by a large pit due to tomb robbery. During the official excavation, only the residual north end of the tomb was revealed, and no burial objects were found. It was said that all the robbed jade artifacts belonged to this tomb, so we named the tomb as tomb M12 for the convenience of recording.

The above findings have already been briefly reported[1], and most unearthed artifacts have also been published in the book of *Jade Artifacts of the Liangzhu Culture*[2].

2. A small pit was found in the southeast of trench T4 and was numbered pit H1. It has an opening under the top soil and its lower part was dug into the sand-weathered rock earth. The circular-shaped pit opening has a diameter of 0.80 m, with a straight inner wall and a flat bottom. The height of the pit is 0.12 m. The pit was filled with grayish-brown fine sand, which was loose in density. Near the bottom of the pit, an extremely thin stratum of plant ash was found, being roughly a rectangular plan with a length of 0.38 m and a width of about 0.16 m, which was located in a southwest-to-northeast direction. There are no other remains inside the pit.

From the surface stratum at the west end of trench T3, five pieces of jade artifacts of Liangzhu culture were unearthed, all white jade. T3:1, long tube, cylinder-shaped, with a hole drilling from both sides; it is 5.4 cm in length, 1.4 cm in diameter, and 0.7 cm in the hole's diameter (Fig. 7: 8). T3:2 and T3:5 are spherical jade beads, on which there were a pair of tunneled-shaped holes, with a diameter of 1.4 cm and 1.5 cm (Fig. 7: 1, 2). T3:3, residual part of crown-shaped object, with only the upper-middle part left (Fig. 7: 4). T3:4, residual part of awl-shaped object, long bar-shaped, broken on both ends, with a length of 2.7 cm and a diameter of 0.35 cm (Fig. 7: 3).

When trench T5 was excavated, the Northern No. 1

[1] Zhejiang Provincial Institute of Cultural Relics and Archaeology, Brief reports on the Excavation of Liangzhu Culture Altar Site, Yuhang Yaoshan, *Cultural Relics*, the first issue in 1988.

[2] Zhejiang Provincial Institute of Cultural Relics and Archaeology, Shanghai Municipal CPAM, Nanjing Museum, *Jade Artifacts of the Liangzhu Culture*, Cultural Relics Press and Liangmu Press, 1989.

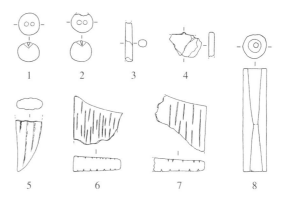

**Fig. 7.** Jade artifacts unearthed from trench T3 and pottery *ding* legs unearthed from the earth upon the northern No. 1 stone revetment

1, 2. jade beads (T3:2, 5); 3. awl-shaped jade object (T3:4); 4. crown-shaped jade object (T3:3); 5–7. pottery *ding* legs; 8. long jade tube (T3:1) (scale: 5–7 are 1/4; the rest are 1/2)

stone revetment was revealed entirely. From the crevice of the stone revetment, shattered stone arrowheads were excavated, judged by rough observation, its section is rhombus-shaped. From the brown mottled earth stacked on the stone revetment, fragments of fin-shaped leg of *ding* were unearthed, with the section being flat and thin (Fig. 7: 5–7). From the deposit stratum and the stone revetment crevice also unearthed some coarse sand-tempered red pottery shards of *gang* vat, which belong to typical Liangzhu culture, all of which are shattered pieces whose whole appearance couldn't be known.

At the west end of trench T5, a tomb which has a rectangle pit with vertical wall was excavated, dating back to the East Zhou dynasty (770 B.C.–221 B.C.), and was assigned the number of Yuyao tomb M13 (Fig. 8).

The tomb is located on the western side of the north end of western No. 1 stone revetment, with a tomb direction of 95°. The tomb pit has a length of 2.70 m and a width of 1.22 m. The inner wall of the pit was straight. The west end of the pit has a depth of around 0.10 m, and the middle part of the pit has a depth of around 0.45 m. The east wall of the tomb pit presented a slope shape by utilizing the western No. 1 stone revetment, with a flat bottom and a slight inclination from east to west. On the northern side of the tomb pit there was a two-stratum terrace, with a width of

**Fig. 8.** Tomb M13

loose in texture. The burial objects were all located in the eastern part of the tomb. Totally five pieces of stamped pottery wares and three pieces of proto-porcelain wares were excavated.

3. Since the principle of protective excavation had been determined, the exposure of the "altar" was done only to the surface and the excavation went no further. No further dissection and confirmation of the construction structure were done, either. As to the scope of the altar relics, the western and northern edge had been defined according to the so-called "slope-protecting earth", which was piled on the western No. 1 and Northern No. 1 stone revetments; the eastern edge was roughly defined according to the fact that the eastern side of the gray earthen ditch were all rocky mountains; and, the southern edge of the relics featuring "earth revetment" was defined with difficulty due to the slight difference between the colors and properties of the earth under the top soil of trench T4. At that time, it was believed that the whole altar and tombs had been fully revealed, so no plans were made to further excavate Yaoshan site. We filled the tomb pit with earth and covered the whole altar relics with earth that was nearly 1 m thick. Then we laid stones on the earth for on-site protection, and afterwards we drew on the stone terrace the plan outlines of the relics and the tombs with bricks and stones, for the purpose of exhibition.

0.15–0.20 m and a height of around 0.18 m. The tomb was filled with grayish-brown mottled earth which was

## Section 2 Excavation in 1996

In the several years following the first excavation, tomb robbery occurred frequently in the neighborhood of the protective stone terrace of Yaoshan site despite of repeated prohibition. In order to strengthen the protection of Yaoshan site, in 1996, according to instructions of the State Administration of Cultural Relics, the Liangzhu Archaeological Station of Zhejiang Provincial Institute of Cultural Relics and Archaeology carried out a second excavation on Yaoshan site, with the expectation to find Liangzhu culture remains in the neighboring area of the first-excavated spot, and further, to confirm its relations with the altar-tomb complex. This excavation began on

May 16, and ended on July 23, 1996, and Rui Guoyao, Ding Pin, Fang Xiangming, Ma Zhushan and Chen Huanle from Zhejiang Provincial Institute of Cultural Relics and Archaeology, and Fei Guoping from Yuhang Management Institute of Liangzhu Cultural Site took part in the excavation.

1. According to the landform of the site and vegetation on site, totally 6 test trenches and test units of different sizes were laid out for exploration, with a total excavation area of 350 square meters. In order to distinguish the units (trenches) laid out this time from those laid out first time, three-digit numbers were assigned to the units (trenches), with the first-

digit number being 2, which referred to the second excavation, and the latter two-digit number being the sequence number (Figs. 9, 10).

Trench T201 was laid in an east–west direction, located on the east side of the stone terrace, with a length of 29.50 m and a width of 2 m. Trench T202 was laid in an east–west direction, located on the east side of the stone terrace, with a length of 40 m and a width of 2 m. After removing the top soil stratum, the flat bedrock was revealed, with some scattered gravels. The west end of these two trenches can be linked to the deposits in the east of the first excavation area. Trench T203 was laid in a north–south direction, located on

the north of the stone terrace, with a length of 26.50 m and a width of 2 m. After removing the top soil stratum, the bedrock which inclined northward was revealed, with some scattered gravels. Trench T205 was laid on the south of the stone terrace in a north–south direction, with a length of 18.85 m and a width of 1 m. After removing the top soil stratum, it was judged that beneath was sandy weathered bedrock.

2. Trench T204 was laid on the west of the stone terrace, with a north–south length of 23.40 m and an east–west width of 5 m. After the discovery of the relics, the trench was extended westward by 1 m at the point of 11 m from southern end of its west wall.

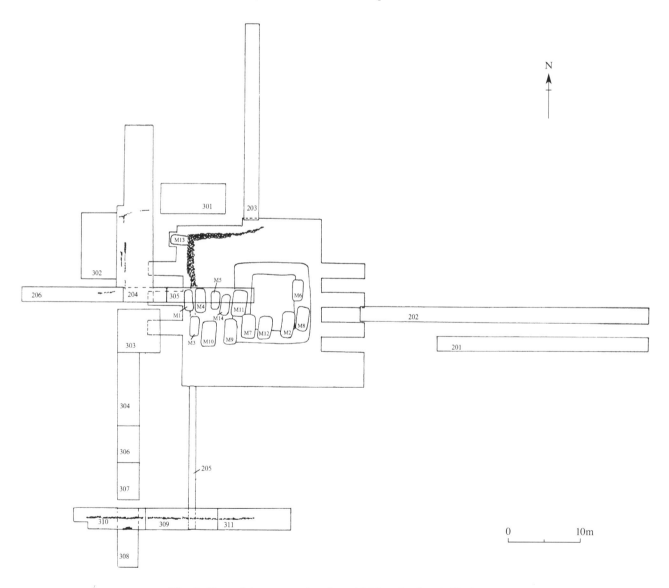

**Fig. 9.** Plan of the excavation from 1996 to the first half of 1997
(three-digit numbers are assigned to the units and trenches)

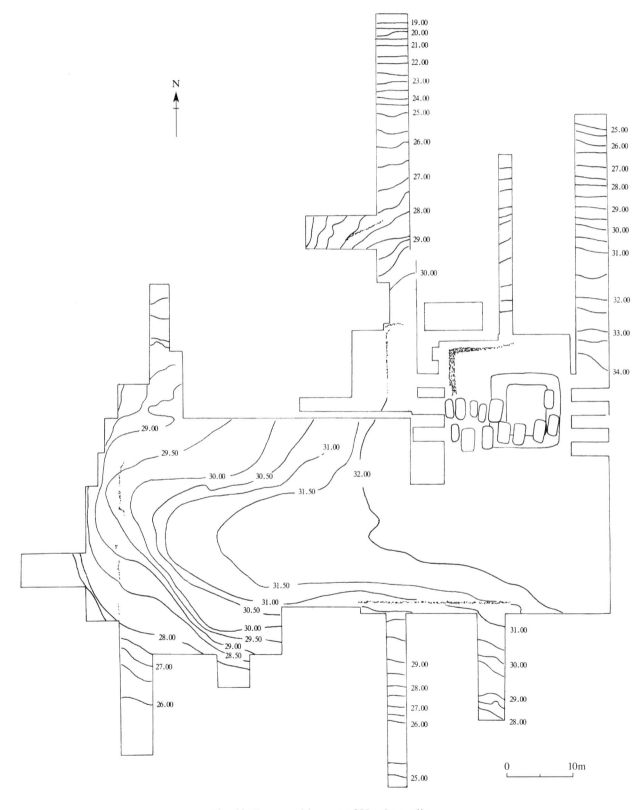

**Fig. 10.** Topographic map of Yaoshan relics

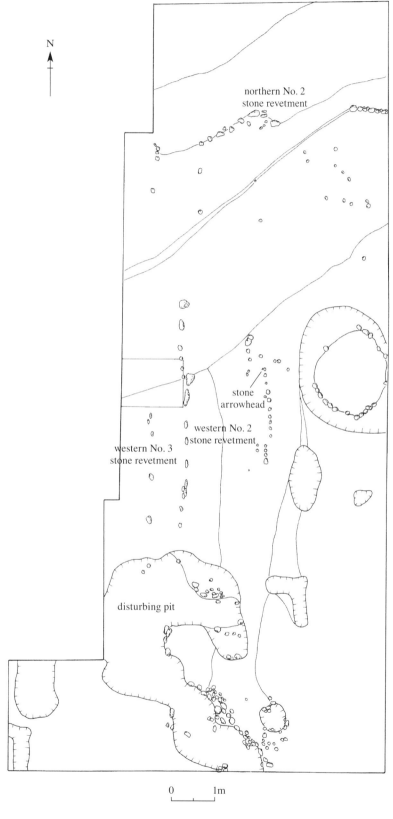

N

northern No. 2
stone revetment

stone
arrowhead

western No. 2
stone revetment

western No. 3
stone revetment

disturbing pit

0        1m

**Fig. 11.** Plan of the mound relics revealed in 1996

Trench T206 was laid on the west of the stone terrace, with its east end linked to trench T204, with an east–west length of 14 m and a north–south width of 2.30 m. After removing the top soil stratum of the two trenches, a sandy reddish-brown earth mound was revealed. Since the principle of protective excavation was determined, exposure went no further beyond the surface of the mound. Observing its plane, we could see that the mound had a stone revetment with a length of about 9 m, which was named western No. 2 stone revetment (Picture 5). There was also a residual stone revetment lying on the northern side, which was named northern No. 2 stone revetment, connected interruptedly, with a length of around 4.50 m. One part of it, as long as 0.8 m, was relatively complete. The two stone revetments were both built by stacking up gravels (Fig. 11). We revealed part of the north end of western No. 2 stone revetment, which had a vertical height of about 0.50 m. The earth covering above was mainly grayish-yellow earth with black brown spots, with loose texture and inclining westward.

Years of looting had already severely damaged the physical features of the relics, affecting our wholistic understanding of the remains. The cement foundation piles set up during the first excavation for the purpose of measurement was damaged in the same year of establishment. So this time, we were unable to measure the relative height difference between the two earthen mounds with stone revetments as seen in the two excavations. Also, since the mound found the first time had been sealed up by the stone terrace, it couldn't be linked with the trench T204 this time. As to whether the two earthen mounds belonged to an unified whole, the excavation team got conclusions from the following features: (1) In the deposits covering western No. 2 stone revetment, some pottery shards of Liangzhu culture were found, while no artifacts of later period were found. Similar artifacts were also found in the crevice of the stone revetment. Hence the relative date of the remains unearthed this season and the archaeological culture they belong to can be confirmed. (2) The way the western No. 2 stone revetment was built and its structure were similar to those of western No. 1 stone revetment. (3) According to the recall of the personnel who involved in the excavation in 1987, the deposits on the "slope-protecting earth" at the west side of the stone revetments found first time could be linked to the sandy reddish-brown earth deposits found this time. Hence it was referred that the mounds with stone revetments found in the two excavations might possibly belong to the same whole. The excavation team held a common view that it was necessary to reveal Yaoshan site more comprehensively, so as to get a further understanding about the overall appearance and building structure of Yaoshan altar relics. Since main members of the excavation team had other excavation plans to carry out in the second half of 1996, further excavation could only be arranged in the following year.

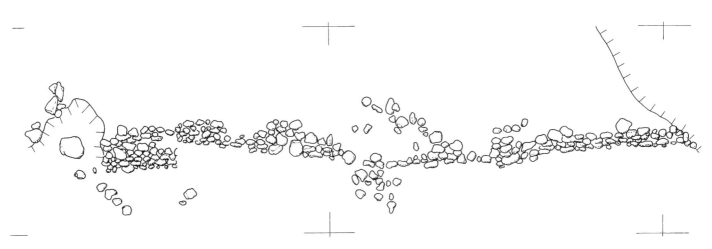

**Fig. 12.** Plan of southern No. 1 stone revetment

# Section 3 Excavation in the First Half of 1997

The main purpose of the excavation this time was to further confirm the area of the relics found last year in the northwest of the protective terrace represented by the stone revetments and the earthen mound, and its relationship with the altar relics found in 1987; to confirm whether there were other remains on the northwest and south of the stone terrace; to conducted out stratigraphic excavation to the relics found in 1987 to confirm its construction structure. Three-digit numbers were assigned for test units laid during this excavation, with the first-digit number being 3, which referred to the third excavation, and the later two-digit number being the sequence number.

To realize the above purposes, unit T301 was laid on the east of the north part of trench T204, unit T302 was laid on the west of the south part of of trench T204. Units T303, T304, T306, T307 and T308 were laid at the south of unit T204. After an east–west stone revetment was found at T308, units T309, T311 and T310 were laid on its east and west sides. Unit T305 was located in the southeast of trench T204, in the same direction with that of trench T206, cutting in the stone terrace sealed in 1987 (see Fig. 9).

This excavation began on April 23 and ended on July 23, 1997. The personnel who were involved in the excavation included Rui Guoyao, Ding Pin, Fang Xiangming, Hu Jigen, Ma Zhushan, Chen Huanle, Fang Zhonghua and Ge Jianliang from Zhejiang Provincial Institute of Cultural Relics and Archaeology, Fei Guoping from Yuhang Management Institute of Liangzhu Cultural Site, and Shi Shiying from Yuhang Liangzhu Cultural Museum.

1. After removing the top soil of unit T301, beneath was the reddish-brown sandy earth of the earthen mound found in 1996. The stratum inclined northwestward, and no other relics were found on the surface of the deposits.

Beneath the top soil of unit T302 was the yellow earth with black brown spots covering the western No. 2 stone revetment found in 1996. The north of the revetment was covered with brown mottled earth, which was inclined northwestward; no other relics were found on the surface of the deposits.

Beneath the top soil of T303, T304, T306, T307 and T308 was reddish-brown sandy earth, which was consistent with the deposits of the mound relic found last year, with the stratum inclining gradually southward. After an east–west stone revetment deposit was found at unit T308, on its both sides we also dug units T309–T311, and an east–west stone revetment was found, which was named southern No. 1 stone revetment, with a length of 24 m (Fig. 12; Pictures 6, 7). At unit T310, a small stratigraphic excavation was conducted to the deposits on the stone revetment, in an

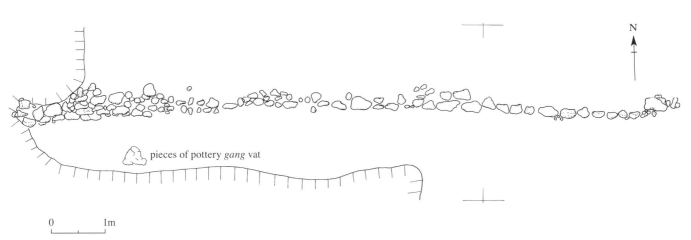

🝖 pieces of pottery *gang* vat

N

0        1m

expectation to get an understanding about the deposits of southern No. 1 stone revetment. The southern No. 1 stone revetment has a slope of 60°, formed by gravels piled upon one another in good order, with a vertical height of 0.70 m. Its top was 31.44 m high above the sea level, and was nearly 3 m lower than the surface of the "altar" in terms of absolute height difference. The west end of the stone revetment was discontinued as damaged by the later-period deposits, and the east end was linked to natural mountains. The outside of the stone revetment was covered with yellow earth with black brown spots, which was stacked in a gentle slope shape, roughly to half of the height of the stone revetment. We noticed during excavation that the yellow mottled earth deposits basically maintained its original state, not fully covering the entire stone revetment.

In the yellow-mottled earth at 1.50 m south of the southern No. 1 stone revetment, an east–west stone revetment was found, with a length of 1.20 m, and was named southern No. 2 stone revetment (Fig. 13). Southern No. 2 stone revetment was lower than southern No. 1 stone revetment, with a height difference of about 0.70 m between their tops. The southern No. 2 stone revetment was stacked up in a similar way to that of southern No. 1 stone revetment,

but with only 2–3 stratums, and inclining slightly southward.

2. In order to confirm the construction structure of western No. 2 stone revetment and the earthen mound, at the north end of west No. 2 stone revetment in the trench T204, an east–west exploration trench was laid in a vertical direction against the stone revetment, with a length of 6 m and a width of 1 m, and it was named the middle trench of T204. Observed from profile of the south wall of the trench, the stratigraphic accumulation was as follows (Fig. 14):

First stratum: surface top soil.

Second stratum: yellow earth with black spots. Western No. 2 stone revetment was revealed underneath the first stratum. On the west side there is also a discontinued north–south stone revetment, which was named western No. 3 stone revetment. The distance between the two stone revetments is around 0.70 m. The deposits in the east of western No. 2 stone revetment, west of western No. 3 stone revetment and between the two stone revetments has the same earth color and earth texture. The stone revetments were mostly formed by 2–3 stratums of gravels (Fig. 16).

Third stratum: brown-mottled earth, located in the western part of the trench, beneath the lower half of western No. 2 stone revetment. The bottom of this stratum had scattered gravels.

Fourth stratum: reddish-brown sandy earth, mingled with a few gravels, inclined westward in a slope shape, thinner in the western part. The bottom of this stratum had scattered gravels.

Fifth stratum: gray-mottled earth, with a few pottery shards unearthed, mingled with scattered gravels.

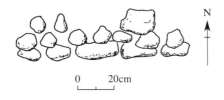

**Fig. 13.** Plan of southern No. 2 stone revetment

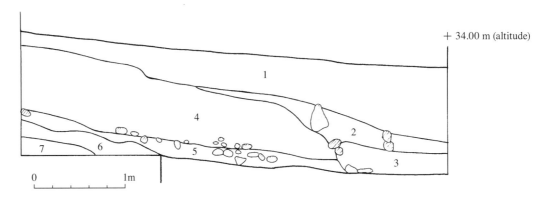

**Fig. 14.** Profile of the south wall of the middle trench T204

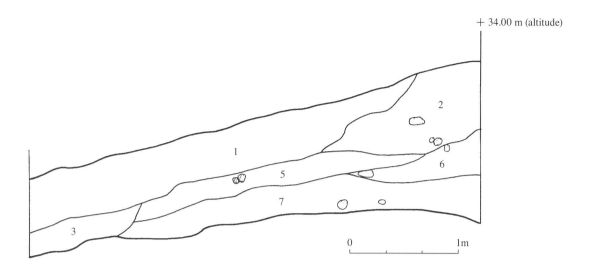

+ 34.00 m (altitude)

0                    1m

**Fig. 15.** Profile of the east wall of the north trench T204

Sixth stratum: light red earth, relatively pure, located in the east part of the test trench.

Underneath the sixth stratum was weathered sandstone.

In order to confirm the construction structure of the northern part of the earthen mound, a north–south test trench was laid closely along the east wall of trench T204, with a length of 5 m and a width of 2 m, and was named north trench of T204. Observed from the profile of the east wall, the stratigraphic accumulation was as follows (Fig. 15):

First stratum: top soil.

Second stratum: yellow earth with black spots, with deposits inclining northward. This stratum was the same as the second stratum of the middle trench of T204.

Third stratum: light grayish-brown earth, with a few Liangzhu culture pottery shards.

Fourth stratum: black gray earth, beneath the third stratum, only located in the northwest of the trench.

Fifth stratum: brown-mottled earth, with a few Liangzhu culture pottery shards and some stones. The bottom of this stratum had irregular pavement of gravels. The northern No. 2 stone revetment was on the edge of this stratum, mostly formed by 1–2 stratums of gravels piled upon one another, with no obvious stone revetment slope found.

Sixth stratum: reddish-brown sandy earth. This stratum was the same as the fourth stratum of the

middle trench of T204.

Seventh stratum: grayish-brown earth. This stratum was the same as the fifth stratum of the middle trench of T204.

According to the further excavation of northwest part of trench T204, the northern No. 2 stone revetment has only a length of 0.50 m in the trench, which extended in a discontinued way westward to constitute a whole length of about 3.20 m. Inferred from the section, the northern No. 2 stone revetment was located at the dividing line between the third, fourth and the fifth and seventh stratums, which was consistent with the situation revealed in the trench.

3. In order to achieve the main purposes of this excavation, we opened another test trench at the south end of T204 closely along its south wall, with a width of 2.30 m, which was named the south trench of T204 and was dug deep into the virgin soil. Meanwhile, we dug T206 deep into the virgin soil. In order to do to get to know the construction structure of the alter relics, we arranged T305 in the southeast of T204 in an east–west direction, straightly cutting into the altar relics.

1) The stratigraphic accumulation of south trench of T204 is to be introduced as follows, citing the profile map of its north wall as an example (Fig. 17):

First stratum: surface top soil and disrupted backfilling earth.

Second stratum: yellow earth with black spots, located at the west end of the trench and extended to

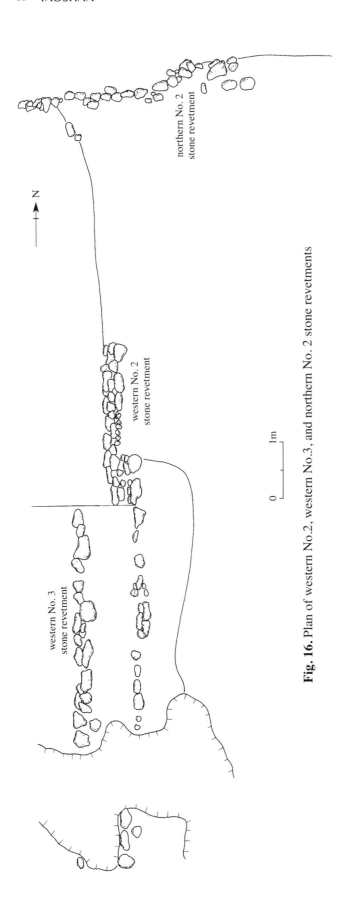

**Fig. 16.** Plan of western No.2, western No.3, and northern No. 2 stone revetments

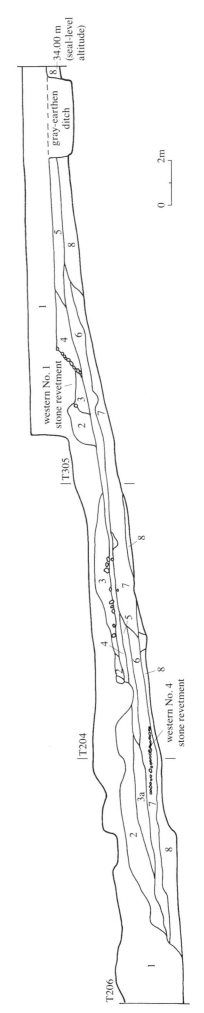

**Fig. 17.** Profile of unit T206 north wall, south trench T204 north wall and unit T305 north wall

trench T206, inclining westward. The earth was pure and no artifacts were found. This stratum was the same as the second stratum of the middle trench of T204.

Third stratum: reddish-brown sandy earth, mingled with a few gravels, mainly located in the eastern half of the trench, slightly inclining westward. This stratum was the same as the fourth stratum of the middle trench of T204.

Fourth stratum: grayish-brown mottled earth, loose in texture, containing a few pottery shards. This stratum is the same with the fifth stratum of the middle trench of T204.

Fifth stratum: tough red earth, pure, no inclusions.

Sixth stratum: brownish-red tough earth, containing many gravel fragments, sandy, mingled with many black mottled earth blocks, located in the western part of the trench. There was a small area of irregular graveled surface, which inclined westward.

Seventh stratum: light red pure earth, with no cultural relics, located in the eastern part of the trench, thick deposits, the thickest part was about 70 cm. This stratum was the same with the sixth stratum of the middle trench of T204.

Eighth stratum: brown-mottled earth, mainly located in the western part of the trench, containing fine sand and a few weathered sandstones.

Underneath the eighth stratum was the virgin soil.

Since the upper half of the trench had been severely disrupted or damaged, the north–south western No. 2 stone revetment and western No. 3 stone revetment were not found in the trench.

2) The stratigraphic accumulation of T206 was comparatively complicated. Here it is introduced as follows, citing the profile of the north wall as an example (Fig. 17):

First stratum: top soil and deposits of late period. It was virgin soil under the top soil at the bottom at the east end.

Second stratum: yellow earth with black spots, mainly located in the eastern part of the trench, inclining westward and becoming thinner southward. This stratum was the same as the second stratum of the south trench of T204.

Third stratum: it was divided into two small stratums. The 3a stratum was brown mottled earth, located in the northeastern part of the trench, inclining northward and westward. This stratum was the same as the third stratum of the middle trench of T204. The 3b stratum was dark brown mottled earth, located in the middle-southern part of the trench, and was not overlapped directly with the 3a stratum.

Fourth stratum: pure red earth, located at the east end of the trench, inclining northwestward. This stratum was the same as the fifth stratum of the south trench of T204. A stone revetment was discovered on the northern edge and was named western No. 4 stone revetment (Fig. 18). Western No. 4 stone revetment basically laid in an east–west direction, inclining northward, with a length of around 2.40 m. It was formed by gravels piled upon one another, at a height of around 0.35 m, and its top had an altitude of 32.10 m. It was deposited directly onto stratum 7 while itself being covered by stratum 3a.

Beneath the fourth stratum in the southern half of

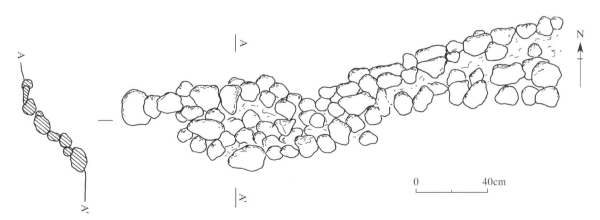

**Fig. 18.** Plan and profile of western No. 4 stone revetment

the trench there were the fifth and sixth stratums of deposits.

Fifth stratum: brownish-red earth, mingled with many gravels and black mottled earth, tough in texture.

Sixth stratum: grayish-brown earth, mingled with much black-mottled earth, tough in texture.

Seventh stratum: brownish-red earth, the same as the sixth stratum of the south trench of T204.

Eighth stratum: yellowish-brown mottled earth, mingled with many gravels, the same as the eighth stratum of the south trench of T204. The deposits of this stratum might be virgin soil.

Underneath the eighth stratum were weathered bedrocks.

3) T305 was arranged in the same direction with that of trench T206 and the south trench of T204, cutting into the sealed stone terrace eastward. The stratigraphic accumulation is introduced as follows, citing the profile map of the north wall of T305 as an example (Fig. 17):

First stratum: original backfilling deposits earth.

Second stratum: reddish-brown earth, the same as the third stratum of the south trench of T204.

Third stratum: yellow earth with black spots, overlying western No. 1 stone revetment, mostly revealed during the excavation in 1987.

Fourth stratum: slightly sandy yellow earth.

Fifth stratum: dark yellow earth, slightly sandy. The fourth and fifth stratums were the deposits of the "gravel - earthen mound" found in the excavation in 1987; the surface of the stratum was basically leveled. The west end of the fourth stratum overlaid western No. 1 stone revetment, and the eastern end of the fifth stratum didn't extend further eastward for it was broken by the "gray-earthen ditch".

Sixth stratum: grayish-brown mottled earth, containing a minute quantity of small pottery shards and gravel stones and was mingled with a few burnt earth particles, inclining westward and extending to the fourth stratum of the south trench of T204.

Seventh stratum: light red earth, compact in texture, no inclusions. Its east end directly covered the eighth stratum, inclining and extending westward. This stratum was the same as the seventh stratum of T204.

Eighth stratum: slightly sandy red earth, loose in texture, in a slope shape, high in the east and lower in the west. Its middle part in the trench was covered by the seventh stratum, and its east end was broken by the gray-earthen ditch. The revealed deposits were the "red-earthen mound" discovered in 1987.

Underneath the eighth stratum were red weathered sandstones, inclined westward. This was the original foundation ground[1].

4) During the excavation of test unit T305, we further dealt with the bottom of tomb M5, and found that there was a shallow groove with a depth of about 7 cm around the tomb pit, thus enabling the tomb bottom to form a low-rise earthen terrace.

At the east end of test unit T305, a ash pit (1997H1) was discovered, with its opening underneath the first stratum, disturbing the fifth and eighth stratums. The eastern part was disturbed by tomb M11. The plane was in irregular rectangle shape in an east–west direction, with a north–south width of 1.50 m, residual length of 1.90 m, and a depth of 0.70 m. The pit wall was not obvious, and the filling earth inside the pit was grayish-brown, relatively loose in texture, mingled with gravels. A small quantity of cinnabar lacquer coat fragments was found at the bottom, with an unclear overall shape, which was difficult to take out (Fig. 19).

Between tombs M5 and M11, a Liangzhu culture tomb was found, which was named Yuyao tomb M14. M14 had its opening beneath the first stratum, disturbing the fifth and sixth stratums till the virgin soil. This should be one of the tombs in the north line, making up for the regret in the excavation of 1987.

For the correspondence of stratum of the northern wall of trench T305, the northern wall of trench T206 and the northern wall of the south trench of T204, see Table 1.

4. After this excavation, the stratigraphic accumulation of the middle part of the Yaoshan site can be summarized into the following stages:

Stage I: above the virgin soil (weathered bedrock

[1] In 2017, for the declaration as a world heritage, this stratum was reconfirmed and judged to be mountain bedrock. The small pebbles supposed contained in the sandy red soil were not transported manually.

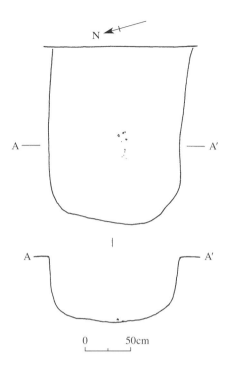

**Fig. 19.** Plan and section of pit 1997H1

**Table 1.** Correspondence table of stratums of some test trenches of Yaoshan site

| Construction stage | T305 | T206 | The south trench of T204 |
|---|---|---|---|
| I | ⑧ | | |
| | ⑦ | | ⑦ |
| | | ⑦ | ⑥ |
| | | ④ | ⑤ |
| II | ⑥ | ③ a | ④ |
| III | ⑤ | | |
| | ④ | | |
| | ③ | | |
| IV | ② | | ③ |
| V | | ② | ② |

and yellowish-brown sandy earth), red earth was stacked up, including the seventh and eighth stratums of unit T305, the fifth, sixth and seventh stratums of T204, and the fourth and seventh stratums of T206, with stone revetments added in certain parts (western No. 4 stone revetment and northern No. 2 stone revetment).

Stage II: above the red earth, grayish-brown mottled earth was stacked up, including the sixth stratum of unit T305 and the fourth stratum of the south trench of T204. Judging from the accumulation form, the texture and the color of earth, the 3a stratum of T206 might also be partial deposits of this stage.

Stage III: the yellow earthen mound was stacked up, including the third to fifth stratums of unit T305, with a basically flat surface. The west side was surrounded by western No. 1 stone revetment, which was covered with black mottled yellow earth (the third stratum of unit T305).

Stage IV: the reddish-brown sandy earthen mound was stacked up, including the second stratum of unit T305, the third stratum of the south trench of T204. The surface of the mound was in a slope shape, and its west side was overlaid with western No. 2 stone revetment and western No. 3 stone revetment.

Stage V: the black mottled yellow earthen mound was stacked up, including the second stratum of the south trench of T204 and the second stratum of trench T206. The surface of the mound was in a slope shape, and its west side area had a boundary that was similar to that of Stage I, hence the constructing of the entire earthen mound was completed.

Stage VI: the enclosing ditch was dug and then filled with pure gray earth to form a strong contrast in the central part with red and gray earth color.

Stage VII: the tomb pits were digged, causing certain damage to the entire big earthen mound.

## Section 4 Excavation in the Second Half of 1997

The excavation in the first half of 1997, together with the previous excavations, enabled us to have a wholly new understanding about Yaoshan site. Especially, the partly stratigraphic excavation of the deposits at the central part of the relics gave us further knowledge about

the construction structure of the altar. Then, it became a primary issue to confirm the plane area of Yaoshan site and its overall layout. Therefore, in the second half of 1997, Zhejiang Provincial Institute of Cultural Relics and Archaeology, Liangzhu Archaeological

Station continued to conducted excavations in this area (Picture 2).

The excavation began on October 14, 1997, and ended on January 10, 1998. Rui Guoyao, Ding Pin, Zhao Ye, Hu Jigen, Ma Zhushan, Fang Zhonghua, Ge Jianliang and Chen Huanle from Zhejiang Provincial Institute of Cultural Relics and Archaeology, Fei Guoping from Yuhang Management Institute of Liangzhu cultural Site, and Shi Shiying from Liangzhu Cultural Museum were involved in the excavation, and

Ding Pin was in charge of on-site issues.

Considering the arranging of test trenches and units in previous two excavations, grid test units were laid this time, with an east–west length of 10 m and a north–south width of 5 m. With the foot of the southwest slope of Yaoshan as the cardinal point, coordinate method was used to assign numbers for the units. These numbers were four-digit ones. The east–west length was calculated 10 m as a unit, which took up the first two digits, and the north–south length was

A. northern No. 1 stone revetment
B. northern No. 2 stone revetment
C. western No. 1 stone revetment
D. western No. 2 stone revetment
E. western No. 3 stone revetment
F. western No. 4 stone revetment
G. western No. 6 stone revetment
H. southern No. 1 stone revetment

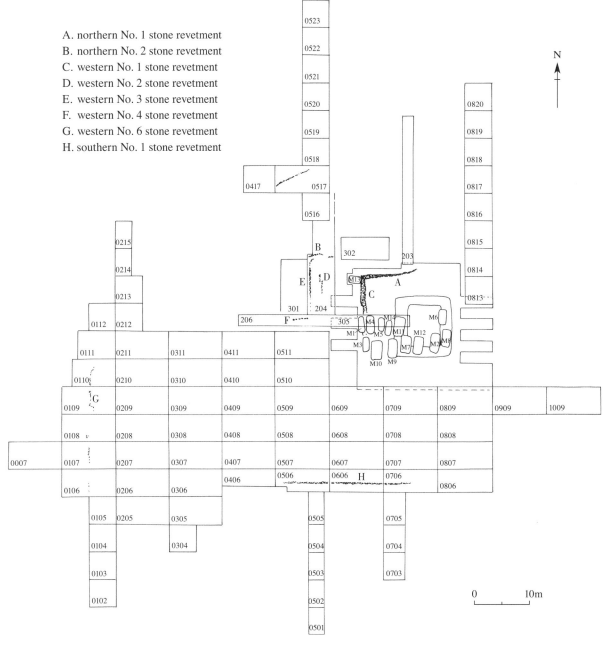

**Fig. 20.** Plan of the excavation from the second half of 1997 to 1998

calculated 5 m as a unit, which took up the later two digits (Fig. 20). The principle for the excavation was that the exposure went no further beyond the stratum of Liangzhu culture.

After removing the top soil with thickness of 20–60 cm and later-period disruptive deposits, the relics was revealed. Its deposits gradually inclined westward, featuring 15° slope inclining southward in the south of the southern No. 1 stone revetment, a relatively flat slope in the west of T0108, T0109 and T0110, a slope inclining northward within the area of the northwestern units T0109, T0209, T0210 and T0211, and a steep slope higher in the south and lower in the north within the area of units T0310 and T0410.

Through the excavation this time, we could confirm that the plane of Yaoshan site was basically in a rectangular shape, its south end bounded by the southern No. 1 stone revetment, its west end bounded by the western edge of T0106–T0109, the middle part of its northern edge bounded by the steep slope of T0310 and T0410, while its eastern boundary was hard to define. Within the area of T0806, T0807 and T0808, weathered sandstones were revealed after the top soil was removed, which had a quite flat and smooth surface, suggesting possible manual handling. Underneath the top soil of units T0707, T0708, T0809 and T0909, there were some Liangzhu culture deposits varying in thicknesses and earth texture. According to the less obvious boundary of these deposits and weathered stones, the eastern boundary could be roughly defined. That was, it went northward from the eastern end of T0706, passed the middle of T0707 to the eastern part of unit T0708, and then passed the northern part of unit T0809 and went northeastward to the middle of unit T1009.

On the eastern part of T0306, a short-length stone revetment was found, which was laid along the same straight line with southern No. 1 stone revetment, suggesting that the two may belong to the same stone revetment. However, in T0406, the southern No. 1 stone revetment was disrupted due to the later-period damage. The deposit above the stone revetment was black mottled yellow earth, forming a northward angle at the western end.

Underneath the top soil of T0206 was a steep slope, on which gravels were densely located, yet with irregular arrangement because of later-period disruption. Some parts were covered by yellowish-brown sandy earth (deposits covered by southern No. 1 stone revetment). This area might be the southwest corner of the site.

The discovery of western No. 5 stone revetment and western No. 6 stone revetment was also the main achievements in this excavation (Fig. 21). The two stone revetments were all in north–south direction, located within the area of units T0106, T0107, T0108, T0109 and T0110. Gravels were seen only on the top of western No. 5 stone revetment, forming a strip shape in north–south direction, the gravels were featuring large size and sparse distribution. The length was hard to determine for the lack of detailed exposure. The western No. 6 stone revetment was formed by small gravels piled upon one another, and had a north–south length of 22 m. Observed from the surface, the deposits on both sides had its earth texture and color consistent with those of the deposits on both sides of southern No. 1 stone revetment.

Underneath the top soil of units T0111 and T0211, a graveled surface was found, which was not fully revealed due to geographical limitations. The gravels were of varied sizes, densely located and flat; the surface was slightly messy, which suggested possible later-period disruption. In unit T0111, a small jade tube and two pottery shards were found on the stratum, which were roughly judged to be coarse sand-tempered pottery *ding* and clay pottery jar.

Besides, a ditch was found within the area of units T0109, T0108, T0107, T0206, T0205 and T0304, with a width of 0.25–0.70 m and a depth of 0.15–0.45 m. It was located at the foot of the southwestern steep slope of Yaoshan site in a northwest-to-southeast direction, its north end reaching the western part of T0109 and its south end reaching the middle of T0304. The ditch had its openning underneath the top soil, disturbed the earthen mound and damaged some of the western No. 6 stone revetment at unit T0108. Obviously, the ditch was built in a time later than when the stone revetment. The filling earth inside the ditch was grayish-brown

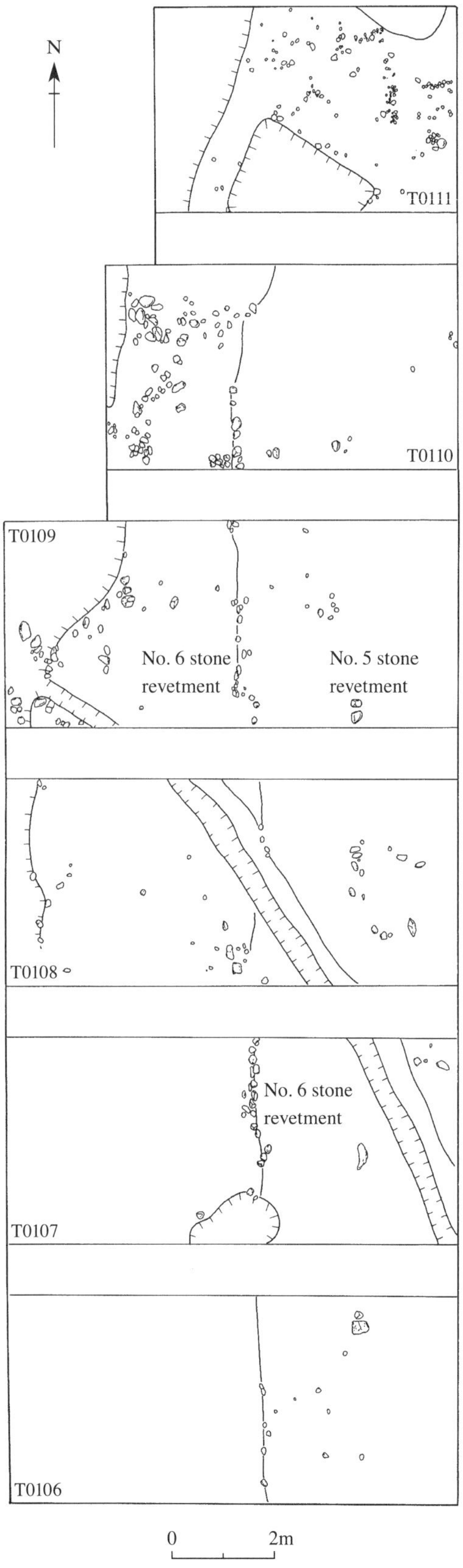

**Fig. 21.** Plan of western No. 5 and No. 6 stone
revetments

mottled sandy, with pure in texture and no artifacts. Hence it was difficult to determine the accurate date of the ditch. According to our excavation experience, the deposits inside the ditch would most probably belong to Liangzhu culture period.

# Section 5 Excavation in 1998

In order to further confirm the planar layout of the Yaoshan site, from April 2 to July 15, 1998, the Liangzhu Archaeological Station of Zhejiang Provincial Institute of Cultural Relics and Archaeology conducted another excavation on Yaoshan site. Rui Guoyao, Ding Pin, Fang Xiangming, Hu Jigen, Lou Hang, Ma Zhushan, Fang Zhonghua, Ge Jianliang and Chen Huanle participated in the excavation, and Ding Pin was the on-site director for the excavation.

1. The principle of protective excavation was still followed this time, as in most of the excavation areas, the excavation went no further beyond the Liangzhu culture stratum. The excavation was mainly carried out in the northeastern, northwestern, southwestern and southern parts of Yaoshan site.

In the northeastern area, the eastern half of excavation units T0813–T0820 was revealed. The whole stratum inclined northward with a height difference of around 9 m between the south and the north. In all the test units, after the top soil was cleared away, red earth mingled with weathered sandstones was revealed, with gravels located on the stratum, and mountainous bedrocks were revealed in some areas. No cultural remains were seen in the stratum, so the deposits were supposed to be virgin soil. Judging from the exposure, these should be outside the relics.

In the northwestern area, the eastern half of excavation units T0417, T0516, T0518–T0523 was revealed. In particular, beneath the top soil from the northern end of unit T0519 to the southern end of unit T0522, a stratum of yellowish-red earth was revealed, hard in texture, suggesting the possible existence of terraces. Yet it was irregularly shaped, and we couldn't exclude the possibility that it was caused by later-period water loss and earth erosion. In other test units, beneath the top soil, weathered mountainous bedrocks were revealed. In the southwestern part of unit T0517, there was a stratum of reddish-brown earth, growing thicker westward, containing scattered Liangzhu culture pottery fragments. Bar-shaped gravels were found on the northern edge of the reddish-brown earth, with a length of around 3.90 m, in a southwest-to-northeast direction, about 6.40 m lower than the surface of T305's second stratum, yet no piling up phenomenon was found (Fig. 22).

In the northwestern area, the western half of excavation units T0212 and T0213 was revealed, as well as the 2 m wide area at the western end of units T0214 and T0215. After the top soil was cleared away, yellowish-red earth deposits were revealed, inclining northwestward. At the north end of unit T0215, the stratum level was 7.90 m lower than the second stratum of T305. At units T0212–T0214, much gravel was located on the stratum, yet no further excavation was made. The deposits of this stratum extended southward and eastward respectively to T0211 and T0311, while the gravel became more and more sparse.

2. The excavation in the southern area was divided into two parts.

1) In the southeastern part of the excavation area, the west half of units T0703–T0705 was revealed. After the top soil was removed, the weathered

mountainous bedrocks appeared. At the northern end of unit T0705, Liangzhu culture deposits were found which were linked to unit T0706. The boundary between the southernmost end and the bedrocks was 3.45 m lower than the surface of T305's second stratum.

In the southwestern part of the excavation area, the eastern half of units T0102–T0105 was revealed. Underneath the top soil was the deposits of yellowish-brown earth and grayish-brown earth, yet the excavation went no further. Shattered Liangzhu culture pottery shards and burned earth particles could be seen on the stratum's surface, yet it was hard to determine whether they were the components of the entire relics. At the southern end of unit T0102, the level of this stratum was about 8.65 m lower than that of T305's second stratum.

2) In order to figure out the construction structure of the large-area gently piled earthen mound in the southern part of the relics, we revealed the eastern half of units T0505 and T0507–T0511, down to the virgin soil. This book only provides the profile map of the east wall of units T0507–T0509 (Fig. 23). Since this excavation was protective, only a 2 m wide area was excavated. Meanwhile, in order to completely preserve the southern No. 1 stone revetment, no

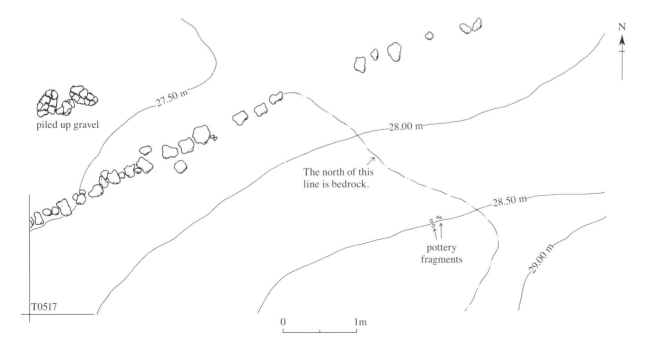

**Fig. 22.** Plan of bar-shaped gravel

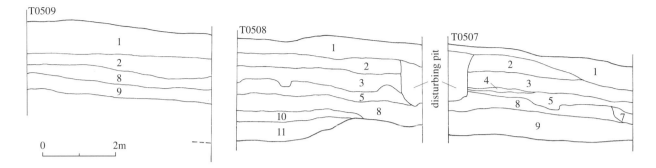

**Fig. 23.** Profile map of the east wall of units T0509, T0508 and T0507

1. top soil; 2. light brown sandy earth; 3. brown coarse sandy earth; 4. yellowish-brown sandy earth; 5. dark brown sandy earth mixed with grayish-white sandy earth; 6. yellow sandy earth; 7. light grayish-white earth; 8. grayish-brown earth; 9. red earth; 10. black mottled light yellow earth; 11. light yellow earth mixed with grayish-white earth

further excavation was carried out at the unit T0506 where the southern No. 1 stone revetment passed. The stratigraphic accumulation in this area could be roughly divided into the following stages:

a. The virgin soil was weathered sandstone, inclining southward. At the northern end, that was unit T0511, the level of the virgin soil was 2.30 m lower than the second stratum of T305; at the south part, that was unit T0507, the level of the virgin soil was 3.60 m lower than the second stratum of T305; and at the south end, that was T0505, the level of the virgin soil was 5.40 m lower than the second stratum of T305.

b. A stratum of relatively pure red earth was stacked up above the virgin soil (the ninth stratum), with a thickness of 35–60 cm, slightly inclining southward. At the north end, that was unit T0511, the stratum was about 1.80 m lower than the second stratum of T305; at the south end, that was unit T0507, the stratum was about 3.30 m lower than the second stratum of T305. This stratum was linked with the seventh stratum of the south trench of T204, both of the stratums belonging to the same Stage I deposits.

c. At unit T0511, above the red earth stratum was a stratum of grayish-brown earth. Because of tomb robbery, only a small amount of deposits were left, with a thickness of only 10 cm. According to the texture and color of earth and the context of deposits, this stratum should be linked with the fourth stratum of the south trench of T204, both belonging to the same Stage II deposits.

d. At units T0507–T0509, brown sandy earth was disposited onto the red earth. The deposits of this stratum and the grayish-brown earth at the northern unit T0511 were all covered by the top soil, without overlap upon one another directly. Hence we were unable to know which stratum was accumulated earlier and the other. The brown sandy earth deposits inclined southward, covering southern No. 1 stone revetment on the edge of T0506. According to the earth quality and color, it was the same as the sandy earthen mound in Stage IV.

After finishing the above excavation, the excavation team believed that the planar layout of Yaoshan site and the deposits and construction process of its main body parts had been basically figured out. The excavation now came to an end. On-site protection and interpretation of Yaoshan site was made under the planning issued by Zhejiang provincial cultural relics departments.

# Chapter III
# Tombs

Over the years, totally 12 Liangzhu culture tombs had been unearthed, mainly concentrated in the northeastern part of Yaoshan site. Judging from the planar distribution, they are all within the Stage III deposits area of the central part. All the tombs are divided into two lines, i. e. the south line and north line, in an orderly arrangement. There are 6 tombs in the north line, respectively tombs M6, M11, M14, M5, M4 and M1 from east to west; and also 6 tombs in the south line, respectively tombs M8, M2, M7, M9, M10 and M3 from east to west. The looted tomb M12 is located between tombs M2 and M7 and will be introduced in Chapter IV.

The tombs are all rectangle pit with vertical wall, basically oriented north–south. Since the Liangzhu culture tombs unearthed in Zhejiang Province are mostly heading southward, hence in the following introduction, except for the tombs whose skeleton remains were found, we all suppose that the tomb headed southward. The burial objects include jade artifacts, pottery vessels and stone artifacts etc., with a number of 754 pieces (sets), and 2,660 individual pieces. In particular, the jade artifacts are the main part, with a number of 678 pieces (sets), and 2,582 individual pieces. The jade artifacts include many types such as crown-shaped object (comb handle), cylindrical object with cover, three-pronged object, set of awl-shaped objects, *yue* axe, *cong*, *cong*-stylistic tube, *huang* semi-circular pendants, round plaque, bracelet, plaque object, belt hook and spindle whorl, yet the main type of jade artifact in Liangzhu culture – *bi* disc is not found.

The shape and burial objects of the tombs will be introduced according to the tombs' serial numbers in this chapter.

## Section 1 Tomb M1

### 1. The Shape of the Tomb

Tomb M1 is located at the westernmost end of the north line of the tombs, with tomb M4 situated to its east. It has its opening under the top soil, and disturbs the stratum that cover the Western No. 1 stone revetment. It is rectangle pit with vertical wall, with an orientation of 183°. Its southern end is slightly wider than the northern end, with a width of 1.18 m in the south and a width of 0.80 m in the north, with a length of 2.84 m and a depth of about 0.20 m. The tomb pit is filled with loose grayish-yellow earth which is relatively pure and contains no other inclusions. Skeleton inside the tomb had rotted away and left no remains (Picture 9).

Burial objects include 4 pottery vessels – a *dou*, a *gang* vat, *a ding* tripod, and also a gray clay pottery whose type couldn't be recognized. These pottery vessels are located at the northern end of the tomb pit, broken severely and hard to be took out.

In the middle part of the pit of tomb M1, there is a horizontally lying jade bracelet (M1:30), a small jade tube (M1:29), about 20 cm higher than the bottom of the tomb, which may indicate certain special meaning. Other jade artifacts are located at the bottom, and are mainly divided into two groups. At the southern end of the tomb, there are a crown-shaped jade object (M1:3), a *huang* semi-circular jade pendant (M1:5)

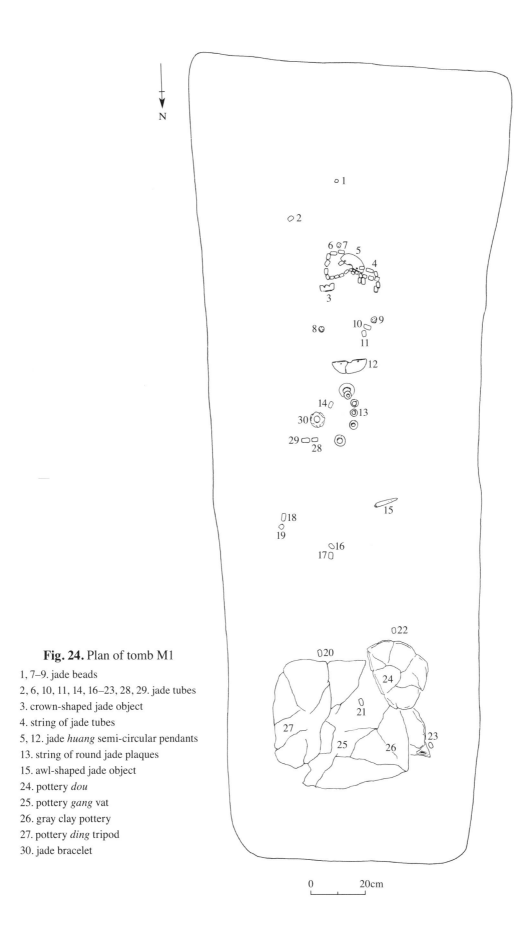

**Fig. 24.** Plan of tomb M1

1, 7–9. jade beads

2, 6, 10, 11, 14, 16–23, 28, 29. jade tubes

3. crown-shaped jade object

4. string of jade tubes

5, 12. jade *huang* semi-circular pendants

13. string of round jade plaques

15. awl-shaped jade object

24. pottery *dou*

25. pottery *gang* vat

26. gray clay pottery

27. pottery *ding* tripod

30. jade bracelet

0      20cm

with a string of tubes (M1:4); in the middle part of the tomb, there are a *huang* semi-circular jade pendant (M1:12), a set of six round jade plaques (M1:13) and a awl-shaped jade object (M1:15) (Picture 10) . Other small jade pieces such as tubes and beads are scattered around these artifacts and between the pottery vessels at the northern end (Fig. 24).

## 2. Burial Objects

The burial objects include jade artifacts and pottery vessels, with a number of 30 pieces (sets), and 61 individual pieces.

(1) Jade artifacts

There is a number of 26 pieces (sets), and 57 individual pieces, mostly white jade, including crown-shaped object, bracelet, *huang* semi-circular pendant, round plaque, awl-shaped object, tube and bead. During the excavation, for the pieces preliminarily determined as belonging to the same set, they are tagged with the same object reference number, under which -1, -2 and -3 ... are marked to indicate each individual piece.

**Crown-shaped object**: one piece (M1:3). It is thin and flat, presenting an upside-down trapezoid in plane, wider at the upper end, with two notches in the middle, forming a shape of semicircle; 3 small holes with the same distance apart are drilled from both sides at the lower end, one of which is broken. It is 2.5 cm in height, 4.5–4.8 cm in width, and 0.2 cm in thickness (Fig. 25; Picture 11).

**Bracelet**: one piece (M1:30). The whole object is in the shape of a wide and flat ring, with straight and smooth inner wall. Same dragon head motifs are carved in the same direction on the four convexities of the outer wall. The wide plane of the outer wall is used to show the front image of the dragon head, and

extend to the upper and lower ends of the bracelet in bas-relief to form the profile of the dragon head, hence forming the there-dimensional dragon head motif. The lower end of the front image is a flat and wide mouth, with straight and flat upper lip, big and regular square-shaped upper teeth. On both sides of the upper lip, there are round raised nostrils. The wide flat nose is in parallel with the upper lip, above which there is a pair of big, round and raised eyeballs, around which are eyepits. Above two eyes, a pair of short horns is carved in intaglio. Between the eyes and the nose there is a rhombus pattern with dual lines, at the center of which a small oblong is carved in intaglio. By the side of the motif, bas-relief and intaglio techniques are used to express the side image of deep and long rictus, nose and head. In the past, such kind of jade artifact was called "Chiyou Ring" (Chiyou: a mythological warrior engaged in the fight with the Yellow Emperor). Its plane and side images indicate that its shape is quite similar to that of the dragon in Chinese mythology. It is 2.65 cm in height, 8.6 cm in diameter, and 6.1 cm in hole diameter (Figs. 26, 27; Pictures 12–14).

***Huang* semi-circular pendants**: two pieces.

M1:5, it has grayish-brown spots. It is undecorated with a half-*bi* shape. The middle of the upper end is semi-circularly concave, with small round holes drilled from both sides on left and right sides, and the bottom is in an arc shape. The whole object is thinner in edges and thicker in the middle. There is a filament-shaped string-cutting mark on its top end and the front surface respectively. It is 4.2 cm in height, 10.1 cm in width, and 0.55 cm in thickness (Fig. 28; Picture 15).

M1:12, it has grayish-green spots. It had already broken into three pieces when unearthed, and is undecorated, with a half-*bi* shape. The middle of the upper end is semi-circularly concave, with small

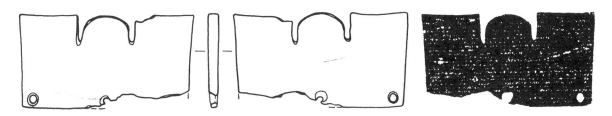

**Fig. 25.** Crown-shaped jade object (M1:3) and its rubbing (1/1)

**Fig. 26.** Jade bracelet (M1:30) and its rubbings (1/2)

round holes drilled from both sides on left and right sides, and the bottom is in an arc shape. There are several groups of cambered string-cutting marks on the surface, mostly on uneven concaves. It is 4.8 cm in height, 11.8 cm in width, and 0.5 cm in thickness (Fig. 28; Picture 16).

**String of tubes:** one set (M1:4). It comprises 27 pieces of tube, five of which are broken. All the tubes are in cylinder shape, with holes drilled from both sides. The tubes are 1.2–1.9 cm in length, 0.8–0.9 cm in diameter. This string of tubes is connected with jade

*huang* semi-circular pendant M1:5 when unearthed, indicating that the two should belong to the same group (Fig. 29; Picture 17).

**Set of round plaques:** one set (M1:13). It comprises 6 round plaques, and they are connected with jade *huang* semi-circular pendant M1:12, indicating that they may belong to the same group. They are flat pie-shaped, with a round hole drilled in the middle. Except M1:13-1, there is a hole drilled from both sides on each piece's edge.

M1:13-1, it has a hole drilled from both sides in

**Fig. 27.** Rubbings of jade bracelet (M1:30) (1/2)

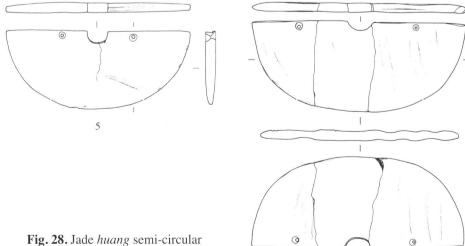

5

**Fig. 28.** Jade *huang* semi-circular
pendants in tomb M1 (1/2)

12

the middle, with spiral marks left on the inner wall of the hole and also has cambered string-cutting marks on the surface. It is 4.5 cm in diameter, 1.7 cm in hole diameter, and 0.5 cm in thickness (Fig. 29; Picture 18).

M1:13-2, it has a hole drilled from one side, with 2.2 cm in diameter, 1 cm in hole diameter, and 0.4 cm in thickness (Fig. 29; Picture 19).

M1:13-3, it has a hole drilled from one side, with 2.25 cm in diameter, 1 cm in hole diameter, and 0.4 cm in thickness (Fig. 29; Picture 20).

M1:13-4, it has a hole drilled from one side, with straight string-cutting marks left on the surface, with 2.2 cm in diameter, 0.9 cm in hole diameter, and 0.3 cm in thickness (Fig. 29; Picture 21).

M1:13-5, it has a hole drilled from one side, with straight string-cutting marks left on the surface, with 2.4 cm in diameter, 0.8 cm in hole diameter, and 0.4 cm in thickness (Fig. 29; Picture 22).

M1:13-6, it has a hole drilled from both sides, with spiral marks left on the inner wall of the hole. It is incomplete, with 2.3 cm in diameter, 1.2 cm in hole diameter, and 0.4 cm in thickness (Fig. 29).

**Awl-shaped object:** one piece (M1:15). It was broken into 5 parts when unearthed. This object is strip shaped, with a rounded square cross-section, on one end is sharp and pointed and the other relatively flat, with a hole drilled from both sides. It is 6.3 cm in length (Fig. 30; Picture 26).

**Tubes:** fifteen pieces, mostly of them are cylinder-shaped with a hole drilled from both sides in the middle.

M1:2, it is 1.2 cm in length, 1 cm in diameter, 0.4 cm in hole diameter (Fig. 30; Picture 23).

M1:6, it is 3 cm in length, 1.2 cm in diameter, 0.6 cm in hole diameter (Fig. 30; Picture 24).

M1:10, it has a three prism shaped cross-section, with 1.9 cm in length, 1.1 cm in diameter and 0.6 cm in hole diameter (Fig. 30; Picture 24).

M1:11, it has cambered string-cutting marks on the surface and on one end face, with 2.1 cm in length, 1.1 cm in diameter, 0.6 cm in hole diameter (Fig. 30; Picture 24).

M1:14, it is 1 cm in length, 0.9 cm in diameter, 0.45 cm in hole diameter (Fig. 30; Picture 23).

M1:16, it has cambered string-cutting marks on one end face, with 2 cm in length, 1.1 cm in diameter,

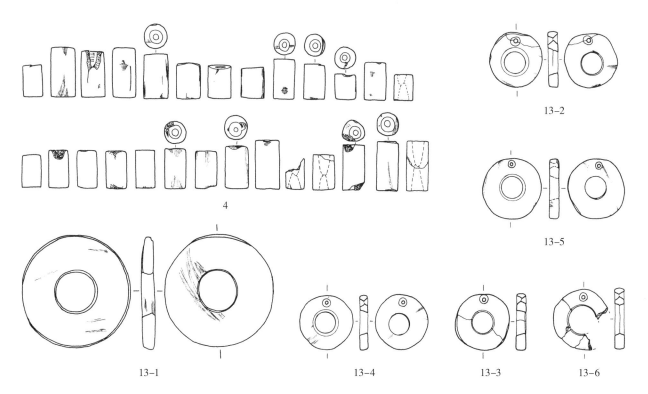

**Fig. 29.** String of jade tubes, string of round jade plaques in tomb M1

4. string of jade tubes; 13-1–13-6. string of round jade plaques (2/3)

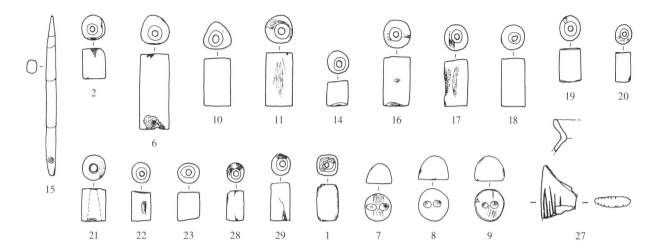

**Fig. 30.** Jade beads, jade tubes, awl-shaped jade pendant and pottery *ding* tripod in tomb M1

1, 7–9. jade beads; 2, 6, 10, 11, 14, 16–23, 28, 29. jade tubes; 15. awl-shaped jade pendant; 27. pottery *ding* tripod (27 is about 1/4, others 2/3)

0.5 cm in hole diameter (Fig. 30; Picture 24).

M1:17, it has cutting marks on the surface and on one end face, with 1.9 cm in length, 1 cm in diameter, 0.4 cm in hole diameter (Fig. 30; Picture 24).

M1:18, it is 1.9 cm in length, 1 cm in diameter, 0.45 cm in hole diameter (Fig. 30; Picture 24).

M1:19, it is 1.3 cm in length, 0.9 cm in diameter, 0.5 cm in hole diameter (Fig. 30; Picture 23).

M1:20, it is 1.1 cm in length, 0.6 cm in diameter, 0.3 cm in hole diameter (Fig. 30; Picture 23).

M1:21, it is cut after drilling from both sides, hence the form of drilling hole is unidirectional, with cambered string-cutting marks on the cutting surface. It is 1.3 cm in length, 1 cm in diameter, 0.6 cm in hole diameter (Fig. 30; Picture 25).

M1:22, it has a concave cutting mark on the surface, with 1.2 cm in length, 0.8 cm in diameter, 0.45 cm in hole diameter (Fig. 30; Picture 25).

M1:23, it is 1.1 cm in length, 0.9 cm in diameter, 0.6 cm in hole diameter (Fig. 30; Picture 25).

M1:28, it is 1.2 cm in length, 0.7 cm in diameter, 0.4 cm in hole diameter (Fig. 30; Picture 25).

M1:29, it is 1.5 cm in length, 0.8 cm in diameter, 0.45 cm in hole diameter (Fig. 30; Picture 25).

**Beads:** four pieces, including two types: waist-drum-shaped and hemispherical.

**Waist-drum-shaped bead:** one piece (M1:1), arc-shaped on upper and lower ends, with a hole drilled from both sides. It is 1.5 cm in length, 0.9 cm in diameter, 0.5 cm in hole diameter (Fig. 30; Picture 23).

**Hemispherical beads:** three pieces, with tunnel-shaped holes drilled laterally on the flat surface.

M1:7, it has cambered string-cutting marks on the surface, with 0.8 cm in thickness and 1.1 cm in diameter (Fig. 30; Picture 27).

M1:8, it is 0.9 cm in thickness and 1.2 cm in diameter (Fig. 30; Picture 27).

M1:9, it has cambered string-cutting marks on the surface, with 1 cm in thickness, 1.2 cm in diameter (Fig. 30; Picture 27).

(2) Pottery vessels: four pieces.

***Ding* tripod:** one piece (M1:27), it is a red sand-tempered pottery and is severely broken, its shape is unidentifiable. It has flared mouth, round lip, flat and straight rim surface, and fin-shaped leg whose cross-section is oblate, thick in the middle while thin on the edge, flat and straight outside (Fig. 30).

***Dou*:** one piece (M1:24), it is a gray clay pottery, and is severely broken, with incomplete trumpet-shaped ring foot.

***Gang* vat:** one piece (M1:25), it is a red sand-tempered pottery, and is loose in body texture, severely broken, whose overall shape is unidentifiable. There are thick basket patterns on the surface.

Besides, there is also a piece of gray clay pottery (M1:26), but is too broken to recognize its shape.

# Section 2 Tomb M2

## 1. The Shape of the Tomb

Tomb M2 is located at the eastern end of the south line of the tombs, with tomb M8 to its east and the robbed tomb M12 to its west. It has its opening under the top soil, and disturbs the southeastern corner of red earthen mound as well as the enclosing grey earthen ditch. It is rectangular pit with vertical wall, with an orientation of 185°. The southwestern part had been damaged by tomb robbers. It is 3.50 m in length and 1.60 m in width, 0.80 m in the deepest point, 0.46 m in the middle part and 0.12 m in the shallowest point. Originally, the tomb contains a single-log coffin because the bottom has a concaved shape. Skeleton inside the tomb had rotten away when excavated and left no remains (Picture 28).

Within the outline of the pit of tomb M2, the texture and color of the earth within a range of north–south 2.70 m by east–west 1.10 m is slightly different, making the earth on the tomb's opening plane presenting a 回-shape. Therefore, we first excavated the whole pit a bit and then excavated the middle part with difference color of earth, and this part was defined as the place where the coffin was laid. The pit wall was cleared out. Most of the burial objects were unearthed from this part. Hence it is a generally correct judgment that there had been a coffin in the tomb. The tomb is filled with grayish-brown mottled earth, which is pure without any artifact. The earth filled outside the coffin outline is relatively tough, and it is found that the earth is in sheet structure, showing that the earth might have been rammed. But the surface of rammed stratums couldn't be identified. The earth filling the coffin outline is relatively loose and soft. Stratigraphic excavation was not conducted so the relationship between the coffin and the tomb pit was not confirmed.

Among the burial objects are four pieces of pottery vessels including one *ding* tripod, two ring-foot jars and two *dou* high-ring foot plates, located at the northern end of the tomb. But they could not be integrally took out due to their loose texture. There are two pieces

of stone *yue* axe of the same type, one (M2:61) being located in the southern end of the tomb and the other (M2:27) in the middle of the tomb, and their blades are both facing the west.

A piece of crown-shaped object (M2:1) was unearthed from west of the southern end of the tomb pit, with its patterned side facing upward, its tenon at the bottom facing the east and cinnabar coats remaining on both the front and back side. There are some traces of wooden fiber extending 10 cm outward from the point at the same width with the tenon, which, however, could not be taken out. Beside the crown-shaped object is a piece of three-pronged jade object (M2:6), being basically connected with a long jade tube (M2:7) when unearthed. There is a set of seven awl-shaped jade objects (M2:8–12) in the middle of the southern end. Moreover, there is a set of cylindrical jade objects with cover (M2:2, 3). The cover is separated from the cylindrical object and the side with tunnel-shaped holes facing upward. The jade *yue* axe (M2:14) is located in the middle by south, with vermilion traces around the hole. There is a *cong*-stylistic jade tube (M2:20) at the top of the *yue* axe and a *cong*-stylistic jade tube (M2:21) 90 cm further north, which might be the lower end ornament at the bottom of the *yue* axe handle. Two pieces of *cong* are unearthed from this tomb. The one (M2:22) in the middle has its top (according to the patterns) facing upward and the other one (M2:23) has its top facing the south (Picture 29). There is an awl-shaped jade object (M2:25) on the west of the middle part. A jade handle (M2:55) and a jade bird (M2:50) were unearthed from the northwest of the pottery *dou* (M2:34) in the north of the tomb. The jade bird was unearthed with the patterned side facing downward and the head facing the north. Besides, a multitude of jade tubes are scattered in the south, middle and north parts with only three sets (M2:38, 40, 59), the rest being individual pieces. What needs noticing is that the round jade plaque unearthed from this tomb is the one and only in the south line of the tombs (Fig. 31).

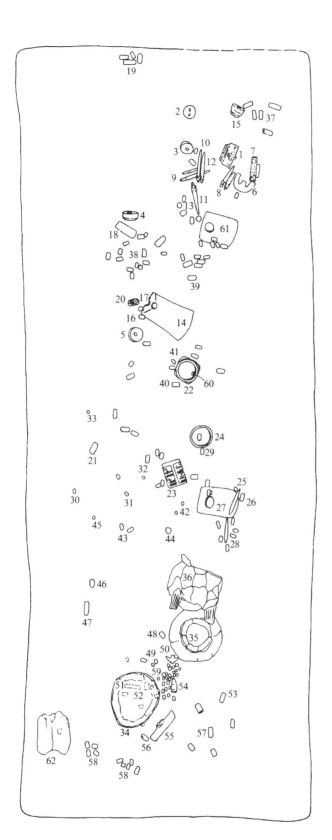

N

0      20cm

**Fig. 31.** Plan of tomb M2

1. crown-shaped jade object
2, 3. cylindrical jade objects with
     cover
4, 5, 16. cylindrical jade objects
6. three-pronged jade object
7, 18. long jade tubes
8–12, 25, 28. awl-shaped jade
     objects
13, 41, 42, 56, 60. jade beads
14. jade *yue* axe
15, 44, 46, 56. jade end ornaments
17. round jade plaque
19, 37, 38, 40, 57–59. strings of
     jade tubes
20, 21. *cong*-stylistic jade tubes
22, 23. jade *cong*
24. jade bracelet
26. jade pendant
27, 61. stone *yue* axes
29, 39, 43, 47, 48, 52, 53. jade
     tubes
30–33, 45, 49. jade particles
34, 62. pottery *dou*
35. pottery ring-foot jar
36. pottery *ding* tripod
50. jade bird
51. jade bar-shaped ornament
55. jade handle

## 2. Burial Objects

The burial objects include jade artifacts, stone artifacts and pottery vessels, with a number of 62 pieces (sets), totaling 190 individual pieces.

(1) Jade artifacts

There is a number of 56 jade pieces (sets), and 184 individual pieces, mostly white jade, including crown-shaped object, cylindrical object with cover, three-pronged object, set of awl-shaped objects, *yue* axe, *cong, cong*-stylistic tube, bracelet, handle, round plaque and awl-shaped object etc.

**Crown-shaped object:** one piece (M2:1). It is flat and a bit concave, presenting an upside-down trapezoid in plane. The middle of the upper end is pointed and 3 small round holes are drilled from both sides equidistantly on the tenon at the bottom. The back side is convex and with no patterns. The front side is concave and carved with sacred animal motif by intaglio technique. The upper part of the motif is carved with a sacred human wearing a feather-like crown. Its face is shaped like an upside-down trapezoid. Eyes, nose, mouth and even two arms are also carved. The lower part of the motif is the sacred animal face with oval eyepits. The double-circles represent the eyes and with triangular canthi. The face has a bulbous nose, under which there are rolling cloud patterns representing the nostrils. The mouth is long and flat with four tusks, among which the two inside are facing upward and the two outside are facing downward. The bottom is decorated with a belt of rolling cloud patterns and two looking-back bird patterns are carved on both the upper left and right corners. There is an oval hole under the sacred animal face. It is 5.8 cm in height, 7.7 cm in width and 0.35 cm in thickness (Fig. 32; Picture 30).

**Cylindrical object with cover:** one set (M2:2, 3). It is so named because it is composed of the cylindrical object and the cover.

M2:2 is the cover. It is round pie shaped with the upper side convex. Its bottom is flat with a tunnel-shaped hole and with cambered string-cutting marks. It is 1.9 cm in thickness and 4.4 cm in diameter (Fig. 33; Picture 32).

M2:3 is the cylindrical object, with blue green spots. The hole in the middle of the cylinder is biased to one side. Cutting marks could be found on the exterior wall of the cylinder object's upper part and the two sets of cambered string-cutting marks intersecting with each other are on the top side. It is 2.5 cm in height and 4.1–4.3 cm in diameter (Fig. 33; Picture 33).

**Three-pronged object:** one piece (M2:6). It is undecorated with gray spots. The two prongs on the left and the right are at the same level while the one in the middle is lower with vertical holes. There is a hole drilled from both sides on both the top end and inner side of the left and right prongs. It is 4.2 cm in height, 6.3 cm in width and 1.1 cm in thickness (Fig. 33; Picture 31).

**Long tubes:** two pieces. They are so named due to

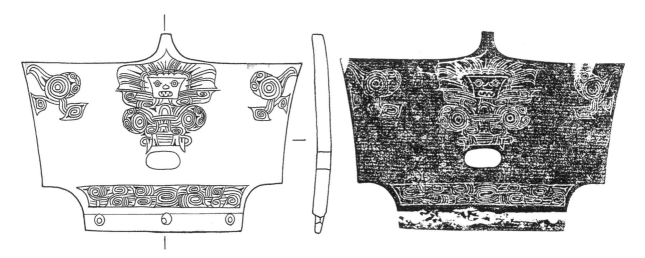

**Fig. 32.** Crown-shaped jade object (M2:1) and its rubbing (1/1)

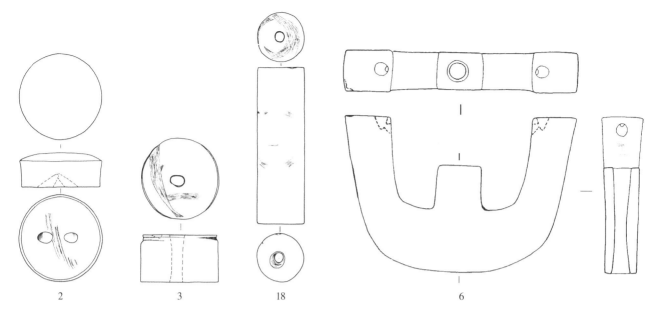

**Fig. 33.** Cylindrical jade object with cover, three-pronged jade object and long jade tube in tomb M2
2. cover; 3. cylindrical object; 6. three-pronged jade object; 18. long tube (6 is 1/1, others 1/2)

their relatively long figure and cylindrical tube shape.

M2:7 is a yellowish white jade artifact. The hole in the middle is not very regular. It has used bas-relief and intaglio carving techniques, and the patterns are divided into the upper, middle and lower group by two circles of ridge pattern. The lower one only has the upper part of the overall pattern. There are four circular projecting blocks on both the upper and lower part of each group, and round circles are intaglioed on the upper circular projecting blocks, and connected with arcs. It is linked with the three-pronged object when unearthed, possibly belonging to one set. It is 6.75 cm in length, 1.4 cm in diameter and 0.5 cm in hole diameter (Fig. 34; Picture 34).

M2:18 has a big brown spot at one end, with a hole drilled from both sides in the middle. It is 8.1 cm in length, 2.6 cm in diameter and 0.5 cm in hole diameter (Fig. 33; Picture 35).

**Set of awl-shaped objects:** one set, composed of seven individual pieces.

M2:8-1 is long arched square cylinder shaped with its head end sharp and with a tenon at the tail end, on which there is a small hole drilled from both sides. Simplified sacred animal motif is carved at the lower part with two belts of thin-line pattern decorated. A small circle is carved on each side to represent the eye.

The flat and convex nose is curved at the corner below. It is 5.6 cm in length and 1.1 cm in diameter (Fig. 35; Picture 36).

M2:8-2 is similar to M2:8-1 in shape, yet slightly longer. The lower part is carved with a relatively complete sacred animal motif. A belt of thin-line pattern is carved on the top of the pattern. The corner under it served as the axis, and the eyes, the nose bridge and the mouth are carved on both adjacent sides. It is 6.5 cm in length and 0.8 cm in diameter (Fig. 35; Picture 37).

M2:9-1 is strip-shaped and without pattern. The head end is round and pointed and the tail end has a flat tenon with a small hole drilled from both sides. It is 11.4 cm in length and 0.8 cm in diameter (Fig. 36; Picture 38).

M2:9-2 is also strip-shaped and without pattern. It is broken into two pieces when unearthed. The head end is round and pointed and the tail end is a little flat with a small hole drilled from both sides. It is 7.8 cm in length and 0.7 cm in diameter (Fig. 36; Picture 39).

M2:10 is strip-shaped. The head end is round and pointed, and the tail end has a tenon with a hole drilled from both sides. The tail end with the tenon presented a arched square cylinder shape, and simplified

**Fig. 34.** Long jade tube (M2:7) and its rubbings (1/1)

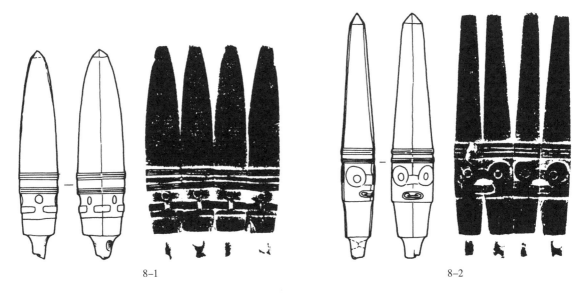

8–1

8–2

**Fig. 35.** Awl-shaped jade objects and their rubbings in tomb M2 (1/1)

sacred animal motifs are carved by bas-relief carving technique on both the front and back sides. The nose is flat and round and the eyes are represented by round projecting blocks at the corner. There is a vertical groove between the two sets of motifs, serving as the division line. It is 9.8 cm in length (Fig. 36; Picture 40).

M2:11 is basically similar to M2:10 in shape. It is 10.2 cm in length (Fig. 36; Picture 41).

M2:12 is strip-shaped without pattern. The head end

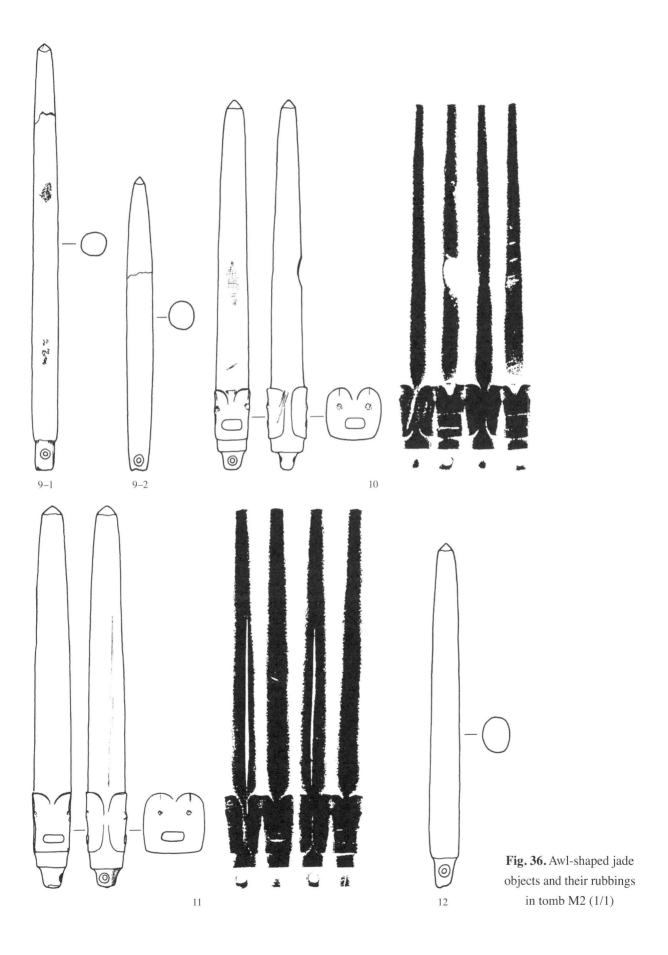

9–1          9–2                              10

11                              12

**Fig. 36.** Awl-shaped jade
objects and their rubbings
in tomb M2 (1/1)

is round and pointed and the tail end has a tenon with a hole drilled from both sides. It is 9.05 cm in length and 0.9 cm in diameter (Fig. 36; Picture 42).

**Yue axe:** one piece (M2:14). It is brown with some red brown spots. It is in shape of rectangle with cambered blade. Broken traces after vertical cutting could be found at the top end, slightly polished. Two round holes are drilled in a vertical line on the upper part, with step-shaped marks left. The upper one with a broken circle at the top end is slightly smaller than the lower one. It is 17.5 cm in length, 9.6 cm in top width, 11.5 cm in blade width and 0.4–0.7 cm in thickness (Fig. 42; Picture 45).

**Cong:** two pieces.

M2:22, with brown spots, it is short cylinder shaped with a round vertical hole, and its exterior wall is slightly convex. There are four rectangular projecting blocks at the corner on which sacred animal motifs are curved, with the corner as the axis. The overall motif is divided into upper and lower part by a horizontal shallow groove. The top is decorated with two belts of patterns composed of line patterns and rolling cloud patterns. Below is engraved with bilaterally symmetric double-circles to represent the eyes, with rolling cloud patterns carved on the horizontal ridge pattern. The lower part of the motif are symmetric oval eyepits carving by bas-relief technique, with double-circles and rolling cloud patterns on it. Between the two eyes is nose carving by bas-relief and intaglio technique. The top end is not even, but polished. It is 5.2 cm in height, 8.2 cm in collar diameter and 6.7 cm in hole diameter (Figs. 37, 38; Picture 43).

M2:23, it is a piece of white jade. It is hollow cylinder shaped with its exterior square and the interior round. The four angles are close to 90 degrees and the exterior wall is slightly convex. The overall motif is divided into two same parts by a crosswise groove, carved with the same simplified sacred animal motif. The double circles by drilling represent the eyes and one short line on each side of the eye represents the canthi. The flat and protruding nose is under the eyes with rolling cloud patterns carved on it. Two belts of bow string patterns are carved above the two eyes to represent the feathered crown. The top end has some

irregular cutting marks, but polished. It is 8.8 cm in height, 7.8 cm in collar diameter and 6.2 cm in hole diameter (Figs. 39, 40; Picture 44).

**Cong-stylistic tubes:** two pieces, similar to jade *cong* in shape but smaller in volume.

M2:20, it is square cylinder shaped with a round hole drilled from both sides in the middle. The motif is divided into three parts of the upper, middle and lower by two belts of crosswise shallow grooves, with the corner as the axis. There are altogether 12 sets of almost same simplified sacred animal motif carved on it. Two belts of bow string patterns are decorated on the top. The circles represent the eyes, with a flat and protruding nose under them. It is 3.3 cm in height, 1.5 cm in collar diameter and 0.65 cm in hole diameter (Fig. 41; Picture 46).

M2:21, it is square cylinder shaped with the hole in the middle drilled from both sides and slightly off-centered. With the shape similar to that of M2:20, it is 3.5 cm in height, 1.4 cm in collar diameter and 0.6 cm in hole diameter (Fig. 41; Picture 47).

**Cylindrical objects:** three pieces. All are cylindrical.

M2:4, it has red brown spots with a hole drilled from both sides in the middle. The tenon-shaped end is slightly narrower than the other. It is 2.2 cm in height, 4 cm in diameter and 0.8 cm in hole diameter (Fig. 42; Picture 48).

M2:5, it has gray spots, and the hole drilled from both sides is slightly off-centered. Fracture faces and cutting marks are found on one end and cambered string-cutting marks are found on the other end. It is 2 cm in height, 4.5 cm in diameter and 0.7 cm in hole diameter (Fig. 42; Picture 49).

M2:16, it has a hole drilled from both sides in the middle. A circle of cutting marks with intervals are found on the exterior wall, and the marks are relatively deep. The cross section is like a triangle with transverse fine string-cutting marks on the cutting surface. Two line traces are on the top of the cylinder. It is 2.5 cm in height, 4.5 cm in diameter and 1.1 cm in hole diameter (Fig. 42; Picture 52).

**Round plaque:** one piece (M2:17). It is flat pie-shaped with a hole drilled from both sides in the middle. Three projecting blocks of bas-relief are on

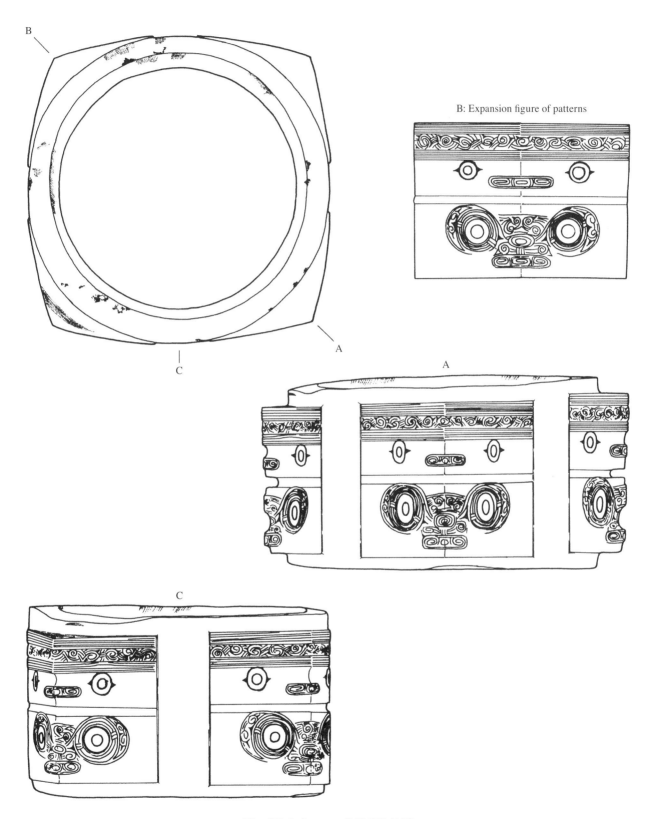

**Fig. 37.** Jade *cong* (M2:22) (1/1)

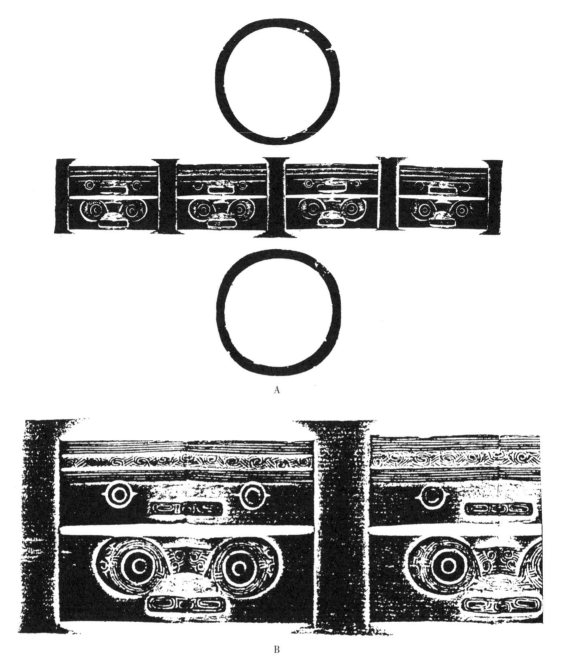

**Fig. 38.** Rubbings of jade *cong* (M2:22) (A is 1/3 and B is 1/1)

the outer rim. Three dragon head motifs are carved in the same direction on them by intaglio and bas-relief technique. A arc double-line rhombus pattern is carved between the motifs. Cambered string-cutting marks are found on the surface. It is 1.1 cm in depth, 4.1 cm in diameter and 1.2 cm in hole diameter (Fig. 43; Pictures 50, 51).

**Bracelet:** one piece (M2:24). It has gray spots with no decoration. Wide-ring shaped, it has a convex inner wall while the outer wall is straight. One end of the surface is left with cambered string-cutting marks. It is 2.6–3.2 cm in height, 8.4 cm in diameter and 6.5 cm in hole diameter (Fig. 42; Picture 53).

**Awl-shaped objects:** two pieces.

M2:25, it is long arched square cylinder shaped. One end is pointed and the other end has a small tenon with a hole drilled from both sides. Simplified sacred animal motifs are carved in the middle, which is divided into upper and lower parts by a shallow groove. A belt of the bow string pattern is carved on

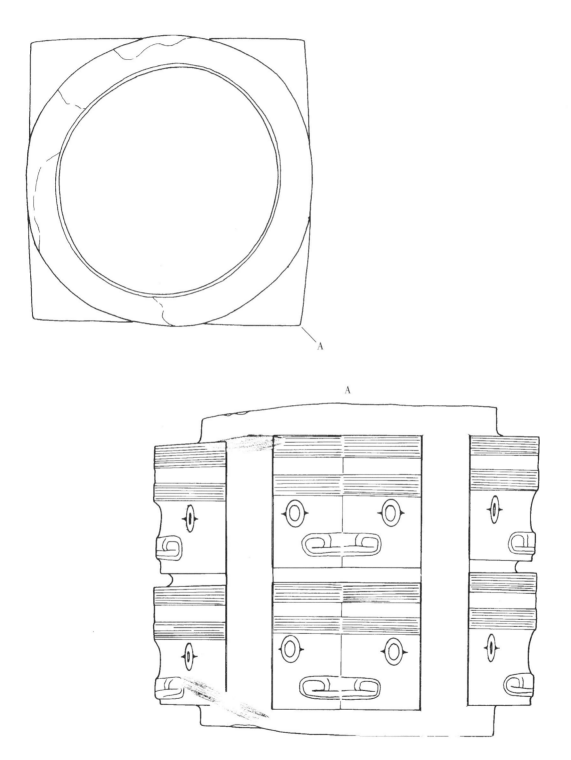

**Fig. 39.** Jade *cong* (M2:23) (1/1)

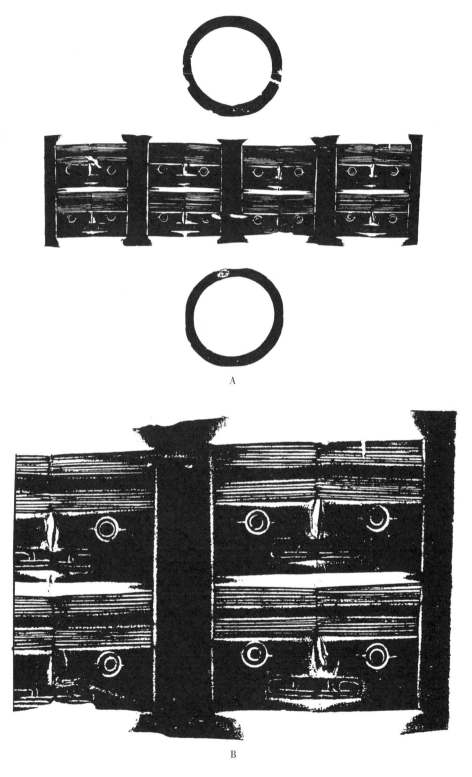

**Fig. 40.** Rubbings of jade *cong* (M2: 23) (A is 1/3 and B is 1/1)

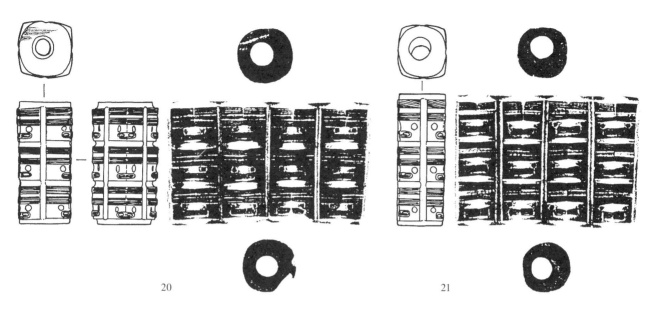

20                    21

**Fig. 41.** *Cong*-stylistic jade tubes (M2:20, 21) and their rubbings (1/1)

each group of the sacred animal motif with the corner as the axis. The adjacent two motifs share one circle representing the eye. It is 8.9 cm in length and 0.95 cm in width (Fig. 44; Picture 55).

M2:28, it is strip-shaped with a slightly oblate cross section. The head end is polished after broken and the tail end has a hole drilled from both sides. It is 9.25 cm in length (Fig. 44; Picture 56).

**Pendant:** one piece (M2:26). It is shaped as a water-drop, without patterns. The lower end is round and pointed and the upper end has a thin and long tenon with a hole drilled from both sides. It is 3.9 cm in length and 1.25 cm in diameter (Fig. 44; Picture 58).

**End ornaments:** four pieces, varying in shapes.

M2:15, it is cylindrical with a hole pierced through in the middle. The hole wall is convex, and the exterior wall is slightly concave. One end of the cylinder presented tenon shaped. The same cutting marks with the cylindrical object M2:16 are found on the exterior wall. It is 3.2 cm in top end diameter, 3.8 cm in bottom end diameter, 3 cm in length and 2.2 cm in hole diameter (Fig. 42; Picture 54).

M2:44, it is cylindrical with blue and gray spots. One end is relatively thin and shaped in a round tenon. Three belts of bow string patterns by intaglio are found on the exterior wall. It is 2.4 cm in length and 1 cm in diameter (Fig. 42; Picture 59).

M2:46, it has the shape and size similar to those of M2:44 (Fig. 42; Picture 60).

M2:54, it is shaped like a flat cylinder and dark green. One end is flat and round and the other end is oval. The thick end is shaped like a tenon with two parallel deeply concave holes. It is 4.55 cm in length and 1.5–2 cm in diameter (Fig. 42; Picture 61).

**Bird:** one piece (M2:50). It is dark green with a few gray and brown spots. The main body is flat yet with the head extending ahead and the two wings stretching. The middle of the bottom is slightly convex. The back side is even and drills with three pairs of tunnel-shaped holes, among which the two holes on the wings are drilled from the wing and the side. The front side of the bird head is carved with the sacred animal motif by bas-relief and intaglio carving technique, representing the mouth and the two eyes. If the bird's beak is turned upside down, the pattern would look like both a bird swooping down and an ox showing off its horns and teeth. It is 3.2 cm in height, 4.6 cm in width and 0.5 cm in depth (Fig. 44; Pictures 62, 63).

**Handle:** one piece (M2:55). It is shaped like a long cylinder with a round-square cross section. The middle is concave, and the two ends are slightly upswept up. A concave hole with a depth of about 0.8 cm is found on two end faces. The middle of the handle is concave with a square projecting block, on which the

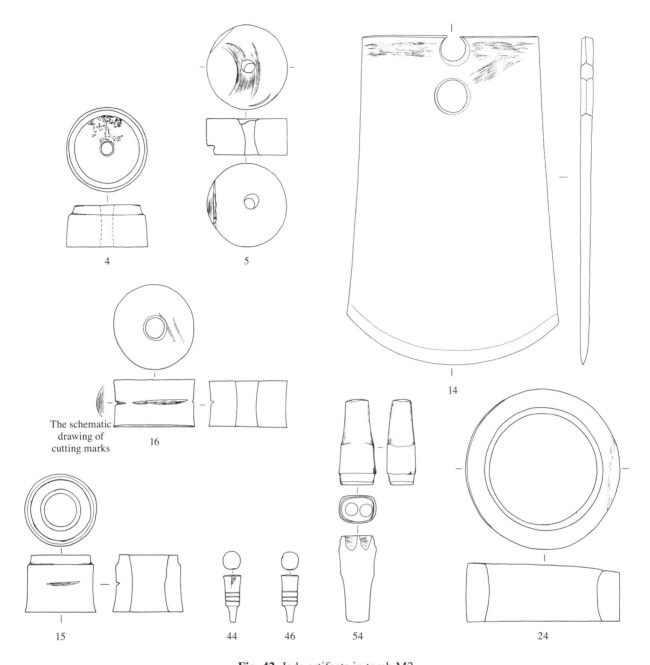

**Fig. 42.** Jade artifacts in tomb M2

4, 5, 16. cylindrical objects; 14. *yue* axe; 15, 44, 46, 54. end ornaments; 24. bracelet (1/2)

The schematic drawing of cutting marks

sacred animal motif is carved. The eyeballs are a bit bulgy with rolling cloud pattern between the eyes, representing the forehead. The lines carved on the two sides of forehead may represent the feather crown. The horizontal rectangular convex represents the nose with rolling cloud patterns decorated on it. Opposite to the projecting block is a concave hole with a depth about 1 cm. The handle is 10.4 cm in length and 2.2 cm in thickness (Figs. 45, 46; Pictures 64, 65).

**Bar-shaped ornament:** one piece (M2:51). Made

of the bluish white jade, without patterns and shaped like a flat rectangular. The two ends are wider than the middle. On either end remains a half hole. It is 5.8 cm in length, 0.95–1.2 cm in width and 0.25 cm in depth (Fig. 45; Picture 57).

**Strings of tubes:** seven sets.

M2:19, it is composed of four individual pieces and identified with the same serial number. With brown spots, they are all cylinder-shaped with holes drilled from both sides in the middle. Their lengths range

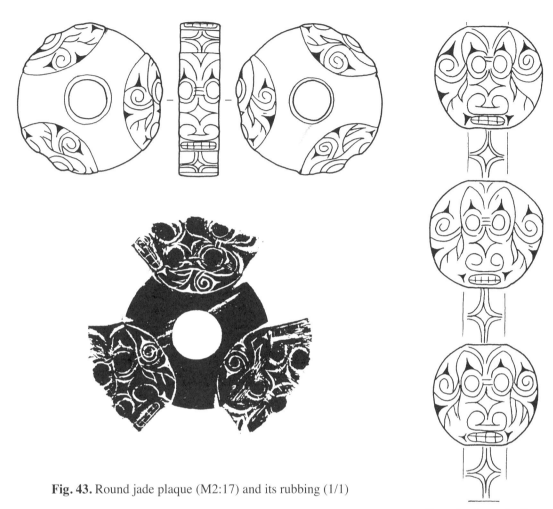

**Fig. 43.** Round jade plaque (M2:17) and its rubbing (1/1)

Expansion figure of patterns

from 2.1 cm to 2.4 cm and their diameters from 1 cm to 1.4 cm (Fig. 47; Picture 70).

M2:37, it is composed of nine individual pieces and numbered as a group during field work. But it is not very probable to classify them as one set, for they are of quite different sizes. All of them are cylinder-shaped with holes drilled from both sides in the middle. They are 1.8–3.15 cm in length, 0.7–1 cm in diameter and 0.5 cm in hole diameter (Fig. 47; Picture 66).

M2:38, it is composed of 28 individual pieces and numbered as one group during field work. But they are quite different in sizes, thus may not belong to one group. Some of the tubes are mingled with gray or brown spots. All of them are cylinder-shaped with holes drilled from both sides in the middle. M2:38-4 is already broken. Their lengths range from 1.5 to 4.8 cm, diameters from 0.7 cm to 1.45 cm and hole diameters from 0.5 cm to 0.7 cm (Fig. 47; Picture 73).

M2:40, it is composed of 30 individual pieces and numbered as one group during field work. But they differ in sizes, thus may not belong to one string. Some of the tubes are mingled with gray or brown spots. They are all cylinder-shaped with holes drilled from both sides in the middle. Their lengths range from 1.2 cm to 3 cm and diameters from 0.7 cm to 1.2 cm (Fig. 47; Picture 67).

M2:57, it is composed of five individual pieces and numbered as one group. All are cylinder-shaped with holes drilled from both sides in the middle. Their lengths range from 1.1 cm to 1.2 cm and diameters from 0.6 cm to 0.7 cm (Fig. 47; Picture 68).

M2:58, it is composed of nine individual pieces and numbered as one group. All are cylinder-shaped with holes drilled from both sides in the middle. One of them is relatively big in size. Their lengths range from 0.9 cm to 1.9 cm, diameters from 0.6 cm to 0.9 cm

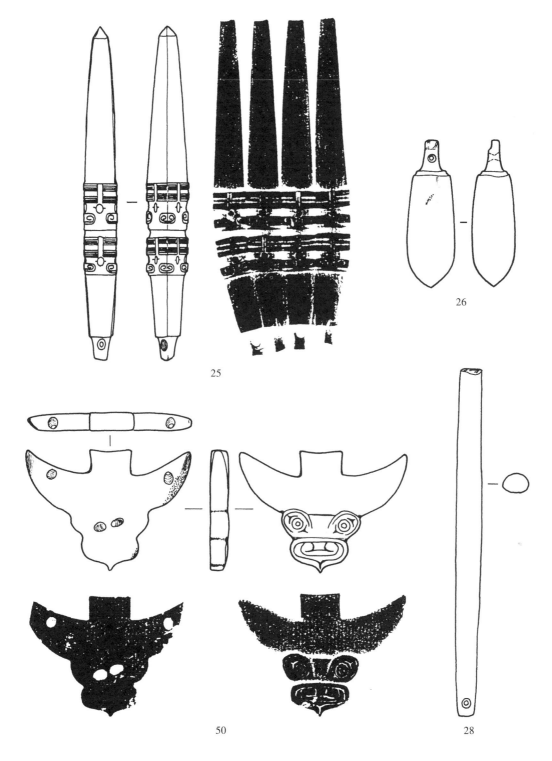

**Fig. 44.** Awl-shaped jade objects, jade pendant and jade bird in tomb M2

25, 28. awl-shaped objects; 26. pendant; 50. bird (1/1)

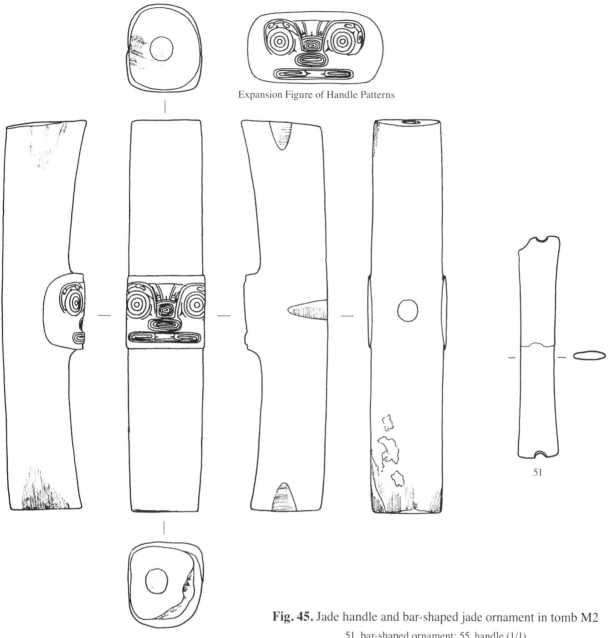

Expansion Figure of Handle Patterns

51

55

**Fig. 45.** Jade handle and bar-shaped jade ornament in tomb M2
51. bar-shaped ornament; 55. handle (1/1)

and hole diameters from 0.09 cm to 0.1 cm (Fig. 47; Picture 69).

M2:59, it is composed of 45 individual pieces, among which three are broken. All are cylinder-shaped and most of them are cutted and splited into two individual pieces after drilling from two ends, thus presenting the form of holes drilled from one side. Their lengths range from 0.7 cm to 1.4 cm and diameters from 0.7 cm to 0.8 cm (Fig. 47; Picture 74).

**Tubes:** eight pieces. All are cylinder-shaped with most of them having holes drilled from both sides in the middle.

M2:29, it is 2.5 cm in length, 2.1 cm in diameter and 0.5 cm in hole diameter (Fig. 48; Picture 72).

M2:39, it is 1.9 cm in length, 0.9 cm in diameter and 0.5 cm in hole diameter (Fig. 48; Picture 71).

M2:43, it is composed of two individual pieces and number as one group. One of the tubes has vertical cutting marks on its exterior wall. They are 1.3–1.4 cm in length, 0.75 cm in diameter and 0.4 cm in hole diameter (Fig. 48; Picture 71).

**Fig. 46.** Rubbings of jade handle (M2: 55) (1/1)

M2:47, it is 4.2 cm in length, 1.5 cm in diameter and 0.65 cm in hole diameter (Fig. 48; Picture 72).

M2:48, it is 1.1 cm in length, 0.7 cm in diameter and 0.35 cm in hole diameter (Fig. 48; Picture 71).

M2:52, the two ends are uneven, it is cutted apart and splited into two individual pieces after drilling from two ends, thus presenting the form of holes drilled from one side. The end with smaller hole diameter has obvious string-cutting marks. It is 1.9 cm in length, 1.3 cm in diameter and 0.35–0.7 cm in hole diameter (Fig. 48; Picture 72).

M2:53, one end is even while the other end has obvious string-cutting marks. Its drilling form is similar to that of M2:52. Thus the two tubes are believed to be cut apart from the same jade artifact. It is 1.9 cm in length, 1.3 cm in diameter and 0.35–0.65 cm in hole diameter (Fig. 48; Picture 72).

**Beads:** seven pieces and could be categorized into hemispherical bead, waist-drum shaped bead and spherical bead.

**Hemispherical beads:** three pieces.

M2:13, it is composed of two individual pieces,

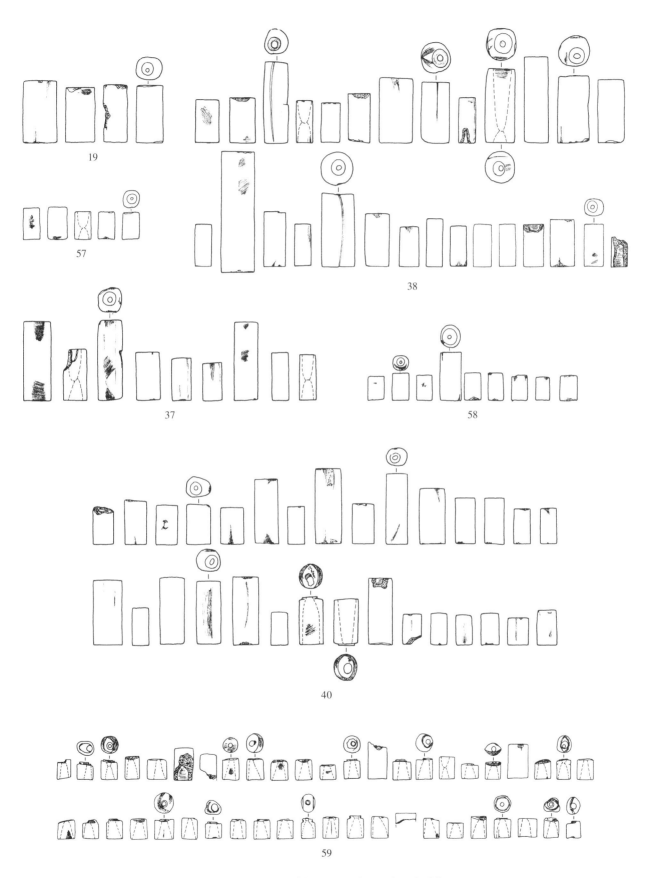

**Fig. 47.** Strings of jade tubes in tomb M2 (2/3)

with 1 cm in height and 1.25 cm in diameter (Fig. 48; Picture 75).

M2:56, drilled with a tunnel-shaped hole on the surface, it is 1.1 cm in height and 2 cm in diameter (Fig. 48).

**Waist-drum shaped beads:** three pieces, all with holes drilled from both sides in the middle.

M2:42, composed of two pieces, it is 1.05 cm in height, 1.05 cm in diameter and 0.4 cm in hole diameter (Fig. 48; Picture 76).

M2:60, it is 0.75 cm in height, 1 cm in diameter and

0.3 cm in hole diameter (Fig. 48; Picture 76).

**Spherical bead:** one piece.

M2:41, it is 1.1 cm in diameter (Fig. 48; Picture 76).

**Particles:** six pieces.

M2:30–33, 45, 49, one side is convex while the other side is even. They might be the imbedded ornaments of some decayed organic artifacts. The lengths range from 0.65 cm to 1.4 cm, the width from 0.45 cm to 0.5 cm and the thickness from 0.25 cm to 0.35 cm (Fig. 48; Picture 77).

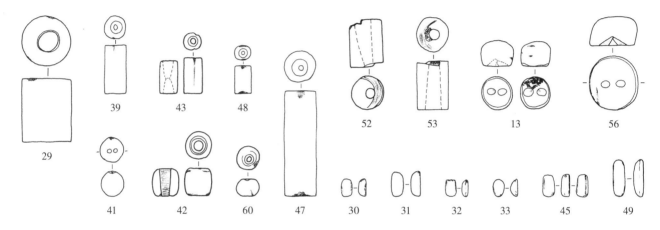

**Fig. 48.** Jade tubes, jade beads and jade particles in tomb M2

13, 56. hemispherical beads; 29, 39, 43, 47, 48, 52, 53. tubes; 30–33, 45,49. particles; 41. spherical bead; 42,60. waist-drum shaped beads

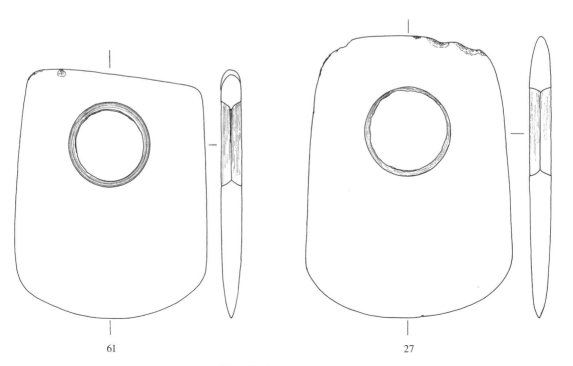

**Fig. 49.** Stone *yue* axes

(2) Stone artifacts

Only one type of stone *yue* axe is found, and the two pieces in all.

M2:27, the plane is like a rectangular with the cambered blade slightly wider than the top. The top is not even and a big round hole is drilled from both sides on the top. It is 15 cm in height, 9 cm in the width of the top and 11.4 cm in the width of the blade (Fig. 49; Picture 78).

M2:61, the plane is like a rectangular, and the end of its blade is slightly wider than the top end. The top end is slant and straight. Big round hole is drilled from both sides on the top. It is 12.9 cm in height, 9.7 cm in the width of the top and 10.5 cm in the width of the blade (Fig. 49; Picture 79).

(3) Pottery vessels: four pieces.

***Ding* tripod:** one piece (M2:36). It is sand-tempered red pottery and severely broken only with its short fin-shaped leg left. The section of leg of the *ding* tripod is slightly flat. The outer side is flat and straight, and slightly thicker than the inner side. The inner corner is round and curved (Fig. 50).

***Dou*:** two pieces.

M2:34, black-coating clay pottery with gray core, severely broken only with the ring foot left. It is 9.6 cm in outer diameter (Fig. 50).

M2:62, black-coating clay pottery with gray core, it is broken into pieces with the shape unidentifiable.

**Ring-foot jar:** one piece (M2:35). It is sand-tempered red pottery and broken into small pieces with the shape unidentifiable.

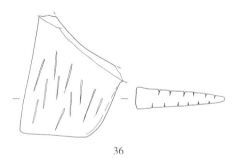
36

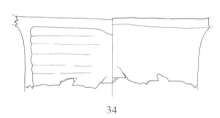
34

**Fig. 50.** Pottery vessels in tomb M2
34. ring foot of *dou*; 36. leg of *ding* tripod (1/2)

# Section 3 Tomb M3

## 1. The Shape of the Tomb

Tomb M3 is located at the westernmost end of the south line of the tombs, with tomb M10 to its east and tomb M4 to its north. It has its opening under the top soil, and disturbs the yellow-earthen mond. It is rectangular pit with vertical wall, with an orientation of 179°. The tomb pit is 2.86 m in length, 1.04 m in width at the northern end, 1.22 m in width at the southern end, the southern end is slightly wider than the northern end, and 0.84 m in depth at the deepest point of the tomb. Farming over the years has led to an uneven opening of the tomb, with the southern side lower than the northern side, with only a depth of 0.3 meters in height. The walls are steep and the bottom

is smooth. It is filled with yellowish-brown mottled earth. Skeleton inside the tomb had rotten away and left no remains (Picture 80).

Four pieces of pottery vessels had been found, scattering at the northern end of the tomb, too broken to be took out. The pottery vessels could be roughly identified as the assemblage of a *ding* tripod, a *dou*, a ring-foot jar, and a *gang* vat.

On the southern end of the tomb, there is a piece of three-pronged jade object with pattern (M3:3), with its carved side facing down when unearthed. Next to M3:3, there are a set of five awl-shaped jade objects (M3:4) and a set of cylindrical jade object with cover (M3:1, 2). When excavated, the whole set of awl-shaped jade objects had been broken into two

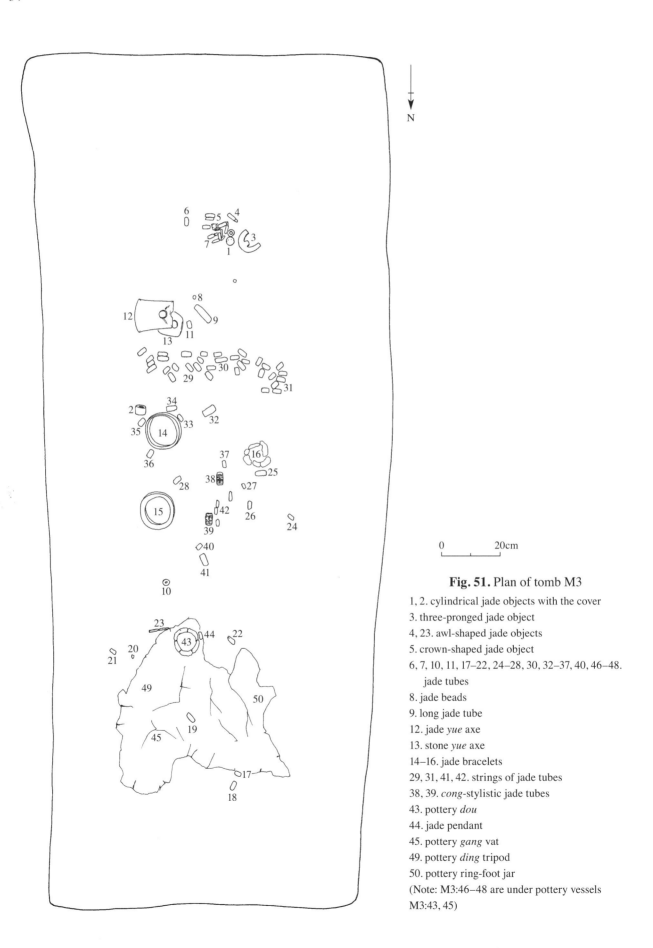

**Fig. 51.** Plan of tomb M3

1, 2. cylindrical jade objects with the cover
3. three-pronged jade object
4, 23. awl-shaped jade objects
5. crown-shaped jade object
6, 7, 10, 11, 17–22, 24–28, 30, 32–37, 40, 46–48.
    jade tubes
8. jade beads
9. long jade tube
12. jade *yue* axe
13. stone *yue* axe
14–16. jade bracelets
29, 31, 41, 42. strings of jade tubes
38, 39. *cong*-stylistic jade tubes
43. pottery *dou*
44. jade pendant
45. pottery *gang* vat
49. pottery *ding* tripod
50. pottery ring-foot jar
(Note: M3:46–48 are under pottery vessels
M3:43, 45)

to five pieces. A piece of crown-shaped jade object (M3:5) overlaid by the awl-shaped objects also has been broken into three pieces when unearthed. The jade beads (M3:8) to the north of the crown-shaped jade object were considered to be earrings. Most jade artifacts were discovered in the middle of the tomb, among which, the blade of a jade *yue* axe (M3:12) is facing the east. Under the jade *yue* axe existed a stone *yue* axe (M3:13). Vermilion coating residue could be found in the round hole on the stone *yue* axe. Two pieces of jade bracelets (M3:14, 15) were found on the right hand in the tomb, and one jade bracelet (M3:16) on the left hand had broken into five pieces. Similar to the set of awl-shaped jade objects and the crown-shaped jade object, the breaking of these objects might be caused by the collapse of funerary container. In addition, there are two pieces of *cong*-stylistic tubes (M3:38, 39) located between the two jade bracelets (M3:15, 16). Next to the *dou* is a piece of awl-shaped jade object (M3:23). Two strings of jade tubes (M3:29, 31) were unearthed from the middle of the tomb. No *cong* was discovered in tomb M3 (Fig. 51).

## 2. Burial Objects

Burial objects include jade artifacts, stone artifacts and pottery vessels, with a number of 50 pieces (sets), and 107 individual pieces.

(1) Jade artifacts

There is a number of 45 pieces (sets), and 102 individual pieces, mostly white jade, including crown-shaped object, cylindrical object with cover, three-pronged object, set of awl-shaped objects, *yue* axe, *cong*-stylistic tube and awl-shaped object etc.

**Crown-shaped object:** one piece (M3:5). It has gray flocs and has been broken into five pieces when unearthed. It is flat and presenting an upside-down trapezoid in plane, with an oval hole in middle of the upper part. The middle part at the top end is concave with a point in the center. The two corners on both sides extend outward. It has a flat tenon on the bottom, with three holes drilled from both sides equidistantly. A group of cambered string-cutting marks are visible on the surface. It is 2.85 cm in height, 5.5–6.4 cm in width and 0.35 cm in thickness (Fig. 52; Picture 83).

**Cylindrical object with cover:** comprising two individual pieces.

M3:1, the cover. It is canary yellow and has brown spots. It is cylinder-shaped, the top is round while the bottom is flat and drilled with tunnel-shaped holes. Cambered string-cutting marks are visible on the bottom end. It is 2.8 cm in height and 3.6 cm in diameter (Fig. 53; Picture 81).

M3:2, the cylindrical object. It is cylinder-shaped with a hole in the middle; the wall of hole is slightly convex and the outer wall is slightly concave. Few cambered string-cutting marks are found on one end. It is 2.8 cm in height, 3.5 cm in diameter and 2 cm in hole diameter (Fig. 53; Picture 82).

**Three-pronged object:** one piece (M3:3). It is canary yellow without patterns. The upper part of the

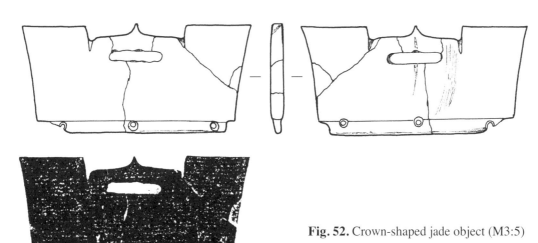

**Fig. 52.** Crown-shaped jade object (M3:5) and its rubbing (1/1)

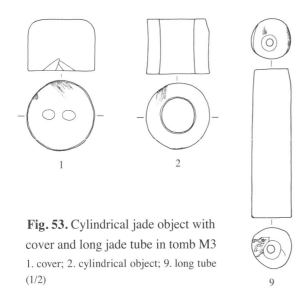

**Fig. 53.** Cylindrical jade object with cover and long jade tube in tomb M3
1. cover; 2. cylindrical object; 9. long tube (1/2)

feather-shaped patterns carved on each side. Below all feather-shaped patterns and around the sacred animal motif are rolling clouds patterns. The upper side edge of the left prong is the fracture surface forming by cutting, and is polished and carved. The lower right side reserves the cutting plane and is only roughly polished. Downward cambered string-cutting marks could be found on the inner side of both the left and right prongs, as well as on the top end face of the prong in the middle. It is 5 cm in height, 6.9 cm in width and 1.2 cm in thickness (Fig. 54; Picture 84).

**Long tube:** one piece (M3:9). It has brown spots, it is irregular cylinder-shaped, with a hole drilled from both sides in the middle. It is 8 cm in length, 2.2 cm in diameter and 0.9 cm in hole diameter (Fig. 53; Picture 85).

**Set of awl-shaped objects:** one set (M3:4). It is composed of five individual pieces (Fig. 55; Picture 86).

M3:4-1, it has gray and brown spots, it is broken into three pieces when unearthed. It is shaped in long strip, with a round and pointed end and a relatively flat end on the other side. Although broken, the hole drilled from both side is still visible. It is 7.7 cm in length, 0.5 cm in diameter (Fig. 55).

M3:4-2, it has gray spots, it is broken into two pieces when unearthed. It is shaped in long strip,

object is three prongs with two prongs on the left and right sides at the same level. The prong in the middle is lower and wider, with a hole drilling on it. It has a round and arc bottom. The front side of the object is carved with the sacred animal motif. Eyepits of the sacred animal are protruding and oval. Its eyes are single-circle and carved in intaglio carving technique. The animal has a wide and flat nose and also a wide mouth and protruding tusks. The right eye is slightly deviated leftward due to a cutting plane next to it and smaller than the left one. The left and right prongs are each decorated with three groups of feather-shaped patterns. There is a vertical projecting ridge in the middle of the middle prong, with two groups of

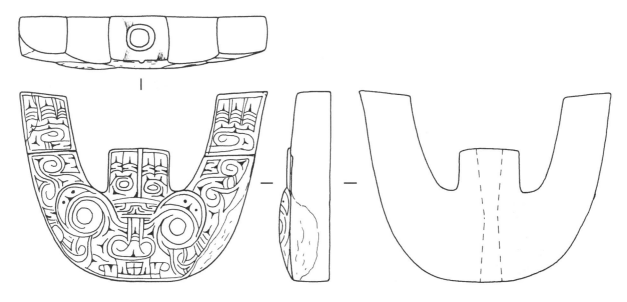

**Fig. 54.** Three-pronged jade object (M3:3) (1/1)

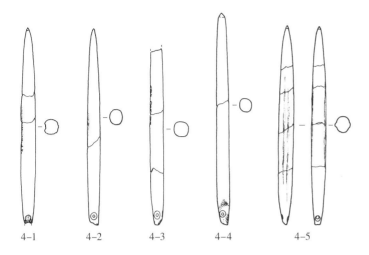

**Fig. 55.** Awl-shaped jade objects in tomb M3 (2/3)

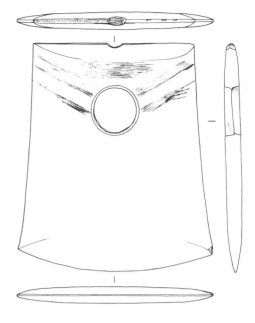

**Fig. 56.** Jade *yue* axe (M3:12) (1/2)

with a round and pointed end and a relatively flat end on the other side with a small hole drilled from both sides. It is 7.9 cm in length and 0.6 cm in diameter (Fig. 55).

M3:4-3, it has gray spots, it is broken into three pieces when unearthed. It is shaped in long strip, with a relatively flat end with a hole drilled from both sides. The other end is broken. It is 7.1 cm in residue length and 0.6 cm in diameter (Fig. 55).

M3:4-4, it has gray spots, it is broken into two pieces when unearthed. It is shaped in long strip, with a round and pointed end, and a relatively flat end with a hole drilled from both sides on the other side. It is 8.4 cm in length and 0.5 cm in diameter (Fig. 55).

M3:4-5, it has gray flocs, it is broken into five pieces when unearthed. It is shaped in long strip, with a round and pointed end, and a relatively flat end with a hole drilled from both sides on the other side. Two stripes of shallow marks caused during blade-cutting could be detected on the surface. It is 7.9 cm in length and 0.6 cm in diameter (Fig. 55).

**Yue** axe: one piece (M3:12). It is grayish-white with cyan spots, with no decoration. It is flat and thin, and its plane presented a trapezoid with an cambered blade. On the middle of the top end, there is a semicircle hole drilled from both sides, and a big round hole drilled from both sides below it. The wall of the hole has spiral marks. Its top end is considered to be broken after cutting since there are broken marks on it, but slightly polished. Two groups of fine

striations stretched from both sides of the round hole to the upper left and right corners and another few horizontally fine striations could be seen above the round hole. It is 12 cm in height, 8.9 cm in top width and 10.9 cm in blade width (Fig. 56; Picture 87).

***Cong*-stylistic tubes:** two pieces (Picture 90).

M3:38, it is square cylinder-shaped, with a hole drilled from both sides in the middle and its surface is divided into two parts by a crosswise shallow groove. It is carved with sacred animal motifs with each corner as the axis. There are two belts of horizontal bow string patterns on the top, presenting the simplified feather crown. Two eyes are carved in intaglio carving technique and short horizontal lines on both sides represent the canthi. It is 3.2 cm in height, 1.4 cm in collar diameter and 0.6 cm in hole diameter (Fig. 57; Picture 88).

M3:39: Its shape, size and pattern are similar to those of M3:38. It is 3.25 cm in height, 1.4 cm in collar diameter and 0.6 cm in hole diameter (Fig. 57; Picture 89).

**Bracelets:** three pieces.

M3:14, it has caesious spots, it is shaped in wide ring, with a slightly convex inner wall and a slightly concave outer wall. One of its ends is incomplete due to cutting of jade raw material, with the arc string-marks still left after slightly polishing. It is 3.1 cm in

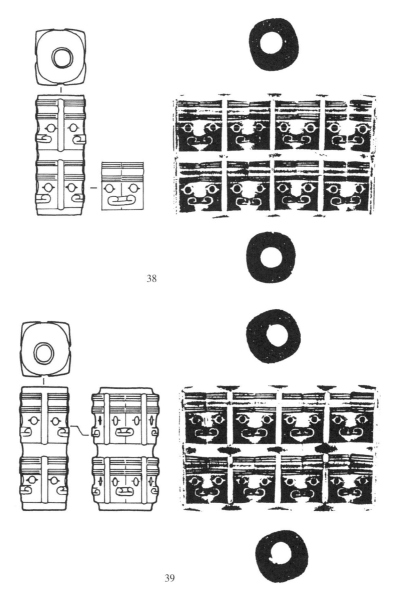

38

39

**Fig. 57.** *Cong*-stylistic jade tubes and their rubbings in tomb M3 (1/1)

height, 9.1 cm in diameter and 6.8 cm in hole diameter (Fig. 58; Picture 91).

M3:15, it has gray spots, it is shaped in wide ring, with a slightly convex inner wall and a slightly concave outer wall. A few spiral cutting marks could be seen on the inner wall. It is 2.8 cm in height, 8.8 cm in diameter and 5.8 cm in hole diameter (Fig. 58; Picture 92).

M3:16, it has gray spots, and broken into five pieces when unearthed. It is shaped in wide ring, with a slightly convex inner wall and a slightly concave outer wall. It is 1.9 cm in height, 7.4 cm in diameter and 6 cm in hole diameter (Fig. 58; Picture 93).

**Awl-shaped object:** one piece (M3:23). It is broken into three pieces and could not be restored since one piece was lost. It is shaped in long strip, with a round and pointed end, and relatively a flat end on the other side. Although broken, the hole drilled from both sides is still visible. It is 5.8 cm in residue length and 0.5 cm in diameter (Picture 94).

**Pendant:** one piece (M3:44). Drop-shaped, it is round and pointed at one end and the other end has a tenon with a small hole drilled from both sides. A slightly arc straight line is left on its surface. It is 2.3 cm in length and 0.9 cm in diameter (Fig. 59; Picture 95).

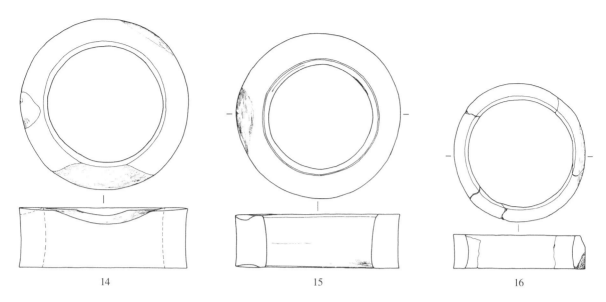

**Fig. 58.** Jade bracelets in tomb M3 (1/2)

**Strings of tubes:** four sets.

M3:29, this string of tubes consists of 23 individual pieces with varying lengths. They are cylinder-shaped, with holes drilled from both sides in the middle. They are 2.15 to 4 cm in length, 1 to 1.2 cm in diameter and 0.4 to 0.6 cm in hole diameter (Fig. 60; Picture 96).

M3:31, this string of tubes consists of 10 individual pieces, of which M3:31-4 is broken. They are cylinder-shaped, with holes drilled from both sides in the middle . They are 1.7 to 2.5 cm in length, 0.9 to 1.2 cm in diameter and 0.4 to 0.6 cm in hole diameter (Fig. 60; Picture 97).

M3:41, this string of tubes consists of 18 individual pieces with varying lengths, cylinder-shaped, with holes drilled from both sides in the middle (Picture 109).

M3:42, four pieces are numbered as one group, of which two pieces are broken, cylinder-shaped, with holes drilled from both sides in the middle. They are 2.5 to 2.9 cm in length, 1.1 cm in diameter and 0.5 to 0.6 cm in hole diameter (Fig. 60; Picture 98).

**Tubes:** twenty seven pieces. All are cylinder-shaped, and mostly have holes drilled from both sides in the middle, with part of them drilled from one side.

M3:6, it is 1.5 cm in length, 0.9 cm in diameter and 0.45 cm in hole diameter (Fig. 61; Picture 99).

M3:7, one of its ends is broken. It is 1.4 cm in residue length, 0.9 cm in diameter and 0.45 cm in hole

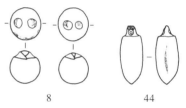

**Fig. 59.** Jade beads and jade pendant in tomb M3
8. beads; 44. pendant (2/3)

diameter (Fig. 61; Picture 99).

M3:10, its surface is slightly concave, with a hole in the center. The wall of hole is convex. The opening of the hole at one end has step-shaped spiral marks, and the other end surface has cambered string-cutting marks. It is 1.8 cm in length, 1.9 cm in diameter and 0.75 cm in hole diameter (Fig. 61; Picture 100).

M3:11, the hole in the middle presents the form of drilling from one side. One of its ends is still left with a sunken unpolished fracture caused by string-cutting, which proved the cutting towards the inner core were from different directions. On the other end, cambered string-cutting marks are visible. It is 1.4 cm in length, 1.95 cm in diameter and 0.6 cm in hole diameter. This jade tube could be matched with M3:48, indicating that these two should have belonged to the same piece of jade tube before it is cut apart after drilling (Fig. 61; Picture 101).

M3:17, this jade tube is cut apart after drilling;

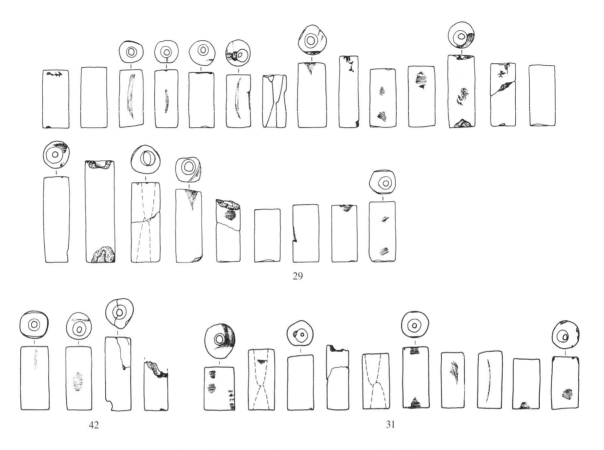

**Fig. 60.** Strings of jade tubes in tomb M3 (2/3)

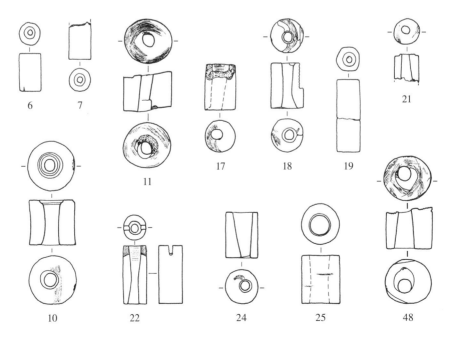

**Fig. 61.** Jade tubes in tomb M3 (2/3)

therefore, the hole presents as if it is drilled from one side. Cambered string-cutting marks are visible on the fracture surface. It is 1.8 cm in length, 1.3 cm in diameter and 0.6 cm in hole diameter (Fig. 61; Picture 102).

M3:18, cutting marks could be found on its surface, with cambered string-cutting marks on one end. It is 1.75 cm in length, 1.35 cm in diameter and 0.6 cm in hole diameter (Fig. 61; Picture 103).

M3:19, it's broken into two pieces. It is 2.9 cm in length, 0.95 cm in diameter and 0.5 cm in hole diameter (Fig. 61; Picture 104).

M3:20, this jade tube is broken into crumbles.

M3:21, one of its ends is broken, the other end is left with step-shaped marks after drilling and cambered string-cutting marks. It is 1.1 cm in residue length, 1 cm in diameter and 0.35 cm in hole diameter (Fig. 61; Picture 99).

M3:22, there is a straight notch on one end, cambered string-cutting marks with the same inward radian could be found on the wall of the notch. Spiral marks could be seen on the inner wall of the tube. It is 2.2 cm in length, 1 cm in diameter and 0.5 cm in hole diameter (Fig. 61; Picture 105).

M3:24, this jade tube is cut apart after drilling;

therefore, the hole presents as if it is drilled from one side. Cambered string-cutting marks are visible on the fracture surface. It is 1.8 cm in length, 1.3 cm in diameter and 0.7 cm in hole diameter (Fig. 61; Picture 102).

M3:25, two stripes of short cutting marks are found on the surface. It is 1.9 cm in length, 1.6 cm in diameter and 0.85 cm in hole diameter (Fig. 61; Picture 104).

M3:26, this jade tube is cut apart after drilling; therefore, the hole presents as if it is drilled from one side. Cambered string-cutting marks are visible on the fracture surface. It is 1.1 cm in length, 1.3 cm in diameter and 0.6 cm in hole diameter (Fig. 62; Picture 102).

M3:27, this jade tube is cut apart after drilling; therefore, the hole presents as if it is drilled from one side. It is 1.8 cm in length, 1.1 cm in diameter and 0.6 cm in hole diameter (Fig. 62; Picture 99).

M3:28, this jade tube is cut apart after drilling; therefore, the hole presents as if it is drilled from one side. A large area of cambered string-cutting marks are visible on the fracture surface. It is 1.9 cm in length, 1.3 cm in diameter and 0.7 cm in hole diameter (Fig. 62; Picture 102).

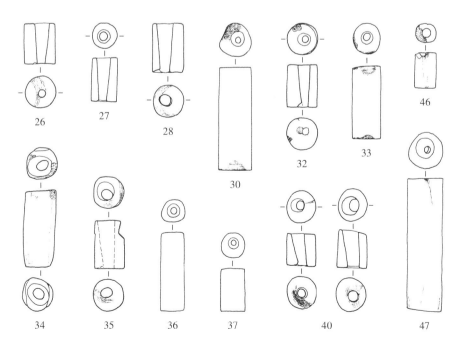

**Fig. 62.** Jade tubes in tomb M3 (2/3)

M3:30, fine string-cutting marks are seen on one end. It is 4.1 cm in length, 1.35 cm in diameter and 0.55 cm in hole diameter (Fig. 62; Picture 106).

M3:32, this jade tube is cut apart after being drilled from both sides. One of its ends is just at the place where the drilling from both sides met. It is 1.7 cm in length, 1.3 cm in diameter and 0.5 cm in hole diameter (Fig. 62).

M3:33, there are cutting marks on one end. It is 2.9 cm in length, 1.2 cm in diameter and 0.5 cm in hole diameter (Fig. 62; Picture 106).

M3:34, it is irregular-shaped. It is 3.1 cm in length, 1.35 cm in diameter and 0.5 cm in hole diameter (Fig. 62; Picture 106).

M3:35, this jade tube is cut apart after drilling; therefore, the hole presents as if it is drilled from one side. Cambered string-cutting marks and fracture surface are visible. It is 1.9 cm in length, 1.2 cm in diameter and 0.7 cm in hole diameter (Fig. 62; Picture 102).

M3:36, it is 3.15 cm in length, 1 cm in diameter and 0.5 cm in hole diameter (Fig. 62; Picture 106).

M3:37, it is 1.7 cm in length, 1 cm in diameter and 0.4 cm in hole diameter (Fig. 62; Picture 99).

M3:40, consists of two individual pieces, this jade tube is cut apart after drilling; therefore, the hole presents as if it is drilled from one side. Cambered string-cutting marks are visible on the fracture surface.

They are 1.3–1.5 cm in length, 1.2 cm in diameter and 0.6 cm in hole diameter (Fig. 62).

M3:46, two stripes of cutting marks are found on the surface. It is 1.4 cm in length, 0.9 cm in diameter and 0.35 cm in hole diameter (Fig. 62; Picture 99).

M3:47, the shape of this jade is irregular, with a stripe of cutting mark on one end. It is 5.3 cm in length, 1.5 cm in diameter and 0.7 cm in hole diameter (Fig. 62; Picture 107).

M3:48, it has reddish-brown spots, it is cut apart after drilling; therefore, the hole in the middle presents as if it is drilled from one side. It is considered to belong to the same complete piece with M3:11. One of its ends remains the convex forming by string-cut, but polished. It is 1.6 cm in length, 1.9 cm in diameter and 0.55–0.9 cm in hole diameter (Fig. 61; Picture 101).

**Beads:** Two pieces of jade beads shared one number (M3:8), spherical, with a tunnel-shaped holes. It is 1.25 cm in diameter (Fig. 59; Picture 108).

(2) Stone artifacts

**Yue axe:** one piece (M3:13). It is fairly thick and shaped like a rectangular with a cambered blade. The top end is flat and straight, a bit narrower than the bottom end. A big round hole is drilled from both sides. It is 12.6 cm in height, 6.5 cm in top width and 8.7 cm in blade width (Fig. 63; Picture 110).

(3) Pottery vessels: four pieces.

**Ding tripod:** one piece (M3:49). It is sand-tempered reddish-brown pottery, severely broken. Research on the broken pieces indicates that it has a flared mouth, with rim face slightly concave, fin legs. The cross section of leg is flat, with a straight outer side and a thinner inner side (Fig. 64).

**Dou:** one piece (M3:43). It is gray clay pottery, severely broken. It has a flared mouth and a flat base, the wall of the plate is slightly open. There is still certain black coating on the ring foot. It is about 18 cm in opening diameter (Fig. 64).

**Ring-foot jar:** one piece (M3:50). It is sand-tempered red pottery, severely broken and only the ring foot could be identified.

**Gang vat:** one piece (M3:45). It is sand-tempered red pottery, so broken that its shape could not be identified.

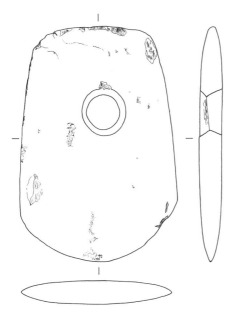

**Fig. 63.** Stone *yue* axe (M3:13) (1/2)

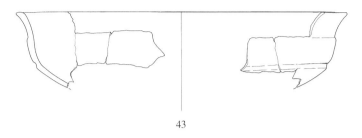

**Fig. 64.** Pottery vessels in tomb M3
43. plate of *dou*; 49. leg of *ding* (1/2)

# Section 4 Tomb M4

## 1. The Shape of the Tomb

Tomb M4 is located at the western end of the north line of the tombs, with tomb M1 to its west, tomb M5 to its east, tomb M3 and tomb M10 to its south. It has its opening under the top soil, and disturbes yellow-earthen mound. It is rectangular pit with vertical wall, with an orientation of 178°. It is 3.30 m in length, 1.68 m in width at the southern end and 1.28 m in width at the northern end. The tomb walls are slant and there is a two-layer terrace at the bottom. The depth from the opening to the terrace ranges from 0.58 m to 0.76 m, and the height of the terrace is 0.08 m. The filling earth is gray-brown mottled earth, somewhat pure, and skeleton inside the tomb had rotten away and left no remains when excavated (Picture 111).

Seven pieces of pottery vessels were found scattering at the northern end of the tomb. The pottery vessels are identified as a *ding* tripod, a *dou*, a *gang* vat, a flat plate, and a ring-foot plate. There are also two pieces of pottery vessels (M4:39, 43) that are too broken to be identified.

Jade artifacts were discovered on the southern part of the tomb. Around the crown-shaped jade object (M4:28), there is a piece of *huang* semi-circular pendant (M4:34), unearthed with its carved side facing up (Fig. 65; Picture 112), and a string of 16 tubes (M4:35). Parts of the string of tubes (M4:35-11, 35-12) are located under the crown-shaped jade object, which were covered by the rest of the string of tubes, indicating a close relationship among *huang* semi-

circular pendant, string of tubes and crown-shaped jade object. North to these, there is a pair of spherical jade beads (M4:30, 32). The distance between the two beads is 8 cm. Next to both spherical jade beads, there is one pair of waist-drum-shaped jade beads (M4:31, 33) respectively. These four pieces of jade beads are probably earrings of the tomb occupant.

In the middle of the tomb, there is a piece of *huang* semi-circular pendant (M4:6) and 8 pieces of round jade plaques (M4:7–14), which were considered to be one set (Picture 113). Right to the middle are two pieces of jade bracelets (M4:15, 16), and another piece is left to the middle (M4:17), which was considered a wrist bracelet. A piece of awl-shaped jade object (M4:18), broken into three pieces, was found above the left jade bracelet. Jade tubes scattered around the tomb (Fig. 66).

## 2. Burial Objects

Burial objects included jade artifacts and pottery vessels, with a number of 45 pieces (sets), 61 individual pieces.

(1) Jade artifacts

There is a number of 38 pieces (sets), 54 individual pieces, mostly white jade, including crown-shaped object, *huang* semi-circular pendant, round plaque, bracelet and awl-shaped object etc.

**Crown-shaped object:** one piece (M4:28). It is without patterns and the color is not pure. It presents an rectangle in shape, with a wider upper end. The bottom has a flat tenon, with 3 round holes drilled

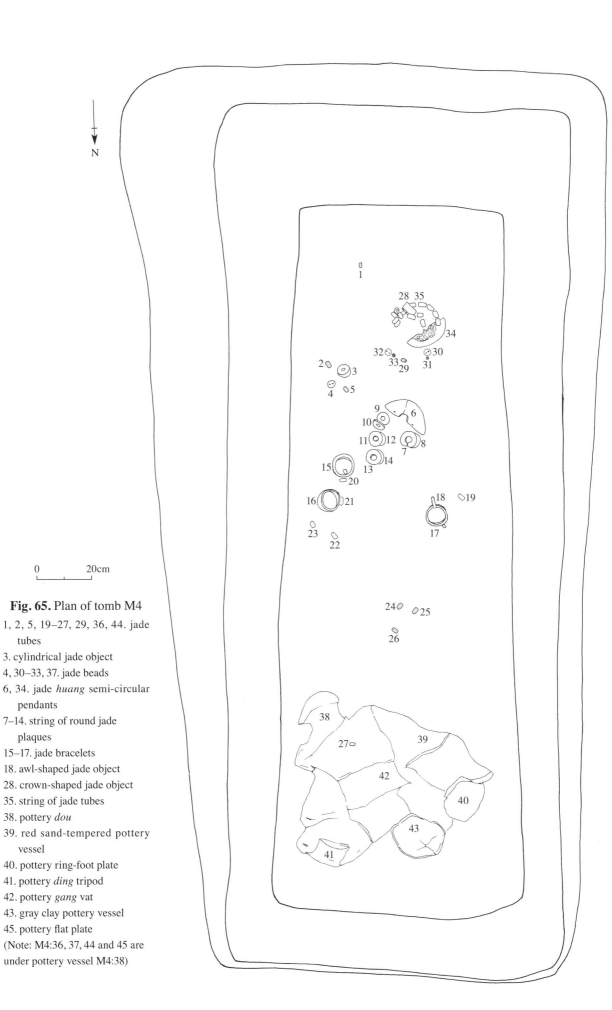

**Fig. 65.** Plan of tomb M4

1, 2, 5, 19–27, 29, 36, 44. jade
  tubes

3. cylindrical jade object

4, 30–33, 37. jade beads

6, 34. jade *huang* semi-circular
  pendants

7–14. string of round jade
  plaques

15–17. jade bracelets

18. awl-shaped jade object

28. crown-shaped jade object

35. string of jade tubes

38. pottery *dou*

39. red sand-tempered pottery
  vessel

40. pottery ring-foot plate

41. pottery *ding* tripod

42. pottery *gang* vat

43. gray clay pottery vessel

45. pottery flat plate

(Note: M4:36, 37, 44 and 45 are
under pottery vessel M4:38)

N

0    20cm

from both sides equidistantly. It is 2.85 cm in height, 5.3–5.56 cm in width and 0.4 cm in thickness (Fig. 67; Picture 114).

***Huang* semi-circular pendants:** two pieces.

M4:6, it is a bit yellowish with brown flocs, shaped in half-*bi*. The middle of the upper end is concave in shape of circular arc, forming by drilling from one direction. There is a small hole drilled from both sides on both sides of the concave respectively. The whole object is thinner in edges and thicker in the middle. Spiral drilling marks could be found on the wall of hole though polished. Although polished, the surface is still not smooth, cutting marks of jade raw material are obvious. It is 6.05 cm in height, 13.7 cm in width and 0.18–0.6 cm in thickness (Fig. 68; Picture 115).

M4:34, it is a light yellow with brown spots, shaped

in half-*bi*. There is a point in the center of the upper end. There is one small round hole on both sides of the concave for stringing and hanging. The front side is carved with the sacred animal motif in intaglio. The two eyes are presented by two holes with circular lines and small triangle pattern, while the wide nose constituted by rolling clouds patterns and curved lines. The rectangular mouth is wide and flat, with sharp teeth and two pairs of protruding tusks. Double-line semicircular lines are carved as the border of the motifs, rolling clouds patters are carved between the mouth and double-line semicircles. The back side is

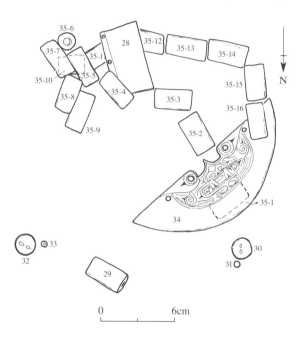

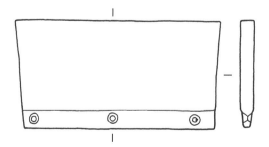

Fig. 66. Provenience of jade *huang* semi-circular pendant (M4:34), crown-shaped jade object (M4:28) and string of jade tubes (M4:35) when unearthed

Fig. 67. Crown-shaped jade object (M4:28) (1/1)

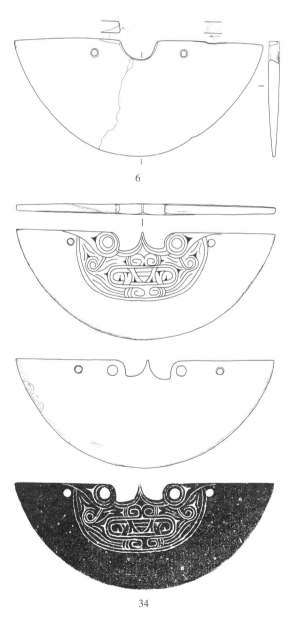

Fig. 68. Jade *huang* semi-circular pendants and the rubbing in tomb M4 (1/2)

smooth without decorations. Polishing marks could be found along edges. It is 5.7 cm in height, 14.3 cm in width (Fig. 68; Picture 116).

**Round jade plaques:** one set, consists of 8 individual pieces. Since being unearthed adjacent to the *huang* semi-circular pendant (M4:6), they possibly belong to the same set of ornaments with the *huang* semi-circular pendant.

M4:7, it has grayish-yellow spots, in the shape of *jue*. It has a gap on one side by string-cutting and a small

hole drilled from both sides on the opposite side. The hole in the middle is flared, probably formed by cutting after it is drilled from both sides. Cambered string-cutting marks could be found slightly concave on the surface. It is 4.7 cm in diameter, 2 cm in hole diameter and 0.7 cm in thickness (Fig. 69; Picture 117).

M4:8, *bi*-shaped, it is flat with a hole drilled from both sides in the center. A few stripes of cambered string-cutting marks are found on the surface. The radian and length of these marks varies on the front

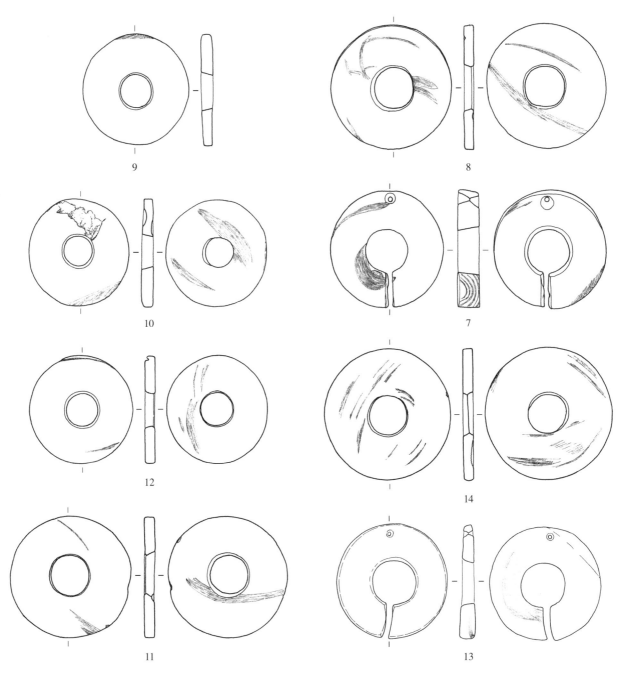

**Fig. 69.** Round jade plaques in tomb M4 (1/2)

and back sides. It is 4.9 cm in diameter, 1.8 cm in hole diameter and 0.4 cm in thickness (Fig. 69; Picture 119).

M4:9, *bi*-shaped, it is flat, with a similar hole to that of M4:7. It is 4.3 cm in diameter, 1.4 cm in hole diameter and 0.4 cm in thickness (Fig. 69; Picture 120).

M4:10, *bi*-shaped, it is flat, with a similar hole to that of M4:7. Two stripes of cambered string-cutting marks are found on one side, with one stripe slightly concave, and there are a few fine string-cutting marks on the edge of the other side. It is 4.2 cm in diameter, 1.35 cm in hole diameter and 0.35 cm in thickness (Fig. 69; Picture 121).

M4:11, *bi*-shaped, it is flat with gray spots. The hole is similar to that of M4:7. One side of the hole is slightly polished. A concave cambered string-cutting mark is visible on one side. It is 5.05 cm in diameter, 1.7 cm in hole diameter and 0.35 cm in thickness (Fig. 69; Picture 122).

M4:12, *bi*-shaped, it is flat, with the similar hole to that of M4:11. Two stripes of cambered string-cutting marks are found on one side, and on the edge of the other side, there is a cutting mark with the same radian as that of the outer edge of the object. It is 4.3 cm in diameter, 1.4 cm in hole diameter and 0.35 cm in thickness (Fig. 69; Picture 123).

M4:13, *jue*-shaped. It is flat and has a gap on one side by string-cutting and a small hole drilled from both sides on the opposite side. The hole is similar to that of M4:7. Cambered string-cutting marks could be found slightly concave on one side of the surface. It is 4.6 cm in diameter, 1.7 cm in hole diameter and 0.7 cm in thickness (Fig. 69; Picture 118).

M4:14, *bi*-shaped, it is flat with a hole drilled from both sides in the center. A few stripes of cambered string-cutting marks are found on the surface, some of which are deeper. It is 5.2 cm in diameter, 1.6 cm in hole diameter and 0.35 cm in thickness (Fig. 69; Picture 124).

**Cylindrical object:** one piece (M4:3). It has grayish-brown flocs, with a small hole drilled from one direction in the center. The inner wall of the hole is slightly polished and a few fine string-cutting marks are visible on one side. It is 2.7 cm in height, 3.6 cm in diameter and 0.9 cm in hole diameter (Fig. 70;

Picture 125).

**Bracelets:** three pieces.

M4:15, it has large brown spots, shaped in wide ring, with a slightly convex inner wall and a slightly arc outer wall. Although incomplete, it is polished, with polishing marks left. It is 2.35 cm in height, 9 cm in diameter and 6.7 cm in hole diameter (Fig. 71; Picture 127).

M4:16, it has brown spots, shaped in wide ring, with a slightly convex inner wall and a flat but slightly concave outer wall. Although incomplete, it is polished, with polishing marks left. It is 2.45–2.6 cm in height, 6.9 cm in diameter and 5.5 cm in hole diameter (Fig. 71; Picture 128).

M4:17, it has brown spots, wide ring shaped, with a slightly arc inner wall and a round and convex outer wall. It is 1.3 cm in height, 7.2 cm in diameter and 5.7 cm in hole diameter (Fig. 71; Picture 129).

**String of tubes:** one set (M4:35). Consist of 16 individual pieces, they should belong to the same set of ornaments with the *huang* semi-circular pendant (M4:34) since they are adjacent to it when excavated. They are cylinder-shaped but not regularly, and most of them have gray flocs. 14 pieces have a hole drilled from both sides in the middle, while the other two are

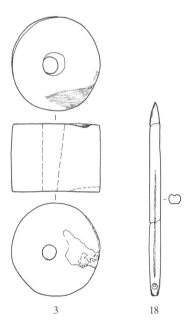

3                18

**Fig. 70.** Cylindrical jade object and awl-shaped jade object in tomb M4

3. cylindrical object; 18. awl-shaped object (2/3)

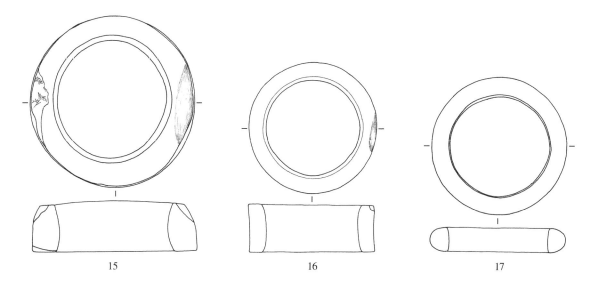

**Fig. 71.** Jade bracelets in tomb M4 (1/2)

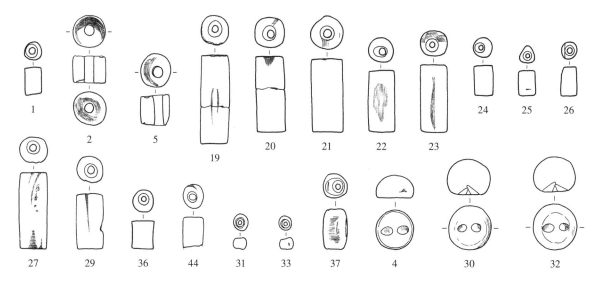

**Fig. 72.** Jade tubes and jade beads in tomb M4
1, 2, 5, 19–27, 29, 36, 44. tubes; 4, 30–33, 37. beads (2/3)

cut apart at the point drilling from both sides meet, with cambered string-cutting marks left. They are 2.1–3.1 cm in length and 1.2–1.3 cm in diameter (Fig. 73; Picture 126).

**Awl-shaped object:** one piece (M4:18). It was broken into 3 pieces when unearthed. It is shaped in strip, with a rounded rectangle cross section. One end is round and pointed while the other is relatively flat, with a small hole drilled from both sides. A straight shallow cutting mark could be seen on the surface. It is 7.7 cm in length and 0.5 cm in diameter (Fig. 70; Picture 130).

**Tubes:** numbered 15 sets, comprising 16 individual pieces. All tubes are cylinder-shaped, most of which have a hole drilled from both sides in the center.

M4:1, it is 1.1 cm in length, 0.7 cm in diameter and 0.45 cm in hole diameter (Fig. 72; Picture 132).

M4:2, it has a straight hole and several cambered string-cutting marks on each end. It is 1.1 cm in length, 1.4 cm in diameter and 0.4 cm in hole diameter (Fig. 72; Picture 131).

M4:5, cambered string-cutting marks can be found concave on the two ends. It is 1.2 cm in length, 1.2 cm in diameter and 0.4 cm in hole diameter (Fig. 72;

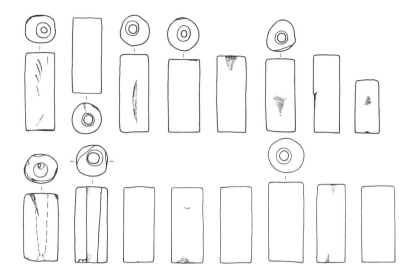

**Fig. 73.** String of jade tubes (M4:35) (2/3)

Picture 131).

M4:19, there are two stripes of vertical cutting marks on the surface. It is 3.5 cm in length, 1.2 cm in diameter and 0.6 cm in hole diameter (Fig. 72; Picture 133).

M4:20, fine string-cutting marks are found on the top end. It is 3 cm in length, 1.2 cm in diameter and 0.55 cm in hole diameter (Fig. 72; Picture 133).

M4:21, it is 2.9 cm in length, 1.3 cm in diameter and 0.6 cm in hole diameter (Fig. 72; Picture 133).

M4:22, there are vertical fine polishing marks on the surface. It is 2.4 cm in length, 1.1 cm in diameter and 0.55 cm in hole diameter (Fig. 72; Picture 133).

M4:23, there are a few fine string-cutting marks on one end, and a vertical stripe of cutting mark on the surface. It is 2.7 cm in length, 1.1 cm in diameter and 0.5 cm in hole diameter (Fig. 72; Picture 134).

M4:24, it is 1.2 cm in length, 0.8 cm in diameter and 0.4 cm in hole diameter (Fig. 72; Picture 132).

M4:25, it is triangular prism shaped, with 1 cm in length, 0.7 cm in diameter and 0.35 cm in hole diameter (Fig. 72; Picture 132).

M4:26, it is 1.15 cm in length, 0.65 cm in diameter and 0.4 cm in hole diameter (Fig. 72; Picture 132).

M4:27, there are cutting marks on the surface. It is 3.1 cm in length, 1.15 cm in diameter and 0.5 cm in hole diameter (Fig. 72; Picture 134).

M4:29, a cutting fracture surface and a vertical stripe of cutting mark are found on the surface. It is

2.2 cm in length, 1.15 cm in diameter and 0.5 cm in hole diameter (Fig. 72; Picture 134).

M4:36, it is 1.1 cm in length, 0.9 cm in diameter and 0.4 cm in hole diameter (Fig. 72; Picture 132).

M4:44, comprising two individual pieces. They are 0.4/1.1 cm in length respectively, 0.5/0.9 cm in diameter respectively and 0.2/0.4 cm in hole diameter respectively (Fig. 72; Picture 135).

**Beads:** six pieces of two types in shape.

**Waist-drum-shaped beads:** three pieces. All these beads have a slightly convex outer wall and a hole drilled from both sides in the center. M4:31 and M4:33 are basically identical in size, which are 0.5 cm in height, 0.7 cm in diameter and 0.35 cm in hole diameter. M4:37 is 1.6 cm in length, 0.9 cm in diameter and 0.4 cm in hole diameter (Fig. 72; Picture 135).

**Hemispheric beads:** three pieces (M4:4, 30, 32). Each is convex on one side and flat on the other side, with a tunnel-shaped hole. They are 1.6/1.8/1.7 cm in diameter respectively, 0.9/1.3/1.3 cm in thickness respectively (Fig. 72; Pictures 136, 137).

(2) Pottery vessels: seven pieces.

***Ding* tripod:** one piece (M4:41). It is a reddish-brown sand-tempered pottery, its rim is severely damaged. It has a bulging abdomen and a approximately flat round bottom, fin-shaped legs (Fig. 74).

**Ring-foot plate:** one piece (M4:40). It is a gray clay pottery, with an orange yellow core. The surface is brightly polished with a red coating. It is severely

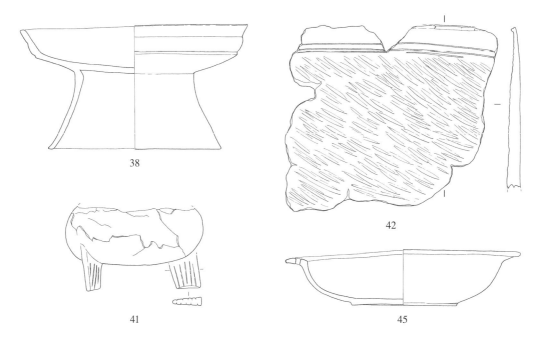

**Fig. 74.** Pottery vessels in tomb M4
38. *dou*; 41. *ding* tripod; 42. *gang* vat; 45. flat plate (1/4)

broken.

**Flat plate:** one piece (M4:45). It is a black-coating clay pottery, with orange red core. It has a wide convex rim, shallow and arc abdomen and a flat bottom, false ring foot. A vertical round hole is found on the rim, and the opposite side is broken, so the existence of a corresponding round hole could not be identified. It is 6 cm in height, 25.8 cm in opening diameter and 11.2 cm in bottom diameter (Fig. 74; Picture 139).

***Dou*:** one piece (M4:38). It is a black-coating gray pottery, with red coating. It has a flared mouth, a folded inner wall and a trumpet-shaped ring foot.

There are two stripes of concave string patterns carved on the outer surface of the plate. It is 12.9 cm in height, 25.2 cm in opening diameter and 19.4 cm in bottom diameter (Fig. 74; Picture 138).

***Gang* vat:** one piece (M4:42). It is a sand-tempered pottery, with brown core and red coating. It has a straight mouth with a sharp lip. The core at the bottom is thicker. It is decorated with oblique basket patterns (Fig. 74).

In addition, there is a piece of red sand-tempered pottery (M4:39) and a piece of gray clay pottery (M4:43), both of which are too broken to be identified.

# Section 5 Tomb M5

## 1. The Shape of the Tomb

Tomb M5 is located in the middle of the north line of the tombs, with tomb M4 to its west, tomb M14 to its east, and tomb M10 to its south. It has its opening under the top soil, and disturbs the yellow-earthen mound. It is rectangular pit with vertical wall, with an orientation of 182°. It is 2.42 meters in length, 0.79 meters in width and 0.34 meters in depth. Around the bottom of the tomb, there is a ditch dug down about

7 cm in depth and 18 cm to 22 cm in width, forming a low terrace there. The filling earth is yellowish-brown mottled earth and skeleton inside the tomb had rotten away and left no remains (Picture 140).

Being numbered into 12 pieces (sets), the burial objects, including jade artifacts and pottery vessels, had been found in tomb M5, is the one with the least number of burial objects. There are three pieces of pottery vessels scattered at the northern end of the tomb, namely, a *ding* tripod, a *dou*, and a pottery vessel severely broken. Jade artifacts were discovered in the southern and middle areas of the tomb. Among which, there is a piece of crown-shaped jade object (M5:3) in the south, surrounded by a set of string of jade tubes (M5:4, 5). Besides, there is a pair of hemispheric jade beads (M5:6) with interval space of 5 cm in between. In the middle of the tomb, two pieces of round jade plaques (M5:8) were found, and the rest one (M5:2) in the south end of the tomb (Fig. 75).

## 2. Burial Objects

Burial objects include jade artifacts and pottery vessels, with a number 12 pieces (sets), 22 individual pieces.

(1) Jade artifact

Jade artifacts are numbered into 9 pieces (sets), 19 individual pieces, including crown-shaped object, round plaque, tube and bead.

**Crown-shaped object:** one piece (M5:3). It has green and brown spots, presenting an upside-down trapezoid in plane, with two notches in the middle of the top end, forming a shape of semicircle. On the bottom there is a flat tenon with three round holes drilled from both sides equidistantly. It is 2.65 cm in height, 4.55–4.85 cm in width and 0.4 cm in thickness (Fig. 76; Picture 141).

**Round plaques:** three pieces.

M5:2, *bi*-shaped, it has a hole drilled from both sides in the middle, slightly biased to one end, indicating that it probably is cut apart after being drilled. It features an uneven thickness, and cambered string-cutting marks remained on the surface. It is 4.3 cm in diameter, 1.6 cm in hole diameter and 0.5 cm in thickness (Fig. 76; Picture 142).

M5:8, it comprises two individual pieces, seemed belong to the same piece before cut apart after drilling. They are in the shape of *jue*, one of them is broken. Obvious string-cutting marks could be found on the gap, and a small hole is drilled from both sides on the opposite part. Cambered string-cutting marks are on the surface, which are polished. Cutting marks could be found on the side edge. They are 4.6 cm in diameter, 1.6–1.8 cm in hole diameter and 0.3–0.7 cm in thickness (Fig. 76; Pictures 143, 144).

**String of tubes:** one set (M5:5). It consists of 8

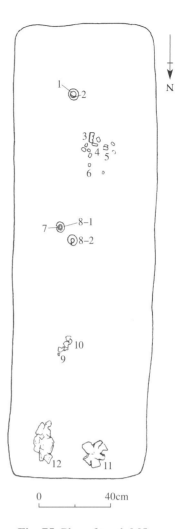

**Fig. 75.** Plan of tomb M5

1,6,7,9. jade beads; 2,8. round jade plaques; 3. crown-shaped jade object; 4. jade tube; 5. string of jade tubes; 10. clay pottery vessel; 11. pottery *ding* tripod; 12. pottery *dou*

single pieces. With gray and brown spots, in the shape of cylinder, they each have a hole drilled from both sides. They are 1.1–1.8 cm in length, 0.8–0.9 cm in diameter (Fig. 77; Picture 145).

**Tubes:** two pieces and they share one number (M5:4). With green spots, cylinder-shaped, each has a hole drilled from both sides. They are 2.5/3.1 cm in length, 1.2/1.4 cm in diameter (Fig. 77; Picture 146).

**Beads:** five pieces and they are divided into hemispheric and waist-drum-shaped.

**Hemispheric beads:** three pieces. One side is convex while the other side is flat, with a tunnel-shaped hole on it.

M5:1, it is 1.35 cm in diameter, 0.9 cm in thickness (Fig. 77; Picture 147).

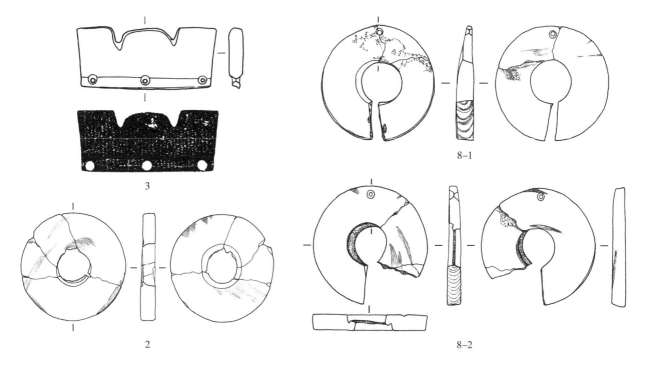

**Fig. 76.** Crown-shaped jade object and round jade plaques

2, 8-1, 8-2. round plaques; 3. crown-shaped object and its rubbing (3 is 1/1 and others are 2/3)

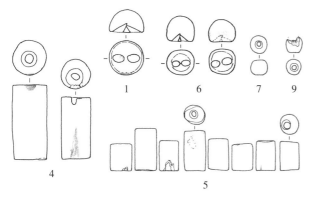

**Fig. 77.** String of jade tubes, jade beads and jade tubes in tomb M5

1, 6, 7, 9. beads; 4. tubes; 5. string of tubes (2/3)

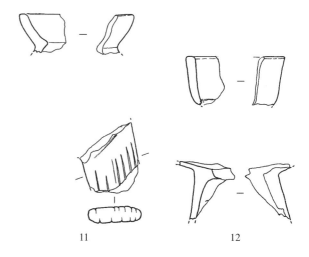

**Fig. 78.** Pottery vessels in tomb M5

11. *ding* tripod; 12. *dou* (1/2)

M5:6, consists of two individual pieces. They are 1.2 cm in diameter and 0.9 cm in thickness (Fig. 77; Picture 147).

**Waist-drum-shaped beads:** two pieces.

M5:7, a hole is drilled from both sides in the middle. It is 0.3 cm in length, 0.6 cm in diameter and 0.3 cm in hole diameter (Fig. 77; Picture 147).

M5:9, broken. It is 0.7 cm in length, 0.7 cm in diameter and 0.3 cm in hole diameter (Fig. 77).

(2) Pottery vessels: three pieces.

**_Ding_ tripod:** one piece (M5:11). It is reddish-brown sand-tempered pottery, and has been severely broken. It has a flared mouth, a sloped lip and fin-shaped legs. The cross section is oval (Fig. 78).

**_Dou_:** one piece (M5:12). It is a black-coating pottery with gray core, decorated with vermilion colored paintings, and has been broken severe (Fig. 78).

There is another black clay pottery (M5:10), covered with orange coating, has been severely broken and its shape is unidentifiable.

# Section 6 Tomb M6

## 1. The Shape of the Tomb

Tomb M6 is located at the easternmost end of the north line of the tombs, with tomb M8 to its south. It has its opening under the top soil, and disturbs the red earth, grey-earthen ditch and virgin soil. It is rectangular pit with vertical wall, with an orientation of 183°. The tomb pit is 2.85 m in length, 0.84 m in width in the southern end and 1.26 m in the northern end, and 0.52 m in depth. The filling earth is yellowish-brown mottled earth, and skeleton inside the tomb had rotten away and left no remains (Picture 148).

Four pieces of pottery burial objects had been found scattered at the northern end of the tomb, being seriously broken. The pottery vessels are roughly identified as a *ding* tripod, a *dou*, a ring-foot jar, and a piece of sand-tempered red pottery (M6:18) whose type could not be recognized.

A few jade artifacts, including a piece of jade spindle whorl (M6:5), scattered around the pottery vessels. Jade artifacts are mainly located in the middle and southern parts of the tomb. Among them, there is a string of eight jade beads (M6:8) placed near one crown-shaped jade object (M6:1), beside them is a piece of *huang* semi-circular pendant (M6:2). In the middle of the tomb, there is a piece of jade bracelet (M6:3, 4) on both the left and right sides respectively. Besides, a piece of awl-shaped jade object (M6:14) was unearthed from the left side of the middle part of the tomb (Fig. 79).

## 2. Burial Objects

Burial objects include jade artifacts and pottery vessels, with a number of 20 pieces (sets), 32 individual pieces.

(1) Jade artifacts

The unearthed jade artifacts are numbered into 16 pieces (sets) 28 individual pieces, including crown-shaped object, *huang* semi-circular pendant, bracelet, awl-shaped object, spindle whorl, cylindrical object, tube, and bead etc.

**Crown-shaped object:** one piece (M6:1). It is caesious with brown spots. It is flat and presents an upside-down trapezoid in plane. The top end is concave, with a point in the center and both corners stretching out. There is an oval hole on the middle of upper part, constituted of 3 holes made by solid drilling. At the bottom is a flat and long tenon, with two holes drilled from both sides. It is 2.7 cm in height, 5–6 cm in width and 0.2–0.4 cm in thickness (Fig. 80; Picture 149).

***Huang* semi-circular pendant:** one piece (M6:2). It has caesious spots, half-*bi*-shaped, thick in the middle and thin in edges. The middle of the upper end is semi-circular concave, with a small round hole drilled from both sides at each side respectively. It is 5.7 cm in height, 10.5 cm in width and 0.1–0.2 cm thickness (Fig. 81; Picture 150).

**String of beads:** are set (M6:8). It consists of eight individual pieces, one of them being severely broken. They are waist-drum-shaped, of them, seven pieces have a hole drilled from both sides, and one has a tunnel-shaped hole. They are placed next to the *huang* semi-circular pendant (M6:2) when unearthed (Fig. 82; Picture 153).

**Bracelets:** two pieces. They are both wide ring shaped, the inner wall is convex and the outer wall is straight.

M6:3, it has red spots. It is 2.8 cm in height, 7.5 cm in diameter and 5.8 cm in hole diameter (Fig. 81; Picture 151).

M6:4, it is 2.3 cm in height, 7 cm in diameter and 5.7 cm in hole diameter (Fig. 81; Picture 152).

**Spindle whorl:** one piece (M6:5). It is caesious with dark green spots, it is flat pie-shaped with a trapezoidal cross section and a slightly convex outer wall. A hole is drilled from both sides in the middle and the wall of the hole has been polished. It is 4.2 cm in diameter, 0.9 cm in thickness and 0.5 cm in hole diameter (Fig. 82; Picture 156).

**Cylindrical object:** one piece (M6:6). It is caesious, shaped in circular truncated cone, with a trapezoidal cross section. A hole is drilled from both

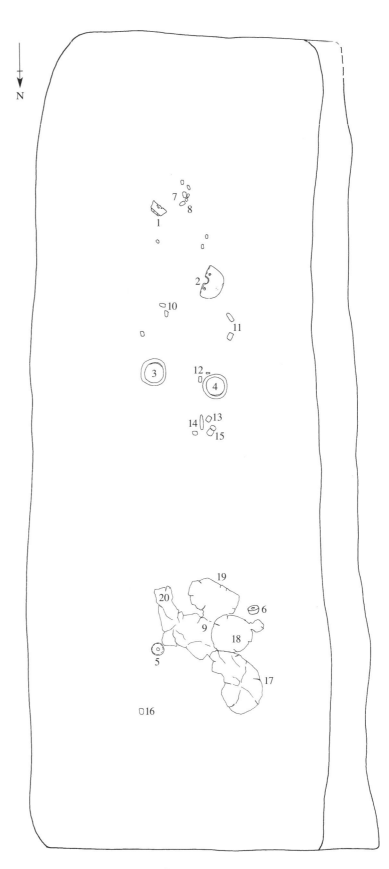

**Fig. 79.** Plan of tomb M6

1. crown-shaped jade object
2. jade *huang* semi-circular pendant
3, 4. jade bracelets
5. jade spindle whorl
6. cylindrical jade object
7, 13, 15. jade beads
8. string of jade beads
9. jade ornament
10–12, 16. jade tubes
14. awl-shaped jade object
17. pottery *dou*
18. red sand-tempered pottery vessel
19. pottery *ding* tripod
20. pottery ring-foot jar

0                    20cm

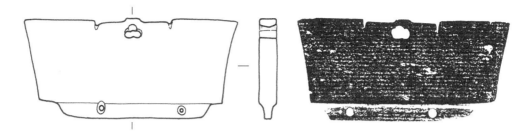

**Fig. 80.** Crown-shaped jade object (M6:1) and its rubbing (1/1)

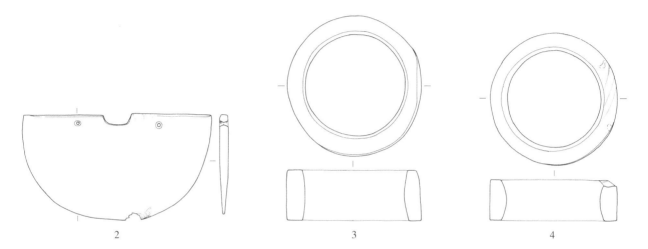

**Fig. 81.** Jade *huang* semi-circular pendant and jade bracelets in tomb M6

2. *huang* semi-circular pendant; 3, 4. bracelets (1/2)

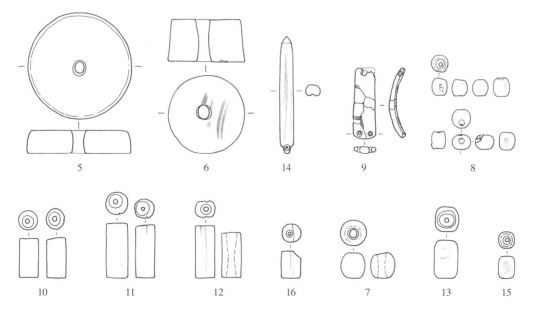

**Fig. 82.** Jade artifacts in tomb M6

5. spindle whorl; 6. cylindrical object; 7,13,15. beads; 8. string of beads; 9. ornament; 10–12,16. tubes; 14. awl-shaped object (2/3)

sides in a position slightly biased to one side instead of in the middle. Cambered string-cutting marks are visible on the surface of one side. It is 1.6 cm in height, 3.2 cm in diameter and 0.5 cm in hole diameter (Fig. 82; Picture 158).

**Awl-shaped object:** one piece (M6:14). It is strip-shaped, slightly presenting multifacets possibly due to the cutting. One end is pointed and the other one has a flat tenon, with a hole drilled from both sides. Lengthwise cutting marks could be found on the surface. It is 4.7 cm in length and 0.6 cm in diameter (Fig. 82; Picture 155).

**Ornament:** one piece (M6:9). It is broken into pieces when unearthed, in wide-curved-strip shape, with a ridge on the convex surface, indicated a possible polished hole drilled from both sides. Two small round holes are drilled from both sides on one end and the residue mark of a round hole could be seen on the edge of the other end which is broken. It is 2.7 cm in length, 0.95 cm in width and 0.32 cm in thickness (Fig. 82; Picture 154).

**Tubes:** seven pieces. All of these are cylinder-shaped with a hole drilled from both sides in the middle.

M6:10, consists of two individual pieces with green spots. They are 1.65 cm in length, 0.8 cm in diameter and 0.55 cm in hole diameter (Fig. 82; Picture 157).

M6:11, consists of two individual pieces, with caesious spots. They are 2.2 cm in length, 0.85 cm in diameter and 0.45 cm in hole diameter (Fig. 82; Picture 157).

M6:12, consists of two individual pieces, with grayish-green spots. They are 1.8/2.1 cm in length, 0.8 cm in diameter and 0.4 cm in hole diameter (Fig. 82;

Picture 157).

M6:16, it is 1.1 cm in length, 0.7 cm in diameter and 0.35 cm in hole diameter (Fig. 82; Picture 157).

**Beads:** five pieces. All of these are waist-drum-shaped with a hole drilled from both sides in the middle.

M6:7, consists of two individual pieces with gray spots. They are 0.9 cm in length, 1 cm in diameter and 0.4 cm in hole diameter (Fig. 82; Picture 159).

M6:13, consists of two individual pieces in similar shape. Cambered string-cutting marks could be found on the surface. They are 1.5 cm in length, 1.1 cm in diameter and 0.5 cm in hole diameter (Fig. 82; Picture 159).

M6:15, there are a few thin string-cutting marks on the surface. It is 0.9 cm in length, 0.7 cm in diameter and 0.3 cm in hole diameter (Fig. 82; Picture 159).

(2) Pottery vessels: four pieces.

***Ding* tripod:** one piece (M6:19). It is reddish-brown sand-tempered pottery, severely broken. It has a flared mouth, slightly concave rim surface and fin-shaped legs, whose outer side of the fracture surface is straight (Fig. 83).

***Dou*:** one piece (M6:17). It is orange-red clay pottery, with a shallow abdomen and a folded wall (Fig. 83).

**Ring-foot jar:** one piece (M6:20). It is red sand-tempered pottery, so broken that its shape could not be identified.

There is another red fine sand-tempered pottery (M6:18). It has cristate ears, and is so broken that its shape could not be identified.

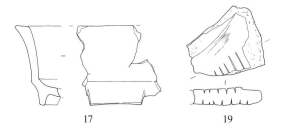

17                    19

**Fig. 83.** Pottery vessels in tomb M6
17. *dou*; 19. leg of *ding* tripod (1/2)

## Section 7 Tomb M7

### 1. The Shape of the Tomb

Tomb M7 is located in the middle of the south line of the tombs, adjacent to tomb M9 on the west and the robbed tomb M12 on the east. Its northwestern corner disturbs the southeastern corner of tomb M11. It has its opening under the top soil, and disturbs the southwestern corner of the middle square red earth area as well as the enclosing gray-earthen ditch. It is rectangle pit with vertical wall, with an orientation of 184°. It is 3.2 meters in length, 1.6 meters in width and 0.64–1.3 meters in depth. Its wall is relatively straight filled with relatively tough grayish-brown mottled earth. At its southern part, rotten human skull and tooth remains were found, suggesting that the occupant's head faced south (Fig. 84; Picture 160).

The burial objects include jade artifacts, stone artifacts, pottery vessels, lacquerware, and animal teeth. Among them, there are four pieces of pottery, namely, one piece of *ding* tripod, one piece of *gang* vat, one piece of ring-foot jar and one piece of *dou*, all placed in the north of the tomb. Close to the pottery is a piece of annular jade artifact (M7:155), surrounded by 13 pieces of jade particles (M7:152) which form a concentric circle. The residue of the vermilion lacquer within the jade particles circle suggest that it is likely to be a piece of lacquerware with jade particles inlaid around its edge. Though taken out in a whole, it could't be restored (Picture 164).

Beneath the pottery *ding* tripod on the northern side, there is a stone *yue* axe (M7:157), with its blade facing left. Additional two pieces of stone *yue* axes are laid in the southern half part of the tomb, one (M7:83) on the western side of the jade *yue* axe (M7:32), with its blade facing inside, and the other (M7:76) on the northern side of the crown-shaped object with its blade also facing inside.

Jade artifacts are mainly located in the middle and southern parts of the tomb. At the southernmost end, there is a string of 29 tubes (M7:5). From the vertical view, they are away from other burial objects.

One possible reason is that they are ornaments of the funerary container. They fell off and moved after the wooden coffin decayed and collapsed. Besides, there is a set of cylindrical objects with cover (M7:8), laid inclining southward. In the south of the skull remains laid a piece of long jade tube (M7:25), closely connected with the middle prong of the three-pronged object (M7:26). This may suggest that the tube should have been used together with the three-pronged object (Fig. 85; Picture 166) which was unearthed with its patterned side facing up. There is a set of ten pieces of awl-shaped objects (M7:22, 23, 24) overlying the three-pronged object and the stone *yue* axe. To the west of the head, there is a piece of crown-shaped object (M7:63) surrounded by 26 small disordered jade particles. Together, they should have been used to decorate the decayed organic body. A string of 18 jade beads lay nearby (M7:60). Judging from its small diameter in circle, it is apparently not worn by the tomb occupant (Fig. 86; Picture 161).

The jade *yue* axe (M7:32) is laid in the east of the tomb with its blade facing westward, indicating that it is held by right hand, and together with the *yue mao* end ornament (M7:31) to its south and the *yue dui* end ornament (M7:33) to its north, they form an intact handled jade *yue* axe. Already decayed, the organic handle of the *yue* axe should have been about 80 cm in length judging from the space between the two end ornaments. At the bottom of the *yue* axe, there is a piece of jade *cong*-stylistic tube (M7:45), which should be a pendant on the *yue* axe (Fig. 88). On the eastern side of the *yue* axe there is a piece of end ornament (M7:29), whose tenon facing southward, opposite to the other end ornament (M7:18) on the right side of the head. They are about 90 cm away from each other, and both might have belonged to the organic handle. Overlying on the jade *yue* axe (M7:32) and the stone *yue* axe (M7:83) is a string of 114 pieces of jade tubes and is located around the tomb occupant's belly, which should have been a hang decoration on the chest (Fig. 87; Picture 162).

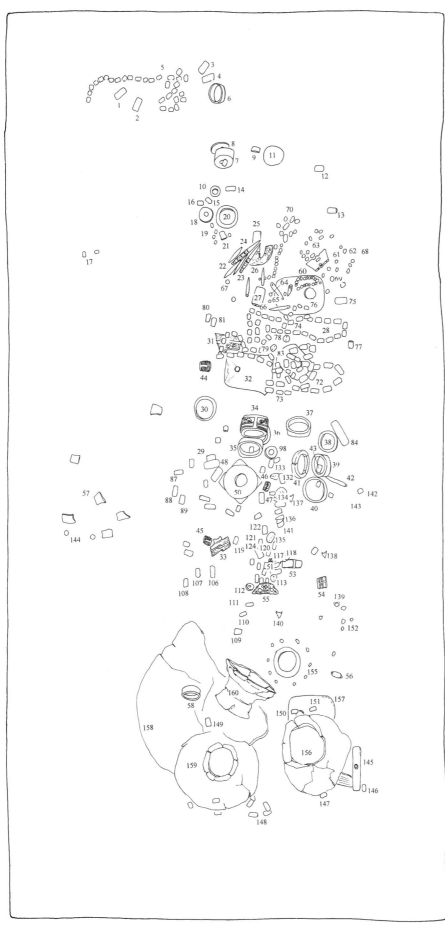

**Fig. 84.** Plan of tomb M7

1–4, 7, 9, 10, 12–16, 21, 48, 75, 77, 85–92, 94–97, 99, 100, 103, 105–111, 117–131, 142, 146, 149, 151, 161. jade tubes

5, 28, 70, 72, 73, 80–82, 102, 104, 114–116, 132, 141, 148. strings of jade tubes

6, 20, 30, 35–41, 57, 58. jade bracelets

8. cylindrical jade object with cover

11. pie-shaped jade ornament

17, 19, 143, 144, 152. jade particles

18, 29. jade end ornaments

22–24, 42. awl-shaped jade objects

25, 84, 145. long jade tubes

26. three-pronged jade object

27, 98. cylindrical jade objects

31. jade *mao* end ornament of *yue* axe

32. jade *yue* axe

33. jade *dui* end ornament of *yue* axe

34, 50. jade *cong*

43–47, 49, 51, 52, 54, 147. *cong*-stylistic jade tubes

53. jade belt hook

55. jade plaque object

56. jade pendant

59, 62, 64–68, 74, 78, 79, 93, 112, 113, 150. jade beads

60, 61, 69, 136. strings of jade tubes

63. crown-shaped jade object and jade particles

76, 83, 157. stone *yue* axes

101, 133–135. semi-circular jade ornaments

137–140. shark teeth

155. jade-inlaid lacquer

156. pottery *ding* tripod

158. pottery *gang* vat

159. pottery ring-foot jar

160. pottery *dou*

(Note: M7:49 is under M7:48; M7:52 is under M7:51; M7:82, 86 are under M7:31; M7:101, 102 are under M7:50; M7:161 is under M7:158; M7:59, 85, 90–97, 99, 100, 103–105, 114–116, 123, 125–131 are all scattered tubes and beads under other artifacts; M7:71, 153 and 154 are null.)

0    20cm

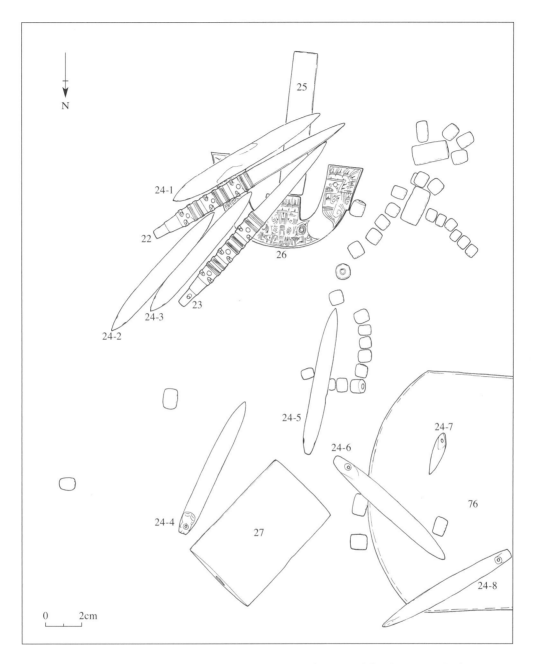

**Fig. 85.** Provenience of three-pronged jade object (M7:26) when unearthed

In the middle part of the coffin chamber are nine pieces of bracelets, which were placed on both sides of the tomb occupant, should be worn on arms and wrists. The one M7:30 laying on the right upper limb could be identified as an armlet. On the east side of the tomb's middle area lays a piece of bracelet (M7:57) which apparently was broken due to falling off and rolling out. It should have been originally placed at the top of the coffin. Therefore, it was speculated that there was a wooden outer coffin outside the inner coffin. There is a piece of awl-shaped object (M7:42) to the west of the bracelet. In the middle area of the tomb are two pieces of jade *cong*. The larger one (M7:50) is placed on proper position while the other (M7:34) was placed on side when unearthed, according to the sacred animal motif (Picture 163).

In the north of the tomb, a triangle-like jade plaque object (M7:55) was found near the pottery vessels with its round end facing southward (Picture 165), surrounded by four pieces of animal teeth.

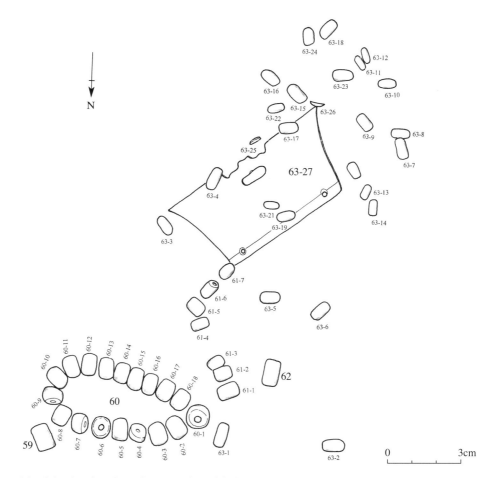

**Fig. 86.** The situation of crown-shaped jade object (M7:63-27) when unearthed

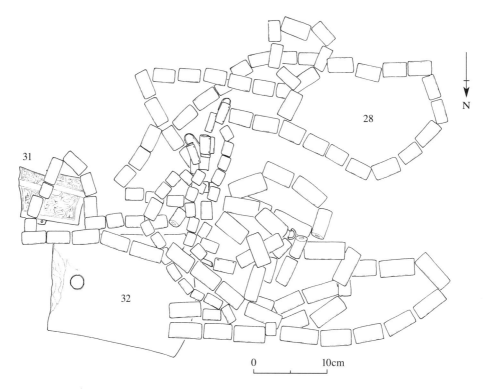

**Fig. 87.** The situation of string of jade tubes (M7:28) when unearthed

**Fig. 88.** The situation of jade *yue* axe (M7:32)
when unearthed

## 2. Burial Objects

There is a number of 158 pieces (sets), and 679 individual pieces. It has the largest number of burial objects in all excavated tombs, including jade artifacts, jade-inlaid lacquer, stone artifacts, pottery vessels and animal teeth.

(1) Jade artifacts

There is a number of 147 pieces (sets), and 667 individual pieces, mostly white jade, including crown-shaped object, cylindrical object with cover, three-pronged object, set of awl-shaped objects, *yue* axe, *cong*, *cong*-stylistic tubes, belt hook, plaque, awl-shaped object, and bracelet etc.

**Crown-shaped object:** one piece (M7:63-27). It has brown spots, it is flat and presents an upside-down trapezoid in shape. The top is concave with the center raising, both of its ends stretching out forming sharp corners. The two sides are indented. There is an oval hole in the middle of the upper part. The bottom has flat tenon with two small holes drilled from both sides. One of its surfaces has two cambered string-cutting marks, but it is polished. It is 3.3 cm in height, 5.4–7.2 cm in width and 0.4 cm in thickness (Fig. 89; Picture 169). When it is unearthed, 26 jade particles (M7:63-1–63-26) are found in a small area nearby (Fig. 86; Picture 161).

**Cylindrical object with cover:** one set (M7:8). It contains a cover and a cylindrical object.

M7:8-1, the cover. It has light gray spots on it with one face flat and the other face convex. There is a pair of tunnel-shaped holes on the plane. It is 1.6 cm in thickness and 3.8 cm in diameter (Fig. 90; Pictures 170, 171).

M7:8-2, the cylindrical object. It has light gray flocs. It is in a flat cylindrical shape with a round hole drilled in the middle. There are string-cutting marks on one side. It is 2.9 cm in height, 5 cm in diameter, 0.7 cm in hole diameter (Fig. 90; Picture 172).

**Three-pronged object:** one piece (M7:26[1]). It has yellow spots. The right and left prongs are at

---

[1] This three-pronged plaque is originally displayed in Shanghai Museum, which provided the line drawing and photos.

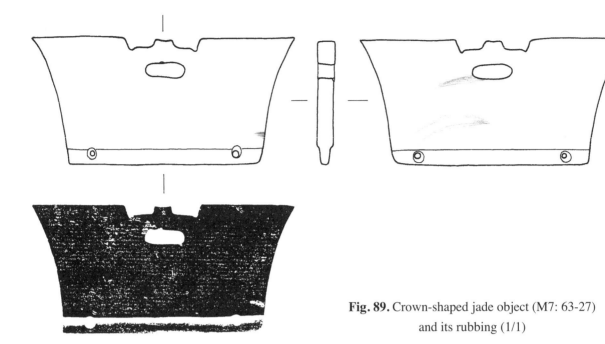

**Fig. 89.** Crown-shaped jade object (M7: 63-27)
and its rubbing (1/1)

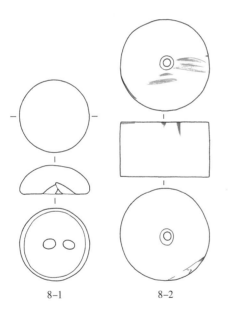

**Fig. 90.** Cylindrical jade object with
cover in tomb M7
8-1. cover; 8-2. cylindrical object

the same level, and the middle prong is lower with a vertical hole. One side is carved while the other is undecorated. The right and left prongs are carved with sacred human motif facing opposite to each other. The sacred human has square face, wearing feathered crowns with single-circle eyes. Two orderly rows of teeth are intaglioed in the mouth. The upper end of the middle prong has five sets of linear feather-like

patterns that represented feathered crown to symbolize the sacred human motif in a frontal position. Sacred animal motif is intaglioed at its lower end, which has symbolic round eyes, nose and tusks. This is another way of combining the sacred human and animal face. It is 4.8 cm in hight, 8.5 cm in width and 0.8 cm in thickness (Fig. 91; Pictures 167, 168).

**Long tubes:** three pieces.

M7:25, it was connected to the middle prong of the three-pronged object (M7:26) when unearthed. They are supposed to be used together. It is cylindrical, light yellow jade with brown spots at one end and a hole drilled from both sides in the middle. Cutting marks could be found on the surface, but have been polished. It is 7.3 cm in Length, 1.3 cm in diameter, 0.8 cm in hole diameter (Fig. 92; Picture 175).

M7:84, it has brown spots at one end, cylindrical, with a hole drilled from both sides. A lengthwise string-cutting mark can be found on its surface and cambered string-cutting marks at its end. It is 6.2 cm in length, 1.8 cm in diameter, 1 cm in hole diameter (Fig. 92; Picture 176).

M7:145, it has light gray flocs. It is long cylinder-shaped, with a hole drilled from both sides. In its middle part is a vertical hole drilled from one side, with spiral lines on the wall. The surface of one end has cambered string-cutting marks, slightly polished.

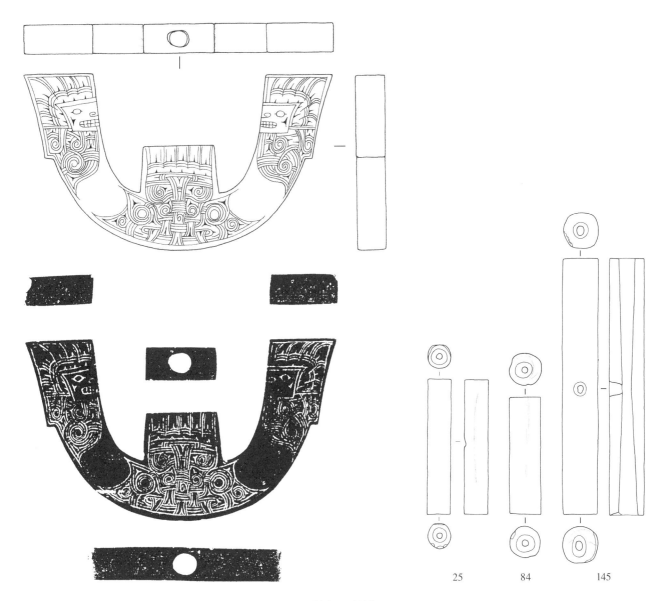

**Fig. 91.** Three-pronged jade object (M7:26) and its rubbings (1/1)

**Fig. 92.** Long jade tubes in tomb M7 (1/2)

It is 13.5 cm in length, 1.9 cm in diameter, 0.9 cm in hole diameter (Fig. 92; Picture 177).

**Set of awl-shaped objects:** one set, comprising 10 individual pieces. They are shaped in long strip, and could be divided into square-cylinder type and cylindrical type by their cross sections.

**Square cylinder type awl-shaped objects:** two pieces.

M7:22, it covered M7:25 and M7:26 when unearthed. It is yellowish-white with some brown spots. It is in a square-column shape, with its front end relatively sharp and bottom end has a bulging flat tenon, with a round hole drilled from both sides. On the lower half part, a simplified sacred animal motif

is carved, which is divided into three segment by two crosswise grooves. Each segment is sculptured with the corner as the central axis. Two neighboring sets share one eye, that is, each of its sides is carved with only one circled eye. It is 12.2 cm in length (Fig. 93; Picture 173).

M7:23, it has the shape similar to that of M7:22, with 12 cm in length (Fig. 93; Picture 174).

**Cylindrical type awl-shaped objects:** eight pieces. All of them are undecorated, their front end are round and sharp and bottom end are flat chisel-like, with round holes drilled from both sides.

M7:24-1, it covered M7:25 and M7:26 when unearthed. Its surface has cutting marks, but polished.

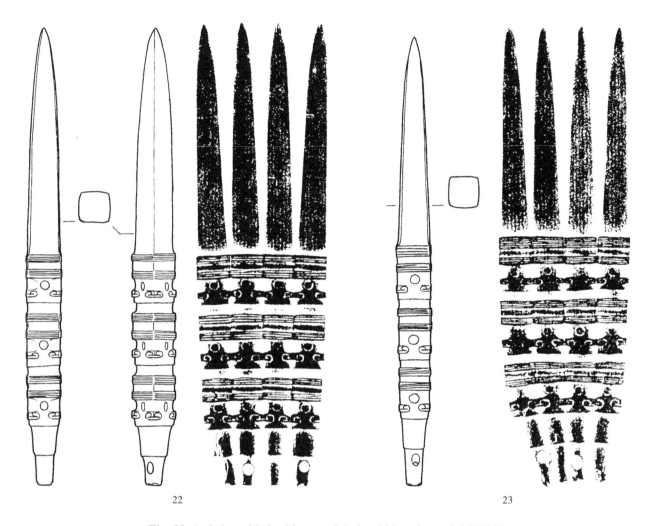

22                                                    23

**Fig. 93.** Awl-shaped jade objects and their rubbings in tomb M7 (1/1)

It is 9.3 cm in length, 1 cm in diameter (Fig. 94; Picture 178).

M7:24-2, its cross section is in square shape with round corner, with 8.6 cm in length, 1 cm in diameter (Fig. 94; Picture 179).

M7:24-3, it covered M7:26 when unearthed, with 9.2 cm in length, 0.9 cm in diameter (Fig. 94; Picture 180).

M7:24-4, fractures surface could be found at the cutting bevel of its end, and it is slightly polished, with 7.9 cm in length, 0.9 cm in diameter (Fig. 94; Picture 181).

M7:24-5, its cross section is oblate, with 7.9 cm in length, 0.72–0.91 cm in diameter: (Fig. 94; Picture 182).

M7:24-6, its end is cut into a bevel, with 8.3 cm in length, 1.05 cm in diameter (Fig. 94; Picture 183).

M7:24-7, it is 7.35 cm in length, 0.9 cm in diameter

(Fig. 94; Picture 184).

M7:24-8, it is 8.3 cm in length, 1 cm in diameter (Fig. 94; Picture 185).

The last three pieces of awl-shaped objects are found overlaying M7:76 stone *yue* axe when unearthed.

**Yue axe:** one set, comprise of the body, *mao* and *dui* end ornaments.

M7:32, the body of *yue* axe, is light greenish white jade with many brown spots. Its body is thin and flat, in shape of trapezoid with the blade cambered. There is a round hole drilled from both sides on the upper part. The top is slightly fractured and the blade has a fracture surface. From both sides of the round hole, there is a set of fine close striations stretching to the side corners. This suggest that the top is originally inserted into the handle with a maximum depth to the horizontal line marks at the top end, tied and fixed aslant using string. Above the horizontal line marks

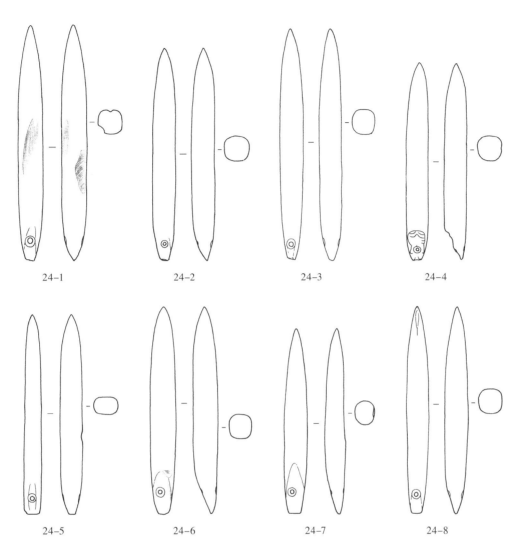

24-1          24-2                    24-3                    24-4

24-5          24-6                    24-7                    24-8

**Fig. 94.** Awl-shaped jade objects in tomb M7 (2/3)

there are slant or vertical line marks in different directions, which possibly are used to increase the friction between the *yue* axe and the handle. It is 16.3 cm in length, 10.3 cm in upper width, 13 cm in blade width, 1.5 cm in hole diameter (Figs. 95, 96; Picture 191). There is a piece of *mao* end ornament at its southern end and a piece of *dui* end ornament at northern end when unearthed.

M7:31, *mao* end ornament, the upper end ornament of *yue* axe. According to the position where it is unearthed, it is speculated that it is originally installed on the top of the *yue* axe's handle. The body is flat, close to a square shape with its top inclined and step-shaped. The bottom is straight with a rectangular tenon in the middle part. The tenon has a horizontal rabbet in the middle and a round hole drilled through it,

vertically. On each side of the tenon, there is a mortise in a ∞ shape, forming by several solid drilling. There are three horizontal raised ridges that run around the body and divide the object into two parts, both carved with vertical feature and sprial patterns. The patterns on front and back surfaces are almost the same, although not completely symmetrical. It is 6.7 cm in height, 7.7 cm in width, 1.5 cm in thickness (Figs. 97, 98; Picture 192).

M7:33, *dui* end ornament, the lower end ornament of *yue* axe. It is roughly in a square shape with olivary cross section. The bottom is also step-shaped, corresponding to the *mao* end ornament. The end connecting the *yue* axe's handle has an oval tenon. The tenon has a horizontal rabbet with a rectangular mortise for easier installation. The mortise is forming

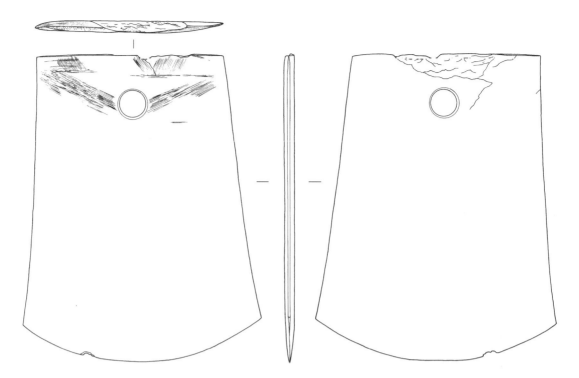

**Fig. 95.** Jade *yue* axe (M7:32) (1/2)

**Fig. 96.** Rubbing of jade *yue* axe (M7:32) (1/2)

by several solid drilling. It has sculptures on its front and back surfaces similar to that of the *mao* end ornament. It is 7.5 cm in width, 3.5 cm in height, 2.4 cm in thickness (Figs. 99, 100; Pictures 193, 194).

**Cong**: two pieces.

M7:34, it has big rufous spots and is in a short

cylinder shape. The inner wall is slightly convex, while the outside looks like a square with round edge. The projecting blocks at the four corners are carved with sacred animal motif with the corner as the axis. Each projecting block is carved with only one group of motifs. The top is decorated with two sets of bow string patterns, symbolizing feathered crown. The eyepits are raised in an oval shape with a fan-shaped forehead in between. The nose is flat, wide and protruding. There are arcs at lower right and left corners to represent the shape of face. It is 4.4 cm in height, 7.5 cm in collar diameter, 6.4 cm in hole diameter (Figs. 101, 102; Picture 189).

M7:50, it has slightly visible gray spots and a rufous spot. It is shaped in a short square cylinder, and has a relatively large hole inside with a shallow round hole on the inner wall. The bottom is not smooth but polished. The irregular form seems to be left after cutting the raw material. Convexities are carved at corners, which are shaped like angle squares and in different sizes due to their irregular body forms. Convexities are carved with a set of simplified sacred animal motif that featured big eyes, horizontal nose, face in arc lines as well as ears represented by

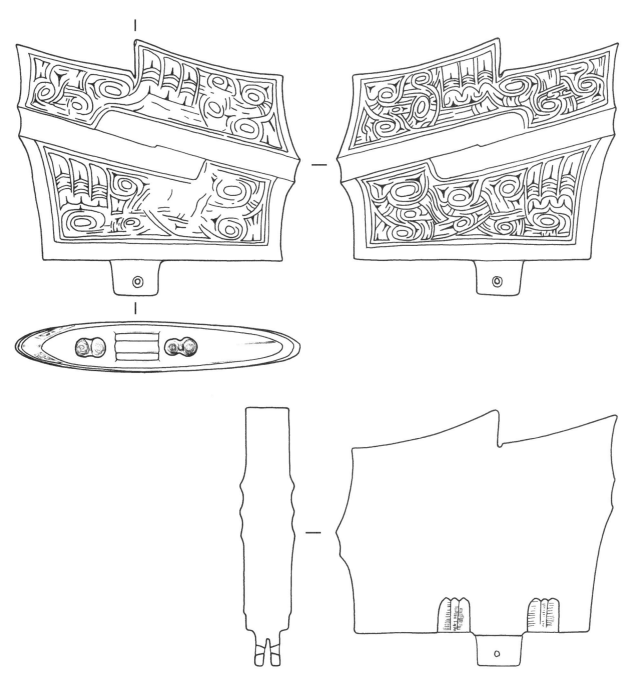

**Fig. 97.** *Mao* end ornament (M7:31) of jade *yue* axe (1/1)

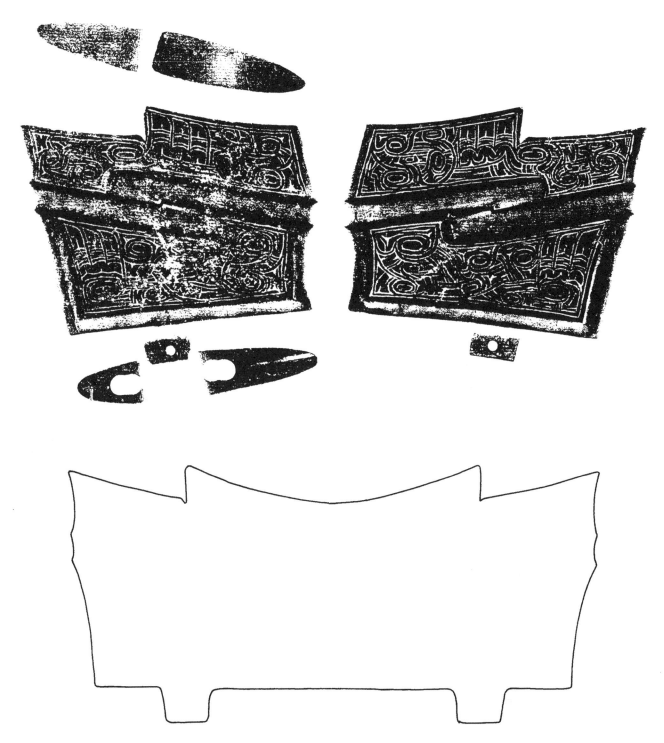

**Fig. 98.** Rubbings of the *mao* end ornament (M7:31) of jade *yue* axe and its expansion plan (1/1)

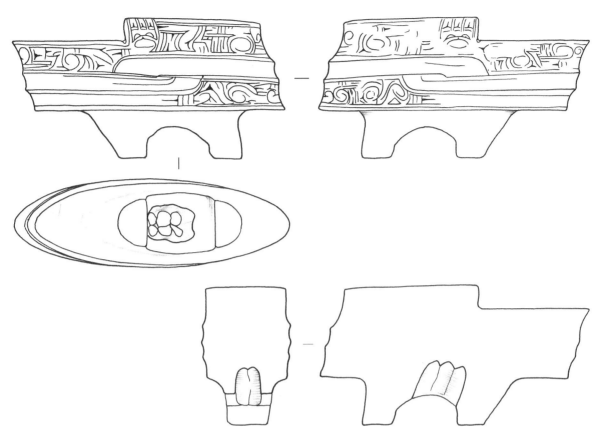

**Fig. 99.** *Dui* end ornament (M7:33) of jade *yue* axe (1/1)

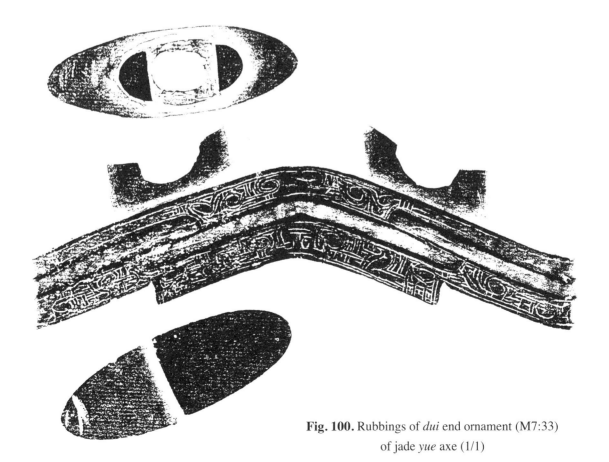

**Fig. 100.** Rubbings of *dui* end ornament (M7:33)
of jade *yue* axe (1/1)

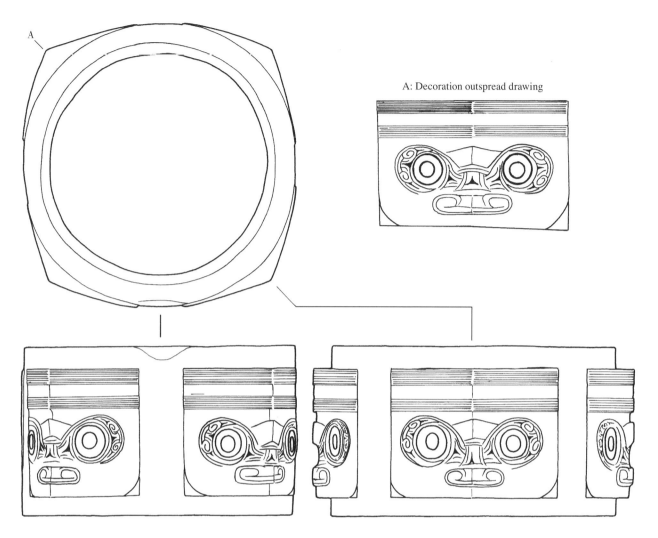

A: Decoration outspread drawing

**Fig. 101.** Jade *cong* (M7:34) (1/1)

semicircular lines intaglioed on both ends. The face is speculated to be drilled with tubular borer, so arcs, though not consecutive, could still be found on the bow string pattern at the top. Its surface is delicately polished. It is 4.2 cm in height, 11.4–11.7 cm in collar diameter, 6.4 cm in hole diameter (Figs. 103, 104; Picture 190).

**Cong-stylistic tube:** ten pieces.

M7:43, it has a square-cylinder body with a hole drilled from both sides in the middle. The crosswise groove cut the sacred animal motif into two parts. Each side is carved with a sacred animal motif using the corner as the axis. The top of the pattern in the upper part is decorated with two belts of bow string patterns. The pattern also features little circular eyes and horizontal nose. In the lower part of the pattern, eyes are oval, eyepits raises, and the horizontal nose

is flat and protruding. It is 2.7 cm in height, 1.5 cm in collar diameter, 1 cm in hole diameter (Fig. 105; Picture 186).

M7:44, it has brown spots, a square-cylinder body with a hole drilled from both sides in the middle. Each corner is decorated with three belts of horizontal bow string patterns. The collar edge at one end has a straight bar-shaped groove. It is 2.65 cm in height, 2.2 cm in collar diameter, 0.9 cm in hole diameter (Fig. 105; Picture 187).

M7:45, it has gray spots, a square-cylinder body with a round hole drilled from both sides in the middle. Each corner is decorated with three belts of horizontal bow string patterns. It is 2.4 cm in height, 2.1 cm in collar diameter and 0.6 cm in hole diameter (Fig. 106; Picture 188).

M7:46, it is square-cylinder shaped with a hole

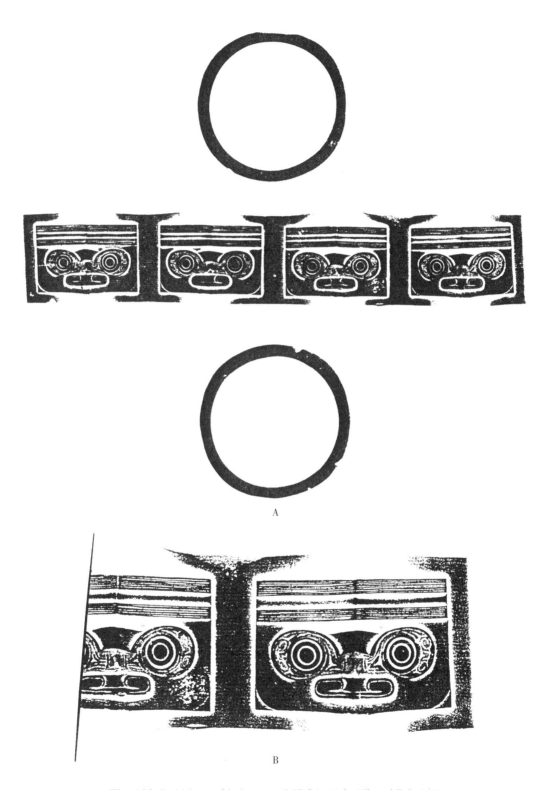

A

B

**Fig. 102.** Rubbings of jade *cong* (M7:34) (A is 1/2 and B is 1/1)

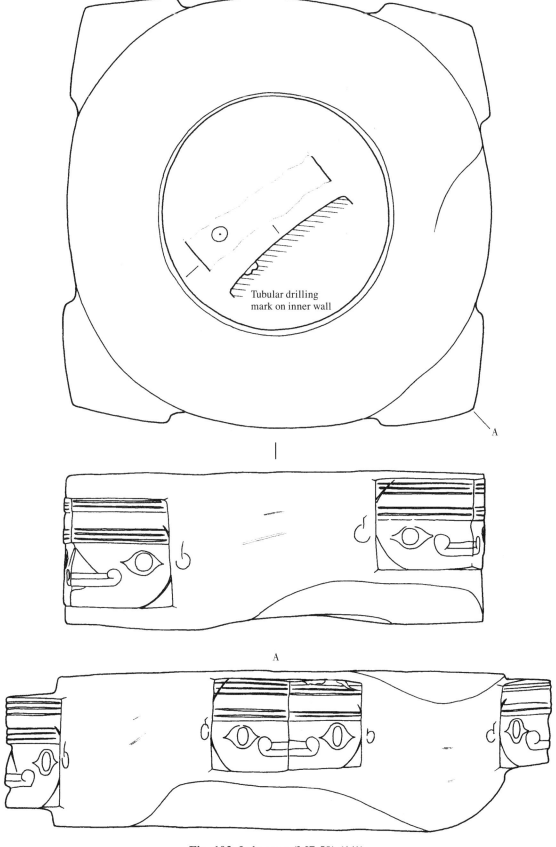

Tubular drilling
mark on inner wall

A

A

**Fig. 103.** Jade *cong* (M7:50) (1/1)

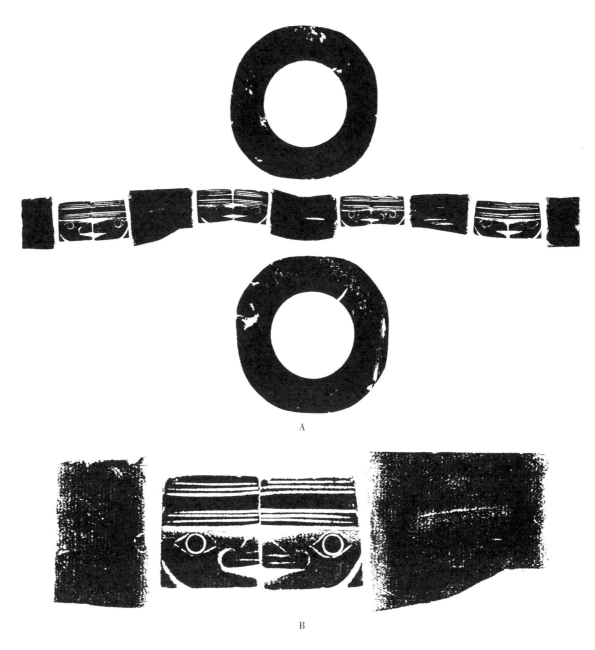

**Fig. 104.** Rubbings of jade *cong* (M7:50) (A is 1/3 and B is 1/1)

drilled from both sides in the middle. Simplified sacred animal motifs are carved with the corner as the axis, and divided into upper and lower parts, each of which has similar patterns carved in similar ways. The upper end is decorated with two belts of bow string patterns. Eyes are represented by round circles, below which there is a horizontal nose, flat and protruding. It is 3.3 cm in height, 1.3 cm in collar diameter, 0.6 cm in hole diameter (Fig. 106; Pictures 195, 197).

M7:47, it has a few gray spots and similar to M7:46

in shape (Fig. 106; Pictures 196, 197).

M7:49, it has many gray spots, square-cylinder shaped with a hole in the middle drilled from both sides. Its shape is irregular, and its corners are decorated with four belts of horizontal bow string patterns. Its surface has slightly concave cutting marks. It is 4.5 cm in height, 1.6 cm in collar diameter, 0.8 cm in hole diameter (Fig. 107; Picture 198).

M7:51, it has a few green spots, square-cylinder shaped with a hole drilled from both sides in the middle. Simplified sacred animal motif is divided into

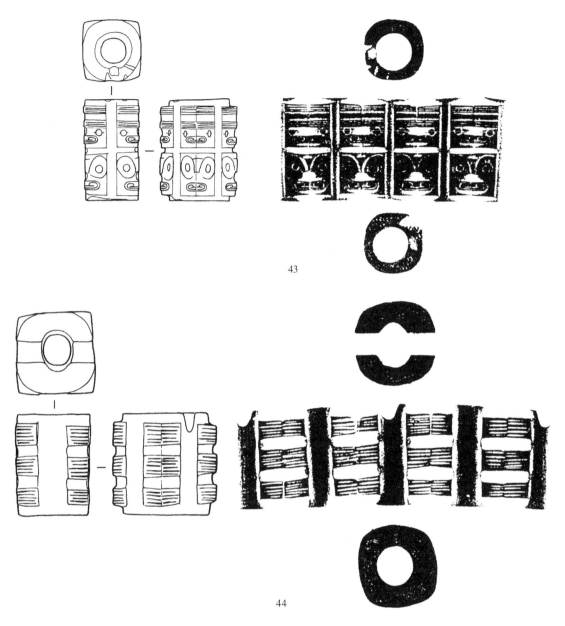

43

44

**Fig. 105.** *Cong*-stylistic jade tubes and their rubbings in tomb M7 (1/1)

upper, middle and lower parts, each having almost the same pattern. The top is decorated with two belts of bow string patterns. Eyes are represented by round circles, below which there is a horizontal nose, flat and protruding. It is 3.9 cm in height, 1.4 cm in collar diameter, 0.7 cm in hole diameter (Fig. 107; Picture 199).

M7:52, its middle hole is drilled from both sides but in malposition. It is similar to M7:51 in shape. It is 3.8 cm in height, 1.3 cm in collar diameter, 0.6 cm in hole diameter (Fig. 108; Picture 200).

M7:54, it has brown spots, short square-cylinder

shaped with the upper part larger than the lower part in size, and a round hole drilled from both sides in the middle, the wall of the hole being polished. Simplified sacred animal motifs are carved at corners, which could be divided into upper and lower parts. The top is decorated with two belts of bow string patterns. Eyes are in the shape of round circles, nose being horizontal, flat and protruding. It is 2.4 cm in height, 2.6 cm in collar diameter, 1 cm in hole diameter (Fig. 107; Picture 201).

M7:147, it is slightly corroded, square-cylinder shaped with a hole drilled from both sides in the

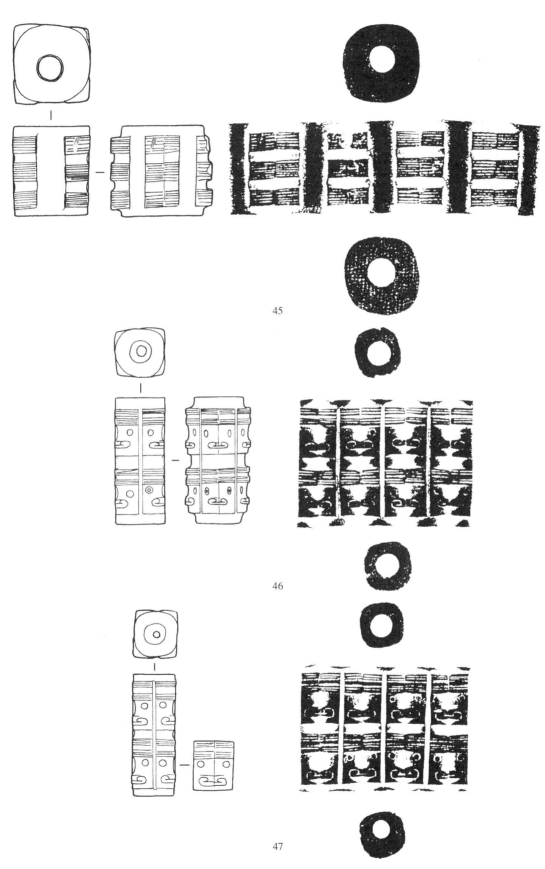

45

46

47

**Fig. 106.** *Cong*-stylistic jade tubes and their rubbings in tomb M7 (1/1)

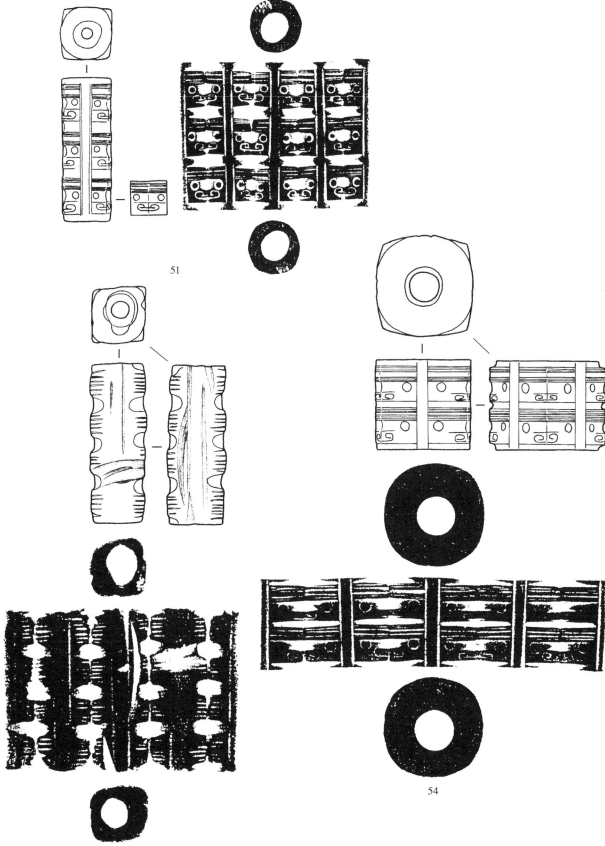

51

54

49

**Fig. 107.** *Cong*-stylistic jade tubes and their rubbings in tomb M7 (1/1)

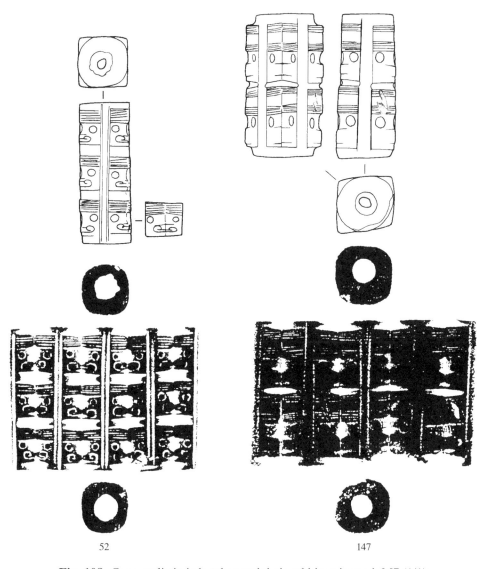

52                          147

**Fig. 108.** *Cong*-stylistic jade tubes and their rubbings in tomb M7 (1/1)

middle. The shape is irregular, its pattern also not very regular. Simplified sacred animal motifs are carved at corners and could be divided into upper and lower parts with similar patterns. The top is decorated with two belts of bow string patterns. Eyes are in the shape of round circles, below which the nose is carved, represented by two fine lines. It is 3.9 cm in height, 1.5 cm in collar diameter, 0.6 cm in hole diameter (Fig. 108; Picture 202).

**Awl-shaped object:** one piece (M7:42). Its tip has reddish brown spots. It is shaped in long and square cylinder. Its top is bluntly pointed, and on the bottom is a small tenon with a small hole drilled from both sides. The lower part is carved with very simplified sacred animal motif that has two belts of bow string patterns. Below the bow string patterns, nose is carved with intaglio lines. From observation, the straight vertical groove that cutted through the sacred anima motif must be carved in the last. It is 6.5 cm in length (Fig. 109; Picture 203).

**Bracelets:** twelve pieces, all without patterns.

M7:6, it is off-white in color with reddish brown spots, wide girdle-shaped, one end with inclined surface. The inner wall is slightly convex, and has step-shaped marks forming by hole drilling. The outer wall is slightly concave. It is 2–2.2 cm in height, 5 cm in diameter, 4.5 cm in hole diameter (Fig. 110; Picture 204).

M7:20, it has light yellow spots, wide girdle-shaped, with the inner wall slightly convex, the outer wall

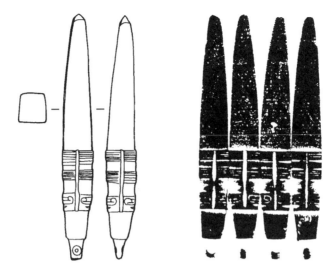

**Fig. 109.** Awl-shaped jade objects (M7:42) and its rubbing (1/1)

concave. It is 1.75 cm in height, 7.3 cm in diameter, 5.7 cm in hole diameter (Fig. 110; Picture 205).

M7:30, it has a few light yellow spots, it is flat ring-like, with the inner wall convex, the outer wall round and convex. It is 0.7 cm in height, 8 cm in diameter, 5.9 cm in hole diameter (Fig. 110; Picture 214).

M7:35, it has light yellow and green spots, it is wide girdle-shaped, with the inner wall slightly convex, the outer wall smooth and straight. It has one slant left due to cutting of raw material, but polished. It is 3 cm in height, 8.6 cm in diameter, 6.7 cm in hole diameter (Fig. 110; Picture 206).

M7:36, it has reddish spots at its end, it is cylinder-shaped, with the inner wall slightly convex, the outer wall relatively straight, one end face inclined and smooth. It is 4.7 cm in height, 8.3 cm in diameter, 6.1 cm in hole diameter (Fig. 110; Picture 207).

M7:37, it has yellow and brown spots, it is cylinder-shaped, with one end slightly inclined and smooth, the outer wall straight and smooth, the inner wall slightly convex. It is 3.9 cm in height, 7.9 cm in diameter, 6.1 cm in hole diameter (Fig. 111; Picture 208).

M7:38, it has brown spots, it is wide girdle-shaped, with the outer wall straight and smooth, the inner wall slightly convex. It is 2.4 cm in height, 7.7 cm in diameter, 6 cm in hole diameter (Fig. 111; Picture 209).

M7:39, it has gray and brown spots, it is cylinder-shaped, with the inner wall slightly convex, the outer

wall straight and smooth. Its wall is relatively thin. Inclined cutting marks can be found on the outer wall. It is 4.2 cm in height, 7.2 cm in diameter, 6.3 cm in hole diameter (Fig. 110; Picture 210).

M7:40, it has brown spots, it is wide girdle-shaped, and has an inclined surface on one of its ends, the inner wall being slightly convex, and the outer wall straight. Cambered string-cutting marks can be found on the end face and outer wall. It is 2.5 cm in height, 8.1 cm in diameter, 5.6 cm in hole diameter (Fig. 111; Picture 211).

M7:41, it has brown spots, it is broken into five pieces when unearthed, ring-like, with the inner wall slightly straight, outer wall convex. Its shape is irregular due to the cutting of the raw material. The inner wall has vertical cambered string-cutting marks. The outer wall also has a few cambered string-cutting marks. It is 0.5–1.1 cm in height, 10.1 cm in diameter, 8.8 cm in hole diameter (Fig. 111; Picture 215).

M7:57, it has lots of brown and gray spots, and quite mottled, it is broken into six pieces when unearthed, wide girdle-shaped, with the outer wall straight and smooth, the inner wall convex. Ring-like cutting marks could be found. It is 2.4 cm in height, 4.9–5.1 cm in diameter, 4.5 cm in hole diameter (Fig. 110; Picture 216).

M7:58, it has yellow spots, one of its ends has inclined cutting marks. There are vertical cambered string-cutting marks on the inner wall. Spiral patterns

**Fig. 110.** Jade bracelets in tomb M7 (1/2)

are more or less visible. It is 1.8–2.2 cm in height, 5.1 cm in diameter, 4.4 cm in hole diameter (Fig. 110; Picture 217).

**Cylindrical objects:** two pieces.

M7:27, it has a few green spots, it is cylinder-shaped, with a small round hole drilled in the middle. There is a horizontal cutting mark in the middle of the outer surface, which is speculated to be left after

drilling. It is 7 cm in height, 4.2 cm in diameter, 0.8 cm in hole diameter (Fig. 111; Picture 212).

M7:98, it has many green spots, it is flat cylinder-shaped, with a small hole drilled in the middle. It is 2.5 cm in height, 4.5 cm in diameter, 1.25 cm in hole diameter (Fig. 111; Picture 213).

**End ornaments:** two pieces.

M7:18, it has caesious and light yellow spots, it is

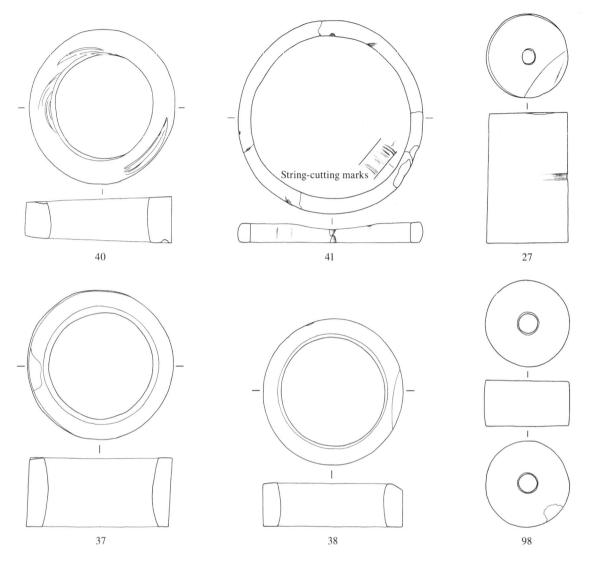

**Fig. 111.** Cylindrical jade objects and jade bracelets in tomb M7
27, 98. cylindrical objects; 37, 38, 40, 41. bracelets (1/2)

circular cone-shaped, with a hole in the middle drilled from both sides. It is 2 cm in height, 4 cm in diameter, 1 cm in hole diameter (Fig. 113; Picture 218).

M7:29, it has reddish brown spots. It looks like a step-like circular cone on the whole. The upper end surface has cambered string-cutting marks. The top has oval cross section with a rectangular mortise carved in the center. The mortise is made by digging and drilling, leaving solid drilling marks on the four corners. The mortise is interlinked with the holes drilled horizontally from both sides. From the middle of the mortise to its bottom, small holes are drilled from both sides. The bottom surface is inclined and smooth. It is 4 cm in height, 5.5 cm in diameter (Fig.

112; Picture 219).

**Belt hook:** one piece (M7:53). It has a few light yellow spots. Shaped like a cuboid, its surface is slightly concave, and its bottom face straight and smooth. One end is penetrated by a round hole with about 0.9 cm in diameter, while the other is carved into a deep groove-like hook. Its surface is polished and bright and its bottom has a arc cutting mark. It is 5 cm in length, 2.75 cm in width, 2.2 cm in thickness (Fig. 113; Pictures 220, 221).

**Plaque object:** one piece (M7:55). The shaped like a triangle in plane with a pointed and cambered bottom. Sacred animal motifs are carved using methods of openwork and intaglio carving technique.

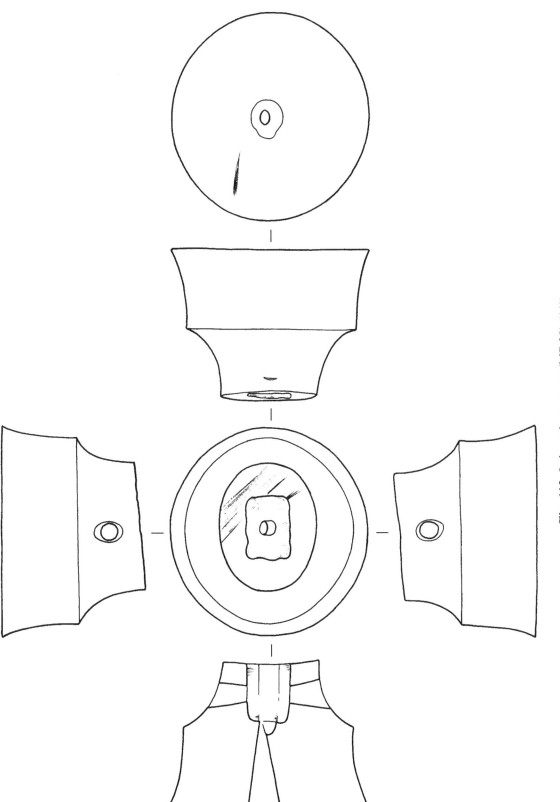

**Fig. 112.** Jade end ornament (M7:29) (1/1)

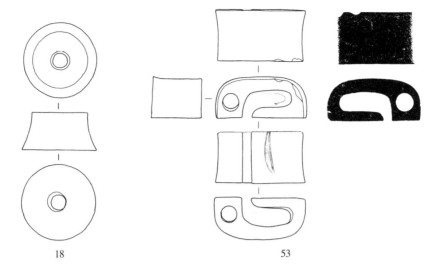

**Fig. 113.** Jade end ornament and jade belt hook in tomb M7
18. end ornament; 53. belt hook (1/2)

Each of the two corners is drilled from both sides with one round hole as the eyes. Arc triangle-shaped holes are made first by cutting, then using string-cutting on both ends of the eyes to form the eyepit and eyelid, which are outlined with intaglio lines. On the forehead between eyes are irregular long strip-type hole formed by openwork. The nostril is represented by spiral pattern using intaglio technique. Below the nose is a hole in the shape of a cross-shaped hole, supposed to be the mouth. Both ends below the eyepit have a jagged protrusion, quite similar to the toes of a frog. The cross-shaped hole and the shapes on its sides resemble very much the hind limbs of a frog. On the whole, it looks like a transformed prostrate frog. It is 7 cm in width, 3.9 cm in height, 0.42 cm in thickness (Fig. 114; Picture 222).

**Pendant:** one piece (M7:56). It is in drop shape. The top end has a round tenon with a small hole drilled from both sides. The bottom is round and pointed. The middle is decorated with a concave bow string pattern that circled the pendant, cutting the surface into two parts. The upper part has no pattern, while the lower part is carved with two eyes and two noses using bas-relief technique and decorated with intaglio lines. It is 3.2 cm in length, 0.95 cm in diameter (Fig. 115; Picture 223).

**Pie-shaped ornament:** one piece (M7:11). It has a color mingled with caesious and reddish-brown, pie-shaped, and one surface is straight, the other convex. It is 5.5 cm in diameter, 1.4 cm in thickness (Fig. 115; Picture 224).

**Semi-circular ornaments:** four pieces.

M7:101, the upper end is concave, the lower end is round and convex, and the right and left corners stretch out upward. On the edge of the upper end, three holes are drilled from both sides with equidistance. The ornament becomes thinner from top to bottom. One side surface has two inclined cutting marks. It is 2.3 cm in height, 3.05 cm in width, 0.35–0.55 cm in thickness (Fig. 115; Picture 225).

M7:133, its upper end is relatively smooth and the lower end is round and convex. The upper end is drilled with 3 small holes from both sides and is slightly thicker than the lower end. One side surface has cutting marks. It is 2.1 cm in height, 3.1 cm in width, 0.6–0.7 cm in thickness (Fig. 115; Picture 226).

M7:134, it has reddish-brown spots, with inclined and smooth upper end and a round and convex lower end. The upper end is drilled with 3 small holes from both sides. One side surface has a arc cutting mark. It is 2.1 cm in height, 3.05 cm in width (Fig. 115; Picture 227).

M7:135, it has reddish-brown spots, with concave upper end and round and concave lower end, the right and left corners stretching out upward. The upper end is drilled with 3 holes from both sides with

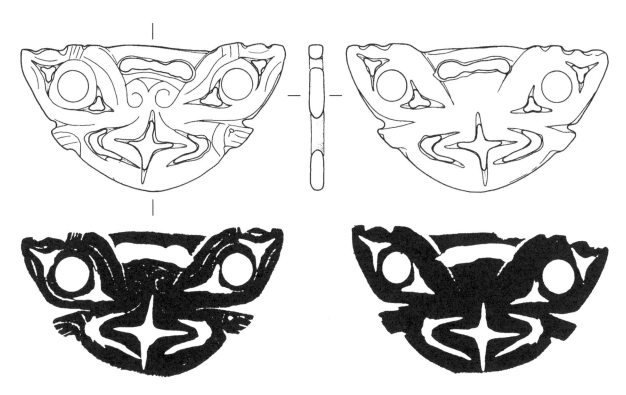

**Fig. 114.** Jade plaque object (M7:55) and its rubbings (1/1)

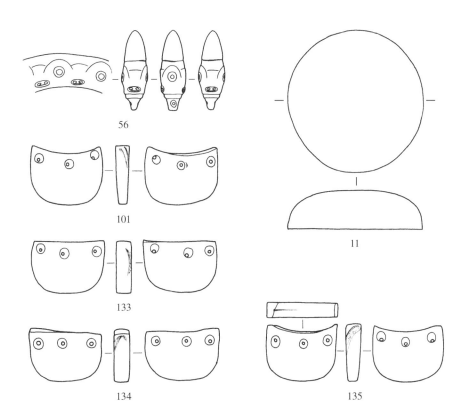

**Fig. 115.** Jade pie-shaped ornament, jade pendant and semi-circular jade ornaments in tomb M7

11. pie-shaped ornament; 56. pendant; 101, 133–135. semi-circular ornaments (2/3)

equidistance. The ornament becomes thinner from top to bottom. One side surface has an arc-shaped cutting mark. The top has a vertical cutting mark. It is 2.3 cm in height, 3 cm in width, 0.35–0.6 cm in thickness (Fig. 115; Picture 228).

**Strings of tubes:** they are summarized into 11 sets by combining field numbers with indoor sorting,

totaling 225 pieces of single jade tubes, all without patterns.

M7:5, it comprises 29 single tubes, with gray and brown spots. Their lengths slightly varied from 0.9 cm to 1.6 cm, diameter from 0.7 cm to 1 cm (Fig. 116; Picture 229).

M7:28, it comprises 114 pieces of single tube (field

**Fig. 116.** String of jade tubes (M7:5) (2/3)

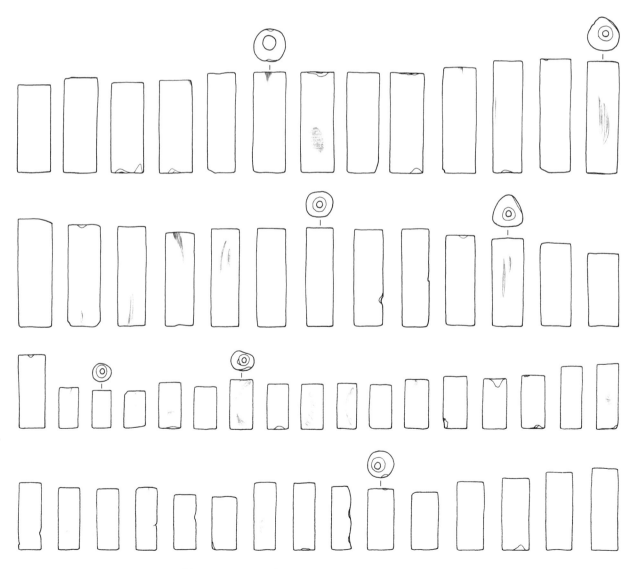

**Fig. 117.** String of jade tubes (Some of M7:28) (2/3)

**Fig. 118.** String of jade tubes (Some of M7:28) (2/3)

numbers 1–66 and 101–148, respectively). Most of them are of white with yellowish-brown spots, cylinder-shaped with varied lengths. Among them, some have a triangle-shaped cross section, some have a hole drilled from both sides, and some have cutting marks. They are 1.4–4.5 cm in length, 0.8–1.3 cm in diameter, 0.45–0.7 cm in hole diameter (Figs. 117, 118; Picture 230).

M7:70, it comprises 10 pieces of single tube, with gray spots. Two of them are numbered into one group in the field. They are cylinder-shaped with holes drilled from both sides. The larger one is 2 cm in length, 0.9 cm in diameter and 0.5 cm in hole diameter, while the smaller one, 0.95 cm in length, 0.7 cm in diameter and 0.3 cm in hole diameter (Fig. 120; Picture 231).

M7:72, it comprises 16 pieces of single tube, with yellow and brown spots and many fractures. Among them, 14 pieces are semicircular and groove-shaped, as if they are cut into two from the middle. Each of the four corners has a hole drilled through from one side. Besides, there is one piece of cylinder-shaped tube and one triangular prism-shaped tube that are seemingly not supposed to be included into this group. They are 1.8–2.8 cm in length, 0.9 cm in diameter (Fig. 119; Pictures 232, 233).

M7:73, it comprises 17 pieces of single tube, with many yellow and brown spots, and all are cylinder-shaped with holes in the middle drilled from both sides. They are 1.2–1.9 cm in length, 0.95 cm in diameter (Fig. 120; Picture 234).

M7:80, it comprises two pieces of single tube, cylinder-shaped with holes drilled from both sides. They are 2.7 cm in length, 1 cm in diameter, 0.6 cm in hole diameter (Fig. 120; Picture 235).

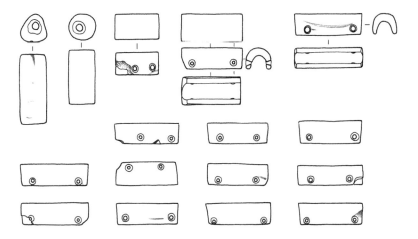

**Fig. 119.** String of jade tubes (M7:72) (2/3)

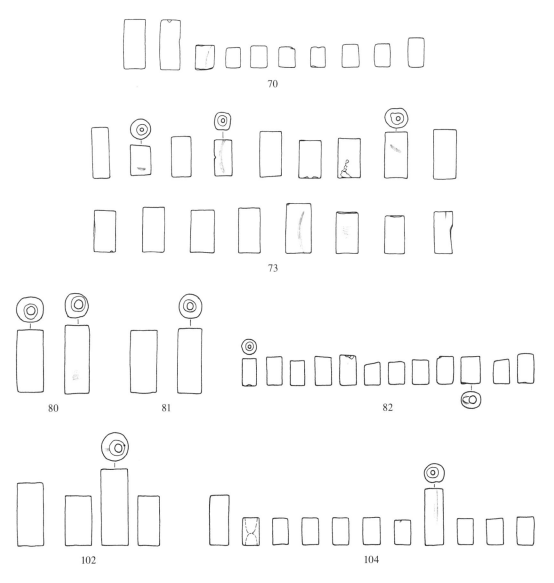

70

73

80    81    82

102    104

**Fig. 120.** Strings of jade tubes in tomb M7 (2/3)

M7:81, it comprises two pieces of single tube, cylinder-shaped with holes drilled from both sides. Ther are 2.55 cm in Length, 1 cm in diameter, 0.5 cm in hole diameter (Fig. 120; Picture 235).

M7:82, it comprises 12 pieces of single tube, cylinder-shaped with holes drilled from both sides. M7:82-4 is 1.2 cm in length, 0.7 cm in diameter, 0.4 cm in hole diameter (Fig. 120; Picture 236).

The above mentioned three groups (M7:80–82) are included into three numbers in the field, but change to one group during indoor sorting. All of them have gray or brown spots.

M7:102, it comprises four pieces of single tube, with gray spots, cylinder-shaped with holes drilled from both sides. They are 2–2.9 cm in length, 0.8–1.1 cm in diameter, 0.4–0.65 cm in hole diameter (Fig. 120; Picture 237).

M7:104, it comprises 11 pieces of single tube, with gray flocs, cylinder-shaped with round holes drilled from both sides. They are 1.1–2.2 cm in length, 0.7–0.8 cm in diameter (Fig. 120; Picture 238).

M7:114, it comprises five pieces of single tube, all with gray spots, cylinder-shaped with holes in the middle drilled from both sides. M7:114-4 has cambered string-cutting marks on its surface. M7:114-5 has blade-like cutting marks on its surface. M7:114-5 is 2.4 cm in length, 1.05 cm in diameter, 0.5 cm in hole diameter (Fig. 121; Picture 239).

M7:115, it comprises three pieces of single tube, with gray spots, cylinder-shaped with round holes drilled from both sides. They are 1.8–3.5 cm in length, 0.9–1.45 cm in diameter (Fig. 121; Picture 240).

M7:116, it comprises seven pieces of single tube, with light gray spots, cylinder-shaped with holes drilled from both sides. M7:116-1 is 2.1 cm in length, 1.2 cm in diameter, 0.65 cm in hole diameter (Fig. 121; Picture 241).

M7:132, it comprises five pieces of single tube, with taupe spots, cylinder-shaped with holes drilled from both sides. They are 1.7–2.6 cm in length, 0.9~1.05 cm in diameter, 0.5–0.6 cm in hole diameter (Fig. 121; Picture 242).

Indoor sorting confirms that M7:114–116 and M7:132 jade tubes (strings) belong to the same grouped

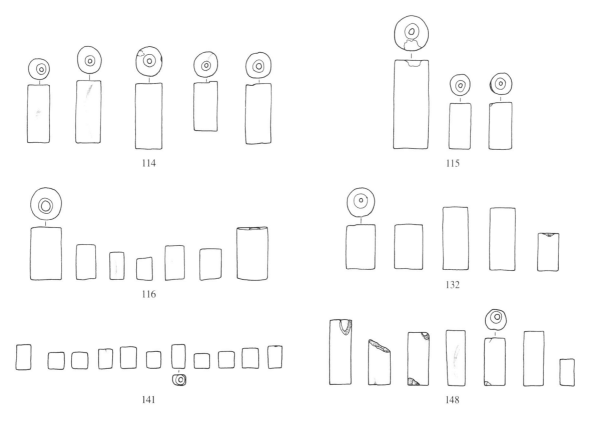

114

115

116

132

141

148

**Fig. 121.** Strings of jade tubes in tomb M7 (2/3)

string of tubes.

M7:141, it comprises 11 pieces of single tube, with gray and brown spots, cylinder-shaped with holes drilled from both sides. One of them has cambered string-cutting marks at its end. M7:141-1 is 0.9 cm in length, 0.65 cm in diameter, 0.3 cm in hole diameter (Fig. 121; Picture 243).

M7:148, it comprises seven pieces of single tube, with a few light gray spots. It is cylinder-shaped with holes drilled from both sides. From M7:148-1 to M7:148-3, one end of them is incomplete. The surface of M7:148-4 has cutting marks. M7:148-1 is 2.6 cm in length, 0.95 cm in diameter, 0.65 cm in hole diameter (Fig. 121; Picture 244).

**Strings of beads:** five groups.

M7:60, it comprises 18 pieces of single bead. The beads are closely connected when unearthed. Some beads have brown spots. They are in the shape of waist drum with holes in the middle drilled from both sides. Their sizes varied slightly. M7:60-1 is 0.75 cm in length, 0.9 cm in diameter, 0.2 cm in hole diameter (Fig. 122; Picture 245).

M7:61, it comprises seven pieces of single bead. With greyish brown spots, they are in the shape of waist drum with holes in the middle drilled from both sides. They are 0.5–0.7 cm in length, 0.6–0.85 cm in diameter (Fig. 122; Picture 246).

M7:69, it comprises 22 pieces of single bead. With many brown spots, they are in the shape of waist drum with holes drilled from both sides. M7:69-1 is 0.6 cm in length, 0.65 cm in diameter, 0.2 cm in hole diameter (Fig. 122; Picture 247).

M7:136, it comprises 170 individual pieces. With gray and brown spots, they are in the shape of waist drum and vary in size. M7:136-3 is 0.5 cm in length, 0.9 cm in diameter (Fig. 122; Picture 248).

In the fieldwork, M7:59, M7:62 and M7:64–68, seven individual pieces in total, are numbered separately; however, they actually may belong to one string. Most having gray and brown spots, they are in the shape of waist drum with holes in the middle drilled from both sides. They are 1.1 cm in length, 0.9–1 cm in diameter, 0.4 cm in hole diameter (Fig. 122; Picture 250).

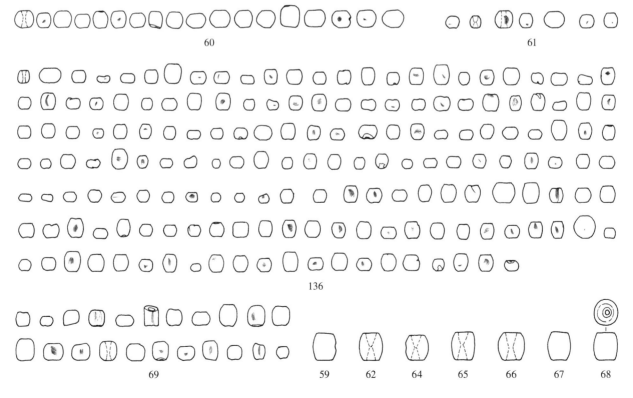

**Fig. 122.** Strings of jade tubes and jade beads in tomb M7
59, 62, 64–68. beads; 60, 61, 69, 136. strings of beads (2/3)

**Tubes:** sixty six pieces. They are mostly cylinder-shaped with holes in the middle drilled from both sides.

M7:1, it has gray spots, 4 cm in length, 1.25 cm in diameter and 0.65 cm in hole diameter (Fig. 123; Picture 252).

M7:2, it is 3.75 cm in length, 1.25 cm in diameter, 0.6 cm in hole diameter (Fig. 123; Picture 252).

M7:3, it has brown spots, with 3.7 cm in length, 1.2 cm in diameter and 0.7 cm in hole diameter (Fig. 123; Picture 252).

M7:4, it has caesious spots, with 3.8 cm in length, 1.1 cm in diameter and 0.6 cm in hole diameter (Fig. 123; Picture 252).

M7:7, it is broken (Fig. 123).

M7:9, it has yellow and brown spots, with 1.35–1.45 cm in length, 2.95 cm in diameter and 1.8 cm in hole diameter (Fig. 123; Picture 251).

M7:10, it has yellow and brown spots, with 1.5–1.6 cm in length, 3 cm in diameter and 2 cm in hole diameter (Fig. 123; Picture 249). Judging from the textures and spots of jade tubes M7:9 and M7:10, they may be made from the same piece of raw material.

M7:12, it is 1.5 cm in length, 0.95 cm in diameter, 0.45 cm in hole diameter (Fig. 123; Picture 253).

M7:13, it is 2.2 cm in length, 0.8 cm in diameter, 0.45 cm in hole diameter (Fig. 123; Picture 253).

M7:14, it has brown spots, with 2.5 cm in length, 1.05 cm in diameter and 0.7 cm in hole diameter (Fig. 123; Picture 254).

M7:15, it has brown spots, with 2.4 cm in length, 1.1 cm in diameter and 0.5 cm in hole diameter (Fig. 123; Picture 253).

M7:16, it has gray flocs, with 1.45 cm in length, 1 cm in diameter and 0.4 cm in hole diameter (Fig. 123; Picture 255).

M7:21, it is 3 cm in length, 1.3 cm in diameter and 0.7 cm in hole diameter (Fig. 123; Picture 254).

M7:48, it has gray spots, with 2.6 cm in length,

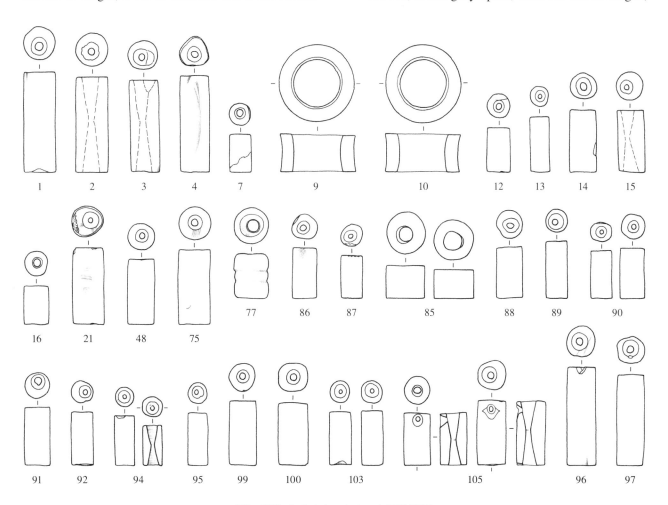

**Fig. 123.** Jade tubes in tomb M7 (2/3)

1.1 cm in diameter and 0.65 cm in hole diameter (Fig. 123; Picture 256).

M7:75, it is 2.9 cm in length, 1.25 cm in diameter, 0.55 cm in hole diameter (Fig. 123; Picture 254).

M7:77, it is cylinder-shaped, with the outer wall round and cambered and the middle part carved with a round of groove. The bottom edge of the groove is convex. It is 1.75 cm in length, 1.3 cm in diameter, 0.5 cm in hole diameter (Fig. 123; Picture: 257).

M7:85, it comprises two individual pieces. It is bluish white and is relatively transparent. It is 1.25 cm in length, 1.6 cm in diameter, 0.6 cm in hole diameter (Fig. 123; Picture 258).

M7:86, it has reddish brown spots, with 2 cm in length, 1.05 cm in diameter and 0.5 cm in hole diameter (Fig. 123; Picture 253).

M7:87, it has gray spots, with 1.6 cm in length, 0.9 cm in diameter and 0.5 cm in hole diameter (Fig. 123; Picture 255).

M7:88, it has caesious spots, with 1.9 cm in length, 1.1 cm in diameter and 0.6 cm in hole diameter (Fig. 123; Picture 253).

M7:89, it has gray flocs, with 2.25 cm in length, 0.85 cm in diameter and 0.6 cm in hole diameter (Fig. 123; Picture 259).

M7:90, it comprises two individual pieces. It is in the south of M7:35, but its position has not been indicated in the field plan. They are 1.9 cm in length, 0.9–1 cm in diameter, 0.5 cm in hole diameter (Fig. 123; Picture 260).

M7:91, it has gray flocs, with 2.3 cm in length, 1.1 cm in diameter and 0.6 cm in hole diameter (Fig. 123; Picture 256).

M7:92, it is in the east of M7:91, but this has not been indicated in the field plan. It is 2.05 cm in length, 0.9 cm in diameter, 0.55 cm in hole diameter (Fig. 123; Picture 259).

M7:94, it comprises two individual pieces. With gray spots, they are located in the southeast of M7:50, but this has not been indicated in the field plan. Spiral marks can be found on the inner wall. They are 1.55–2 cm in length, 0.8–0.85 cm in diameter, 0.5 cm in hole diameter (Fig. 123; Picture 261).

M7:95, it has gray spots. It was in the east of M7:50, but this has not been indicated in the field plan. It is 2.1 cm in length, 0.8 cm in diameter, 0.5 cm in hole diameter (Fig. 123; Picture 259).

M7:96, it has gray spots, with 3.8 cm in length, 1.2 cm in diameter and 0.8 cm in hole diameter (Fig. 123; Picture 254).

M7:97, it has gray spots, with 3.6 cm in length, 1.1 cm in diameter and 0.6 cm in hole diameter (Fig. 123; Picture 262).

M7:99, it is 2.6 cm in length, 1.1 cm in diameter and 0.5 cm in hole diameter (Fig. 123; Picture 262).

M7:100, it has gray spots, with 2.4 cm in length, 1.1 cm in diameter and 0.5 cm in hole diameter (Fig. 123; Picture 256).

M7:103, it comprises two individual pieces and are 2.1–2.2 cm in length, 0.8–0.85 cm in diameter and 0.5 cm in hole diameter (Fig. 123; Picture 260).

M7:105, it comprises two individual pieces with greyish brown spots. The side surface of one end has a hole inwards drilled through from one direction. They are 2.5 cm in length, 1.1 cm in diameter, 0.6 cm in hole diameter (Fig. 123; Picture 263).

M7:106, it has gray flocs, with 2.8 cm in length, 1.35 cm in diameter and 0.7 cm in hole diameter (Fig. 124; Picture 262).

M7:107, it is 2.1 cm in length, 0.9 cm in diameter and 0.5 cm in hole diameter (Fig. 124; Picture 259).

M7:108, it is 1.95 cm in length, 0.95 cm in diameter and 0.5 cm in hole diameter (Fig. 124; Picture 259).

M7:109, it has gray flocs, with 1.85 cm in length, 1.15 cm in diameter and 0.4 cm in hole diameter (Fig. 124; Picture 264).

M7:110, it is 1.4 cm in length, 0.75 cm in diameter and 0.4 cm in hole diameter (Fig. 124; Picture 255).

M7:111, it is 1.3 cm in length, 0.7 cm in diameter and 0.5 cm in hole diameter (Fig. 124; Picture 255).

M7:117, it is 2.1 cm in length, 1.2 cm in diameter and 0.65 cm in hole diameter (Fig. 124; Picture 264).

M7:118, it is 1.4 cm in length, 0.85 cm in diameter and 0.4 cm in hole diameter (Fig. 124; Picture 255).

M7:119, it has reddish brown spots, with 2.4 cm in length, 1.1 cm in diameter and 0.5 cm in hole diameter (Fig. 124; Picture 264).

M7:120, it comprises two individual pieces. With

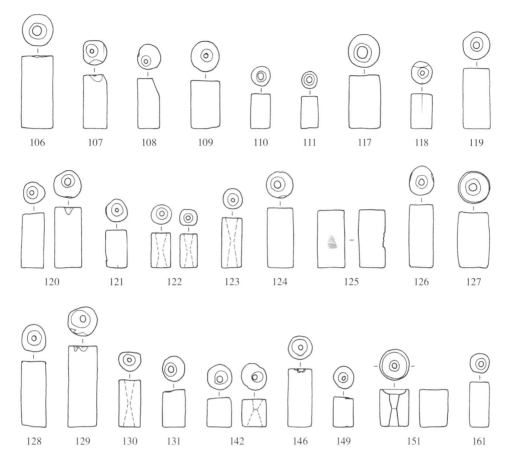

**Fig. 124.** Jade tubes in tomb M7 (2/3)

gray flocs, they are 2.2–2.4 cm in length, 0.9–1.1 cm in diameter and about 0.4 cm in hole diameter (Fig. 124; Picture 260).

M7:121, it has gray spots, with 1.45 cm in length, 0.85 cm in diameter and 0.4 cm in hole diameter (Fig. 124; Picture 265).

M7:122, it comprises two individual pieces. They are close to M7:121, but this has not been indicated in the field plan. They are 1.35 cm in length, 0.8 cm in diameter and 0.4 cm in hole diameter (Fig. 124; Picture 261).

M7:123, it has gray spots, with 1.95 cm in length, 0.8 cm in diameter and 0.5 cm in hole diameter (Fig. 124; Picture 265).

M7:124, it is 2.35 cm in length, 1.1 cm in diameter and 0.55 cm in hole diameter (Fig. 124; Picture 256).

M7:125, it has gray flocs, with 2.3 cm in length, 1.1 cm in diameter and 0.6 cm in hole diameter (Fig. 124; Picture 264).

M7:126, it has gray spots, with 2.5 cm in length, 1.1 cm in diameter and 0.55 cm in hole diameter (Fig. 124; Picture 266).

M7:127, it has gray spots, with 2.2 cm in length, 1.25 cm in diameter and 0.6 cm in hole diameter (Fig. 124; Picture 266).

M7:128, it is 2.55 cm in length, 1 cm in diameter and 0.6 cm in hole diameter (Fig. 124; Picture 256).

M7:129, it has brown spots, with 3.2 cm in length, 1.2 cm in diameter and 0.6 cm in hole diameter (Fig. 124; Picture 262).

M7:130, it has reddish brown spots, with 1.8 cm in length, 0.9 cm in diameter and 0.45 cm in hole diameter (Fig. 124; Picture 265).

M7:131, it had gray flocs, with 1.5 cm in length, 0.9 cm in diameter and 0.45 cm in hole diameter (Fig. 124; Picture 265).

M7:142, it comprises two individual pieces with faded gray spots. They are 1.2 cm in length, 1 cm in diameter and 0.5 cm in hole diameter (Fig. 124; Picture 261).

M7:146, it has faded gray flocs, with 2.3 cm in length, 0.95 cm in diameter and 0.5 cm in hole diameter (Fig. 124; Picture 266).

M7:149, it is 1.2 cm in length, 0.9 cm in diameter and 0.4 cm in hole diameter (Fig. 124; Picture 265).

M7:151, it is 1.5 cm in length, 1.2 cm in diameter and 0.5 cm in hole diameter (Fig. 124; Picture 266).

M7:161, it is 1.8 cm in length, 0.8 cm in diameter and 0.5 cm in hole diameter (Fig. 124; Picture 265).

**Beads:** ten pieces. They are mostly white.

M7:74, it comprises three individual pieces sharing one number. They have gray and brown spots and are in the shape of waist drum with holes drilled from both sides. They are 1.05 cm in length, 0.95 cm in diameter, 0.5 cm in hole diameter (Fig. 125; Picture 267).

M7:78, it is in a spherical shape with two tunnel-shaped holes, and is 2.1 cm in diameter (Fig. 125; Picture 268).

M7:79, its structure is the same as that of M7:78. It is 2.2 cm in diameter (Fig. 125; Picture 269).

M7:93, it comprised two individual pieces. They are in the shape of waist drum with holes drilled from both sides. They are 1.1 cm in length, 1 cm in diameter,

0.45 cm in hole diameter (Fig. 125; Picture 267).

M7:112, it has brown spots and is in a hemispherical shape with two tunnel-shaped holes on its plane. It is 2.1 cm in diameter, 1.1 cm in thickness (Fig. 125; Picture 270).

M7:113, it has gray spots and is in a hemispherical shape with two tunnel-shaped holes on its plane. It is 2.2 cm in diameter, 1 cm in thickness (Fig. 125; Picture 270).

M7:150, it has gray spots and is in a spherical shape with two tunnel-shaped holes on its plane. It is 1.4 cm in diameter (Fig. 125; Picture 271).

**Particles:** fifty five pieces.

M7:63-1 to M7:63-26, 26 individual pieces, located around the crown-shaped objects (M7:63-27) when unearthed. With oval planes, they are in similar shape, with one surface smooth and the other convex. They are 0.7–1.2 cm in length, 0.4–0.7 cm in width, 0.25–0.5 cm in thickness (Fig. 125; Picture 274).

M7:17, it comprises two individual pieces. They are close to a rectangle in shape, with one surface convex and the other surface smooth. They are 0.7 cm in length, 0.5 cm in width, 0.4 cm in thickness (Fig. 125;

**Fig. 125.** Jade particles and jade beads in tomb M7

17, 19, 63-1–63-26, 143, 144, 152. particles; 74, 78, 79, 93, 112, 113, 150. beads (2/3)

Picture 272).

M7:19, it comprises 6 individual pieces, located around the bracelet M7:20 when unearthed. They are white with green color inside and in an oval shape, one surface being smooth and the other surface convex. They are 0.6–0.9 cm in length, 0.3–0.35 cm in width, 0.2 cm in thickness (Fig. 125; Picture 273).

M7:143, it comprises six individual pieces. They are in an oval shape, with one surface convex and the other surface smooth. Three of them are larger with 0.9 cm in length, 0.6 cm in width and 0.5 cm in thickness, and the rest smaller with 0.6 cm in length, 0.3 cm in width and of 0.25 cm in thickness (Fig. 125; Picture 275).

M7:144, it comprises two individual pieces with its plane in a ring shape. One of its surfaces is convex and the other smooth. They are 1.1 cm in diameter, 0.6 cm in thickness (Fig. 125; Picture 276).

M7:152, it comprises 13 individual pieces and serves as the outer edge of the jade-inlaid lacquer (M7:155). Their planes are in an oval shape, with one surface convex and the other surface smooth. M7:152-2 is 0.9 cm in length, 0.5 cm in width, 0.4 cm in thickness (Fig. 125; Picture 277).

(2) Jade-inlaid lacquer

There is one piece of jade-inlaid lacquer. Its plane has a circular shape with a piece of annular jade artifact (M7:155) in the middle. The piece of jade artifact is about 10 cm in diameter with its outer edge circled in a diameter of about 14 cm by 13 pieces of orderly oval jade particles. The residue of the vermilion lacquer object which lied in the jade particle circle suggests that it is likely to be a piece of lacquer with jade particles inlaid around its outer edge (Fig. 126; Picture 164).

(3) Stone artifacts: three pieces.

Only stone *yue* axe is found.

M7:76, it is black brown in color, its surface has irregular holes and dots. It looks slightly like a rectangle. Its top end is slightly cambered and the edge is arc-shaped. It is flat and thin, and has a hole drilled from both sides. It is 17.9 cm in height, 11.8–13 cm in width, 4.2 cm in hole diameter (Fig. 127; Picture 278).

M7:83, it is black brown in color, it is flat and thin with its plane slightly looking like a rectangle. Its top end is smooth and straight and the edge is arc-shaped. Inside the hole, spiral lines could be found. It is 14.7 cm in height, 9.4–10.5 cm in width, 3.8 cm in

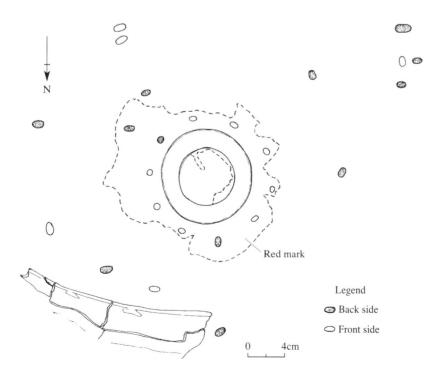

Fig. 126. Provenience of jade-inlaid lacquer (M7:155) when unearthed

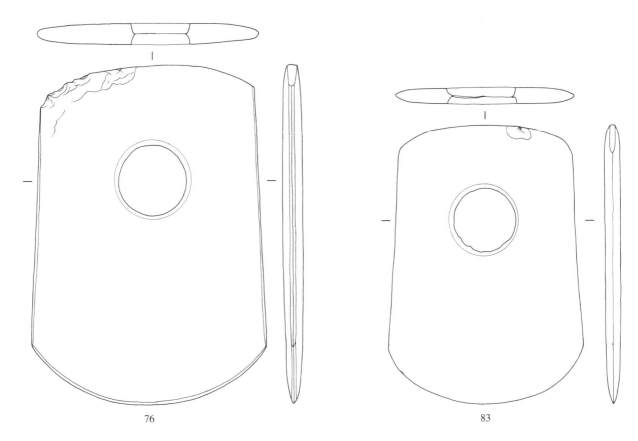

76                                                                                83

**Fig. 127.** Stone *yue* axes in tomb M7 (1/2)

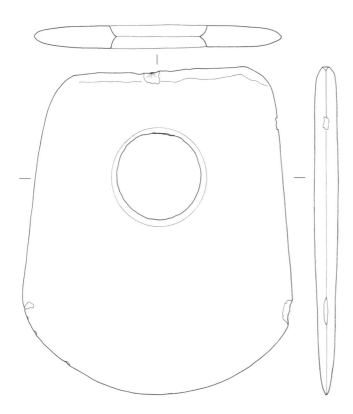

**Fig. 128.** Stone *yue* axe (M7:157) (1/2)

hole diameter (Fig. 127; Picture 279).

M7:157, it is black brown in color, its surface has irregular holes and dots. It looks slightly like a rectangle. Its top end is slightly inclined and the edge is arc-shaped. Fracture surface could be found on its edge. There is a hole drilled from both sides with spiral lines inside, and fracture surface could be found at the drilling junction. It is 17 cm in height, 9.3–14.8 cm in width, 5.3 cm in hole diameter (Fig. 128; Picture 280).

(4) Pottery vessels: four pieces.

**Ding tripod:** one piece (M7:156). It is sand-tempered reddish-brown pottery, its surface is polished, appeared orange. It has been severely broken, with only its fin-shaped legs identifiable.

**Dou:** one piece (M7:160). It is clay pottery, it has multi-layer core. From the inside out, its core is gray and then orange in color. Its surface is black with polished red coating. It has been severely broken and its shape is unidentifiable.

**Ring-foot jar:** one piece (M7:159). It is sand-tempered red pottery. It has been severely broken and its shape is unidentifiable.

***Gang* vat:** one piece (M7:158). It is sand-tempered pottery and has a charcoal gray core with red surface. Its texture is loose and the surface corroded severely. It has been broken totally into pieces and its shape is unidentifiable.

(5) Shark tooth

There are four pieces of animal teeth, among which M7:137 is broken. White in color and shaped in a triangle, with two bevel thorny edges, while the other edge is broken and hollow, and the surface texture is visible. It is 2.1 cm in length, 1.5 cm in width (Fig. 129, 1; Pictures 281, 282). M7:138, M7:139 and M7:140 are all severely broken with only tooth tips visible (Fig. 129).

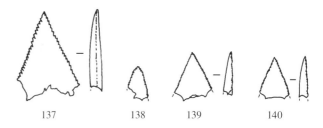

137          138     139        140

**Fig. 129.** Shark teeth in tomb M7 (1/1)

# Section 8 Tomb M8

## 1. The Shape of the Tomb

Tomb M8 is located at the eastern end of the south line of the tombs, with tomb M1 to its west. It has its opening under the top soil, and disturbs gray earth of enclosing ditch. It is rectangular pit with vertical wall, with an orientation of 183°. It is 3.08 m in length, 1.54 m in width and 0.36 m in depth. The tomb is filled with tough gray-brown mottled earth.

In the tomb, there is a rectangle relic outline, approximately 2.60 m in length and 1 m in width, showing the location of the funerary container like coffin, the existence of which was confirmed again after a stratum of earth of about 10 cm was removed within the tomb pit. When the excavation reached the bottom within the coffin-like area, it was found that all the burial objects were buried within the relic outline, which generally proved our judgment of the location of the coffin. Since the filling earth of the tomb is tough with indistinguishable colors, it was rather difficult to reveal the funerary container. The "pit walls" are thus steep and not likely to present their original situation. Skeleton inside the tomb had rotten away and left no remains (Picture 283).

Among the burial objects, pottery vessels are located in the north of the tomb, including a *ding* tripod, a ring-foot jar, a *gang* vat, a *dou*, all being so severely broken that its form could not be recognized.

There is a set of cylindrical stone objects with cover (M8:2) at the southernmost of the funeral container. In the whole south line of the tombs, tomb M8 is the only one with cylindrical stone objects with cover instead of cylindrical jade objects with cover.

Jade artifacts, such as crown-shaped jade object (M8:3) and three-pronged jade object (M8:8) are primarily found in the south of the tomb. The projecting tenon of the crown-shaped object point to southwest, and the prongs of the three-pronged object point to southeast, with the sides with tunnel-shaped holes faced the ground. A set of awl-shaped jade objects (M8:10), comprising 5 awl-shaped objects, were found on the north of the three-pronged object, a few of which were found covered on a jade *yue* axe (M8:14). The jade *yue* axe laid in east–west direction with the top facing the tomb wall and the blade facing inward the tomb. Lying vertically to the *yue* axe in south–north direction, 11 jade particles (M8:13) were possibly inlaid in the handle of M8:14. Based on the length of the arrangement of jade particles, it could be estimated that the handle is more than 60 cm in length. On the side facing down, vermilion was found around the hole at the top of the *yue* axe. In the tomb, except a jade bracelet (M8:29) and 2 awl-shaped jade objects (M8:30, 31), the remaining objects are scattered jade tubes and beads, some of which could be identified as string ornaments. For example, stringed ornaments M8:32 comprised 10 jade

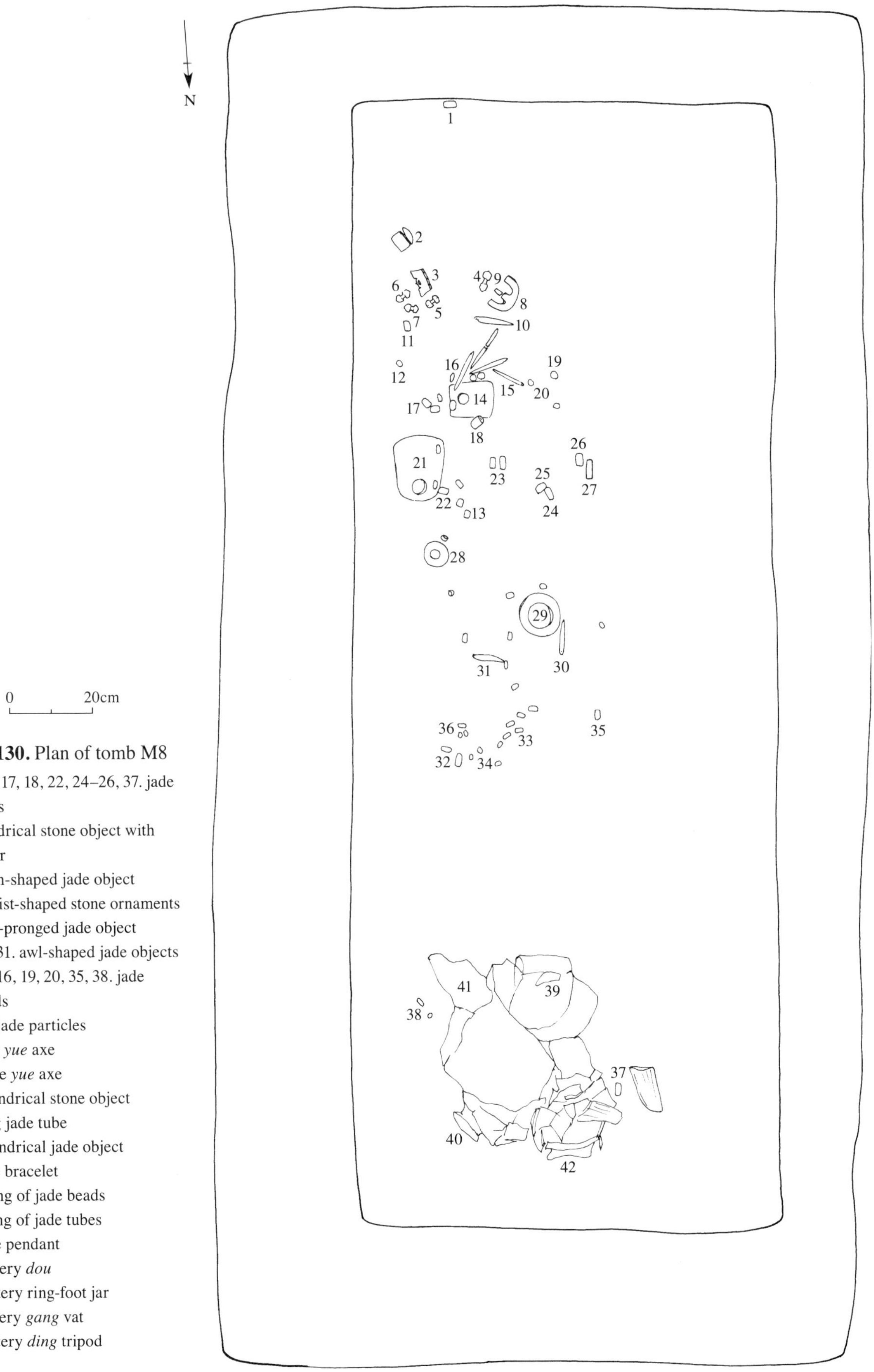

**Fig. 130.** Plan of tomb M8

1, 9, 11, 17, 18, 22, 24–26, 37. jade
    tubes
2. cylindrical stone object with
    cover
3. crown-shaped jade object
4–7. waist-shaped stone ornaments
8. three-pronged jade object
10, 30, 31. awl-shaped jade objects
12, 15, 16, 19, 20, 35, 38. jade
    beads
13, 36. jade particles
14. jade *yue* axe
21. stone *yue* axe
23. cylindrical stone object
27. long jade tube
28. cylindrical jade object
29. jade bracelet
32. string of jade beads
33. string of jade tubes
34. jade pendant
39. pottery *dou*
40. pottery ring-foot jar
41. pottery *gang* vat
42. pottery *ding* tripod

beads; string ornament M8:33 comprised 7 jade tubes. No jade *cong* was unearthed (Fig. 130).

## 2. Burial Objects

The burial objects are numbered into 42 pieces (sets), 80 individual pieces, including jade artifacts, stone artifacts and pottery vessels.

(1) Jade artifacts

There is 31 pieces (sets), 68 pieces of jade artifacts were unearthed. Most of them are white and a few are gray, all being simple with no pattern, including crown-shaped object, three-pronged object, set of awl-shaped object, *yue* axe, awl-shaped object, and bracelet.

**Crown-shaped object:** one piece (M8:3). With gray spots, it is flat and presented an upside-down

trapezoid in shape. Its left and right corner on the top slightly extend outward, and the middle is concave with a point. Under the point, there is an oblate hole left with marks by drilling on the edge, which indicat that the hole is enlarged by string-cutting after being drilled. There is a flat tenon at the bottom of the object with three equidistant round holes on it. It is 3.1 cm in height, 6.3–7 cm in width and 0.2–0.3 cm in thickness (Fig. 131; Picture 284).

**Three-pronged object:** one piece (M8:8). It's left and right prongs are at the same level, and there are holes drilled from both sides at the top end and inner side, and two pairs of tunnel-shaped holes at the two edges of the back side respectively. The middle prong is comparatively short, with a vertical hole. It is 4.6 cm in height, 6.4 cm in width and 1–1.1 cm in thickness

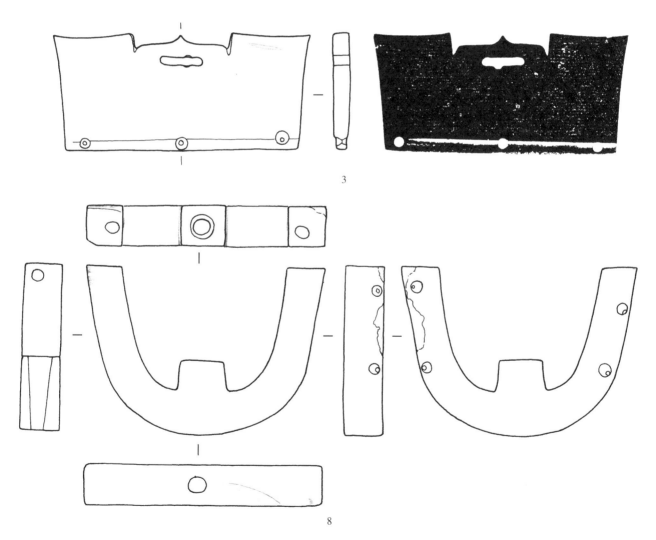

**Fig. 131.** Crown-shaped jade object and three-pronged jade object in tomb M8

3. crown-shaped object (M8:3) and its rubbing; 8. three-pronged object (1/1)

(Fig. 131; Pictures 285, 286).

**Set of awl-shaped objects:** one set (M8:10), comprising five pieces.

M8:10-1, it is shaped in long strip, whose one end is round and pointed while the other end is slightly fragmentary and flat with a hole drilled from both sides. There is a lengthwise cutting marks on the surface. It is 8.2 cm in length, 0.65 cm in diameter (Fig. 132; Picture 288).

M8:10-2, it is shaped in long strip, whose one end is round and pointed while the other end is flat and pointed with a hole drilled from both sides. There are two lengthwise cutting marks on the surface. It is broken into two pieces when unearthed, is 10.2 cm in length, 0.6 cm in diameter (Fig. 132; Picture 288).

M8:10-3, it is shaped in long strip, whose one end is round and pointed while the other end is slightly flat, presenting the shape of tenon, with a small hole drilled from both sides. It is 10 cm in length, 0.6 cm in diameter (Fig. 132; Picture 288).

M8:10-4, it is shaped in long strip, whose one end is round and pointed while the other end is slightly flat, with a small hole drilled from both sides. It has an approximately square cross section. It is 10.4 cm in length, 0.6 cm in diameter (Fig. 132; Picture 288).

M8:10-5, it is shaped in long strip, whose one end is round and pointed while the other end is flat with a hole drilled from both sides. There are two lengthwise

cutting marks on the surface, making the cross section irregular. It is 7.7 cm in length, 0.7 cm in diameter (Fig. 132; Picture 288).

**Awl-shaped objects:** two pieces.

M8:30, it is shaped in long strip, whose one end is round and pointed while the other end is flat with a hole drilled from both sides. It is 7.7 cm in length, 0.65 cm in diameter (Fig. 132; Picture 289).

M8:31, it is shaped in long strip, whose one end is round and pointed, and the other end has a round projecting tenon with a hole drilled from both sides. With an approximately square cross section, it is 6.6 cm in length, 0.9 cm in diameter (Fig. 132; Picture 290).

***Yue* axe:** one piece (M8:14). It is caesious, with vermilion painting on the back when unearthed, it is in an approximately rectangular plane with the blade wider than the top end. Its top end is flat and its blade is arc. There is a hole drilling from both sides at the upper part with step-shaped marks inside. There are polished lengthwise cutting marks on the top end, and not very obvious cambered string-cutting marks on the surface. It is 12.6 cm in height, 8.2 cm in top width, 11.4 cm in blade width, 0.8 cm in thickness and 2.2 cm in hole diameter (Fig. 133; Picture 287).

**Cylindrical object:** one piece (M8:28). It has yellow spots, cylindrical-shaped, it has a hole drilled from both sides with step-shaped marks and spiral

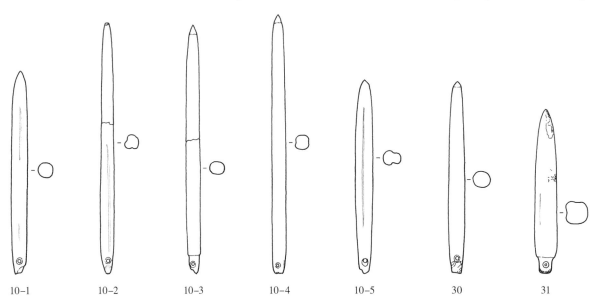

| 10–1 | 10–2 | 10–3 | 10–4 | 10–5 | 30 | 31 |

**Fig. 132.** Awl-shaped jade objects in tomb M8 (2/3)

marks on the wall of the hole. It is 1.5 cm in height, 4.5 cm in diameter, 1.4 cm in hole diameter (Fig. 134; Picture 292).

**Bracelet:** one piece (M8:29). It has gray-green spots, in the shape of a wide ring with the inner wall slightly convex. It is 10.3 cm in diameter, 6.6 cm in hole diameter, and 1.8 cm in thickness (Fig. 134; Picture 293).

**Pendant:** one piece (M8:34). In purple color and water drop shape, it is unlikely made of nephrite. The upper end is round and pointed, with a hole drilled from both sides. It is 11.5 cm in length, 0.7 cm in diameter (Fig. 134; Picture 294).

**Long tube:** one piece (M8:27). It is cylindrical-shaped with a hole drilled from both sides. There are string-cutting marks on the surface. It is 7 cm in length, 2 cm in diameter and 0.9–1.1 cm in hole diameter (Fig. 134; Picture 291).

**String of tubes:** one set.

M8:33, it comprised 7 individual pieces, two of which are comparatively larger. They has gray spots, cylindrical-shaped with a hole drilled from both sides. The tubes are 1.45–2 cm in length, 0.8–0.9 cm in diameter and 0.4–0.55 cm in hole diameter (Fig. 134; Picture 295).

**String of beads:** one set.

M8:32, it comprised 10 pieces of beads in the shape

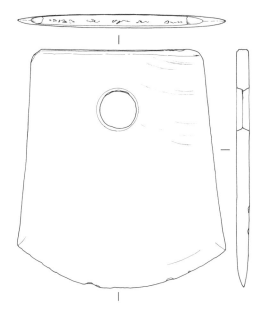

**Fig. 133.** Jade *yue* axe (M8:14) (1/2)

of waist drum with holes drilled from both sides. Some of the beads has cutting marks on the surface. They are 1 cm in length, 0.6 cm in diameter and 0.3 cm in hole diameter (Fig. 134; Picture 296).

**Tubes:** fourteen pieces.

M8:1, it is cylindrical-shaped, with a hole drilled from both sides. It is slant at the two ends. It is 1.2 cm in length, 0.8 cm in diameter and 0.5 cm in hole diameter (Fig. 135; Picture 297).

M8:9, it is cylindrical-shaped, with a hole drilled

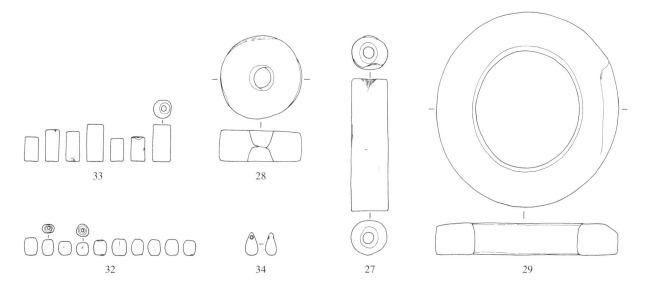

**Fig. 134.** Jade artifacts in tomb M8

27. long tube; 28. cylindrical object; 29. bracelet-shaped artifact; 32. string of beads; 33. string of tubes; 34. pendant (1/2)

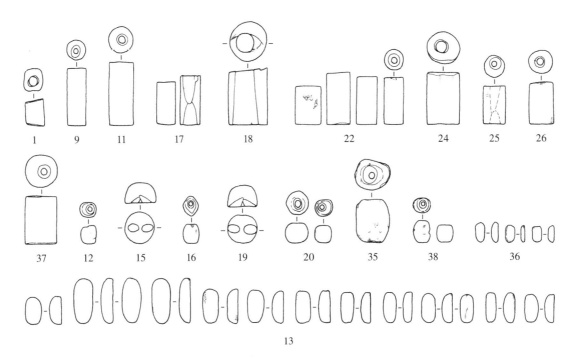

**Fig. 135.** Jade tubes, jade beads and jade particles in tomb M8
1, 9, 11, 17, 18, 22, 24–26, 37. tubes; 12, 15, 16, 19, 20, 35, 38. beads; 13, 36. particles (2/3)

from both sides. It is 2.35 cm in length, 0.75 cm in diameter and 0.5 cm in hole diameter (Fig. 135; Picture 297).

M8:11, it is cylindrical-shaped, with a hole drilled from both sides. It is 2.5 cm in length, 1.1 cm in diameter and 0.4 cm in hole diameter (Fig. 135; Picture 297).

M8:17, it is comprised of 2 individual pieces. They are cylindrical-shaped with a hole drilled from both sides respectively. They are 1.7–1.9 cm in length, 0.8 cm in diameter and 0.4–0.6 cm in hole diameter (Fig. 135; Picture 297).

M8:18, it is cylindrical-shaped and cut after being drilled from both sides, so the hole looked like being drilled from one side. One of its ends has cambered string-cutting marks. It is 2.2 cm in length, 1.6 cm in diameter and 0.8–1 cm in hole diameter (Fig. 135; Picture 298).

M8:22, it comprises 4 individual pieces. They has gray-green spots, cylindrical-shaped with a hole drilled from both sides respectively. They are 1.5–2.05 cm in length, 0.8–1.05 cm in diameter and 0.4–0.5 cm in hole diameter (Fig. 135; Picture 299).

M8:24, it has brown spots, cylindrical-shaped,

with a round hole drilled from both sides. It is 2.1 cm in length, 1.45 cm in diameter and 0.8 cm in hole diameter (Fig. 135; Picture 299).

M8:25, it has brown spots, cylindrical-shaped, with a hole drilled from both sides. It is 1.5 cm in length, 0.9 cm in diameter and 0.4 cm in hole diameter (Fig. 135; Picture 297).

M8:26, it is gray with brown spots, cylindrical-shaped with a hole drilled from both sides. It is 1.8 cm in length, 1 cm in diameter and 0.3 cm in hole diameter (Fig. 135; Picture 300).

M8:37, it has brown spots, cylindrical-shaped, with a hole drilled from both sides. It is 1.9 cm in length, 1.3 cm in diameter and 0.5 cm in hole diameter (Fig. 135; Picture 298).

**Beads:** nine pieces in the shape of waist drum or hemisphere.

**Waist drum shaped beads:** seven pieces.

M8:12, in the shape of waist drum, it has a hole drilled from both sides. It is 0.75 cm in length, 0.6 cm in diameter and 0.4 cm in hole diameter (Fig. 135; Picture 302).

M8:16, in the shape of waist drum, it had a hole drilled from both sides. It is 0.8 cm in length, 0.55 cm in diameter and 0.3 cm in hole diameter (Fig. 135; Picture 302).

M8:20, it is comprised of 2 pieces. In the shape of waist drum, each one has a hole drilled from both sides respectively. They are 0.7–0.8 cm in length, 0.6–0.7 cm in diameter and 0.35 cm in hole diameter (Fig. 135; Picture 302).

M8:35, it has brown spots. In the irregular shape of waist drum, it has a hole drilled from both sides. It is 1.7 cm in length, 0.9 cm in diameter and 0.55 cm in hole diameter (Fig. 135; Picture 301).

M8:38, it comprises two beads. In the shape of waist drum, each one has a hole drilled from both sides. They are 0.7–0.9 cm in length, 0.5–0.6 cm in diameter and 0.3 cm in hole diameter (Fig. 135; Picture 302).

**Hemispherical beads:** two pieces.

M8:15, hemispherical, it has a tunnel-shaped hole on the flat surface. It is 0.85 cm in thickness and 1.25 cm in diameter (Fig. 135; Picture 303).

M8:19, hemispherical, it has a tunnel-shaped hole on the flat surface. It is 0.8 cm in thickness and 1.2 cm in diameter (Fig. 135; Picture 303).

**Particles:** fourteen pieces.

M8:13, it comprises 11 individual pieces. They are oval in plane, with one convex side and one flat side. They are 1.1–1.75 cm in length, 0.45–0.85 cm in width and 0.45–0.6 cm in thickness (Fig. 135; Picture 304).

M8:36, it comprises 3 individual pieces. They are oval in plane, with one convex side and one flat side. They are 0.75 cm in length, 0.4 cm in width and 0.3 cm in thickness (Fig. 135; Picture 305).

(2) Stone artifacts: eight pieces.

There is one set of cylindrical stone object with cover (M8:2), including a cylinder and a cover.

M8:2-1, the cover, it was made of quartz and shaped as a round pie, has one convex side and one flat side with a tunnel-shaped hole on it. It is 4.7 cm in diameter and 1.7 cm in thickness (Fig. 136; Pictures 308, 309).

M8:2-2, the cylindrical object, it was made of sandstone and shaped as a cylinder, has a hole running from one end to the other. It is 2.6 cm in height, 4.3 cm in diameter and 0.8 cm in hole diameter (Fig. 136; Picture 309).

**Narrow waist-shaped ornaments:** four pieces. They are slightly rectangular in plane with two ends pointed and a transverse straight groove carved in the middle. One side is flat and the other side is slightly convex (Fig. 136).

M8:4, it is 3.3 cm in length, 1.9 cm in width and 0.7 cm in thickness (Picture 306).

M8:5, it is 3.3 cm in length, 1.9 cm in width and 0.6 cm in thickness (Picture 307).

M8:6, it's fragmentary, 3.3 cm in length, 1.8 cm in width and 0.6 cm in thickness.

M8:7, it's fragmentary, 3.3 cm in length, 1.7 cm in width and 0.6 cm in thickness.

**Cylindrical object:** one piece (M8:23). It was made of sandstone, it's severely broken, and likely to be a cylindrical object. There are spiral marks on the wall of the hole (Fig. 136).

**Yue axe:** one piece (M8:21). It is dark brown, slightly rectangular, with a slant top end and looked

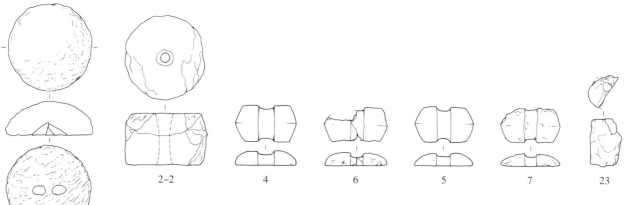

2–2    4    6    5    7    23

2–1

**Fig. 136.** Cylindrical-shaped stone artifacts and stone tubes with narrow middle part in tomb M8
2. cylindrical-shaped artifact with cover; 4–7. tubes with narrow middle part; 23. cylindrical-shaped artifacts (M8:23) (1/2)

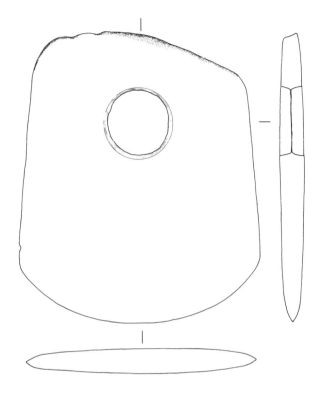

**Fig. 137.** Stone *yue* axe (M8:21) (1/2)

crude and coarse. There is a hole drilled from both sides on the upper part with spiral marks on the hole's wall.

The lower part is a little wider with a cambered blade. The whole object is thick in general. It is 15.3 cm in height, 13.2 cm in blade width, 3.8 cm in hole diameter and 1.3 cm in thickness (Fig. 137; Picture 310).

(3) Pottery vessels: four pieces.

***Ding* tripod:** one piece (M8:42). It is sand-tempered pottery, reddish-brown inside and ash black outside. It is so broken that its original shape could not be recognized. It has fin-shaped legs, the outer parts of which were flat and a little thick.

***Dou*:** one piece (M8:39). It is clay pottery, orange-red inside and black outside. It is too broken that its original shape could hardly be recognized, and only a trumpet-shaped ring foot remained.

**Ring-foot jar:** one piece (M8:40). It is reddish-brown fine sand-tempered pottery, with the surface polished. It is severely broken that its original shape could not be recognized.

***Gang* vat:** one piece (M8:41). It is red sand-tempered pottery, decorated with basket patterns on the surface. It is too broken that its original shape could not be recognized.

# Section 9 Tomb M9

## 1. The Shape of the Tomb

Tomb M9 is located to the western of the middle part of the south line of the tombs, with tomb M10 to the west, tomb M7 to the east and tomb M11 and M14 to the north. It has its opening under the top soil and disturbed gray earthen ditch and yellow-earthen mound. It is rectangular pit with vertical wall, with the southern end slightly wider than the northern end and with an orientation of 183°. The opening of the tomb is wider than the bottom, and the tomb walls are sloped. The opening is 4 m in length, 1.95 m in width in the north and 2.2 m in width in the south; the bottom is 3.15 m in length and 1.32 m in width; and the depth is 1.30 m from the opening to the bottom of the tomb. The tomb is filled with gray-brown mottled earth without inclusion. Skeleton inside the tomb had rotten away and left no remains (Picture 311).

A set of pottery vessels, including a *ding* tripod, a *dou*, a ring-foot jar and a *gang* vat, was found at the northern end of the tomb. They are severely broken when unearthed due to their loose texture. A piece of jade-inlaid lacquer (M9:78) was found to the south of the pottery. The core of the lacquer had decayed, but according to the shape of the lacquer coating, the original shape of the object could be generally identified. It is a pity that the lacquer coating could not be taken out.

Jade burial objects were mainly unearthed from the south and middle of the tomb. There is a string of jade tubes (M9:77) lying in east–west direction in the south of the tomb. They were found higher than other burial objects, presumably because they were placed outside the funerary container. In addition, another string of jade tubes (M9:70, 71) compromising 22 tubes were excavated to the south of the pottery *ding* tripod. A triangular jade plaque (M9:68) was found to the south of the pottery in the north of the tomb.

A three-pronged object (M9:2) was unearthed with the convex side facing the ground and the prongs pointing at southeast. It is approximately 20 cm away from a long jade tube (M9:3), and there is a relative height difference between the two, which was speculated to be caused by the collapse of the funerary container. There is a set of cylindrical jade object with cover (M9:1) near the three-pronged object, which are the only cylindrical objects carved with patterns found in Yaoshan Cemetery. The patterns were in right position when unearthed, but the covers laid under the cylindrical objects.

A set of awl-shaped jade objects (M9:7–10, 17–19), comprising 7 pieces, were unearthed from the tomb. It laid to the east of a crown-shaped jade object (M9:6) with a set of jade particles totaling 20 pieces scattered in it. There may be some relation among the three.

A jade *yue* axe (M9:14) was unearthed from the middle of the tomb with its blade facing west and a stone *yue* axe (M9:13) laying in east–west direction on the top of it. There is a *cong*-stylistic jade tube (M9:11) to the west of M9:14, and another *cong*-stylistic jade tube (M9:12) of the same shape is found 58 cm away to the north of M9:14, which is similar to what was found in tomb M7. The two pieces of *cong*-stylistic tubes are presumably the ornaments of the handle of M9:14. Between the two *cong*-stylistic jade tubes are five long strip-shaped jade particles (M9:32, 33, 34) in south–north direction, which were possibly inlaid in the organic handle of M9:14. Jade *cong* (M9:4) laid on its side to the north of M9:14. According to the pattern on M9:4, its top might face the south. Two cylindrical jade objects (M9:35, 36) are on the two sides of M9:4, which may have some implication.

There are a string of tubes (M9:31) located between jade *cong* and *yue* axe, which comprising 39 pieces, are presumably the pectoral ornament of the tomb occupant. To the west of the middle of the tomb, a jade bracelet (M9:4) and an awl-shaped object (M9:14) were found (Fig. 138).

## 2. Burial Objects

The burial objects are numbered into 82 pieces (sets), 268 individual pieces, including jade artifacts, stone artifacts, pottery vessels and jade-inlaid lacquer.

(1) Jade artifacts

There is 76 pieces (sets), 262 individual pieces of jade artifacts were unearthed, mostly white, including crown-shaped object, cylindrical object with cover, three-pronged object, set of awl-shaped object, *yue* axe, *cong*, *cong*-stylistic tube, awl-shaped object, bracelet, plaque, etc.

**Crown-shaped object:** one piece (M9:6). It is bluish-white, flat and presented an upside-down trapezoid in shape. Its two upper corners on the top slightly extend outward, and the middle is concave with a point. An oblate hole is under the point. There is a flat tenon at the bottom of the object, on which there are three holes drilled from both sides equidistantly. It is 3.7 cm in height, 5.5–6.9 cm in width and 0.15–0.3 cm in thickness (Fig. 139; Picture 312).

**Cylindrical object with cover:** one set (M9:1). It comprises a cover and a cylindrical object (Picture 313).

M9:1-1, the cover, shaped like a round pie, has one convex side and one flat side with a tunnel-shaped hole on its plane. It is 4.5 cm in diameter and 1 cm in thickness (Fig. 140; Picture 314).

M9:1-2, the cylindrical object has three protruding blocks which are respectively carved with the sacred animal motif in bas-relief and intaglio carving techniques. The middle of upper end of the motif are decorated with three sets of feathers, below which are two slightly convex eyepits, and the double-circles inside represented eyes. Below the eyes are a wide nose and a flat and wide mouth, from which two inner tusks sticking upward and two outer tusks sticking downward. The rest part is filled with intaglioed lines and rolling cloud patterns as the ground-tint. It is 3.5 cm in height, 4.8 cm in diameter and 2.6–2.7 cm in hole diameter (Fig. 140; Picture 315).

**Three-pronged object:** one piece (M9:2). It has brown spots, flat on one side and convex on the other side, in the shape of a trident. It's left and right prongs are at the same level, with oval holes drilled on the top end, and small holes drilled through the back and front. The oval hole is drilled with two or three solid

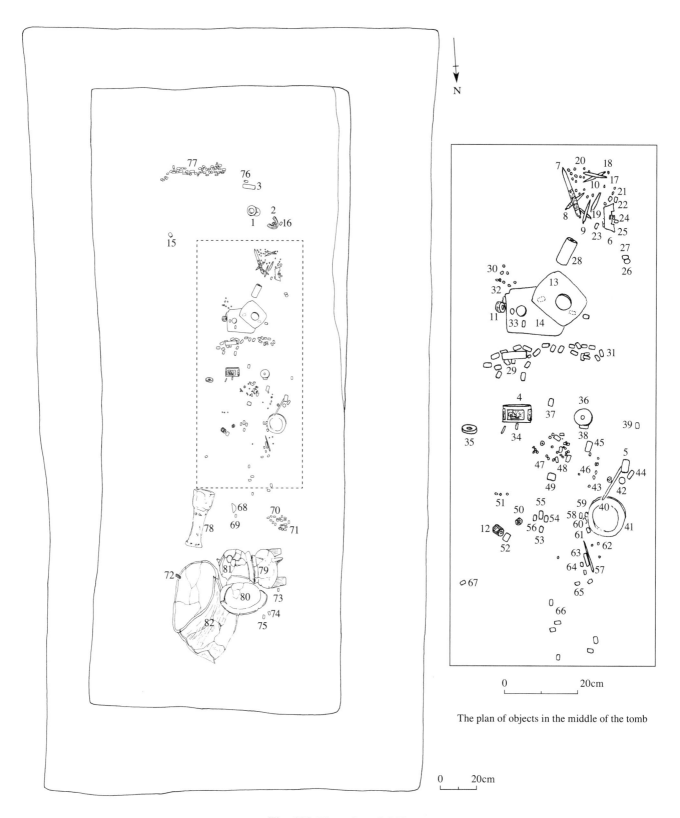

**Fig. 138.** Plan of tomb M9

1. cylindrical jade object with cover; 2. three-pronged jade object; 3, 28, 29. long jade tubes; 4. jade *cong*; 5. jade tube with carved patterns; 6. crown-shaped jade object; 7–10, 17–19, 40. awl-shaped jade objects; 11, 12, 49, 50, 72. *cong*-stylistic jade tubes ; 13. stone *yue* axe; 14. jade *yue* axe; 15, 16, 21–23, 25, 27, 37–39, 44, 45, 52–56, 58–61, 63, 65, 67, 69, 73–76. jade tubes; 20, 30, 32–34, 46, 47, 51, 62. jade particles; 24, 26, 42, 43. jade beads; 31, 48, 66, 70, 71, 77. strings of jade tubes; 35, 36. cylindrical jade objects; 41. jade bracelet; 57. strip-shaped jade object; 68. jade plaque object; 78. jade-inlaid lacquer; 79. pottery *ding* tripod; 80. pottery *dou*; 81. pottery ring-foot jar; 82. pottery *gang* vat

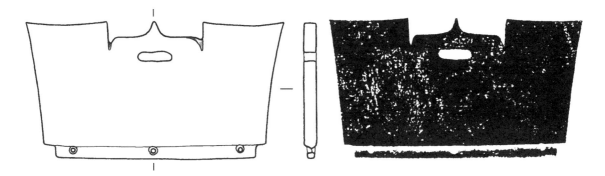

**Fig. 139.** Crown-shaped jade object (M9:6) and its rubbing (1/1)

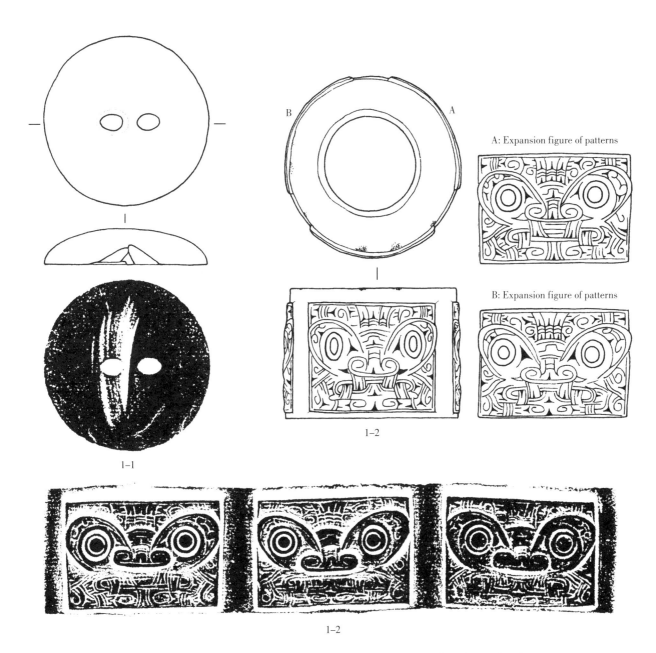

A: Expansion figure of patterns

B: Expansion figure of patterns

1–1

1–2

1–2

**Fig. 140.** Cylindrical jade object with cover and their rubbings in tomb M9

1-1. cover of cylindrical object; 1-2. cylindrical object (1/1)

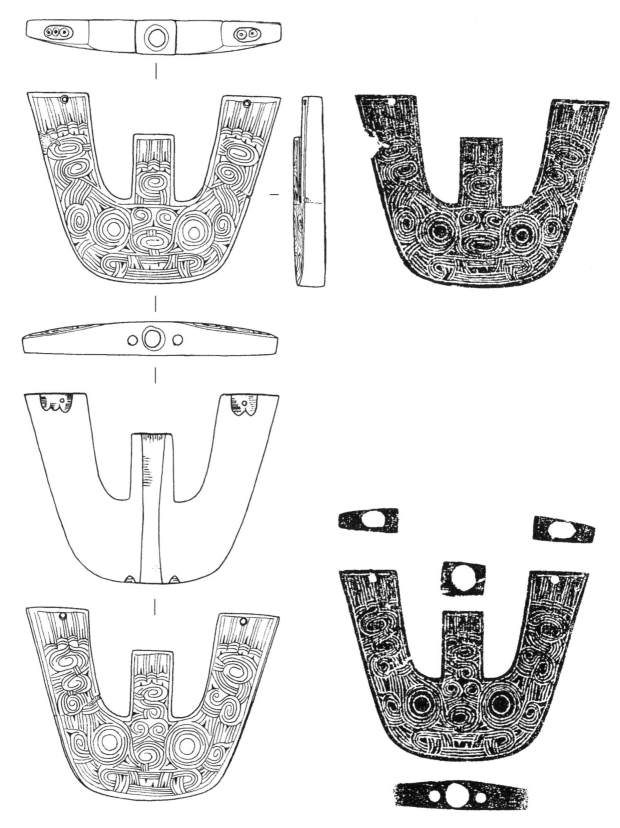

**Fig. 141.** Three-pronged jade object (M9:2) and its rubbings (1/1)

drilling. The middle prong is comparatively short, with a vertical oval hole running through, and with two small shallow holes at the two sides of the bottom of the oval hole. The front and back side of the object are carved with the same motifs. The upper parts of the two long prongs are carved with feather patterns and the lower part was carved with the sacred animal motif with round eyes, wide mouth and two groups of tusks sticking out. The rest part is intaglioed with rolling cloud patterns. It is 5.05 cm in height, 6.8 cm in width and 0.4–0.6 cm in thickness (Fig. 141; Pictures 316, 317).

**Long tubes:** three pieces.

M9:3, with brown spots, it is cylindrical-shaped with a hole drilled from both sides. The depths of the drilling from both sides are quite different. It is 6.4 cm in length, 1.7 cm in diameter and 0.65–0.75 cm in hole diameter (Fig. 142; Picture 318). It was found approximately 20 cm away from the three-pronged jade object. According to the similar situation found in other tombs in Yaoshan Cemetery, it was inferred that the long jade tube formed a complete set together with the three-pronged object.

M9:28, it is cylindrical-shaped, with a hole drilled from both sides and its shape and the hole were all irregular. There are cambered string-cutting marks on the surface and one end of the tube. It is 6.9 cm in height, 3.2 cm in diameter and 1.15 cm in hole diameter (Fig. 142; Picture 319).

M9:29, it is cylindrical-shaped, irregular, with a hole drilled from both sides. The hole on one side is drilled by two solid drilling, and the depths of drilling from both sides are quite different. There are cambered string-cutting marks on the surface and two ends of the tube. It is 7 cm in height, 1.8 cm in diameter and 1 cm in hole diameter (Fig. 142; Picture 320).

**Set of awl-shaped object:** one set, comprising seven pieces.

M9:7, in the shape of a long square cylinder, it is pointed at the upper end and had small projecting tenon at the lower end with a hole drilled from both sides. The object is divided equally into the upper and lower parts by a belt of bow string pattern. The upper part is smooth without patterns, and the lower part is

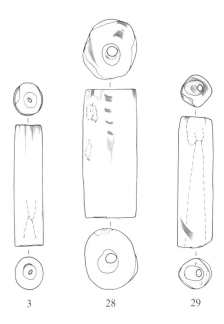

**Fig. 142.** Long jade tubes in tomb M9

carved with the simplified sacred animal motif. Two sets of patterns are carved with the corner as the axis. The sacred animal has oval and convex eyepits and slightly bulging eyeballs. The area between two eyes is carved cloud patterns in intaglio as its forehead, above which carved several parallel thin bow strings which symbolized the feathered crown. The flat ridge, which is carved in intaglio with rolling cloud patterns, presented the nose. It is 5.9 cm in length (Fig. 145; Picture 323).

M9:8, in the shape of a long square cylinder, it is pointed at the upper end and had a round projecting tenon at the other end with a hole drilled from both sides. The lower part of the object is carved with simplified sacred animal motif, which is divided into the upper and lower parts by a crosswise shallow groove. There are totally 8 sets of patterns. The top of each set is decorated with thin bow string pattern, single-circled eyes and a flat, wide and protruding nose. It is 8.1 cm in length and 1 cm in width (Fig. 145; Picture 324).

M9:9, with a small number of blue spots, it is pointed at the top end and had a round projecting tenon at the other end with a hole drilled from both sides. The lower part of the object is carved with the sacred animal motif. There are two sets of motifs divided by four corners with the nose as the central axis.

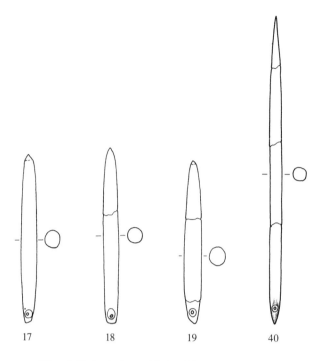

17    18    19    40

**Fig. 143.** Awl-shaped jade objects in tomb M9

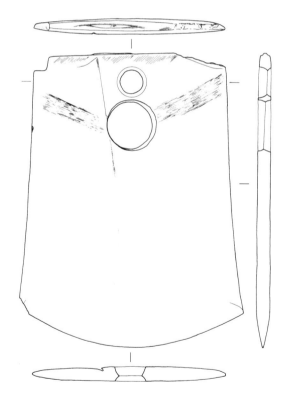

**Fig. 144.** Jade *yue* axe (M9:14) (1/2)

On the bas-relief belt is rolling cloud pattern, which symbolized the sacred human. Convex eyepits with bulging eyes and surrounded by the cloud pattern were carved in two corresponding corners. The prominent

noses decorated with the cloud pattern are carved in the other corners. It is 6.9 cm in length (Fig. 145; Picture 325).

M9:10, it was broken into three pieces when unearthed, in the shape of a long square cylinder, it is pointed at the top end and had a round projecting tenon at the other end with a hole drilled from both sides. The lower part was carved with sacred animal motif and was divided into the upper, middle and lower parts by crosswise shallow grooves. Therefore, there are totally 12 sets of the same patterns. At the top of each set are two belts of bow string patterns, below which are oval eyepits and two single-circle eyes, a flat and wide nose, and a wide mouth with two tusks sticking downward. It is 13.5 cm in length and 0.85 cm in width (Fig. 145; Picture 326).

M9:17, shaped in long strip, it has a round cross section, one end is round and pointed while the other end has a hole drilled from both sides. It is 6.7 cm in length and 0.65 cm in diameter (Fig. 143; Picture 327).

M9:18, it is shaped in long strip and broken into two pieces when unearthed, it has a round cross section, one end is round and pointed while the other end has a hole drilled from both sides. It is 7.05 cm in length and 0.65 cm in diameter (Fig. 143; Picture 327).

M9:19, it is shaped in long strip and broken into three pieces when unearthed, it has a round cross section, one end is round and pointed while the other end has a hole drilled from both sides. It is 6.5 cm in length and 0.7 cm in diameter (Fig. 143; Picture 327).

**Yue axe:** one piece (M9:14). It has an approximately rectangular plane with the blade wider than the top. One corner of the blade is broken. There are two holes, one big and one small, on the upper part. The top end has cambered string-cutting marks and fracture surfaces, roughly polished. Vertical cutting marks, which are carved aslant on the surface, could be seen on one side of the upper hole. There is a group of thin striations on the two sides of the lower hole to the two corners of the top end respectively, with 1 cm in width. Slant thin striations could also been seen at the edge of the top end. It is 15.6 cm in height, 10.6 cm in top width, 11.6 cm in blade width, 1.55 cm in upper hole diameter, 2.2 cm in lower hole diameter and 0.8 cm in

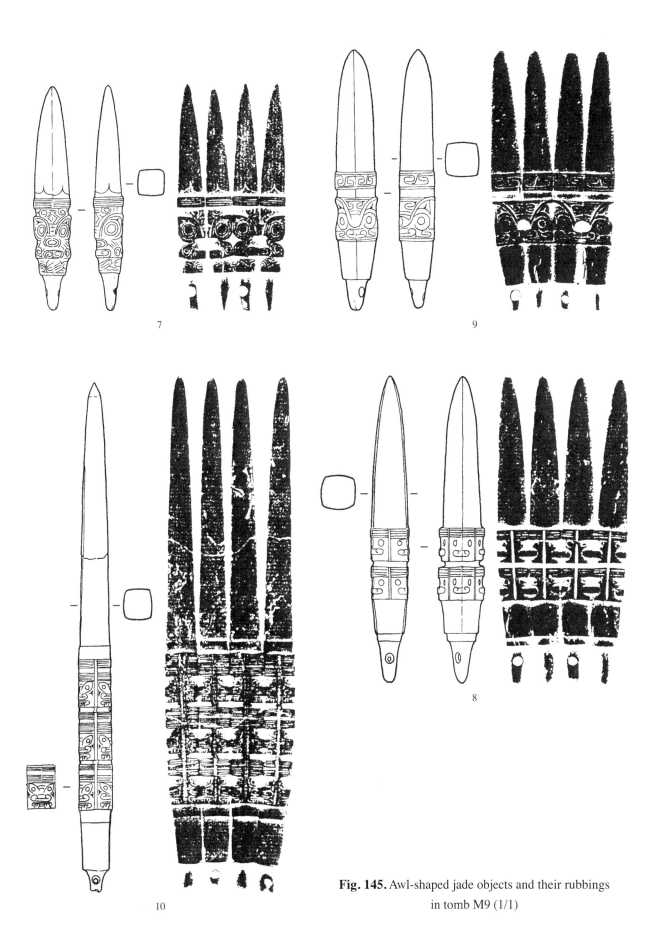

7

9

8

10

**Fig. 145.** Awl-shaped jade objects and their rubbings
in tomb M9 (1/1)

thickness (Fig. 144; Picture 322).

**Cong:** one piece (M9:4). With gray-brown spots, it is cylinder-shaped with slightly convex hole wall which is polished. There are four symmetrical rectangular protruding blocks on the surface, which are carved with almost the same sacred animal motif respectively. On each set of motif, there are the oval eyepits, forehead and nose carved in bas-relief technique, round eyes forming by tubular drilling; slightly protruding nose with wide nose wings; intaglioed nostrils; flat wide and convex mouth; and two pairs of tusks carved in intaglio with two inner tusks sticking upward and the two outer tusks sticking downward. Between the main motif there are filled with dense rolling cloud patterns in intaglio technique.

In addition, on each set of pattern, above the sacred animal motif are three belts of the feather pattern, which symbolizing the sacred crown. It is 4.5 cm in height, 7.95 cm in collar diameter and 6.3 cm in hole diameter (Figs. 146, 147; Pictures 328, 329).

**Carved tube:** one piece (M9:5). It is cylindrical-shaped and with a hole drilled from both sides in the middle. It is carved with crosswise shallow grooves at both ends to highlight the pattern. There are four round projecting blocks on the upper and lower parts, with arc lines carved around the projecting blocks and rhombuses carved between the round projecting blocks. The hole at the two ends are not regular. It is 3.7 cm in height, 2 cm in diameter and 0.6 cm in hole diameter (Fig. 148; Picture 321).

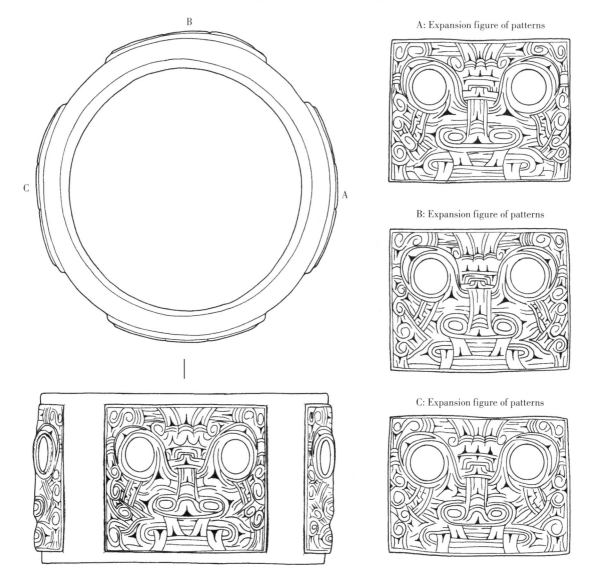

A: Expansion figure of patterns

B: Expansion figure of patterns

C: Expansion figure of patterns

**Fig. 146.** Jade *cong* (M9:4) (1/1)

A

B

**Fig. 147.** Rubbings of jade *cong* (M9:4) (A is 1/2 and B is 1/1)

**Cong-stylistic tubes:** five pieces.

M9:11, with gray spots, it is in the shape of a square cylinder with a hole drilled from both sides in the middle. There are four protruding blocks on the surface, with the corner as the axis. Simplified sacred animal motifs, which are basically the same, are carved on them. The upper part of the motif is decorated with two belts of bow string patterns, below which are single-circle round eyes and a protruding nose. It is 3 cm in height, 2.8 cm in collar diameter and 1.3 cm in hole diameter (Fig. 149; Pictures 330, 333).

M9:12, it is similar to M9:11 in shape and size (Fig. 149; Pictures 331, 333).

M9:49, in the shape of a square cylinder, it is cut

**Fig. 148.** Jade tube (M9:5) with carved patterns and its rubbings (1/1)

from the middle; and only the lower part is found. cambered string-cutting marks could be seen on the section. The sacred animal motifs carved on the upper part of the tube only remained lower part. Sacred animal motifs are carved with the corner as the axis on the lower part of the tube. The upper part of each set of the sacred animal motif decorated two belts of bow string patterns, below which are double-circled eyes and nose. It is 1.7 cm in height, 1.6 cm in collar diameter and 0.6 cm in hole diameter (Fig. 150; Picture 332).

M9:50, it is in the shape of a square cylinder, and

the hole is irregular around. Two sets of simplified sacred animal motifs are carved on the four corners respectively. The upper part of each set of the sacred animal motif decorated bow string pattern, below which are round single-circled eyes and nose, with arc lines at two sides representing the shape of face. It is 2 cm in height, 1.6 cm in collar diameter and 0.6 cm in hole diameter (Fig. 150; Picture 335).

M9:72, in the shape of a square cylinder, it has a hole drilled from both sides in the middle. Three belts of bow string patterns are carved on the four corners respectively. It is 3.55 cm in height, 1.5 cm in

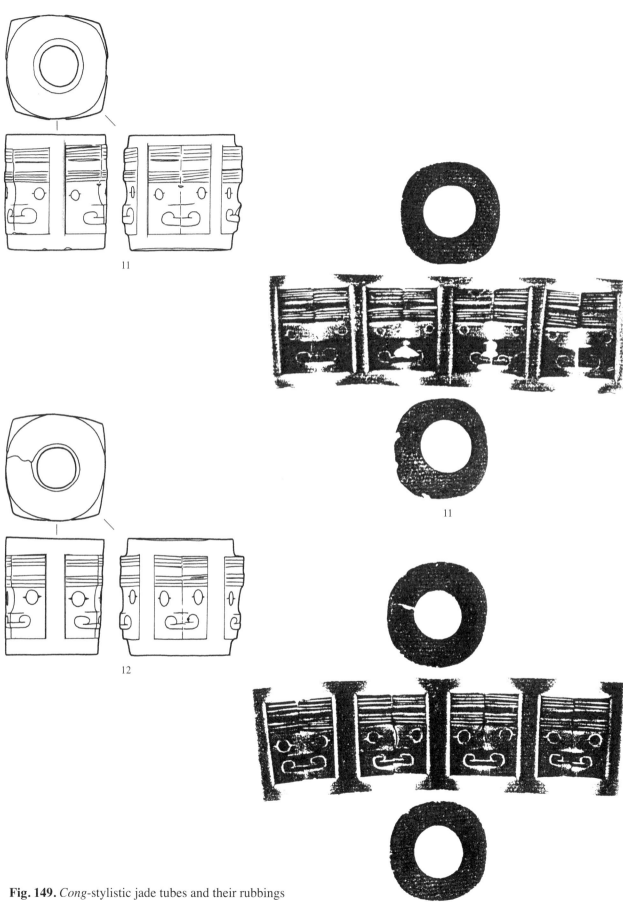

**Fig. 149.** *Cong*-stylistic jade tubes and their rubbings
in tomb M9 (1/1)

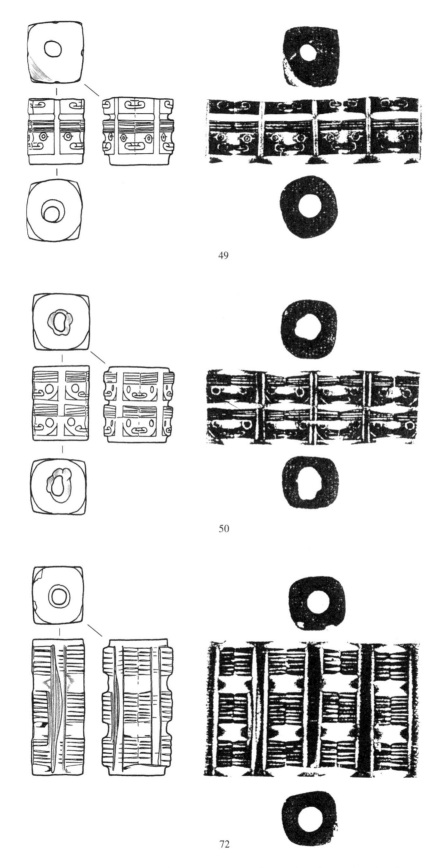

49

50

72

**Fig. 150.** *Cong*-stylistic jade tubes and their rubbings in tomb M9 (1/1)

collar diameter and 0.6 cm in hole diameter (Fig. 150; Picture 334).

**Bracelet:** one piece (M9:41). With gray spots, it is in the shape of a wide ring. The inner wall is convex and the outer wall is straight. It is 3 cm in height, 9.8 cm in diameter and 6.4 cm in hole diameter (Fig. 151; Picture 336).

**Cylindrical objects:** two pieces.

M9:35, it has brown spots, cylindrical-shaped with a hole drilled from one side, cambered string-cutting marks could be seen on one end. It is 1.55 cm in height, 4.3 cm in diameter and 1 cm in hole diameter (Fig. 152; Picture 337).

M9:36, it is cylindrical-shaped, with a hole drilled from one side, cambered string-cutting marks could be seen on one end. It is 1.55 cm in height, 4.4 cm in diameter and 1.2 cm in hole diameter (Fig. 152; Picture 338).

**Plaque object:** one piece (M9:68). It is white, made by a sheet of jade. It is in the shape of an upside-down triangle, thick in the middle and thin around the edge. A hole at the lower edge and two holes on the upper edge are drilled from both sides. One side is convex, with slightly polished rough surfaces while the other side is flat with many polished cambered string-cutting marks. It is 4.1 cm in length, 5.5 cm in width

and 0.8 cm in thickness (Fig. 152; Pictures 340, 341).

**Awl-shaped object:** one piece (M9:40). It is broken into 4 pieces when unearthed. It is shaped in long strip with one end sharp and pointed while one end flat and pointed with a hole drilled from both sides. It is 12.4 cm in length and 0.5 cm in diameter (Fig. 143; Picture 339).

**Strip-shaped object:** one piece (M9:57). It is bluish white, shaped in long strip with an oval cross section. Horizontal cutting marks could be seen on one end, and half of a drilling hole trace is left on the other end. It is 9.2 cm in length and 0.5 cm in diameter (Fig. 151; Picture 342).

**Strings of tubes:** six sets, comprising 133 individual pieces.

M9:31, it comprises 39 individual pieces. They are cylindrical-shaped, primarily white, and some had gray-brown spots. Most of them has holes drilled from both sides, and a few has holes which seem like being drilled from one side due to the fact that they were cut apart after being drilled from both sides. Cambered

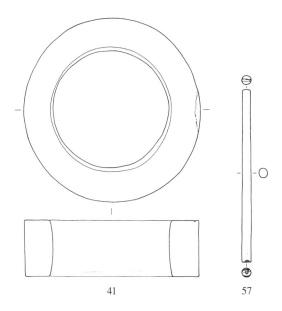

**Fig. 151.** Jade bracelet and bar-shaped jade object in tomb M9

41. bracelet; 57. bar-shaped object (1/2)

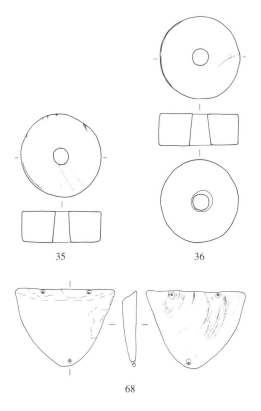

**Fig. 152.** Cylindrical jade objects and jade plaque object in tomb M9

35, 36. cylindrical objects; 68. plaque (1/2)

string-cutting marks could be seen on the ends and surface. They are 2.2–3.6 cm in length, 1.1–1.2 cm in diameter and 0.5–0.6 cm in hole diameter (Fig. 153; Picture 344).

M9:48, it comprises 8 individual pieces. They are cylindrical-shaped, had gray spots with holes drilled from both sides. Cambered string-cutting marks could be seen on the surface of a few tubes. They are 1.4–1.9 cm in length, 0.9–0.95 cm in diameter and 0.4–0.5 cm in hole diameter (Fig. 154; Picture 343).

M9:66, it comprises 8 individual pieces. They are cylindrical-shaped, with holes drilled from both sides, they were primarily white, and some had gray-brown spots. They are 1.4–1.7 cm in length, 0.8–0.9 cm in diameter and 0.4 cm in hole diameter (Fig. 154; Picture 345).

**Fig. 153.** String of jade tubes (M9:31) (2/3)

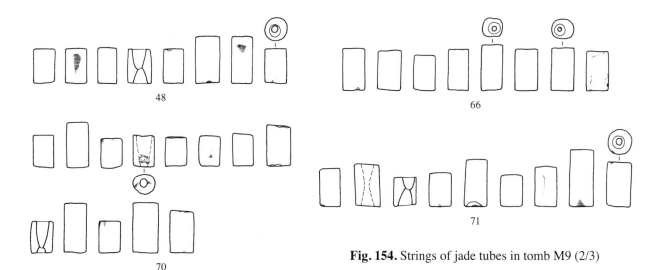

48

66

70

71

**Fig. 154.** Strings of jade tubes in tomb M9 (2/3)

M9:70, it comprises 13 individual pieces. They are cylindrical-shaped, with holes drilled from both sides, they are primarily white, and some had gray-brown spots. The hole of one piece seems like being drilled from one side, but it was actually cutted apart after being drilled from both sides. They are 1.25–1.9 cm in length, 0.9–1.05 cm in diameter and 0.4–0.5 cm in hole diameter (Fig. 154; Picture 346).

M9:71, it comprises 9 individual pieces. They are cylindrical-shaped, with holes drilled from both sides, they are primarily white, and some had gray spots. They are 1.2–2.2 cm in length, 0.8–1 cm in diameter and 0.4 cm in hole diameter (Fig. 154; Picture 347).

M9:77, it comprises 56 individual pieces. With holes drilled from both sides, they are primarily white, and some has gray-brown spots. Most of the tubes are cylindrical-shaped, and a few had triangle or square sections. Cambered string-cutting marks could be seen on surface of some tubes. They are 1–3.4 cm in length, 0.85–1.2 cm in diameter and 0.4–0.6 cm in hole diameter (Fig. 155; Picture 348).

**Tubes:** thirty pieces.

M9:15, it is cylindrical-shaped, with a hole drilled from both sides, it has cambered string-cutting marks

on two ends. It is 1.5 cm in length, 1.7 cm in diameter and 0.5–0.6 cm in hole diameter (Fig. 156; Picture 349).

M9:16, it is cylindrical-shaped, with a hole drilled from both sides, it has cambered string-cutting marks on one end. It is 2.05 cm in length, 1.05 cm in diameter and 0.5 cm in hole diameter (Fig. 156; Picture 354).

M9:21, it is cylindrical-shaped, with a hole drilled from both sides, it has cambered string-cutting marks on the surface. It is 1.2 cm in length, 0.9 cm in diameter and 0.4 cm in hole diameter (Fig. 156; Picture 354).

M9:22, it is cylindrical-shaped, with a hole drilled from both sides, it has step-shaped marks caused by cutting. It is 1.1 cm in length, 0.9 cm in diameter and 0.4 cm in hole diameter (Fig. 156; Picture 350).

M9:23, with gray spots, it is cylindrical-shaped with a hole drilled from both sides. It is 1.3 cm in length, 0.9 cm in diameter and 0.5 cm in hole diameter (Fig. 156; Picture 350).

M9:25, it is cylindrical-shaped, with a round hole drilled from both sides. It is 1.1 cm in length, 0.7 cm in diameter and 0.4 cm in hole diameter (Fig. 156; Picture 350).

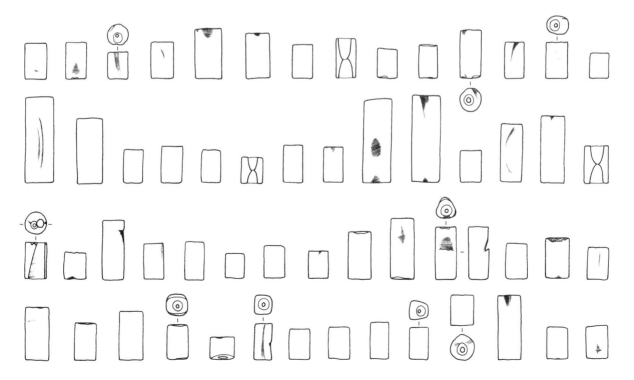

**Fig. 155.** String of jade tubes (M9:77) (2/3)

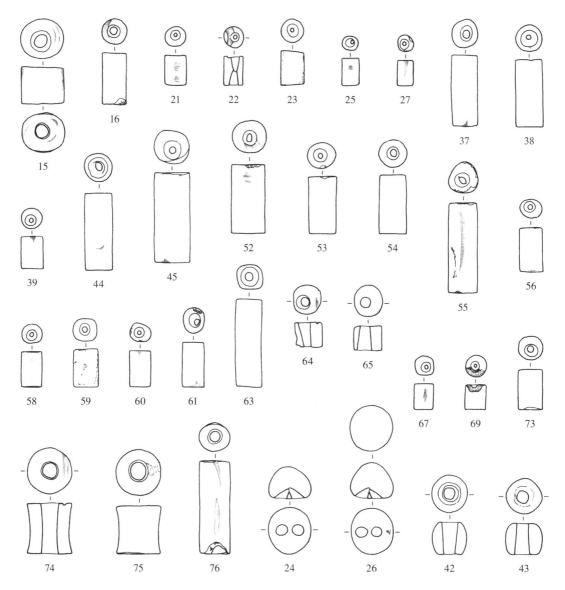

**Fig. 156.** Jade tubes and jade beads in tomb M9
24, 26, 42, 43. beads; others. tubes (2/3)

M9:27, it is cylindrical-shaped, it has a hole drilled from both sides with cambered string-cutting marks on the surface. It is 1 cm in length, 0.65 cm in diameter and 0.3 cm in hole diameter (Fig. 156; Picture 350).

M9:37, with gray spots, cylindrical-shaped, it has a round hole drilled from both sides. It is 2.85 cm in length, 1.1 cm in diameter and 0.5 cm in hole diameter (Fig. 156; Picture 351).

M9:38, with many gray spots, cylindrical-shaped, it has a hole drilled from both sides. It is 2.7 cm in length, 1.1 cm in diameter and 0.7 cm in hole diameter (Fig. 156; Picture 351).

M9:39, it is cylindrical-shaped, with a hole drilled

from both sides. It is 1.3 cm in length, 0.8 cm in diameter and 0.4 cm in hole diameter (Fig. 156; Picture 350).

M9:44, it is cylindrical-shaped, with a hole drilled from both sides. It is 3.05 cm in length, 1.15 cm in diameter and 0.7 cm in hole diameter (Fig. 156; Picture 351).

M9:45, it has gray-brown spots, cylindrical-shaped, with a hole drilled from both sides. It is 3.5 cm long with a diameter of 1.5 cm and a hole diameter of 0.6 cm (Fig. 156; Picture 351).

M9:52, with brown spots, cylindrical-shaped, it has a hole drilled from both sides and cambered string-cutting marks on one end. It is 2.7 cm in length, 1.4 cm in diameter and 0.5–0.6 cm in hole diameter (Fig. 156; Picture 351).

M9:53, with gray spots, cylindrical-shaped, it has a hole drilled from both sides. It is 2.3 cm in length, 1.1 cm in diameter and 0.4 cm in hole diameter (Fig. 156; Picture 352).

M9:54, with gray spots, cylindrical-shaped, it has a hole drilled from both sides. It is 2.3 cm in length, 1.1 cm in diameter and 0.4 cm in hole diameter (Fig. 156; Picture 352).

M9:55, it is cylindrical-shaped, with a hole drilled from both sides. It is 3.6 cm in length, 1.15 cm in diameter and 0.5 cm in hole diameter (Fig. 156; Picture 352).

M9:56, it is cylindrical-shaped, with a hole drilled from both sides. It is 1.75 cm in length, 0.9 cm in diameter and 0.4 cm in hole diameter (Fig. 156; Picture 350).

M9:58, with brown spots, cylindrical-shaped, it has a hole drilled from both sides and cutting marks on the surface. It is 1.4 cm in length, 0.9 cm in diameter and 0.4 cm in hole diameter (Fig. 156; Picture 353).

M9:59, with gray spots, cylindrical-shaped, it has a hole drilled from both sides and a square section with round corners. It is 1.5 cm in length, 1 cm in diameter and 0.5 cm in hole diameter (Fig. 156; Picture 353).

M9:60, with gray spots, cylindrical-shaped, it has a hole drilled from both sides. It is 1.4 cm in length, 0.8 cm in diameter and 0.4 cm in hole diameter (Fig. 156; Picture 353).

M9:61, with brown spots, cylindrical-shaped, it has a hole drilled from both sides. It is 1.8 cm in length, 1 cm in diameter and 0.5 cm in hole diameter (Fig. 156; Picture 353).

M9:63, with brown spots, square cylindrical-shaped, it has a hole drilled from both sides. It is 3.5 cm in length, 1.05 cm in diameter and 0.6 cm in hole diameter (Fig. 156; Picture 352).

M9:64, it is cylindrical-shaped, with a hole which seems like being drilled from one side due to the fact that it was cut after being drilled from both sides. It is 1 cm in length, 1.2 cm in diameter and 0.55 cm in hole diameter (Fig. 156; Picture 353).

M9:65, it is cylindrical-shaped, with a hole which seems like being drilled from one side due to the fact that it was cut after being drilled from both sides. It is 0.9 cm in length, 1.2 cm in diameter and 0.6 cm in hole diameter (Fig. 156; Picture 349).

M9:67, it is cylindrical-shaped, with a hole drilled from both sides and cutting marks on the surface. It is 1 cm in length, 0.8 cm in diameter and 0.4 cm in hole diameter (Fig. 156; Picture 354).

M9:69, it is cylindrical-shaped, with a hole drilled from both sides. It is 1 cm in length, 0.9 cm in diameter and 0.3 cm in hole diameter (Fig. 156; Picture 354).

M9:73, with yellowish-brown spots, cylindrical-shaped, it has a hole drilled from both sides. It is 1.65 cm in length, 1 cm in diameter and 0.4 cm in hole diameter (Fig. 156; Picture 354).

M9:74, with many gray spots, cylindrical-shaped, it has a hole drilled from both sides. Its outer wall is concave and polished. It is 2 cm in length, 1.85 cm in diameter and 0.7 cm in hole diameter (Fig. 156; Picture 355).

M9:75, with many gray spots, cylindrical-shaped, it has a hole drilled from both sides. Its outer wall is concave and polished. It is 1.9 cm in length, 1.85 cm in diameter and 0.85 cm in hole diameter (Fig. 156; Picture 357).

M9:76, with gray spots, cylindrical-shaped, it has a hole drilled from both sides and cambered string-cutting marks on the surface. It is 3.7 cm in length, 1.3 cm in diameter and 0.5 cm in hole diameter (Fig. 156; Picture 352).

**Beads:** four pieces.

M9:24, hemispherical, it has a tunnel-shaped hole on the plane. It is 1.3 cm in thickness and 1.8 cm in diameter (Fig. 156; Picture 356).

M9:26, hemispherical, it has a tunnel-shaped hole on the plane. It is 1.3 cm in thickness and 1.8 cm in diameter (Fig. 156; Picture 356).

M9:42, in the shape of waist drum, it has a hole drilled from one side. It is 1.3 cm long with a diameter of 1.4 cm and a hole diameter of 0.65 cm (Fig. 156; Picture 358).

M9:43, in the shape of waist drum, it has a hole

drilled from one side. It is 1.25 cm in length, 1.3 cm in diameter and 0.6 cm in hole diameter (Fig. 156; Picture 358).

**Particles:** sixty seven pieces.

M9:20, it comprises 20 individual pieces. Approximately oval in plane, they are flat on one side and convex on the other side. They are 0.6–1.1 cm in length, 0.3–0.6 cm in width and 0.2–0.4 cm in thickness (Fig. 157; Picture 359).

M9:30, it comprises 8 individual pieces. Approximately oval in plane, they are flat on one side and convex on the other side. They are 0.5–0.9 cm in length, 0.4 cm in width and 0.3 cm in thickness (Fig. 157; Pictures 360, 361).

M9:32, it comprises two individual pieces. Shaped in long strip, they are flat on one side and convex on the other side. They are 3.5, 3.75 cm in length, 0.6 cm in width and 0.45 cm in thickness (Fig. 157; Picture 362).

M9:33, with grayish-green spots, shaped in long strip, it is flat on one side and convex on the other side. It is 3.05 cm in length, 0.6 cm in width and 0.55 cm in thickness (Fig. 157; Picture 363).

M9:34, it comprises two individual pieces. Shaped in long strip, they are flat on one side and convex on the other side. They are 2.7, 2.9 cm in length, 0.5 cm

in width and 0.5 cm in thickness (Fig. 157; Picture 362).

M9:46, it comprises eight individual pieces. Oval in plane, they are flat on one side and convex on the other side. They are 0.8–1 cm in length, 0.55 cm in width and 0.3 cm in thickness (Fig. 157; Picture 364).

M9:47, it comprises 19 individual pieces. Approximately oval in plane, they are flat on one side and convex on the other side. They are 0.4–1.1 cm in length, 0.2–0.6 cm in width and 0.2–0.4 cm in thickness (Fig. 157; Picture 365).

M9:51, it comprises 3 individual pieces. Approximately oval in plane, they are flat on one side and convex on the other side. They are 0.5–0.6 cm in length, 0.3 cm in width and 0.2 cm in thickness (Fig. 157; Picture 366).

M9:62, it comprises 4 individual pieces. Approximately oval in plane, they are flat on one side and convex on the other side. They are 0.85–1.1 cm in length, 0.45–0.6 cm in width and 0.4–0.5 cm in thickness (Fig. 157; Picture 367).

(2) Stone artifacts

**Yue axe:** one piece (M9:13). Black-brown, it is approximately rectangular in plane with slightly arc top end. The cambered blade is wider than the top end, and there is a hole drilled from both sides on the upper

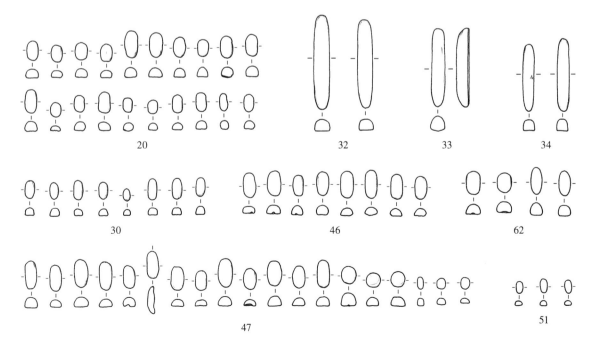

**Fig. 157.** Jade particles in tomb M9 (2/3)

part with spiral marks on the hole's wall. It is 13 cm in height, 9.6 cm in top width, 10.8 cm in blade width, 3.9 cm in diameter and 1.1 cm in thickness (Fig. 158; Picture 369).

(3) Jade-inlaid lacquer

**Lacquer cup:** one piece (M9:78). Cylinder-shaped, it has a open mouth and a thin and tall trumpet-shaped ring foot. Its core was decayed when unearthed, and could not be taken out. The lacquer coating was evenly distributed vermilion, still glossy when unearthed. Jade particles were inlaid around the joint of the cup body and ring foot and around the exterior surface of the ring foot's bottom. These particles are convex on the front side and flat on the back side. Since the interior and exterior lacquer coatings are still in their original looks when unearthed, it is inferred from the excavation that the lacquer cup is 2–3 mm in thickness, 29 cm in height, 11 cm in opening diameter and 12 cm in ring foot diameter (Picture 368).

(4) Pottery vessels: four pieces.

***Ding* tripod:** one piece (M9:79). It is fine sand-tempered pottery, its core is reddish-brown inside and ash black outside. It has a flared mouth, concave rim

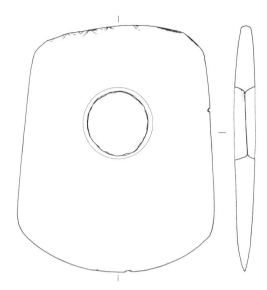

**Fig. 158.** Stone *yue* axe (M9:13) (1/2)

surface, a bulging abdomen and a round bottom. It has flat fin-shaped legs, the outer parts of which are flat and slightly thick, and the inner corners are arc. It is 18.4 cm in height, 14.8 cm in opening diameter (Fig. 159; Picture 370).

***Dou:*** one piece (M9:80). It is a gray clay pottery, and its core is orange-red outside. With a flared mouth and an inclined lip, it has a folded abdome, with a

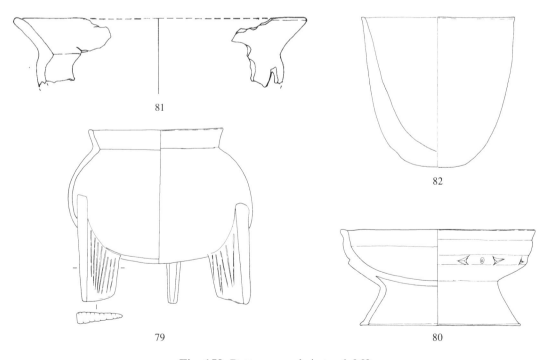

81

79

82

80

**Fig. 159.** Pottery vessels in tomb M9

81. ring-foot jar; 82. *gang* vat; 79. *ding* tripod; 80. *dou* (82 is 1/8, others are 1/4)

short trumpet-shaped ring foot. The outer surface of the plate is decorated with a belt of the bow string pattern and a decorative belt comprising two triangles with concave arc sides and a round incompletely penetrated hole. Based on observation, it is inferred that the round hole was forming by tubular drilling. It is 10.3 cm in height, 21.8 cm in opening diameter and 18.6 cm in foot diameter (Fig. 159; Picture 371).

**Ring-foot jar:** one piece (M9:81). It is red sand-tempered pottery, with orange-red coating and is polished. It has a flared mouth, and the rim surface is sloped. It is so broken that its original shape could not be recognized (Fig. 159).

***Gang* vat:** one piece (M9:82). It is reddish sand-tempered pottery. It has a sharp lip, deep abdomen with an approximately flat bottom. It is irregular in shape, and is thick in the lower abdomen and bottom. It is 32.4 cm in height, 32–33.5 cm in mouth diameter (Fig. 159; Picture 372).

# Section 10 Tomb M10

## 1. The Shape of the Tomb

Tomb M10 is located in the western of the south line of the tombs, with tomb M3 to its west and tomb M9 to its east, and adjacent to tombs M4 and tomb M5 on the north. It has its opening under top soil, and disturbed the yellow-earthen mound. It is rectangular pit with vertical wall, with an orientation of 184°. The tomb is 3.35 meters in length, 1.75 meters in width and 1.34 meters in depth. The pit walls and bottom are comparatively even, filled with gray mottled earth, with no inclusions in it. Skeleton inside the tomb had rotten away and left no remains (Picture 373).

In the north of the tomb, four pieces of pottery vessels were unearthed, including one *ding* tripod, one *dou*, one ring-foot jar, and one *gang* vat. All of them are very loose in texture, and are seriously broken when unearthed. Some jade tubes are scattered around the pottery vessels. And there is also a long jade (M10:21) tube with carved patterns above the *dou*. To the south of the pottery vessels is a triangular jade plaque (M10:20), which is unearthed with its carved pattern side downward.

Jade artifacts are mainly located in the middle and south of the tomb. In the south, there are three-pronged object, crown-shaped object, cylindrical object with cover, and a set of awl-shaped objects. Among them, the three-pronged object (M10:6) covered the set of awl-shaped object (M10:5) comprising 11 pieces, with its carved side facing downward. The end of the three-pronged object and the end of the awl-shaped objects both point to the southwest (Picture 375). There is a jade bracelet (M10:3) above the awl-shaped objects. To its north is the crown-shaped object (M10:4), whose tenon point to the north. Beside the awl-shaped object is a stone *yue* axe, whose blade facing the east (M10:8). In the southern end of the tomb laid a string of jade tube (M10:65) in the east–west direction, totaling 114 single tubes. Between the string of jade tubes and the three-pronged object, there is a set of cylindrical object with cover (M10:2), and the cover is separated from the cylindrical jade object. Furthermore, when the cylindrical jade object (M10:1) was unearthed, it is 30 cm higher than the bottom of the tomb, which indicated that possibly it is originally places above the funerary container.

In the middle of the tomb, many jade bracelets, three pieces of jade *cong* and a jade *yue* axe (Picture 374) were found. Among them, the double-holed jade *yue* axe (M10:14), with its blade facing the east, is covered by the stone *yue* axe (M10:13). Jade *congs* were near the jade *yue* axe. According to the pattern, the top end of the jade *cong* M10:15 points to the north, and that of M10:16 and M10:19 points upward. To the west of the jade *cong*, there are many pieces of jade bracelets, and some of them are overlapped on each other. Among the above-mentioned objects, the scattered 69 pieces of jade tubes belonged to a string (M10:63), and this might be the pectoral ornament of the tomb occupant. There was no singleton of awl-

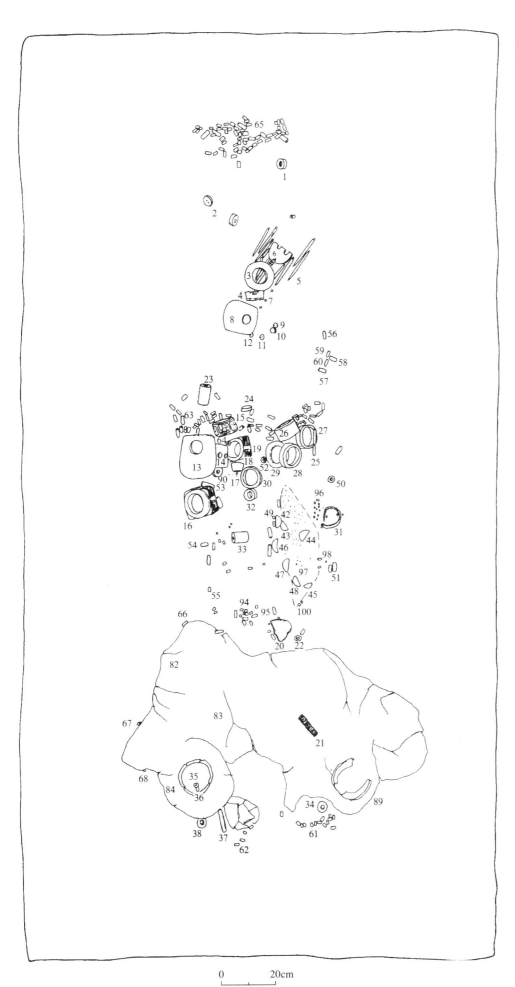

**Fig. 160.** Plan of tomb M10

1, 17, 23, 32–34, 38, 90. cylindrical jade objects

2. cylindrical jade object with cover

3, 26–31. jade bracelets

4. crown-shaped jade object

5. awl-shaped jade object

6. three-pronged jade object

7, 95, 96, 98, 107. jade particles

8, 13. stone *yue* axes

9–12, 35, 50, 64, 94, 100, 103, 105. jade beads

14. jade *yue* axe

15, 16, 19. jade *cong*

18, 24. jade end ornaments

20. jade plaque object

21, 37, 53. long jade tubes

22. ring-shaped jade ornament

25. strip-shaped jade ornament

36, 39, 40, 41, 51, 52, 54–60, 62, 66, 68, 69, 71, 72, 74–81, 85–88, 91, 93, 101, 102, 104, 106. jade tubes

42–45, 48, 99. semi-circular jade ornaments

46, 47. crescent jade ornaments

49, 61, 63, 65, 97. strings of jade tubes

67, 70. bullet-shaped jade ornaments

82. pottery *dou*

83. pottery *gang* vat

84. pottery ring-foot jar

89. pottery *ding* tripod

(Note: M10:69 is under M10:84; M10:70–81, 100–106 are under M10:82; M10:85–88, 91, 93 are under M10:84; M10:99 is under M10:97; M10:39–41 are scattered under other artifacts; M10:73 and M10:92 are vacant numbers.)

0        20cm

shaped object found in the tomb, but the strip-shaped jade object (M10:25), according to its unearthed place, might have taken place of the function of the singleton awl-shaped object. In the north-central of the tomb, seven pieces of jade ornaments (M10:42–48) were unearthed and their plane present as a semicircle or a crescent. Judging from their thin bodies and multi tunnel-shaped holed edge, they might be objects used to be sewn on something. Around them, there are also some stringed ornaments (M10:97), comprising 201 pieces of jade tubes (Fig. 160).

## 2. Burial Objects

The burial objects include jade artifacts, stone artifacts and pottery vessels, and they are numbered into 105 pieces (sets), 562 individual pieces.

(1) Jade artifacts

There is 96 pieces (sets), 556 individual pieces of jade artifacts were unearthed, mostly white and many had reddish-brown spots. The types include crown-shaped object, cylindrical object with cover, three-pronged object, set of awl-shaped object, *yue* axe, *cong*, bracelet, plaque object and bullet-shaped ornament, and so on.

**Crown-shaped object:** one piece (M10:4). With gray spots, it presents an upside-down trapezoid in plane; wider at the upper end, and the middle is concave with a point in the center. Under the concave is an oval hole. And there is a flat tenon at the bottom, with three little holes drilled from both sides equidistantly. It is 3.15 cm in height, 6.4 cm in width and 0.4 cm in thickness (Fig. 161; Picture 376).

**Cylindrical object with cover:** one set (M10:2). It comprises a cover and a cylindrical object.

M10:2-1, the cover. It is flat and looked like a round pie. One side is convex while the other side is flat. The flat side has a tunnel-shaped hole with some spiral marks inside. It is 4.1 cm in diameter, 1.3 cm in thickness (Fig. 162; Picture 377).

M10:2-2, the cylindrical object. It is cylinder-shaped, with a hole drilled from both sides and obvious step-shaped marks. The outside wall is slightly concave, and has a crosswise cutting mark. It is 3 cm in height, 4.5 cm in diameter and 1.7 cm in hole diameter (Fig. 162; Picture 378).

**Three-pronged object:** one piece (M10:6). It has reddish-brown spots. Its three prongs are at the same level, with a vertical straight hole on the middle prong, and its bottom is arc-shaped. The front side is carved with the sacred animal motif in bas-relief and intaglio carving techniques, among which three sets of feather patterns are carved on the upper parts of the three prongs respectively. On the middle part, two double-circled round eyes with arc-shaped eyepits outside them are carved. Strip-shaped nose bridge is

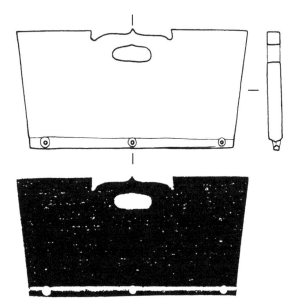

**Fig. 161.** Crown-shaped jade object (M10:4) and its rubbing (1/1)

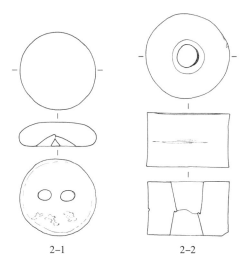

2–1                2–2

**Fig. 162.** Cylindrical jade object with cover (M10:2)
2-1. the cover of the cylindrical object;
2-2. cylindrical object (1/2)

between the eyes, and the nose wings are quite wide. Under the nose, there is a wide arc-shaped mouth, with two pairs of tusks stretching outwards. The inside pair faces upward while the outside pair faces downward. Around the main carved motifs there are rolling cloud patterns. The back side is even and smooth without patterns. It is 5.2 cm in height, 7.4 cm in width and 1.3 cm in thickness (Fig. 163; Pictures 379, 380).

**Set of awl-shaped objects:** one set, comprising 11 individual pieces, and all of them are even and smooth without carved patterns.

M10:5-1, with brown spots, it is strip-shaped, one end is pointed and the other end is flat with a hole drilled from both sides. It is 11.5 cm in height, 0.7 cm in diameter (Fig. 164; Picture 381).

M10:5-2, livid with brown spots, it is strip-shaped, one end is pointed and the other end is flat with a hole drilled from both sides. It is 11.7 cm in length and 0.8 cm in diameter (Fig. 164; Picture 381).

M10:5-3, with brown spots, it is strip-shaped, one end is pointed and the other end is flat with a hole drilled from both sides. It is 11.7 cm in length and 0.8 cm in diameter (Fig. 164; Picture 381).

M10:5-4, it is broken into two pieces when unearthed. With brown spots, it is strip-shaped, one end is pointed and the other end is flat with a hole drilled from both sides. It is 11.9 cm in length 11.9 cm and 0.9 cm in diameter (Fig. 164; Picture 381).

M10:5-5, it is broken into two pieces when unearthed. It is strip-shaped, one end is pointed and the other end is flat with a hole drilled from both sides. It is 11.8 cm in length and 0.8 cm in diameter (Fig. 164; Picture 381).

M10:5-6, it is gray, strip-shaped, one end is pointed

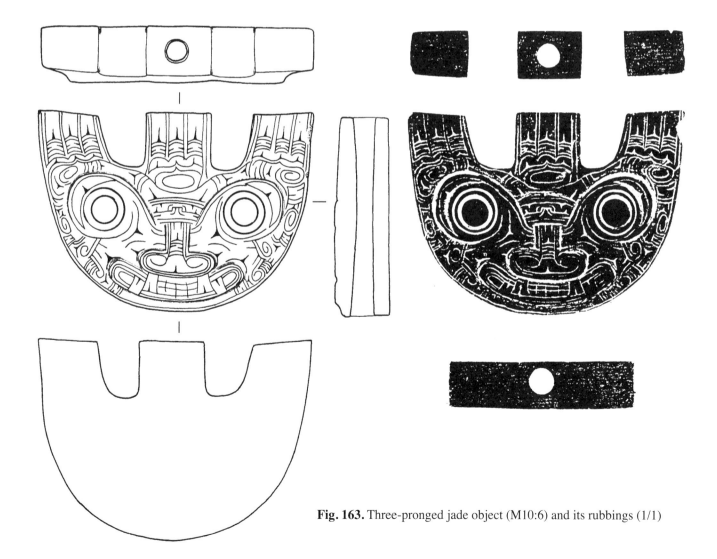

**Fig. 163.** Three-pronged jade object (M10:6) and its rubbings (1/1)

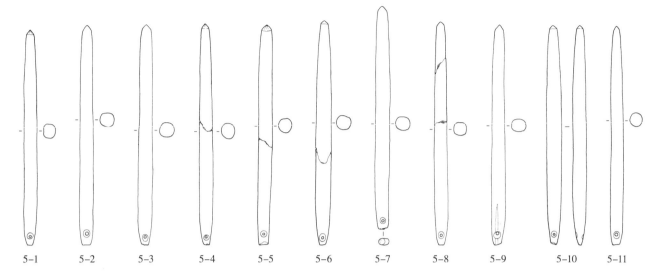

**Fig. 164.** Awl-shaped jade objects in tomb M10 (1/2)

and the other end is flat with a hole drilled from both sides. It is 12 cm in length and 0.9 cm in diameter (Fig. 164; Picture 381).

M10:5-7, it has brown spots, strip-shaped, one end is pointed and the other end is flat with a hole drilled from both sides. It is 11.9 cm in length and 0.8 cm in diameter (Fig. 164; Picture 381).

M10:5-8, it is broken into three pieces when unearthed. With gray flocs, it is strip-shaped, one end is pointed and the other end is flat with a hole drilled from both sides. It is 11.8 cm in length and 0.8 cm in diameter (Fig. 164; Picture 381).

M10:5-9, it is caesious, strip-shaped, one end is pointed and the other end is flat with a hole drilled from both sides and with straight cutting marks on this end. It is 11.8 cm in length and 0.8 cm in diameter (Fig. 164; Picture 381).

M10:5-10, it is caesious, strip-shaped, one end is pointed and the other end is flat with a hole drilled from both sides. It is 11.6 cm in length and 0.8 cm in diameter (Fig. 164; Picture 381).

M10:5-11, it is caesious, strip-shaped, one end is pointed and the other end is flat with a hole drilled from both sides. It is 11.7 cm in length and 0.7 cm in diameter (Fig. 164; Picture 381).

**Yue axe:** one piece (M10:14). With large brown spots, its body is flat and thin, and in a trapezoid plane. The top end is straight and the blade is cambered.

Two small round holes are drilled on the upper part. Besides, the upper hole has crosswise lines on both sides and the lower hole has one oblique lines on both sides respectively, about 0.5 cm in width and stretching to the top corners. There are also step-shaped marks on the wall of the holes. It is 15.6 cm in height, 8.2 cm in top width, 10.6 cm in blade width, 0.8 cm in thickness, 1.45 cm in upper hole diameter, 1.95 cm in lower hole diameter (Fig. 165; Picture 383).

**Cong:** three pieces.

M10:15, with greyish brown spots, it is cylinder shaped, and there is a big hole drilled from both sides in the middle, with the wall polished. On the surface, there are four symmetrical rectangle protruding blocks, each of which is decorated with sacred animal motif. The outline of eyes, forehead, nose are carved in bas-relief technique, and the eyeballs, nosewings, mouth, lips and two pairs of tusks are carved in intaglio. On the top of the pattern there are two belts of paralleled bow string patterns. Around the main pattern is decorated with dense rolling cloud patterns. It is 4.5 cm in height, 8.3 cm in collar diameter and 6.4 cm in hole diameter (Figs. 166, 167; Picture 382).

M10:16, with reddish-brown spots, it is short cylindrical-shaped, and the middle hole is slightly bigger. The outside wall is slightly convex, and the angle is larger than 90 degrees. The four protruding blocks are carved with sacred animal motif respectively, with the

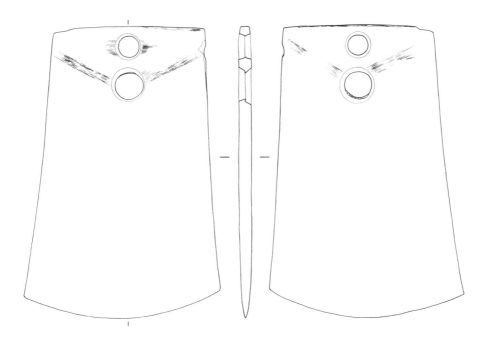

**Fig. 165.** Jade *yue* axe (M10:14) (1/2)

A: Expansion figure of patterns

B: Expansion figure of patterns

C: Expansion figure of patterns

**Fig. 166.** Jade *cong* (M10:15) (1/1)

**Fig. 167.** Rubbings of jade *cong* (M10:15) (A is 1/2 and B is 1/1)

corner as the axis. Crosswise ridges are on the top and two belts of bow string patterns are carved over and below the ridge respectively. Twisted-rope patterns are carved between the bow string patterns to represent the feathered crown. Round double-circled eyes with sharp corner are carved on both sides. Oval patterns are carved between eyes, with wedge-shaped eye corners on both left and right corner. There are oval pattern between the eyes, with sharp corner carved on the top left and top right corners. The nose under eyes raise up in bas-relief, with nosewings outlined with arc and sharp corner on both sides. The cheeks of the sacred animal motif are decorated by variant bird motif. The top of the object is not smooth due to its jade material, but it is carefully polished. In the middle of the hole wall, there is a crosswise cutting mark. It is 5.8 cm in height, 10.1 cm in collar diameter and 5.9 cm in hole diameter (Figs. 168, 169; Picture 385).

M10:19, with grayish brown spots, it is shaped in a short cylinder, with a hole drilled in the middle and the wall of the hole is polished. The exterior wall is slightly convex, and the corner angle is larger than

90 degree. Four sets of sacred animal motifs are carved with the corner as the axis, and each set of the motif is divided into the upper and lower segments by a crosswise shallow groove in the middle. The upper segment is the sacred human motif. The top is decorated two belts of paralleled bow string patterns representing the feathered crown. Below which are two intaglioed eyes and protruding wide nose. The lower

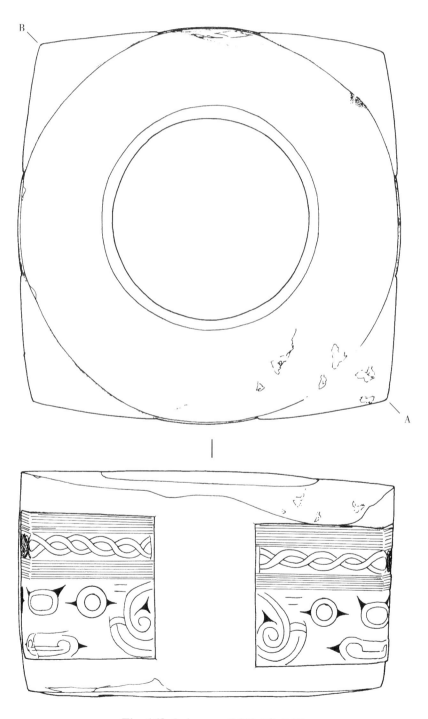

**Fig. 168.** Jade *cong* (M10:16) (1/1)

B: Expansion figure of patterns

A

**Fig. 169.** Jade *cong* (M10:16) and its rubbing (1/1)

segment is the sacred animal face. The oval eyepits are convex and inside them are intaglioed double-circled eyes. Its forehead is represented by bridge-shaped convexity and its flat nose is raising. Under the nose was carved with its wide flat mouth with two pairs of

tusk inside. Dense rolling cloud patterns are around the main patterns as decoration. It is 5.2 cm in height, 8.2 cm in collar diameter and 6.4 cm in hole diameter (Figs. 170, 171; Picture 386).

**Cylindrical object:** eight pieces.

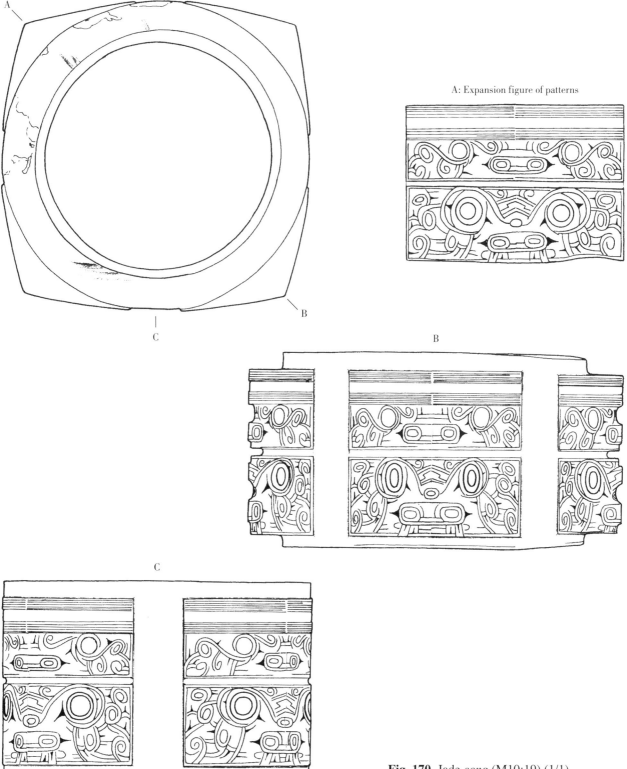

Fig. 170. Jade *cong* (M10:19) (1/1)

**Fig. 171.** Rubbings of jade *cong* (M10:19) (A is 1/2 and B is 1/1)

M10:1, with yellow spots, it is cylinder-shaped with a irregular hole drilled in the middle. One end has cambered string-cutting marks. It is 2.4 cm in height, 4 cm in diameter and 1.7 cm in hole diameter (Fig. 172; Picture 384).

M10:17, it is cylinder-shaped with a hole drilled in the middle, and the wall of the hole is slightly convex. One of the ends has cambered string-cutting marks. It is 2.05 cm in height, 4.3 cm in diameter and 1.2 cm in hole diameter (Fig. 172; Picture 387).

M10:23, with some brown spots on one end of it, it is cylinder-shaped with a hole drilled from both sides in the middle. The wall of the hole is polished. It is 6.95 cm in height, 4 cm in diameter and 1.1–1.2 cm in hole diameter (Fig. 172; Picture 389).

M10:32, with gray spots, it is cylinder-shaped with a hole drilled from both sides in the middle and step-shaped marks remained. There are cambered string-cutting marks on both ends. There are unnoticeable vertical line marks on the wall of the hole. It is 2 cm in height, 4.2 cm in diameter and 2.1 cm in hole diameter (Fig. 172; Picture 390).

M10:33, it is cylinder-shaped with a hole drilled from both sides in the middle and the hole is polished. The outer wall is slightly concave. Both ends has cambered string-cutting marks. It is 5.4 cm in height, 4.3 cm in diameter and 0.9 cm in hole diameter (Fig. 172; Picture 391).

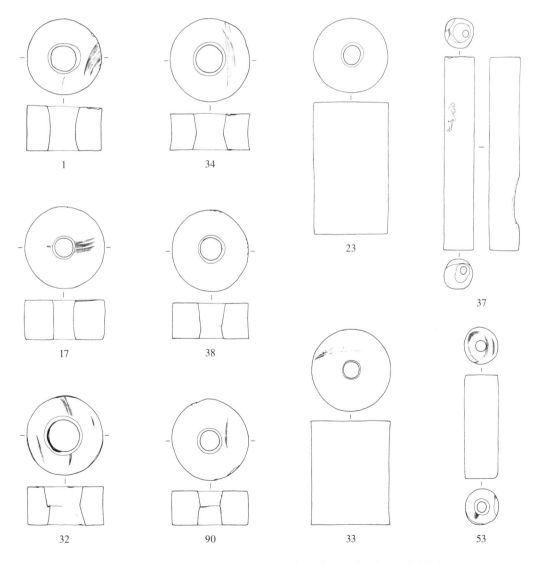

**Fig. 172.** Cylindrical jade objects and long jade tubes in tomb M10
1, 17, 23, 32–34, 38, 90. cylindrical objects; 37, 53. long tubes (1/2)

M10:34, with gray spots, it is cylinder-shaped with a round hole drilled from both sides. The outer wall is slightly concave. Both ends has cambered string-cutting marks. It is 1.9 cm in height, 4.4 cm in diameter and 1.8 cm in hole diameter (Fig. 172; Picture 388).

M10:38, with greyish brown spots, it is cylinder-shaped with a hole drilled from both sides. There are spiral marks on the wall of the hole. It is 1.85 cm in height, 4.3 cm in diameter and 1.4 cm in hole diameter (Fig. 172; Picture 392).

M10:90, with greyish brown spots, it is cylinder-shaped with a hole drilled from both sides. There are spiral marks on the wall of the hole. It is 1.75 cm in height, 4.2 cm in diameter and 1.4 cm in hole diameter (Fig. 172; Picture 393).

**Long tube:** three pieces.

M10:21, it is cylinder-shaped with a irregular hole in the middle. The patterns are carved on the surface using bas-relief and intaglio carving techniques, and divided into three parts by two circles of vertical grooves. On each part, there are four round protruding blocks, and on each of them, three irregular circles are intaglioed to represent eyes. Above the eyes, a continuous semicircular line is carved. Between two eyes, there is a double-line rhombus patterns and the nose is intaglioed under the rhombuses. The whole pattern could be interpreted as four dragon's heads that shared eyes. It is 8 cm in length and 1.8 cm in diameter (Fig. 173; Picture 394).

M10:37, it is cylinder-shaped and has a hole drilled from both sides which was off-center. The surface has some defects left due to cutting of jade raw material, but polished later. It is 10.2 cm in length, 1.6 cm in diameter and 0.8 cm in hole diameter (Fig. 172; Picture 395).

M10:53, with greyish brown spots, it is cylinder-shaped with a hole drilled from both sides. Both ends has cambered string-cutting marks. It is 5.5 cm in length, 1.9 cm in diameter and 0.5–0.9 cm in hole

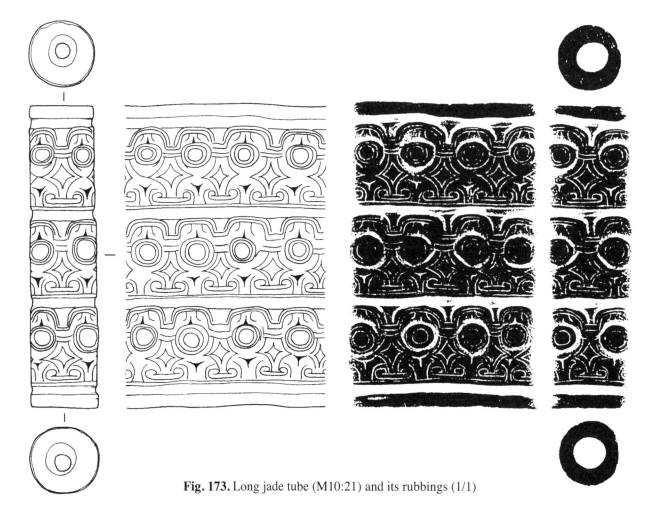

**Fig. 173.** Long jade tube (M10:21) and its rubbings (1/1)

diameter (Fig. 172; Picture 396).

**Bracelets:** seven pieces.

M10:3, with gray and brown spots, it is flat ring-shaped, and the inner wall is slightly convex. One end has defects left due to cutting of jade raw material. It is 10.3 cm in diameter, 6.1 cm in hole diameter and 1.35 cm in thickness (Fig. 174; Picture 397).

M10:26, it is cylindrical-shaped, and the body is flat and thin. The outer wall is straight while the inner wall is slightly convex. It is comparatively delicately made. It is 4.2 cm in height, 7.35 cm in diameter and 6.4 cm in hole diameter (Fig. 174; Picture 399).

M10:27, with brown spots, it is cylinder-shaped. The inner wall is convex while the outer wall is concave. It is 3.7 cm in height, 8.2 cm in diameter and 6.5 cm in hole diameter (Fig. 174; Picture 400).

M10:28, with brown spots, it is wide ring-shaped. The inner wall is convex with crosswise cutting marks. It is 2.3 cm in height, 8.8 cm in diameter and 6.6 cm in hole diameter (Fig. 174; Picture 398).

M10:29, with gray spots, it is wide ring-shaped. The inner wall is slightly arc and convex while the outer wall is round and convex. It is 1.7–2.2 cm in height, 9.3 cm in diameter and 6.3 cm in hole diameter (Fig. 174; Picture 401).

M10:30, it is wide ring-shaped. The inner wall is slightly convex while the outer wall is slightly concave. It is 2.75 cm in height, 8.1 cm in diameter and 6.1 cm in hole diameter (Fig. 174; Picture 402).

M10:31, it is broken into four parts when unearthed. It is circular shaped, and the hole drilled from both sides made the inner wall pointed and convex. It is

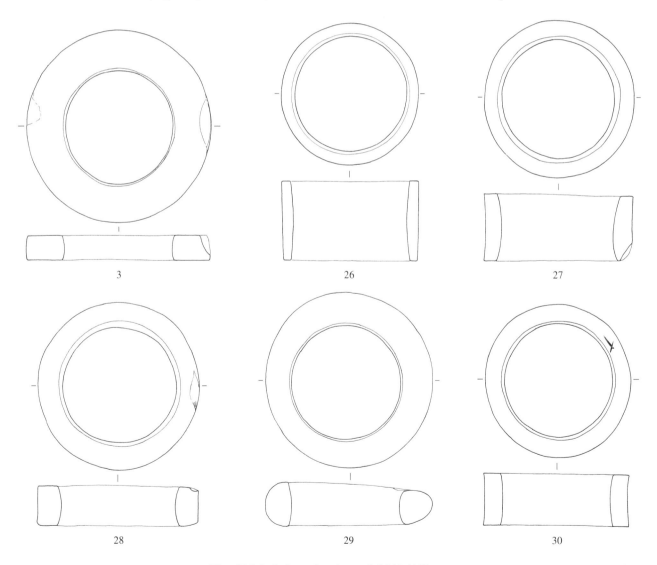

3      26      27

28      29      30

**Fig. 174.** Jade bracelets in tomb M10 (1/2)

0.9 cm in height, 10.1 cm in diameter and 9.1 cm in hole diameter (Fig. 175; Picture 403).

**End ornaments:** two pieces.

M10:18, it is approximately truncated cone-shaped, and the outer wall is concave. One end is convex, while the other is round tenon-shaped with a crosswise rabbet. Two holes are drilled in the rabbet with solid drilling to form one oval hole. The inner wall of the hole has spiral marks and crosswise and vertical line marks remained in the rabbet. It is 2.9 cm in height and 4.5 cm in diameter (Fig. 176; Pictures 404, 405).

M10:24, it is truncated cone-shaped, and the outer wall is slightly concave. One end is convex while the other is flat. A small wafer about 0.4 cm in thickness was put in the middle hole of the convex end. There are cambered string-cutting marks on the flat end. It is 2.25 cm in height, 3.85 cm in upper diameter and 3.6 cm in lower diameter (Fig. 176; Picture 406).

**Plaque object:** one piece (M10:20). With brown spots, its plane looked slightly like a triangle. There is a ridge in the middle of the top end. The bottom is circularly cambered. The front side is carved with sacred animal motif in bas-relief and intaglio carving techniques. At the top is an oblong bas-relief sacred human motif. The sacred human wear a feather-like crown that consist of 11 sets of radical feather patterns. The sacred human motif has a face shaped in an upside-down trapezoid, olive shaped eyes, single-circled eyeballs, a bulbous nose, an oblate mouth with two even rows of teeth inside. On either side of the head, there are some hollowed-out holes to outline the slender neck. Beneath the sacred human motif is the sacred animal's face in bas-relief. The animal has oval eyepits with two protruding eyeballs with quadruple circles outside, of which two circles are tubular drilled, the others carved in intaglio. It has a straight and raised nose, with a wide wing of nose carved with rolling cloud patterns. Along the bottom is the animal's wide mouth with two rows of teeth inside. Each side of its mouth is carved with two pair of tusks. The space between the sacred human and animal motif is filled with rolling cloud patterns. The back side is smooth and flat, with four pairs of small tunnel-shaped holes drilled slantingly, of which 3 pairs are at the upper end and the other at the bottom. It is 6.1 cm in height, 8.2 cm in width and 0.6–1.28 cm in thickness (Fig. 177; Pictures 418–420).

**Semi-circular ornaments:** six pieces.

M10:42, it has blue and brown spots. The upper end is smooth and flat, and the lower end is cambered.

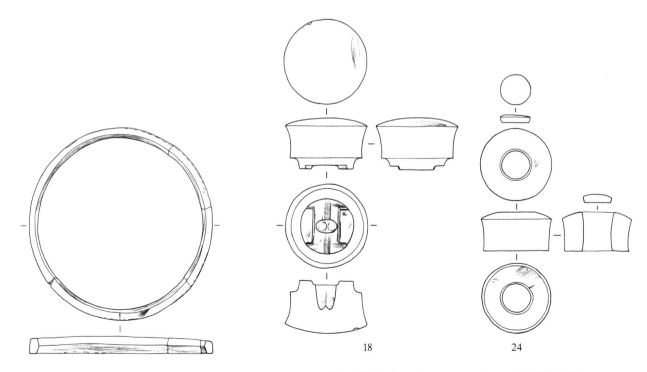

**Fig. 175.** Jade bracelet (M10:31) (1/2)

**Fig. 176.** Jade end ornaments in tomb M10 (1/2)

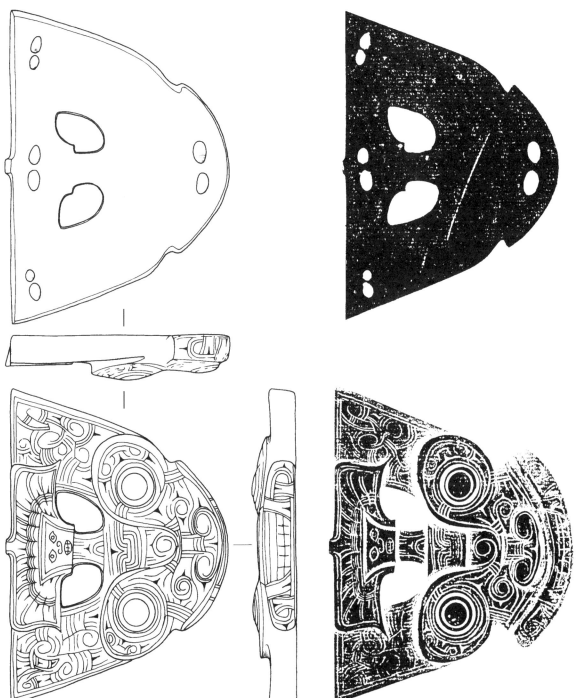

**Fig. 177.** Jade plaque (M10:20) and its rubbings (1/1)

Each of the upper corners has a hole drilled from both sides. The hole on one corner was drilled through to the top end, and the other was drilled through to the back. The bottom also has a hole drilled from both sides. It is 2.55 cm in height, 4.7 cm in width and 0.5 cm in thickness (Fig. 178; Pictures 407, 408).

M10:43, it has blue and brown spots, roughly similar to M10:42 in shape. It is 2.7 cm in height, 4.75 cm in width and 0.5 cm in thickness (Fig. 178; Picture 409).

M10:44, it has many blue and brown spots, similar to M10:42 in shape, but with a crosswise cutting mark on its top end. It is 2.3 cm in height, 4.7 cm in width and 0.5 cm in thickness (Fig. 178; Pictures 410, 411).

M10:45, it has many blue and brown spots, roughly similar to M10:42 in shape, but the bottom has a hole drilled from both sides through to the back. The back has a hole that has not been drilled through, and the top end has cutting marks. It is 2.05 cm in height, 3.9 cm in width and 0.5 cm in thickness (Fig. 178; Picture 412).

M10:48, it has many blue and brown spots, similar to M10:45 in shape. It is 2.1 cm in height, 3.75 cm in width and 0.4 cm in thickness (Fig. 178; Picture 413).

M10:99, it has many blue and brown spots, similar to M10:45 in shape. The top end has cutting marks. It is 2.3 cm in height, 4.05 cm in width and 0.4 cm in thickness (Fig. 178; Picture 414).

**Crescent-shaped ornaments:** two pieces.

M10:46, it has many brown spots. The lower end is cambered, and the upper end is concave with the two corners stretching upward. The upper end is thicker than the lower end. Each of the corner has a hole drilled from both sides. The front was slightly convex, and the back is flat with 3 pairs of tunnel-shaped holes. The top end has crosswise cutting marks. It is 1.95 cm in height, 4.75 cm in width and 0.9 cm in thickness (Fig. 179; Pictures 415, 416).

M10:47, it has many brown spots, similar to M10:46 in shape. It is 2 cm in height, 4.5 cm in width and 0.65 cm in thickness (Fig. 179; Picture 417).

**Ring-shaped ornament:** one piece (M10:22). It is yellowish brown, with truncated and cone-shaped, with a hole drilled from both sides in the middle. The outer wall is slanting and the inner wall is slightly convex. It is 0.8 cm in height, 2.6 cm in diameter and

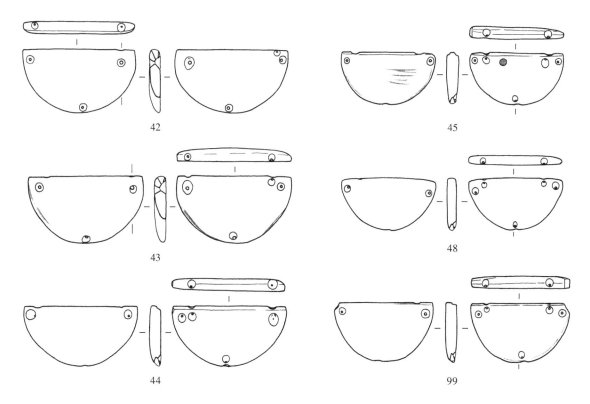

**Fig. 178.** Semi-circular jade ornaments in tomb M10 (2/3)

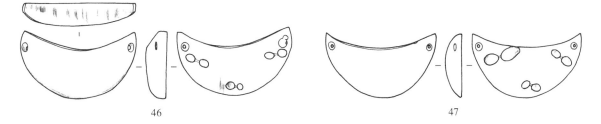

46　　47

**Fig. 179.** Crescent jade ornaments in tomb M10 (2/3)

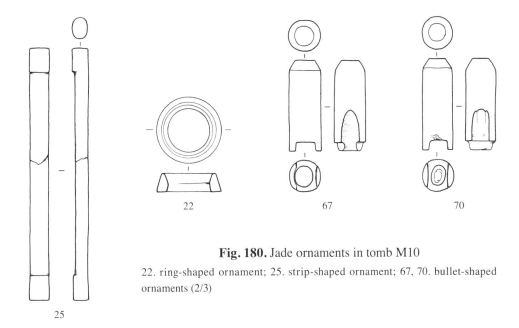

22　67　70

25

**Fig. 180.** Jade ornaments in tomb M10

22. ring-shaped ornament; 25. strip-shaped ornament; 67, 70. bullet-shaped ornaments (2/3)

1.85 cm in hole diameter (Fig. 180; Picture 421).

**Strip-shaped ornament:** one piece.

M10:25, it has many gray spots, and is broken into two pieces when unearthed. It is shaped like a strip, and the end face is oval. Both the ends are smooth and flat with a bulging part. It is 10.1 cm in length and 0.8 cm in diameter (Fig. 180; Picture 423).

**Bullet-shaped ornaments:** two pieces.

M10:67, it is grayish-white and cylinder-shaped, like a bullet. The top is truncated cone-shaped. The bottom has a crosswise notch and a round hole that has not been drill through. The hole wall has solid drilling marks. It is 3.6 cm in length, 1.3 cm in diameter and 0.7 cm in hole diameter (Fig. 180; Picture 424).

M10:70, it is grayish-white with brown spots, similar to M10:67 in shape and size (Fig. 180; Picture 425).

**String of jade tubes:** five sets, 461 individual pieces in total.

M10:49, it consists of 18 individual pieces varying in length. They all has gray spots, and most are shaped like cylinder while some are like round triangles. They has holes drilled from both sides, and some has cutting marks on the surface. They are 2.3–4.4 cm in length, 1–1.5 cm in diameter (Fig. 181; Picture 426).

M10:61, it consists of 14 individual pieces varying in length. They are grayish-white with brown spots. They are cylinder-shaped and has holes drilled from both sides. They are 0.8–1.3 cm in length and 0.6–0.7 cm in diameter (Fig. 181; Picture 422).

M10:63, it consists of 69 individual pieces, of which one is badly damaged. They are cylinder-shaped and has holes drilled from both sides, and some has cambered string-cutting marks. They are 1.7–3.2 cm in length and 1.1–1.5 cm in diameter (Fig. 182; Picture 427).

M10:65, it consists of 114 individual pieces. They are cylinder-shaped and has holes drilled from both

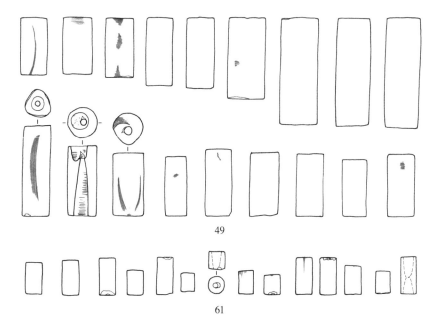

**Fig. 181.** Strings of jade tubes in tomb M10 (2/3)

sides, and some were cut apart after being drilled from both sides. They are 1.3–3.6 cm in length and 0.8–1.4 cm in diameter (Figs. 183, 184; Picture 428).

M10:97, it consists of 201 individual pieces. They varies in colors: white, yellow, green, brown, or mixed color. Some of brown ones may not be jade. Some of them has cambered string-cutting marks on the end or surface. The middle holes are mostly drilled from both sides, but some were cut apart after drilling from both sides, as if the holes are drilled from one side. They are 0.4–1.4 cm in length and 0.65–0.75 cm in diameter (Fig. 185; Picture 429).

**Tubes:** forty four pieces.

M10:36, it is cylinder-shaped. The wall of the hole drilled from both sides has been polished, and two ends tilt and are concave inward. It is 1.8 cm in length, 1.95 cm in diameter and 0.95 cm in hole diameter (Fig. 186; Picture 430).

M10:39, it is triangular-prism-shaped and has a hole drilled from both sides. There are two cambered string-cutting marks on the surface. It is 3.6 cm in length, 1.4 cm in diameter and 0.6 cm in hole diameter (Fig. 186; Picture 431).

M10:40, it is cylinder-shaped and has a hole drilled from both sides. It is 3.6 cm in length, 1.4 cm in diameter and 0.6 cm in hole diameter (Fig. 186;

Picture 431).

M10:41, with brown spots, it is cylinder-shaped, and has a hole drilled from both sides, with cutting marks on its surface. It is 1.8 cm in length, 1 cm in diameter and 0.5 cm in hole diameter (Fig. 186; Picture 433).

M10:51, it consists of two individual pieces. They are grayish-white, cylinder-shaped, with holes drilled from both sides. One piece has cambered string-cutting marks on its ends and surface. They are 2.75–2.85 cm in length, 1.6 cm in diameter and 0.5 cm in hole diameter (Fig. 186; Picture 432).

M10:52, it is cylinder-shaped and has a hole drilled from both sides, with step-shaped marks inside the hole. It is 1.5 cm in length, 2.1 cm in diameter and 1.1 cm in hole diameter (Fig. 186; Picture 434).

M10:54, with many yellowish brown spots, it is cylinder-shaped, with a hole drilled from both sides. Both of the ends has cambered string-cutting marks. It is 4 cm in length, 1.7 cm in diameter and 0.8–1.1 cm in hole diameter (Fig. 186; Picture 435).

M10:55, it is cylinder-shaped and has a hole drilled from both sides, with step-shaped marks remained inside the hole. It is 1.4 cm in length, 2 cm in diameter and 0.8–1.1 cm in hole diameter (Fig. 186; Picture 436).

M10:56, with brown spots, it is cylinder-shaped

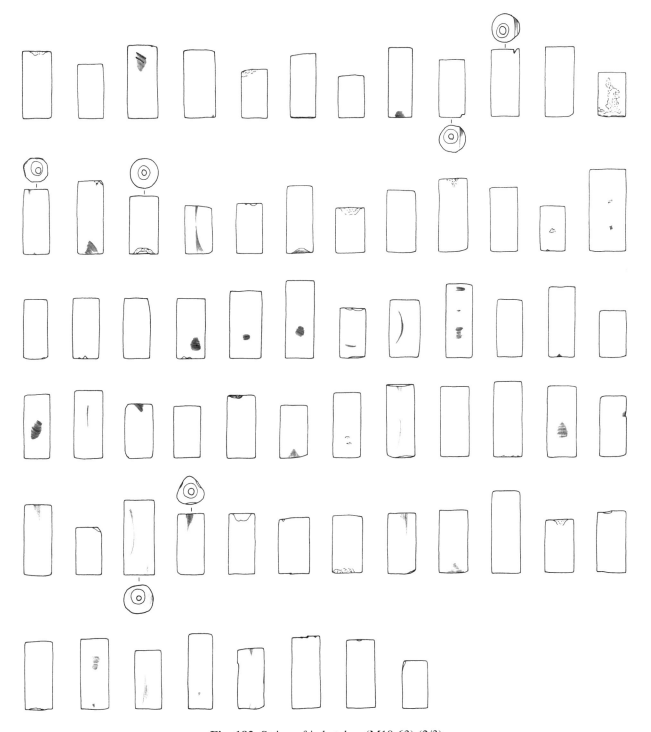

**Fig. 182.** String of jade tubes (M10:63) (2/3)

but not regular in shape, with a hole drilled from both sides. It is 3.8 cm in length, 1.6 cm in diameter and 0.6 cm in hole diameter (Fig. 186; Picture 435).

M10:57, with gray spots, it is cylinder-shaped, with a hole drilled from both sides. It is 3.6 cm in length, 1.25 m in diameter and 0.7 cm in hole diameter (Fig. 186; Picture 431).

M10:58, with gray spots, it is cylinder-shaped, with a hole drilled from both sides. It is 3.6 cm in length, 1.6 cm in diameter and 0.6 cm in hole diameter (Fig. 186; Picture 435).

M10:59, with red brown spots, it is triangular-prism-shaped, with a hole drilled from both sides. It is 2.4 cm in length, 1.1 cm in diameter and 0.6 cm in

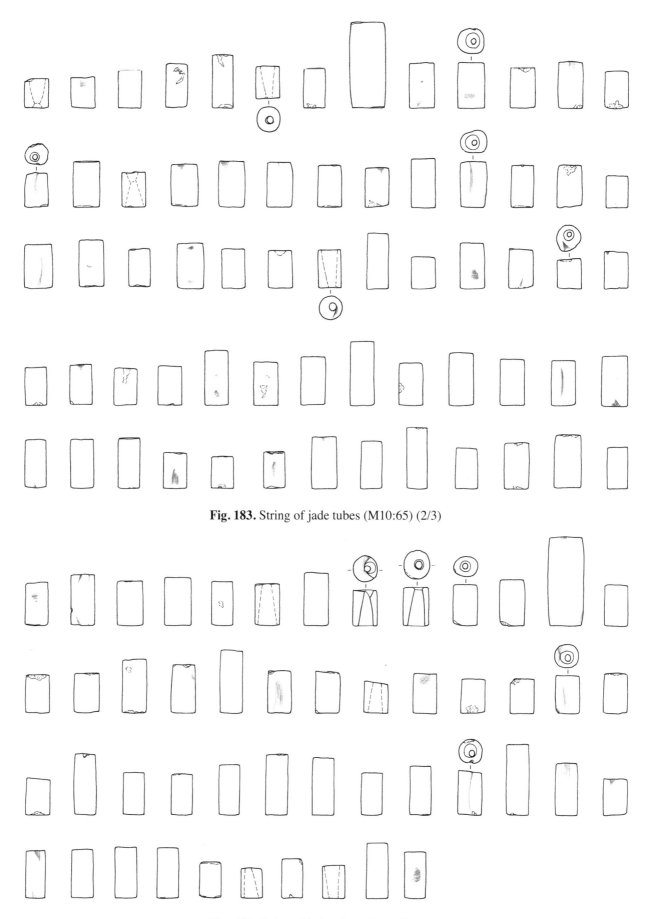

**Fig. 183.** String of jade tubes (M10:65) (2/3)

**Fig. 184.** String of jade tubes (M10:65) (2/3)

**Fig. 185.** String of jade tubes (M10:97) (2/3)

hole diameter (Fig. 186; Picture 433).

M10:60, with gray spots, it is cylinder-shaped, with a hole drilled from both sides. It is 2.4 cm in length, 1.1 cm in diameter and 0.55 cm in hole diameter (Fig. 186; Picture 431).

M10:62, it consists of 4 individual pieces, with gray spots, cylinder-shaped, with a hole drilled from both sides. They are 1.1–1.5 cm in length, 0.65–0.7 cm in diameter and 0.4 cm in hole diameter (Fig. 186; Picture 437).

M10:66, with brown spots, it is cylinder-shaped, with a hole drilled from both sides. It is 2.1 cm in length, 1 cm in diameter and 0.5 cm in hole diameter (Fig. 186; Picture 431).

M10:68, it is cylinder-shaped and has a round

hole drilled from both sides, with cutting marks on its surface and ends. It is 2.2 cm in length, 1.05 cm in diameter and 0.5 cm in hole diameter (Fig. 186; Picture 438).

M10:69, it is cylinder-shaped and has a hole drilled from both sides, with cutting marks on its surface. It is 2.8 cm in length, 1.1 cm in diameter and 0.6 cm in hole diameter (Fig. 186; Picture 438).

M10:71, it is cylinder-shaped and has a round hole drilled from both sides. It is 2.85 cm in length, 1.2 cm in diameter and 0.6 cm in hole diameter (Fig. 186; Picture 438).

M10:72, it is cylinder-shaped and has a hole drilled from both sides. It is 1.95 cm in length, 1.1 cm in diameter and 0.55 cm in hole diameter (Fig. 186;

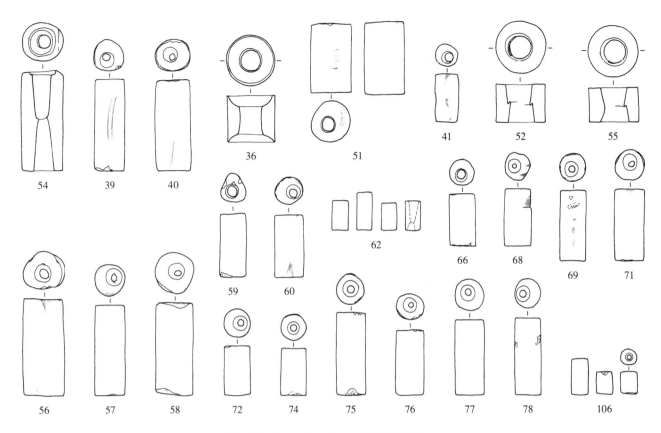

**Fig. 186.** Jade tubes in tomb M10 (2/3)

Picture 438).

M10:74, with caesious spots, it is cylinder-shaped, with a hole drilled from both sides. It is 1.8 cm in length, 1 cm in diameter and 0.5 cm in hole diameter (Fig. 186; Picture 432).

M10:75, it is in the shape of cylinder, with a hole drilled from both sides. It is 3.3 cm in length, 1.3 cm in diameter and 0.5 cm in hole diameter (Fig. 186; Picture 438).

M10:76, with gray spots, it is cylinder-shaped, with a hole drilled from both sides. It is 2.6 cm in length, 1.15 cm in diameter and 0.55 cm in hole diameter (Fig. 186; Picture 439).

M10:77, with red brown spots, it is cylinder-shaped, with a hole drilled from both sides. It is 3 cm in length, 1.2 cm in diameter and 0.5–0.6 cm in hole diameter (Fig. 186; Picture 439).

M10:78, with red brown spots, it is cylinder-shaped, with a hole drilled from both sides. It is 3 cm in length, 1.1 cm in diameter and 0.7 cm in hole diameter (Fig. 186; Picture 439).

M10:79, it is cylinder-shaped with a hole drilled from both sides. It is 2.8 cm in length, 1.2 cm in diameter and 0.45 cm in hole diameter (Fig. 187; Picture 439).

M10:80, it is cylinder-shaped and has a hole drilled from both sides, with cutting marks on its surface. It is 2.9 cm in length, 1.4 cm in diameter and 0.55 cm in hole diameter (Fig. 187; Picture 440).

M10:81, it is cylinder-shaped and has a hole drilled from both sides. It is 2.55 cm in length, 1.4 cm in diameter and 0.45 cm in hole diameter (Fig. 187; Picture 440).

M10:85, with gray spots, it is cylinder-shaped, with a hole drilled from both sides. It is 1.5 cm in length, 0.7 cm in diameter and 0.4 cm in hole diameter (Fig. 187; Picture 443).

M10:86, it is yellowish-brown, cylinder-shaped and has a hole drilled from both sides, with a hole drilled from the outer wall on one end. It is 3.2 cm in length, 1 cm in diameter and 0.55 cm in hole diameter (Fig. 187; Picture 440).

M10:87, it is cylinder-shaped and has a hole drilled from both sides, with a straight cutting mark on one end. It is 2.55 cm in length, 1.1 cm in diameter and

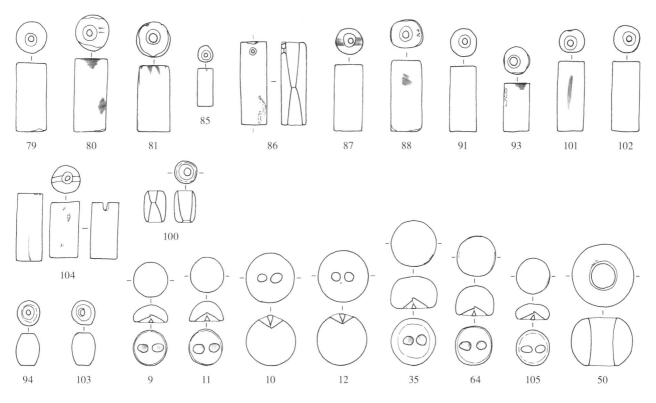

**Fig. 187.** Jade tubes and jade beads in tomb M10
9–12, 35, 50, 64, 94, 100, 103, 105. beads; others. tubes (2/3)

0.5 cm in hole diameter (Fig. 187; Picture 440).

M10:88, it is cylinder-shaped and has a hole drilled from both sides, with cutting marks on its surface. It is 2.7 cm in length, 1.2 cm in diameter and 0.5 cm in hole diameter (Fig. 187; Picture 441).

M10:91, it is yellow and white, cylinder-shaped, with a hole drilled from both sides. It is 2.55 cm in length, 1.1 cm in diameter and 0.5 cm in hole diameter (Fig. 187; Picture 440).

M10:93, with livid spots, it is cylinder-shaped, with a hole drilled from both sides. It is 1.9 cm in length, 1.1 cm in diameter and 0.5 cm in hole diameter (Fig. 187; Picture 433).

M10:101, it is brown, cylinder-shaped, and has a hole drilled from both sides, with cambered string-cutting marks on its surface. It is 2.8 cm in length, 1.1 cm in diameter and 0.5 cm in hole diameter (Fig. 187; Picture 433).

M10:102, it is cylinder-shaped with a hole drilled from both sides. It is 2.8 cm in length, 1.1 cm in diameter and 0.5 cm in hole diameter (Fig. 187; Picture 433).

M10:104, it consists of two individual pieces. They are cylinder-shaped with holes drilled from both sides. One piece has a notch on its end. They are 2.2, 2.7 cm in length and 1.1 cm in diameter (Fig. 187; Picture 442).

M10:106, it consists of three individual pieces, of which two were grayish-white. They are cylinder-shaped with holes drilled from both sides. They are 0.85–1.4 cm in length, 0.7 cm in diameter and 0.3 cm in hole diameter (Fig. 186; Picture 443).

**Beads:** twelve pieces.

M10:9, with brown spots, it is hemisphere-shaped, with a tunnel-shaped hole drilled on the plane. It is 1.45 cm in diameter and 0.65 cm in thickness (Fig. 187; Picture 447).

M10:10, it is sphere-shaped with a tunnel-shaped hole. It is 1.9 cm in diameter (Fig. 187; Picture 445).

M10:11, it is hemisphere-shaped, with a tunnel-shaped hole drilled on the plane. It is 1.3 cm in diameter and 0.75 cm in thickness (Fig. 187; Picture 447).

M10:12, it is sphere-shaped, with a tunnel-shaped

hole. It is 2 cm in diameter (Fig. 187; Picture 444).

M10:35, it is hemisphere-shaped, with a tunnel-shaped hole drilled on the plane. It is 1.9 cm in diameter and 1.7 cm in thickness (Fig. 187; Picture 449).

M10:50, with brown spots, it is waist-drum-shaped, with a large hole drilled in middle. It is 1.8 cm in length, 2.45 cm in diameter and 1.1 cm in thickness (Fig. 187; Picture 450).

M10:64, it is hemisphere-shaped, with a tunnel-shaped hole drilled on the plane. It is 1.7 cm in diameter and 1.2 cm in thickness (Fig. 187; Picture 449).

M10:94, it is waist-drum-shaped, with a hole drilled from both sides. It is 1.2 cm in length, 0.6 cm in diameter and 0.5 cm in hole diameter (Fig. 187; Picture 451).

M10:100, it consists of two individual pieces. With red brown spots, they are waist-drum-shaped, with holes drilled from both sides. They are 1.2 cm in length, 0.7 cm in diameter and 0.35–0.6 cm in hole diameter (Fig. 187; Picture 451).

M10:103, it is waist-drum-shaped and has a hole drilled from both sides. It is 1.2 cm in length, 0.55 cm in diameter and 0.35 cm in hole diameter (Fig. 187; Picture 451).

M10:105, it is hemisphere-shaped with a tunnel-shaped hole drilled on the plane. It is 1.3 cm in diameter and 0.6 cm in thickness (Fig. 187; Picture 446).

**Particles:** thirty two pieces.

M10:7, it consists of 3 individual pieces. They are oval in plane, with one side flat and the other convex. They are 0.8 cm in length, 0.35 cm in width and 0.3 cm in thickness (Fig. 188; Picture 454).

M10:95, it consists of 2 individual pieces. They are oval in plane, with one side flat and the other convex. They are 0.85–0.95 cm in length, 0.5–0.55 cm in width and 0.4 cm in thickness (Fig. 188; Picture 455).

M10:96, it consists of 12 individual pieces. They are oval in plane, with one side flat and the other convex. They are 0.75–0.8 cm in length, 0.35–0.5 cm in width and 0.3 cm in thickness (Fig. 188; Picture 456).

M10:98, it consists of 9 individual pieces. They are oval in plane, with one side flat and the other convex. They are 0.7–1 cm in length, 0.45–0.55 cm in width and 0.4 cm in thickness (Fig. 188; Picture 457).

M10:107, it consists of 6 individual pieces. They are oval in plane, with one side flat and the other convex. They are 0.8–0.9 cm in length, 0.5 cm in width and 0.3 cm in thickness (Fig. 188; Picture 458).

(2) Stone artifacts: two pieces.

Only stone *yue* axe.

M10:8, it is black brown, slightly square in plane. The top is slightly cambered; it has an cambered blade with its lower end wider than the upper. It has a hole drilled from both sides with spiral marks. It is 11.8 cm in height, 11.3 cm in top width, 12 cm in blade width, 3.3 cm in hole diameter and 1.3 cm in thickness (Fig. 189; Picture 448).

M10:13, it is black brown, slightly square in plane. It has a smooth and flat top end, and an cambered

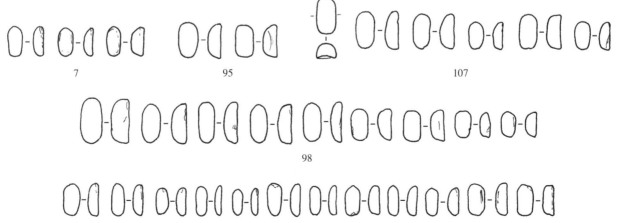

7          95                    107

98

96

**Fig. 188.** Jade particles in tomb M10 (1/1)

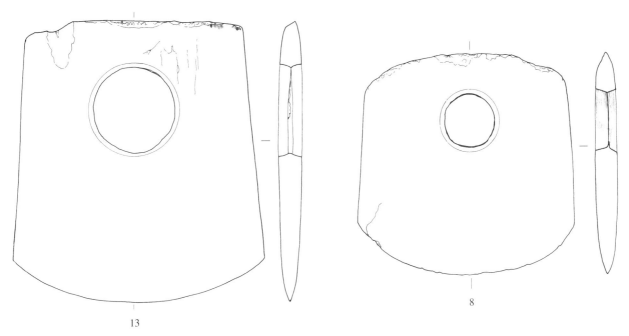

13                                    8

**Fig. 189.** Stone *yue* axe in tomb M10 (1/2)

blade with its lower end wider than the upper. It has a hole drilled from both sides with a step-shaped mark. It is 15 cm in height, 12 cm in top width, 13.8 cm in blade width, 5 cm in hole diameter and 1.2 cm in thickness (Fig. 189; Picture 453).

(3) Pottery vessels: four pieces.

***Ding* tripod:** one piece (M10:89). It is reddish-brown sand-tempered pottery. It is so broken that its shape could not be recognized.

***Dou:*** one piece (M10:82). It is clay pottery, with grayish-red body and black coating. Besides, it has a round lip and a straight wall with 3 belts of concave bow string patterns. The lower part of the slender handle is badly damaged and hard to be restored. It is 20.4 cm in opening diameter (Fig. 190; Picture 452).

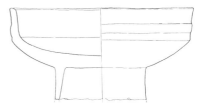

**Fig. 190.** Pottery *dou* (M10:82) (1/4)

**Ring-foot jar:** one piece (M10:84). It is reddish-brown sand-tempered pottery. It is so broken that its shape could not be recognized.

***Gang* vat:** one piece (M10:83). It is sand-tempered pottery. It has a red core, and its surface is covered with thick liquid which made it smooth and gray black. No patterns are on it. It is so broken that its shape could not be recognized.

# Section 11 Tomb M11

## 1. The Shape of the Tomb

The tomb M11 is located in the middle of the north line tombs, with tomb M14 to its west and, tomb M9 to its south, adjacent to square red earth on the east. It has its opening under the top soil and disturbed the enclosing gray earthen ditch, ash pit 97H1 and yellow-

earthen mound, and its southeastern corner was broken by tomb M7. It is a rectangle pit with vertical wall, with an orientation of 183°. The tomb pit is 3.15 m in length, 1.70 m in width and 1.58 m in width. The pit walls of the tomb are vertical, and the bottom is even. The tomb is filled with gray mottled earth. Skeleton inside the tomb had rotten away and left no remains

(Picture 459).

There is a rectangle area at the bottom of the tomb, covered by plank ashes, 2.80 m in length and 0.96 m in width, which should be the coffin's position. All of the artifacts were unearthed here, so the burial objects could be assumed to have been placed in the coffin.

The burial objects include jade artifacts, turquoise beads and pottery vessels. The pottery vessels are mainly located in the north of the tomb, 7 pieces in all. They are two pieces of *ding* tripods, one piece of *dou*, one piece of ring-foot jar, one piece of *gang* vat, one piece of *zeng* steamer and one piece of filter. The broken fragment of pottery *gang* vat were scattered in a large area, and were covered by the filter, ring-foot jar and *ding* tripod as well as a jade spindle whorl with a jade stick (M11:16) and a jade handle (M11:15). When the jade spindle whorl was unearthed, the stick pierced through the middle hole of the spindle whorl, pointing to the south (Picture 463). To the south of the pottery *gang* vat are 7 pieces of jade ornaments (M11:30) on the pottery *dou*, lying in order, shaped like bullets, pointing to the north.

The jade artifacts are located in the middle of the tomb. In addition to the scattered tubes, beads and petal-shaped jade ornaments, the main jade artifacts are stringed jade *huang* semi-circular pendant and bracelets (Picture 460). When unearthed, the jade *huang* semi-circular pendant (M11:54) is a little tilting with its arc facing the north. The surrounding 12 round pendants (M11:53-1–53-4, M11:55–62), according to the congeneric artifacts in the tomb M4, together with the jade *huang* semi-circular pendant, should have been of the same set, which is possibly the pectoral ornament of the tomb's occupant. To the west of the presumed pectoral ornament was an awl-shaped object, with its tail end facing north. The bracelets consist of nine pieces, of which four (M11:68–71) were overlapped in north–south direction (Picture 461). Between the bracelets and the jade *huang* semi-circular pendant is a cylindrical object, which, according to its patterns, is facing the south. Among the jade tubes and jade beads, there are three sets of strings (string of jade tubes M11:76, string of jade tubes M11:77 and string of beads

M11:78) that belonged to stringed ornaments. The unidentified ones are the scattered pedal-shaped jade ornaments (M11:81, 82) in the tomb, 75 in total, with similar shape but different sizes. These pedal-shaped jade ornaments have tunnel-shaped holes on their flat surface, so they might be the stitching ornaments of organic clothes.

In the south of the tomb, there are two sets of string of jade tubes (M11:95, 96) and one jade *huang* semi-circular pendant under two sets of string of jade tubes, another jade *huang* semi-circular pendant (M11:83) was overlaid on the string of jade tubes. Besides, another one jade *huang* semi-circular pendant (M11:94) laid between two sets of string of tubes (Picture 462), and to its south is a crown-shaped with the tenon facing east (M11:86), flanked by a pair of hemisphere-shaped beads (M11:87). In the southern end is a cylindrical object with cover (M11:89), which is the only one of this kind found in M11 in the north line of the tombs (Figs. 191, 192).

## 2. Burial Objects

The burial objects are numbered into 96 pieces (sets), 546 individual pieces, including jade artifacts, pottery vessels, and turquoise beads.

(1) Jade artifacts

There is 87 pieces (sets), 537 individual pieces, mostly white, including crown-shaped object, cylindrical object with cover, *huang* semi-circular pendant, round plaque, bracelet, awl-shaped object, spindle whorl and bullet-shaped ornaments, and so on.

**Crown-shaped object:** one piece (M11:86). With gray spots, it is flat and thin, presenting an upside-down trapezoid in plane. The middle of the upper end is concave with a point. Under the concave there is an oval hole. The bottom of the object has a flat tenon, with 5 holes drilled from both sides equidistantly. Both sides are carved with the sacred animal motif in intaglio technique. The sacred animal motif has round double-circled eyes, oval eyepits, wide nose wings, and wide mouth with two pairs of tusks. The frames are carved all around the whole object. The main motifs are accompanied by rolling cloud patterns. It is 3.4 cm in height, 6.35 cm in width, 0.32 cm in

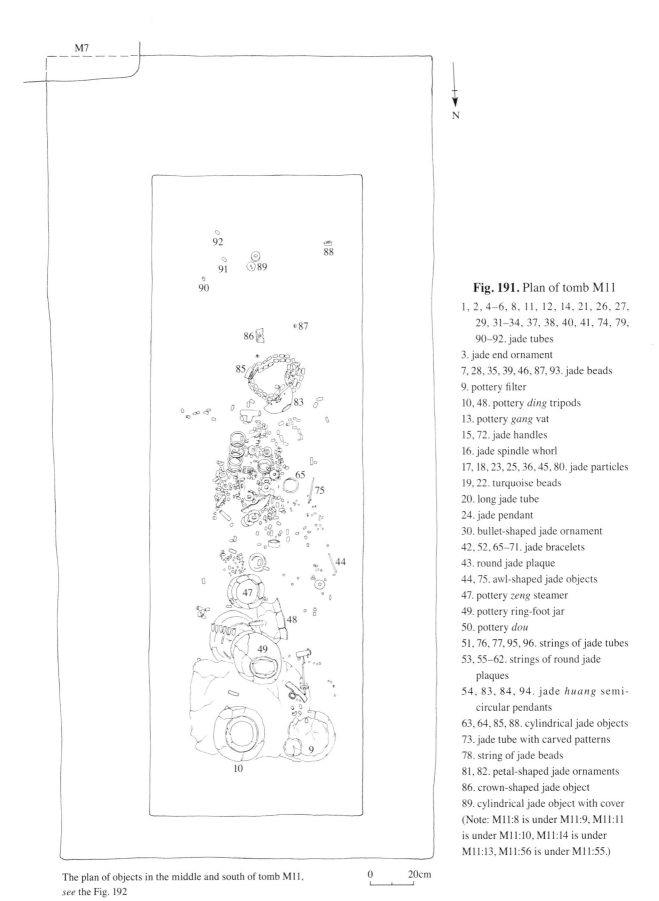

**Fig. 191.** Plan of tomb M11

1, 2, 4–6, 8, 11, 12, 14, 21, 26, 27, 29, 31–34, 37, 38, 40, 41, 74, 79, 90–92. jade tubes

3. jade end ornament

7, 28, 35, 39, 46, 87, 93. jade beads

9. pottery filter

10, 48. pottery *ding* tripods

13. pottery *gang* vat

15, 72. jade handles

16. jade spindle whorl

17, 18, 23, 25, 36, 45, 80. jade particles

19, 22. turquoise beads

20. long jade tube

24. jade pendant

30. bullet-shaped jade ornament

42, 52, 65–71. jade bracelets

43. round jade plaque

44, 75. awl-shaped jade objects

47. pottery *zeng* steamer

49. pottery ring-foot jar

50. pottery *dou*

51, 76, 77, 95, 96. strings of jade tubes

53, 55–62. strings of round jade plaques

54, 83, 84, 94. jade *huang* semi-circular pendants

63, 64, 85, 88. cylindrical jade objects

73. jade tube with carved patterns

78. string of jade beads

81, 82. petal-shaped jade ornaments

86. crown-shaped jade object

89. cylindrical jade object with cover
(Note: M11:8 is under M11:9, M11:11 is under M11:10, M11:14 is under M11:13, M11:56 is under M11:55.)

The plan of objects in the middle and south of tomb M11, *see* the Fig. 192

0        20cm

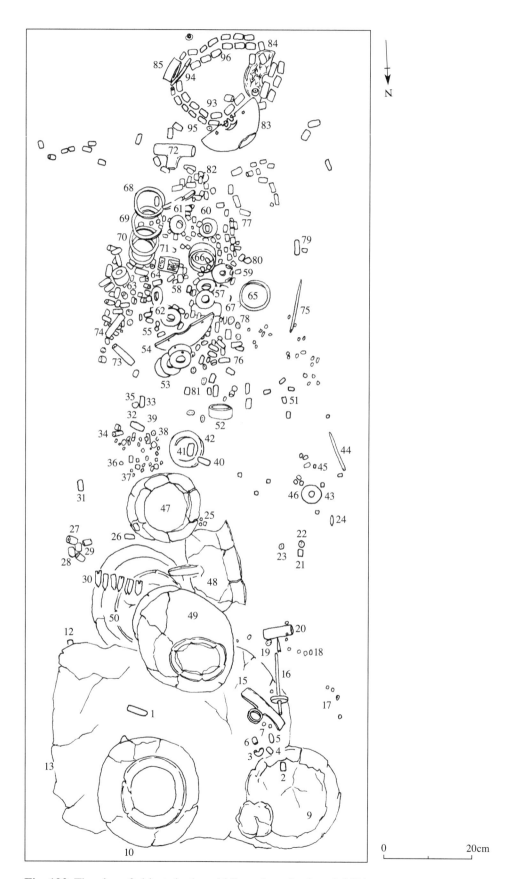

**Fig. 192.** The plan of objects in the middle and south of tomb M11

thickness (Fig. 193; Pictures 466, 467).

**Cylindrical object with cover:** one set (M11:89). It comprises a cover and a cylindrical object.

M11:89-1, the cover is shaped like a flat pie. One side is convex while the other is flat and even. A tunnel-shaped hole is drilled on the plane, and out-inside cambered cutting marks remained on it. It is 4 cm in diameter, 1.1 cm in thickness (Fig. 194; Picture 468).

M11:89-2, the cylindrical object is cylinder-shaped with a hole drilled from both sides and the hole was polished. It is 3.6 cm in height, 3.9 cm in diameter, and 0.8 cm in hole diameter (Fig. 194; Picture 469).

***Huang* semi-circular pendants:** four pieces.

M11:54, with gray flocs, it is in half-*bi* shape. The middle of the upper end is concave, with a hole drilled from both sides on both sides. Its body is comparatively thick, while the bottom is a bit thin. It is 6.3 cm in height, 15.6 cm in width, and 0.6 cm in thickness (Fig. 194; Picture 472).

M11:83, it is in half-*bi* shape. The object was flat and thin. The middle of the upper end is concave, with a point in the center. Under the point there is a crosswise crescent-shaped hollowed-out hole. On each side of the concave there is a hole drilled from both sides, and on the edge of each side there are two

holes drilled from both sides, one on the upper and the other lower. There is a crosswise cutting concave on the surface, while a vertical arc cutting mark on the other side, both having been polished. It is 7.45 cm in height, 15.8 cm in width, 0.4 cm in thickness (Fig. 194; Picture 465).

M11:84, it is in half-*bi* shape. There is a hole on both sides of the concave notch on the upper end respectively. The sacred animal motifs are carved by openwork and intaglio techniques on both sides. The eyes are chestnut-shaped with the canthi curling upward. Eyeballs are represented by circular holes. Between the eyes, cambered crosses or triangular hollowed-out holes are used to represent the bridge and wings of nose. A wide mouth is outlined by arc-shaped holes and intaglio, with the corners stretching upward. The rest parts are carved with irregular holes and intaglioed lines. The pattern could be interpreted as two opposite dragons. The hollowed-out holes are all formed by solid drilling first and expanded by string-cutting later. The object is even and thin, and the cambered edge in the bottom is thinner. And the bottom, though with slight defect, has been polished. It is 4.8 cm in height, 12.7 cm in width (Fig. 195; Picture 464).

M11:94, with some gray spots, it is bridge-shaped,

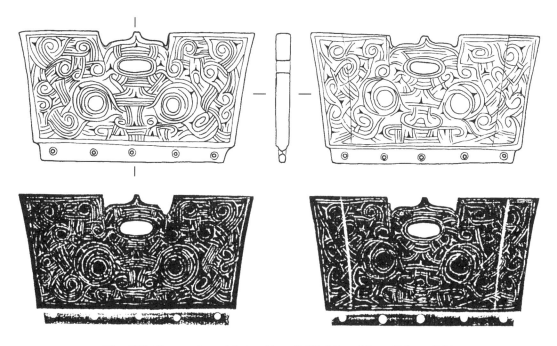

**Fig. 193.** Crown-shaped jade object (M11:86) and its rubbings (1/1)

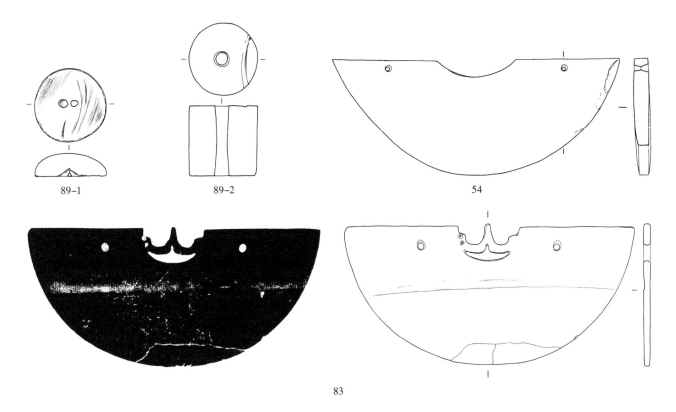

**Fig. 194.** Cylindrical jade object with cover and jade *huang* semi-circular pendants in tomb M11
54, 83. *huang* semi-circular pendants; 89-1. the cover of the cylindrical object; 89-2. cylindrical object (1/2)

and the middle of the object is a bit thicker. Two small holes are drilled from both sides on both top ends. Four dragon head motifs are curved on the edge of cambered bottom by bas-relief and intaglio carving techniques, which point to the same direction and are equidistant from each other vertically. The dragon heads motif has a pair of short horns, convex round eyes, rhombus-shaped nose and wide mouth. It is 2.9 cm in height, 8 cm in width (Fig. 196; Pictures 470, 471).

**String of round plaques:** with 12 individual pieces as one set, they are basically shaped in round pie and looked like small-sized jade *bi*. Holes are drilled in the middle and the wall of the hole is slant. A small round hole is drilled from both sides on the outer edge of the object.

M11:53-1, there are out-inside cambered string-cutting marks on the surface. It is 4.6 cm in diameter, 1.6 cm in hole diameter and 0.4 cm in thickness (Fig. 197; Picture 473).

M11:53-2, the cross section is in the shape of trapezoid. The wall of the hole is slant and with spiral marks. There are cambered string-cutting marks on the surface. It is 4.4 cm in diameter, 1.8 cm in hole diameter, and 0.4 cm in thickness (Fig. 197; Picture 474).

M11:53-3, there are cambered string-cutting marks on the surface. It is 4.4 cm in diameter, 1.7 cm in hole diameter, 0.4 cm in thickness (Fig. 197; Picture 475).

M11:53-4, there are out-inside cambered string-cutting marks on the surface. It is 4.4 cm in diameter, 1.8 cm in hole diameter and 0.3 cm in thickness (Fig. 197; Picture 476).

M11:55, there are cambered string-cutting marks on the surface. It is 4.4 cm in diameter, 1.6 cm in hole diameter and 0.4 cm in thickness (Fig. 197; Pictures 478, 479).

M11:56, there are cambered string-cutting marks on the surface. It is 4.5 cm in diameter, 2 cm in hole diameter and 0.4 cm in thickness (Fig. 197; Picture 477).

M11:57, it is broken into two pieces when unearthed.

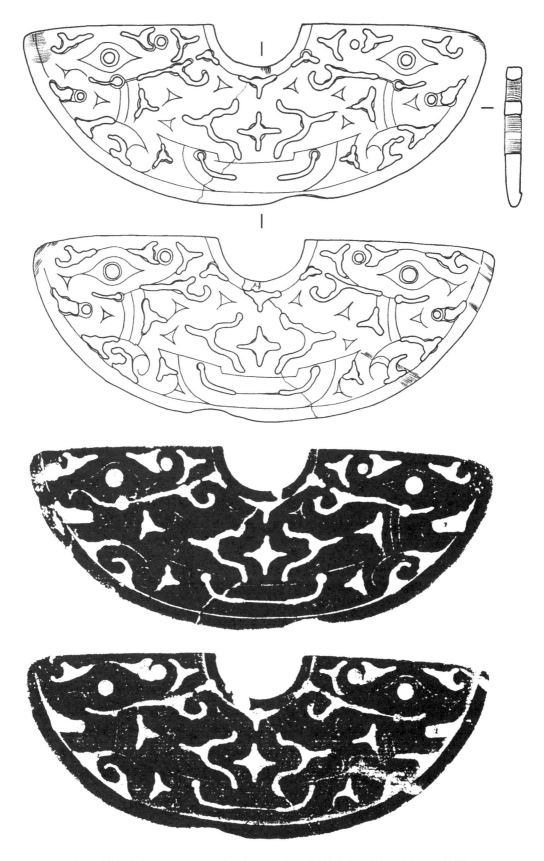

**Fig. 195.** Jade *huang* semi-circular pendant (M11:84) and its rubbings (1/1)

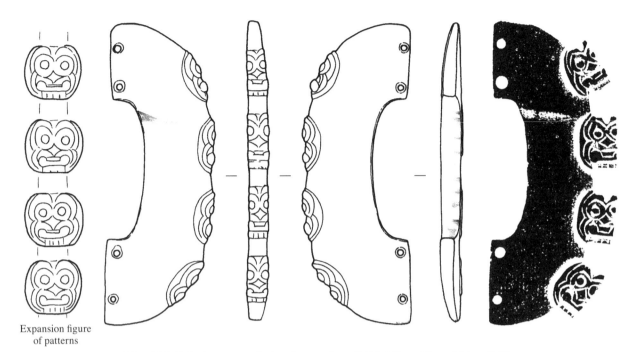

Expansion figure
of patterns

**Fig. 196.** Jade *huang* semi-circular pendant (M11:94) and its rubbing (1/1)

It is 4.15 cm in diameter, 1.6 cm in hole diameter and 0.4 cm in thickness (Fig. 197; Picture 480).

M11:58, the middle hole has step-shaped marks. The outer edge has a small round hole drilled from both sides. There are cambered string-cutting marks on the surface and cutting mark on the outer side. It is 4.5 cm in diameter, 1.6 cm in hole diameter and 0.4 cm in thickness (Fig. 197; Picture 481).

M11:59, the hole is drilled from one side, with spiral marks remained on the wall of the hole. There are three equidistant bas-relief convexities on the edge, which are the dragon head motifs in the same direction. The body is uneven in thickness, with cambered string-cutting marks remained on it. It is 4.7 cm in diameter, 1.1–1.3 cm in hole diameter, and 0.5–0.9 cm in thickness (Fig. 198; Pictures 482, 483).

M11:60, there are cambered string-cutting marks on the surface. It is 4.4 cm in diameter, 2 cm in hole diameter and 0.35 cm in thickness (Fig. 197; Picture 485).

M11:61, the surface is uneven with arc and linear cutting marks on it. It is 4.4 cm in diameter, 1.9 cm in hole diameter and 0.35 cm in thickness (Fig. 197; Picture 486).

M11:62, the hole in the middle has step-shaped

marks, and cambered string-cutting marks on the surface. It is 4.4 cm in diameter, 1.8 cm in hole diameter and 0.35 cm in thickness (Fig. 197; Picture 484).

Most of the round plaques above has holes presenting the feature of drilling from one side. In fact, it was made in such a way: at first holes were drilled from both sides on the cylindrical-shaped objects, and then the cylindrical-shaped objects were cut horizontally. The five round plaques in Fig. 197 (M11:53-1, 53-3, 53-4, 55, 56) were made by cutting the same piece of object. In addition, the M11:60, 61, 53–2 in Fig. 197 were made in the same way.

**Round plaque:** one piece.

M11:43, it is broken into three pieces when unearthed. It is pie-shaped with a hole drilled from one side. The surface is uneven with out-inside cambered string-cutting marks. It is 4.2 cm in diameter, 1.2 cm in hole diameter and 0.3 cm in thickness (Fig. 197; Picture 487).

**Bracelets:** nine pieces.

M11:42, with brown spots, it is annular-shaped, with a round outer wall and an convex inner wall. It is 2.1 cm in height, 8.2 cm in diameter, and 5.9 cm in hole diameter (Fig. 199; Picture 490).

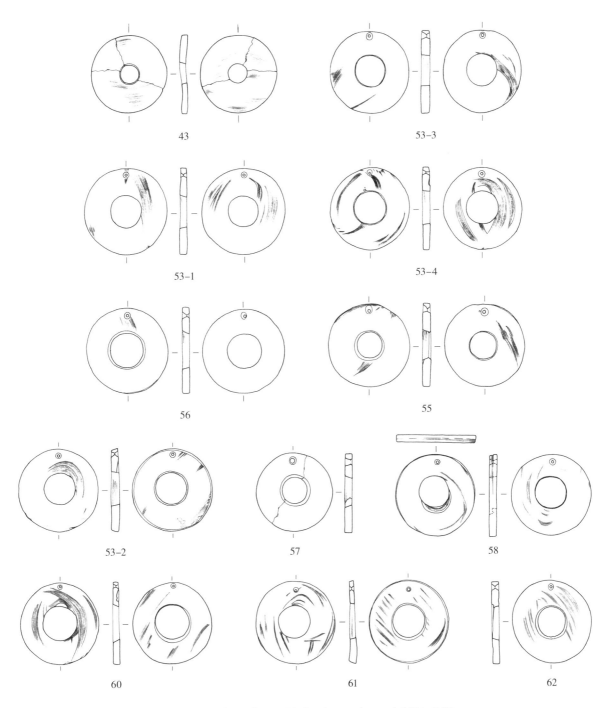

43

53-3

53-1

53-4

56

55

53-2

57

58

60

61

62

**Fig. 197.** String of round jade plaques in tomb M11 (1/2)

M11:52, it is truncated cone-shaped with a hole in the middle. The outer wall is inclined straight and the inner wall is slightly cambered. It is 1.7 cm in height, 5.3–5.8 cm in diameter, 4.7 cm in hole diameter (Fig. 199; Picture 488).

M11:65, with caesious spots, it is annular-shaped, with convex outer wall. It is 1.2 cm in height, 6.9 cm in diameter, and 5.7 cm in hole diameter (Fig. 199;

Picture 491).

M11:66, it is wide annular-shaped, with a round outer wall and a slightly convex inner wall. It is 3.3 cm in height, 6.9 cm in diameter, and 5.7 cm in hole diameter (Fig. 199; Picture 489).

M11:67, with gray spots, it is cylinder-shaped. The outer wall is slightly concave and the inner wall is convex. It is 3.7 cm in height, 6.6 cm in diameter, and

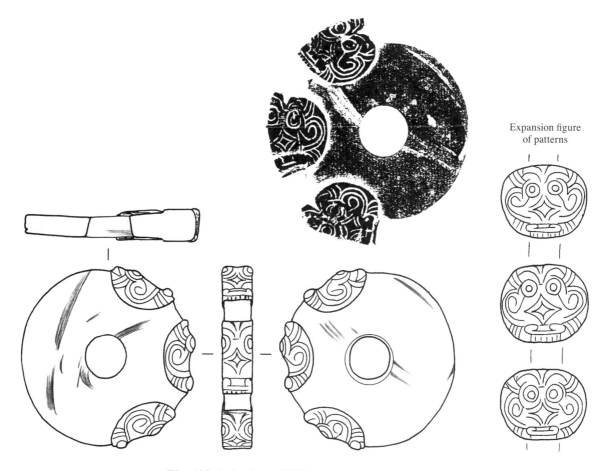

**Fig. 198.** Jade plaque (M11:59) and its rubbing (1/1)

5.7 cm in hole diameter (Fig. 199; Picture 492).

M11:68, with dark green and reddish-brown spots, it is wide ring-shaped. The inner wall is straight and the outer wall is carved with a circle of parallel oblique ridge, that is twisted thread pattern. This pattern is the only one found in Liangzhu culture jade bracelets. It is 2.3 cm in height, 6.5 cm in diameter, and 5.7 cm in hole diameter (Fig. 199; Picture 493) [1].

M11:69, it is annular-shaped. The outer wall is round and the inner wall is slightly convex. It is 1 cm in height, 7.25 cm in diameter, and 5.6 cm in hole diameter (Fig. 199; Picture 494).

M11:70, it is caesious and annular-shaped. The outer wall is round and the inner wall is slightly convex. It is 1.3 cm in height, 6.85 cm in diameter, and 5.7 cm in hole diameter (Fig. 199; Picture 495).

M11:71, it is annular-shaped. The outer and inner walls are convex. The shape is irregular. It is1.4 cm in height, 6.5 cm in diameter, and 5.8 cm in hole diameter (Fig. 199; Picture 496).

**Cylindrical objects:** four pieces.

M11:63, with gray spots, it is cylinder-shaped. There is a hole drilled from both sides in the middle with step-shaped marks left. It is 2.6 cm in height, 4.6 cm in diameter, and 1.5 cm in hole diameter (Fig. 200; Picture 497).

M11:64, it is cylinder-shaped with 3 convexities on the surface, each convexity is carved with the sacred animal motif which differed slightly from each other by intaglio and bas-relief carving technique. The middle of upper end of the motif is carved with three belts of feather patterns. The double-circled round eyes are slightly convex, the eyepits are oval. The nose is carved in intaglio between the eyes. The wing of a nose is wide and the mouth is flat and wide. There are

[1] This jade bracelet is displayed in Shanghai Museum. The artifact chart and pictures are provided by Shanghai Museum.

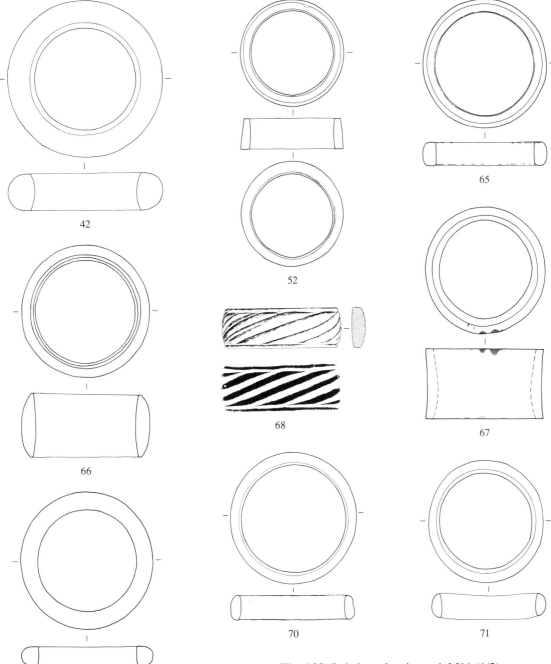

**Fig. 199.** Jade bracelets in tomb M11 (1/2)

two tusks sticking upward in the middle of the mouth and two tusks sticking downward in the outer side. The intaglioed lines and rolling cloud patterns are carved in intaglio around the main patterns as ground-tint. Both ends has cambered string-cutting marks. It is 3.3 cm in height, 5 cm in diameter, 1.4 cm in hole diameter (Fig. 201; Picture 498).

M11:85, it is cylinder-shaped with a hole in the middle. It is 2.2 cm in height, 4.1 cm in diameter, and

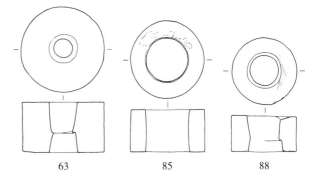

**Fig. 200.** Cylindrical jade objects in tomb M11 (1/2)

C: Expansion figure of patterns

B: Expansion figure of patterns

A

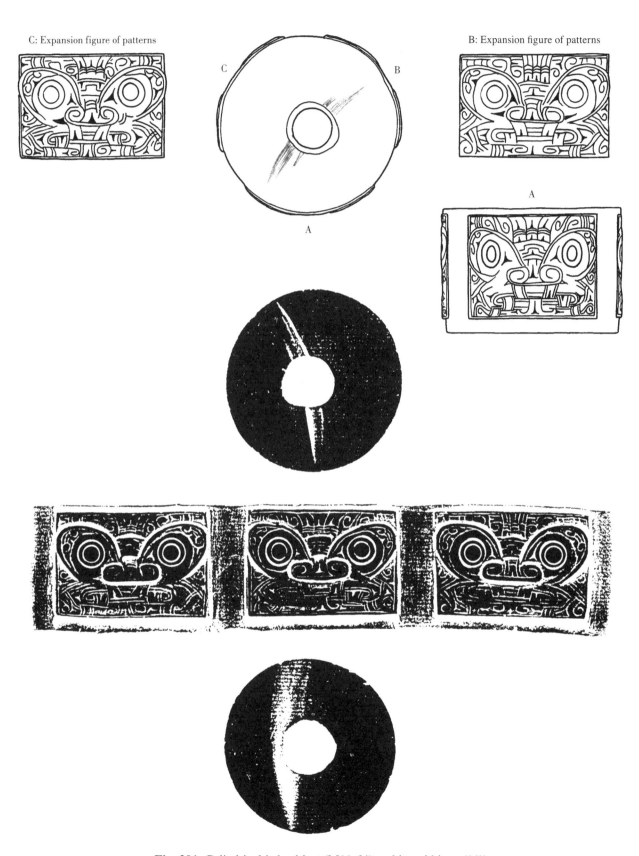

**Fig. 201.** Cylindrical jade object (M11:64) and its rubbings (1/1)

2.25 cm in hole diameter (Fig. 200; Picture 499).

M11:88, with gray spots, it is cylinder-shaped. There is a hole drilled from both sides in the middle, which, although polished, is left with step-shaped marks. One end has cambered string-cutting marks. It is 1.9 cm in height, 3.6 cm in diameter, and 1.9 cm in hole diameter (Fig. 200; Picture 500)

**Awl-shaped objects:** two pieces.

M11:44, strip-shaped, it is broken into two pieces when excavated. One end has a small hole drilled from both sides, and the other end is flat. It is 8.8 cm in length, 0.55 cm in diameter (Fig. 202 Picture 501).

M11:75, strip-shaped, it is broken into two pieces when excavated. One end is pointed, and the other end has a small hole drilled from both sides. It is 11.5 cm in length, 0.5 cm in diameter (Fig. 202; Picture 501).

**Long tube:** one piece (M11:20). It is cylinder-shaped with a hole drilled from both sides. It is 6.7 cm in length, 2.15 cm in diameter and 0.8 cm in hole diameter (Fig. 202; Picture 502).

**End ornament:** one piece (M11:3). It is hemispherical. One end is convex, the other end is flat, with a straight notch. Both sides of the notch looked like trumpet, with cutting marks left. The hole in the middle is not thoroughly drilled. It is 2.6 cm in diameter, and 1.6 cm in thickness (Fig. 202; Pictures 519, 520).

**Handles:** two pieces.

M11:15, with brown spots, it is flat and strip-shaped. The top is connected with a ring, and the inner and outer walls of the ring are concave, with a hole drilled from both sides. The handle's top is concave, with the two corners stretching upward; the bottom is flat, with a shallow groove running through the middle. It is 4.5 cm in height, 11.7 cm in width (Fig. 203; Picture 504).

M11:72, with brown spots, it presents a " 凸 " shape by side-view. The transverse part is slightly concave, and the fracture surface is round; the protruding part is carved with a crosswise shallow groove, in which are several oval mortises made by solid drilling. It is 5.2 cm in height, 8.7 cm in width (Fig. 204; Pictures 503, 505).

**Spindle whorl:** one piece (M11:16). It comprised

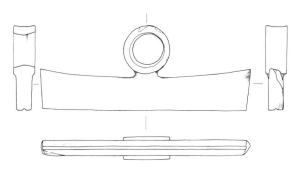

**Fig. 203.** Jade handle (M11:15) (1/2)

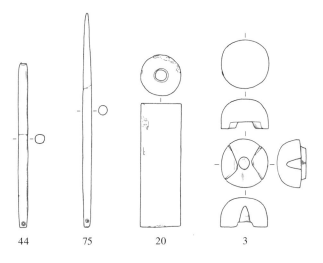

**Fig. 202.** Jade end ornament, long jade tube and awl-shaped jade objects in tomb M11

3. end ornament; 20. long tube; 44, 75. awl-shaped objects (1/2)

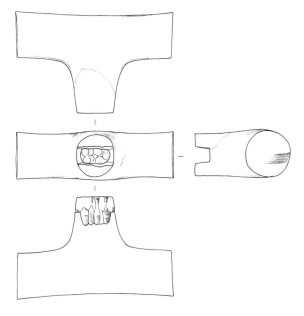

**Fig. 204.** Jade handle (M11:72) (1/2)

of a spindle whorl and a stick. The spindle whorl is white, and the pole is blue. The spindle whorl is circular pie-shaped, and its cross section presents trapezoid, with a polished hole drilled from both sides. The pole is strip-shaped, of which, the top end is pointed with a small hole drilled from both sides, and the bottom was left with marks of drilling from both side. It is 4.3 cm in diameter, 0.6 cm in hole diameter, 0.9 cm in thickness and the pole was 16.4 cm in length (Fig. 205; Picture 506).

**Bullet-shaped ornament:** one set. It comprises 7 individual pieces in the same size (M11:30). When unearthed, the seven pieces are juxtaposed, with their pointed ends facing north. They looked like bullets, one end being tapered and pointed and the other end being hollowed with a crosswide groove. Spiral marks are left on the wall of the hole in the middle. It is 3.1 cm in length, 1.1 cm in diameter and 0.6 cm in hole diameter (Fig. 206; Picture 507).

**Carved tubes:** two pieces.

M11:73-1, it is shaped in triangular prism with a hole drilled in the middle. One end is cut off, left with cambered string-cutting marks. The surface is carved with a circle of lines, and there are 4 protruding round eyes, with single-circle round eye, straight line carved in intaglio between eyes and a circle of ridges carved above the eyes. It is 1.1 cm in height, 1.5 cm in diameter (Fig. 205; Picture 508).

M11:73-2, it is shaped in triangular prism with a hole drilled in the middle. One end was cut off, left with cambered string-cutting marks. The surface is similar to that of the previous one. It is 1.2 cm in height, 1.4 cm in diameter (Fig. 205; Picture 509).

The two curved tubes were cut apart from one piece of object, judging from

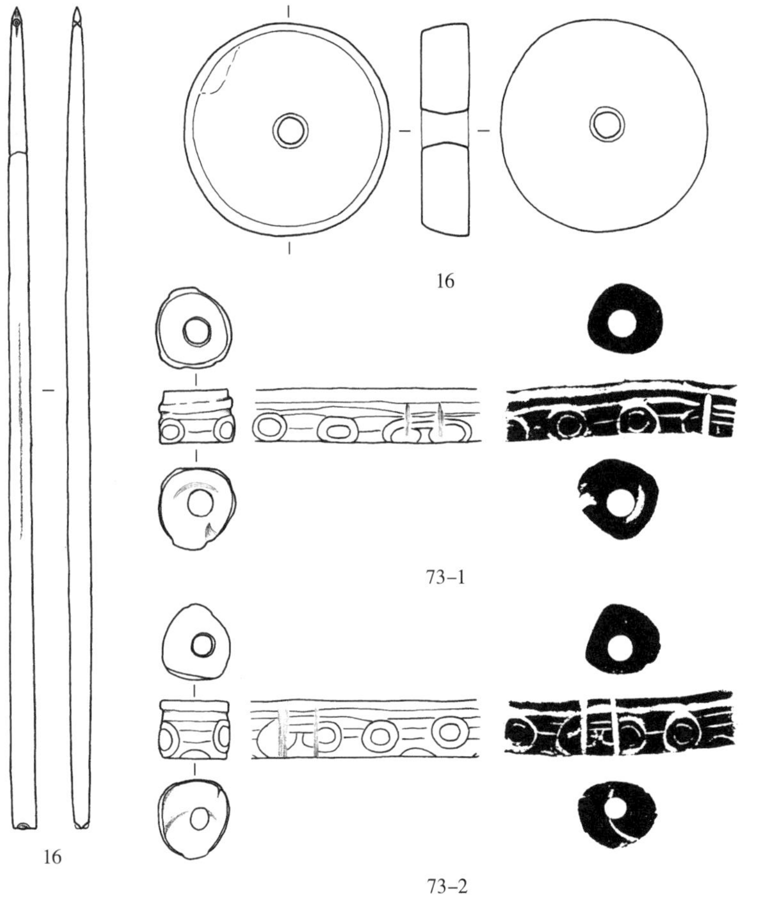

**Fig. 205.** Jade spindle whorl and jade tubes with carved patterns in tomb M11

16. spindle whorl and pole; 73-1, 73-2. carved tubes

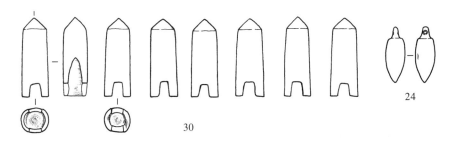

**Fig. 206.** Jade pendant and bullet-shaped jade ornaments in tomb M11

24. pendant; 30. bullet-shaped ornaments (2/3)

the shape and patterns, but they could not be connected straightly, possibly because the middle part is lost.

**Pendant:** one piece (M11:24). It is in the shape of olive, one end being sharp and the other end having a small tenon with a hole drilled from both sides. It is 2.25 cm in length (Fig. 206; Picture 510).

**Strings of tubes:** five sets, totaling 253 individual pieces.

M11:51, it consists of five individual pieces, they are cylinder-shaped with holes drilled from both sides. They are 1.25 cm in length, 0.9 cm in diameter and 0.4 cm in hole diameter (Fig. 209).

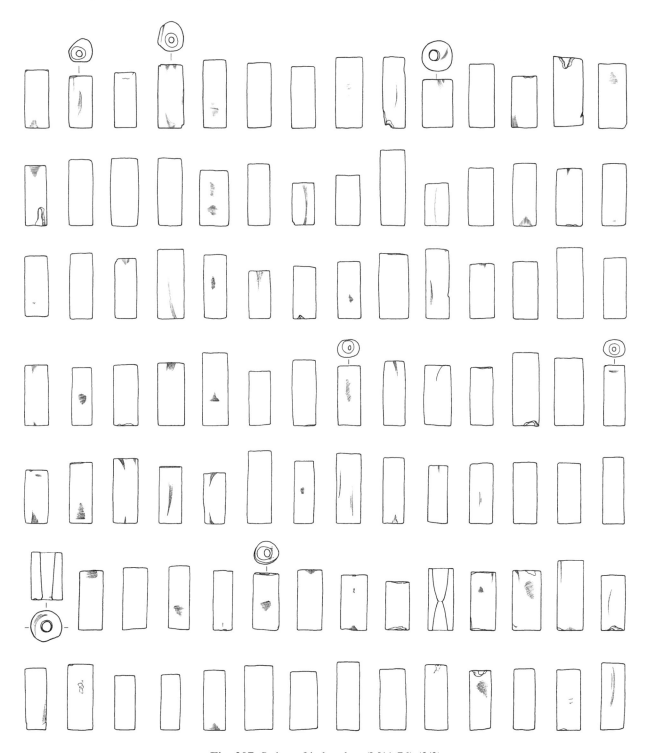

**Fig. 207.** String of jade tubes (M11:76) (2/3)

M11:76, it consists of 98 individual pieces, of which some has gray spots. They are cylinder-shaped with holes drilled from both sides. Parts of the tubes are left with cambered string-cutting marks on the surface and the end. They are 1.7–3 cm in length, 0.9–1.2 cm in diameter and 0.3–0.5 cm in hole diameter (Fig. 207; Picture 511).

M11:77, it consists of 110 individual pieces, with caesious and brown spots. They are cylinder-shaped, most of which has holes drilled from both sides, and a few were cut apart after drilling, thus presenting holes drilled from one side. Part of the tubes are left with cambered string-cutting marks on the surface and the end. They are 0.75–2 cm in length, 0.7–1.1 cm in

diameter and 0.3–0.6 cm in hole diameter (Fig. 208; Picture 512).

M11:95, it consists of 23 individual pieces, of which some has gray spots. They are cylinder-shaped, most of which has holes drilled from both sides, and a few were cut apart after drilling, thus presenting holes drilled from one side. Parts of the tubes are left with cambered cutting marks on the surface and the end. They are 2.2–2.5 cm in length, 1–1.4 cm in diameter and 0.4–0.6 cm in hole diameter (Fig. 209; Picture 513).

M11:96, it consists of 17 individual pieces. They are cylinder-shaped, most of which has holes drilled from both sides, and a few were cut apart after drilling,

**Fig. 208.** String of jade tubes (M11:77) (2/3)

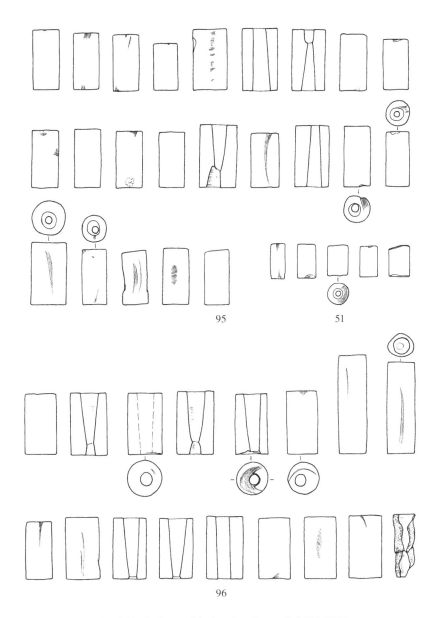

**Fig. 209.** Strings of jade tubes in tomb M11 (2/3)

thus presenting holes drilled from one side. Parts of the tubes are left with cambered string-cutting marks on the surface and the end. They are 2.4–3.9 cm in length, 1.1–1.3 cm in diameter and 0.5–0.8 cm in hole diameter (Fig. 209; Picture 514).

**String of beads:** one set (M11:78). It consisted of 34 individual pieces, of which some had gray spots. They are waist-drum-shaped, with holes drilled from both sides or drilled from one direction. Parts of the beads are left with cambered string-cutting marks on the end. They are 0.3–0.6 cm in diameter (Fig. 210; Picture 515).

**Petal-shaped ornaments:** seventy five pieces.

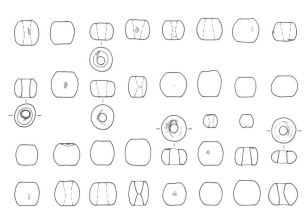

**Fig. 210.** String of jade beads (M11:78) (1/1)

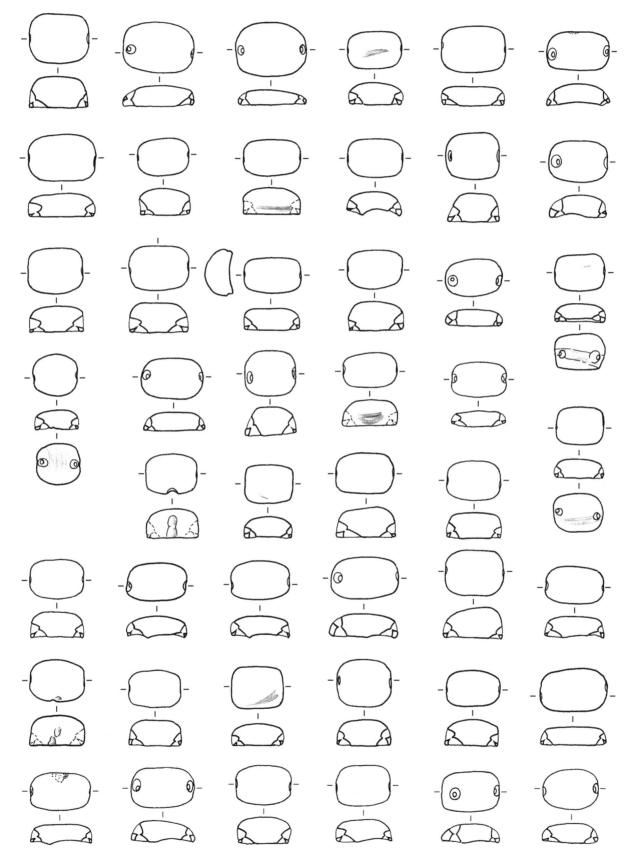

**Fig. 211.** Petal-shaped jade ornaments (M11:81) (1/1)

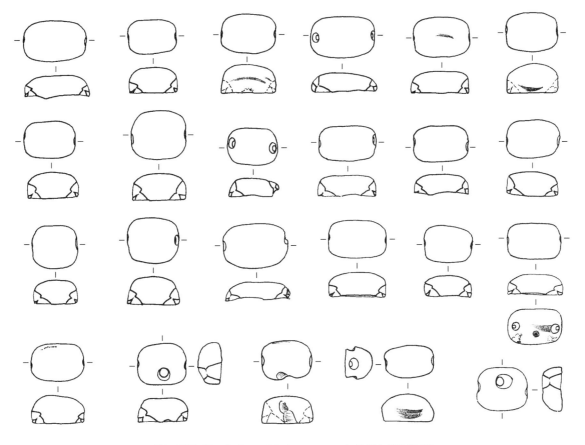

**Fig. 212.** Petal-shaped jade ornaments (M11:81) (1/1)

M11:81, this number contains 69 individual pieces. With brown spots, they are oval in shape, one side being flat and the other side being convex. Both ends are respectively drilled with one hole. Parts of the surfaces are left with cambered string-cutting marks. They are 1.6–1.75 cm in length, 0.95–1.3 cm in width and 0.5–0.8 cm in thickness (Figs. 211, 212; Picture 516).

M11:82, this number contains 6 individual pieces. With brown spots, they are oval or rectangle in shape; both ends are drilled with tunnel-shaped holes, and three pieces were drilled with tunnel-shaped holes in the plane. They are 2.2–2.5 cm in length, 1.4–1.55 cm in width and 0.5 cm in thickness (Fig. 213; Pictures 517, 518).

**Tubes:** twenty eight pieces.

M11:1, with grayish-green spots, it is shaped in triangular prism. There is a hole drilled from both sides, and cambered string-cutting marks are left on the surface. It is 4.4 cm in length, 1.2 cm in diameter and 0.6 cm in hole diameter (Fig. 214; Picture 521).

M11:2, it is cylinder-shaped with a hole drilled from both sides. Cambered string-cutting marks were left on the surface of the end. It is 1.4 cm in length, 1.4 cm in diameter and 0.8 cm in hole diameter (Fig. 214; Picture 522).

M11:4, it is cylinder-shaped with a hole drilled from both sides. It is 1.7 cm in length, 0.8 cm in diameter and 0.4 cm in hole diameter (Fig. 214; Picture 522).

M11:5, it is cylinder-shaped with a hole drilled from both sides. It is 1.7 cm in length, 1 cm in diameter and 0.45 cm in hole diameter (Fig. 214; Picture 522).

M11:6, it is cylinder-shaped with a hole drilled from both sides. It is 0.9 cm in length, 0.8 cm in diameter and 0.3 cm in hole diameter (Fig. 214; Picture 522).

M11:8, it is cylinder-shaped, and was cut apart after the hole drilled from both sides. The fracture surface is left with cambered string-cutting marks, and the surface has oblique cutting marks. It is 1.9 cm in length, 1.2 cm in diameter and 0.6 cm in hole diameter (Fig. 214; Picture 522).

M11:11, it is cylinder-shaped with a hole drilled

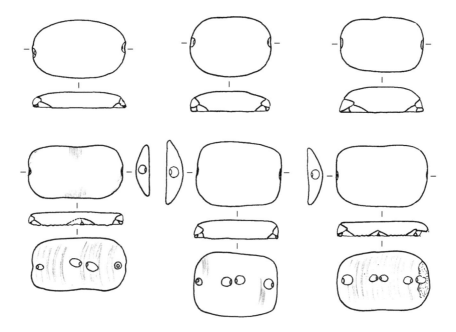

**Fig. 213.** Petal-shaped jade ornaments (M11:82) (1/1)

from both sides. It is 1.6 cm in length, 1.7 cm in diameter and the 0.9 cm in hole diameter (Fig. 214; Picture 523).

M11:12, with grayish-brown spots, it is cylinder-shaped with a hole drilled from both sides. Cambered string-cutting marks are left on the surface. It is 2.5 cm in length, 0.9 cm in diameter and 0.6 cm in hole diameter (Fig. 214; Picture 522).

M11:14, it is cylinder-shaped with a hole drilled from both sides. It is 2.2 cm in length, 1 cm in diameter and 0.5 cm in hole diameter (Fig. 214; Picture 522).

M11:21, it is cylinder-shaped with a hole drilled from both sides. One end has a slot. It is 1.4 cm in length, 0.9 cm in diameter and 0.4 cm in hole diameter (Fig. 214; Picture 522).

M11:26, it is cylinder-shaped, and was cut apart after drilled the hole from both sides. The fracture surface is left with cambered string-cutting marks. It is 1.4 cm in length, 1 cm in diameter and 0.5 cm in hole diameter (Fig. 214; Picture 522).

M11:27, one end has brown spots. It is shaped in triangular prism, and was cut apart after drilled the hole from both sides. The fracture surface is left with cambered string-cutting marks. It is 2.1 cm in length, 1.65 cm in diameter and 1.1 cm in hole diameter (Fig. 214; Picture 523).

M11:29, this number contains 2 individual pieces. With brown spots, they are cylinder-shaped with a hole drilled from both sides. They are 2.2 cm in length, 1 cm in diameter and 0.5 cm in hole diameter (Fig. 214; Picture 524).

M11:31, with gray spots, it is cylinder-shaped with a hole drilled from both sides. It is 2.5 cm in length, 0.9 cm in diameter and 0.5 cm in hole diameter (Fig. 214; Picture 524).

M11:32, it is cylinder-shaped, and there is a hole drilled from both sides with step-shaped marks left. It is 3.3 cm in length, 1.2 cm in diameter and 0.6 cm in hole diameter (Fig. 214; Picture 524).

M11:33, with brown spots, it is cylinder-shaped with a hole drilled from both sides. It is 2.7 cm in length, 1 cm in diameter and 0.4 cm in hole diameter (Fig. 214; Picture 524).

M11:34, with gray spots, it is cylinder-shaped with a hole drilled from both sides. It is 2.9 cm in length, 1 cm in diameter and 0.5 cm in hole diameter (Fig. 214; Picture 525).

M11:37, it is cylinder-shaped with a hole drilled from both sides. It is 2.4 cm in length, 1.2 cm in diameter and the 0.6 cm in hole diameter (Fig. 214; Picture 525).

M11:38, with dark green spots, it is cylinder-shaped

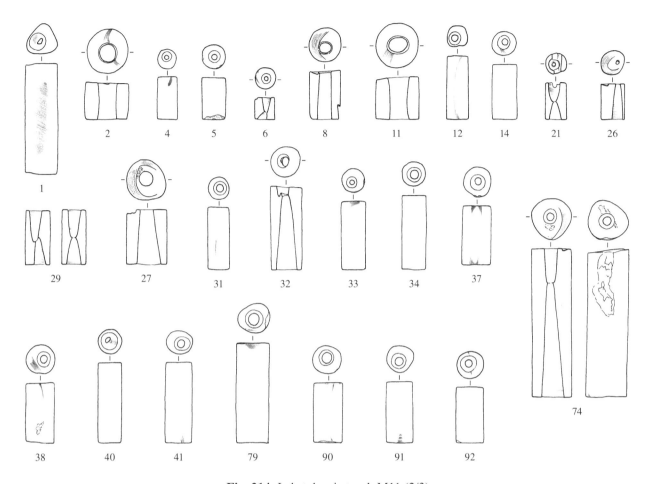

**Fig. 214.** Jade tubes in tomb M11 (2/3)

with a hole drilled from both sides. cambered string-cutting marks are left on the end surface. It is 2.4 cm in length, 1.2 cm in diameter and 0.6 cm in hole diameter (Fig. 214; Picture 525).

M11:40, with grayish-brown spots, it is cylinder-shaped with a hole drilled from both sides. It is 3.15 cm in length, 1 cm in diameter and 0.7 cm in hole diameter (Fig. 214; Picture 525).

M11:41, with grayish-green spots, it is cylinder-shaped with a hole drilled from both sides. It is 3.2 cm in length, 1.1 cm in diameter and 0.5 cm in hole diameter (Fig. 214; Picture 526).

M11:74, this number contains 2 individual pieces. They are shaped in triangular prism, with a round hole drilled from both sides. One piece is left with cambered string-cutting marks on the end surface. They are 5.9 cm in length, 1.6 cm in diameter and 0.55 cm in hole diameter (Fig. 214; Picture 527).

M11:79, with grayish-brown spots, it is cylinder-shaped with a hole drilled from both sides. It is 4 cm in length, 1.2 cm in diameter and 0.6 cm in hole diameter (Fig. 214; Picture 521).

M11:90, it is cylinder-shaped with a hole drilled from both sides. It is 2.4 cm in length, 1.2 cm in diameter and 0.6 cm in hole diameter (Fig. 214; Picture 526).

M11:91, it is cylinder-shaped with a hole drilled from both sides. It is 2.4 cm in length, 1.1 cm in diameter and 0.6 cm in hole diameter (Fig. 214; Picture 526).

M11:92, it is cylinder-shaped with a hole drilled from both sides. It is 2.15 cm in length, 1.1 cm in diameter and 0.55 cm in hole diameter (Fig. 214; Picture 526).

**Beads:** thirteen pieces.

M11:7, this number contains 2 individual pieces. They are waist-drum-shaped with a hole drilled from both sides. They are 0.8 cm in length, 0.7 cm

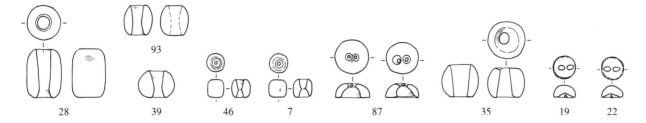

**Fig. 215.** Turquoise beads and jade beads in tomb M11
19, 22. turquoise beads; others. jade beads (2/3)

in diameter and 0.35 cm in hole diameter (Fig. 215; Picture 528).

M11:28, this number contains 2 individual pieces. They are waist-drum-shaped with a hole drilled from both sides. They are 1.9 cm in length, 1.3 cm in diameter and 0.6 cm in hole diameter (Fig. 215; Picture 529).

M11:35, this number contains 2 individual pieces. They are waist-drum-shaped, and one piece has a hole drilled from one side, the other was cut apart after the drilling a hole from one side, with cambered string-cutting marks left on the cutting surface. They are 1.3 cm in length, 1.4 cm in diameter and 0.8 cm in hole diameter (Fig. 215; Picture 531).

M11:39, it is waist-drum-shaped with a hole drilled from both sides. It is 1.1 cm in length, 1.4 cm in diameter and 0.5 cm in hole diameter (Fig. 215; Picture 531).

M11:46, this number contains 2 individual pieces. They are waist-drum-shaped with a hole drilled from both sides. They are 0.7 cm in length, 0.75 cm in diameter and 0.5 cm in hole diameter (Fig. 215; Picture 528).

M11:87, this number contains 2 individual pieces. They are hemispherical, with a concave hole drilled on the flat surface and two small holes drilled on the convex surface. They are 1.4 cm in diameter and 0.5 cm in thickness (Fig. 215; Picture 529).

M11:93, this number contains 2 individual pieces. They are waist-drum-shaped with a hole drilled from both sides. They are 1.2 cm in length, 1.2 cm in diameter and 0.5 cm in hole diameter (Fig. 215; Picture 531).

**Particles:** eighty four pieces.

M11:17, this number contains 5 individual pieces, one of which is incomplete. They are oval in plane, one surface being flat and the other being cambered and protruding. They are 0.7 cm in length, 0.4 cm in width and 0.25 cm in thickness (Fig. 216; Picture 532).

M11:18, this number contains 9 individual pieces, one of which was incomplete. They are slightly oval in plane, one surface being flat and the other being cambered protruding. They are 1 cm in length, 0.5 cm in width and 0.35 cm in thickness (Fig. 216; Picture 533).

M11:23, with brown spots, it is oval in plane, one surface being flat and the other being cambered and protruding. It is 0.8 cm in length, 0.6 cm in width and 0.4 cm in thickness (Fig. 216; Picture 530).

M11:25, this number contains 4 individual pieces. They are blue-white and oval in plane, one surface being flat and the other being cambered and protruding. They are 0.5 cm in length, 0.4 cm in width and 0.25 cm in thickness (Fig. 216; Picture 534).

M11:36, this number contains 32 individual pieces. With brown spots, they are oval or round in plane, one surface being flat and the other being cambered and protruding. Among the all, four pieces are relatively large, one of which had cutting marks on the surface from outside to inside. The oval ones are 0.5–0.8 cm in length and 0.3–0.5 cm in width, the round ones are 0.6–1.3 cm in diameter and 0.2–0.4 cm in thickness (Fig. 216; Picture 536).

M11:45, this number contains 10 pieces. With mixed color, they are oval, one surface being flat and the other being cambered and protruded. They are 0.6–1.6 cm in length, 0.6 cm in width and 0.3–0.5 cm in thickness (Fig. 216).

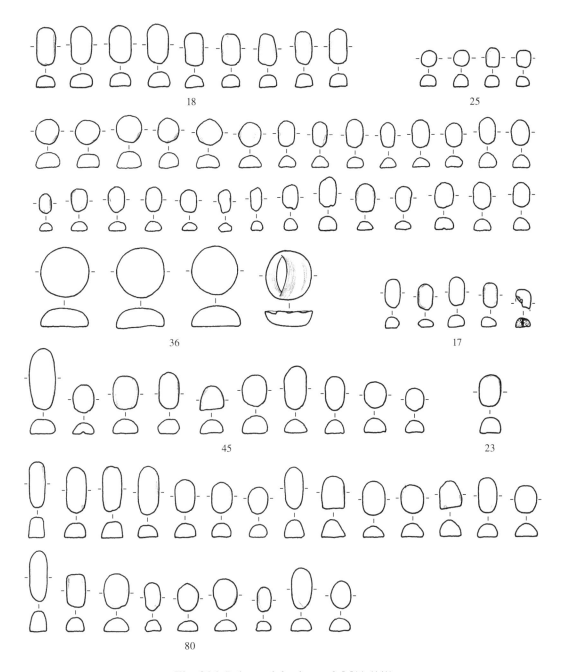

**Fig. 216.** Jade particles in tomb M11 (1/1)

M11:80, this number contains 23 pieces. There are brown spots. They are a little oval, one surface being flat and the other being cambered and protruded. They are 0.8–1.2 cm in length, 0.5–0.6 cm in width and 0.3–0.6 cm in thickness (Fig. 216; Picture 535).

(2) Turquoise beads

Two pieces, the same type.

M11:19, it is hemispherical, with a tunnel-shaped hole on the flat. It is 0.8 cm in diameter, 0.55 cm in thickness (Fig. 215; Picture 537).

M11:22, it is hemispherical, with a tunnel-shaped hole on the flat. It is 0.8 cm in diameter, 0.55 cm in thickness (Fig. 215; Picture 537).

(3) Pottery vessel: seven pieces.

***Ding* tripod:** two pieces.

M11:10, it is reddish-brown sand-tempered pottery, and the inner wall of the rim was covered with red coating, with a smooth surface. It has a flared mouth, flat rim surface, bulging abdomen and round bottom, fin-shaped legs, with the cross section is flat outer side

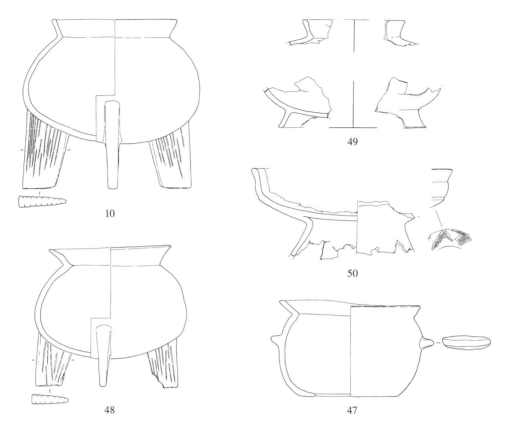

**Fig. 217.** Pottery vessels in tomb M11

10, 48. *ding* tripods; 47. *zeng* steamer; 49. ring-foot jar; 50. *dou* (1/4)

and a round arced corner. It is 18 cm in height and 13.9 cm in opening diameter (Fig. 217; Picture 540).

M11:48, it is sand-tempered reddish-brown pottery, with polished surface. It has a flared mouth, uneven rim, bulging abdomen and round bottom. It has short fin-shaped leg, with cross section and outer side flat. It is 14.8 cm in height and the 13.6 cm in opening diameter (Fig. 217; Picture 539).

**Dou:** one piece (M11:50). It is clay pottery, it has a gray and an orange core respectively. It has a flared mouth and a slightly folded wall, trumpet-shaped ring foot. The bottom is too broken to be restored. Both outer wall and ring feet are painted with vermilion painting but the pattern was unclear. It is 23.4 cm in opening diameter (Fig. 217).

**Ring-foot jar:** one piece (M11:49). It is sand-tempered reddish pottery, with a polished and smooth surface. There are many broken parts. It has a flared mouth, concave rim surface, with a bulging abdomen, and outward-stretching short ring foot. It is about 11 cm in opening diameter and 16 cm in foot diameter (Fig. 217).

**Gang vat:** one piece (M11:13). It is red sand-tempered pottery. There are so many broken parts that its shaped could not be recognized.

**Zeng steamer:** one piece (M11:47). It is reddish-brown fine sand-tempered pottery. The surface is covered with slurry so that its color appeared dark brown and smooth. It has a flared mouth, with a straight rim surface, a bulging abdomen, flat bottom and a big hole in the bottom. It is 10.3 cm in height, 15.5 cm in opening diameter, and 10.2 cm in bottom diameter (Fig. 217; Picture 538).

**Filter:** one piece (M11:9). It is gray clay pottery. It is broken into too many parts to be recognized precisely.

# Section 12 Tomb M14

## 1. The Shape of the Tomb

Tomb M14 is located in the middle of the north line of the tombs, adjacent to tomb M5 on the west and with tomb M11 to the east. It had its opening under the top soil, and disturbed the yellow-earthen mound. It is rectangular pit with vertical wall, with an orientation of 182°, with a length of 2.8 m, a width of 1–1.15 m, and a depth of about 0.6 m. The tomb pit is a little oblique inwards and the pit wall was easy to reveal.

Deposits in the tomb could be divided into five stratums. The first stratum is grayish-yellow mottled earth; the second is grayish-brown mottled earth, and the third is reddish clay. The 1st-3rd stratums of earth are loose in texture and partly contained gravel, the earth bottom is concave and arc-shaped. It is due to the collapse of funerary containers according to the situation. Under 3rd stratum there is some raised gray silt which is located in the northern and western sides of the pit. It may be the ash marks of funerary containers. The 4th stratum is dense gray silty earth. Burial objects were mostly excavated from here. The 5th stratum is very thin gray silt, and it should belong to the alluvial earth at the bottom of the tomb. Skeleton inside the tomb had rotten away and left no remains (Picture 541).

Burial objects concentrated in the central and northern of the tomb. Pottery vessels excavated from northern tomb are preserved poorly. Four pieces of pottery vessels could be identified: one piece of *ding* tripod, one piece of ring-foot jar, one piece of *dou*, one piece of *gang* vat.

The tenon of crown-shaped jade object (M14:10) is facing south, scattered around a set of string ornaments (M14:1–9) which comprised of nine pieces of jade tubes. One pair of identical hemispherical beads (M14:11, 12) are probably earrings. The two beads are very close probably due to the collapse of funerary containers. Adjacent to jade *huang* semi-circular pendant (M14:25) unearthed a round jade plaque, there are two bracelets (M14:39, 36) on both left and

right side. One piece of awl-shaped jade object was unearthed (M14:37), which has been broken into four parts and the top overlaid the jade bracelet (M14:36) (Fig. 218).

## 2. Burial Objects

There are 52 pieces of burial artifacts, 4 pieces of pottery vessels. The others are jade artifacts.

(1) Jade artifacts

48 pieces.

Crown-shaped jade object: one piece (M14:10). It has gray spots and broken into two pieces when excavated. It presents an upside-down trapezoid in shaped. Its top end is slightly wider and it is concave in the middle, with a half round protrusion. The bottom has a flat tenon, with three holes drilled from both sides equidistantly. The top corner of one side has cambered string-cutting marks and has been polished. There are vertical string-cutting marks on the concave parts. It is 2.3 cm in height, 5.35–5.65 cm in width, 0.42 cm in thickness (Fig. 219; Picture 542).

**Awl-shaped object:** one piece (M14:37). It has gray spots and broken into four pieces when unearthed. It is shaped in long strip. Both sides are sharp and pointed, with a hole drilled from both side on one end. It is 11.8 cm in length (Fig. 220; Picture 543).

*Huang* **semi-circular pendant:** one piece (M14:25). It has gray spots. It is half-*bi* shaped, both sides are slightly sharp. There are two holes drilled from both sides on both sides of the top end. It is 4.85 cm in height, 12.3 cm in width and 0.5 cm in thickness (Fig. 220; Picture 544).

**Bracelets:** two pieces.

M14:36, it has gray and brown spot. It is flat and annular, the inner side is straight and the outer side is convex. It is 1.65 cm in height, 9.25 cm in the diameter and 6.05 cm in hole diameter (Fig. 220; Picture 545).

M14:39, it is annular, the inner side is straight and the outer side is convex. It is 1.75 cm in height, 7.05 cm in diameter, and 5.1 cm in hole diameter (Fig. 220; Picture 546).

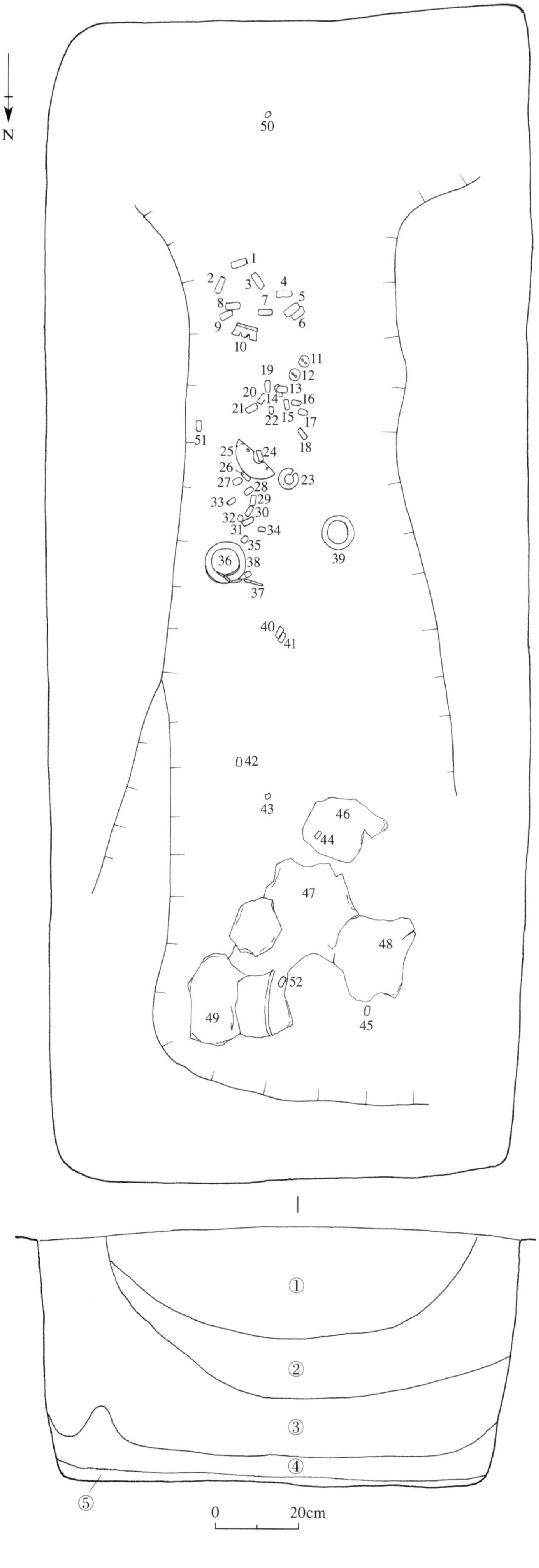

**Fig. 218.** Plan and cross-section of
tomb M14

1–9, 13–22, 24, 26–33, 40–45, 50–52. jade
   tubes
10. crown-shaped jade object
11, 12. jade beads
23. round jade plaque
25. jade *huang* semi-circular pendant
34, 35, 38. petal-shaped jade ornaments
36, 39. jade bracelets
37. awl-shaped jade object
46. pottery *dou*
47. pottery *ding* tripod
48. pottery ring-foot jar
49. pottery *gang* vat
① grayish yellow motted earth
② grayish brown motted earth
③ reddish clay
④ gray silt
⑤ gray alluvial soil

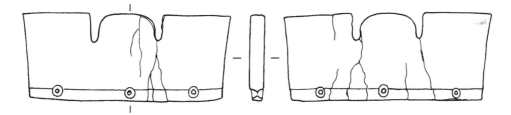

**Fig. 219.** Crown-shaped jade object (M14:10) (1/1)

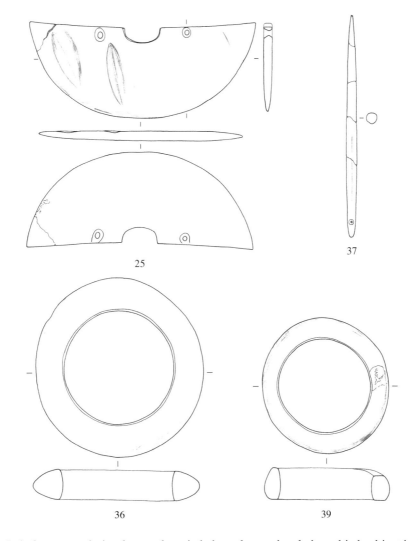

**Fig. 220.** Jade *huang* semi-circular pendant, jade bracelets and awl-shaped jade object in tomb M14

25. *huang* semi-circular pendant; 36, 39. bracelets; 37. awl-shaped object (1/2)

**Round plaque:** one piece (M14:23). With gray spots, it is flat and annular, with a big hole drilled from both sides in the middle. A narrow gap was made by string-cutting method. The side opposite to the gap was drilled with a small hole. The surface has cambered string-cutting marks, with a hole drilled from both sides and slightly polished. It is 4.45 cm in diameter,

1.95 cm in hole diameter, and 0.6 cm in thickness (Fig. 221; Picture 547).

**Petal-shaped ornaments:** three pieces.

M14:34, it is a little oval, one side being flat and the other side being convex. There are two oblique holes drilled from both sides. It is 1.55 cm in length, 1.3 cm in width, 0.58 cm in thickness (Fig. 221; Picture 548).

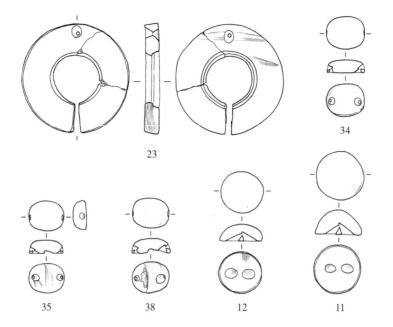

**Fig. 221.** Jade beads, round jade plaque and petal-shaped jade ornaments in tomb M14
11, 12. beads; 23. round plaque; 34, 35, 38. petal-shaped ornaments

M14:35, it is a little oval, one side being flat and the other side being convex. There are two oblique holes drilled from both sides. It is 1.45 cm in length, 1.22 cm in width and 0.55 cm in thickness (Fig. 221; Picture 548).

M14:38, it is oval, one side being flat and the other side being convex. There are two oblique holes drilled from both sides. It is 1.55 cm in length, 1.3 cm in width, and 0.6 cm in thickness (Fig. 221; Picture 548).

**Beads:** two pieces.

M14:11, it is hemispherical and drilled with a tunnel-shaped hole. Cambered string-cutting marks are left. It is 1.9 cm in diameter, 1 cm in thickness (Fig. 221; Picture 549).

M14:12, it has brown spots. It is hemispherical and drilled with a tunnel-shaped hole. It is 1.75 cm in diameter, 0.75 cm in thickness (Fig. 221; Picture 549).

**Tubes:** thirty seven pieces.

M14:1, it is cylindrical and with a hole drilled from both sides. It is 3.5 cm in length, 1.05 cm, in diameter (Fig. 222; Picture 550).

M14:2, it is cylindrical and with hole drilled from both sides. It is 3.65 cm in length, 1.05 cm in diameter (Fig. 222; Picture 550).

M14:3, there are gray spots. It is cylindrical and has a hole drilled from both sides. It is 3.3 cm in length, 1 cm in diameter (Fig. 222; Picture 550).

M14:4, it was cylindrical and had a hole drilled from both sides. It was 2.65 cm in length, 1.05 cm in diameter (Fig. 222; Picture 550).

M14:5, it has gray spots. It is cylindrical and has a hole drilled from both sides. It is 3.2 cm in length, 1.05 cm in diameter (Fig. 222; Picture 550).

M14:6, it has gray spots. It is shaped in triangular prism and has a hole drilled from both sides. It is 2.95 cm in length, 1.25 cm in diameter (Fig. 222; Picture 551).

M14:7, it is cylindrical and has a hole drilled from both sides. It is 3.2 cm in length, 1.05 cm in diameter (Fig. 222; Picture 551).

M14:8, it is cylindrical and has a hole drilled from both sides. It is 3.3 cm in length, 1.1 cm in diameter (Fig. 222; Picture 551).

M14:9, it is cylindrical and has a hole drilled from both sides, and the cross-section was irregular. It is 2.3 cm in length, 1.2 cm in diameter (Fig. 222; Picture 551).

M14:13, it is cylindrical and has a hole drilled from both sides. It is 2.05 cm in length, 0.95 cm in diameter (Fig. 222; Picture 551).

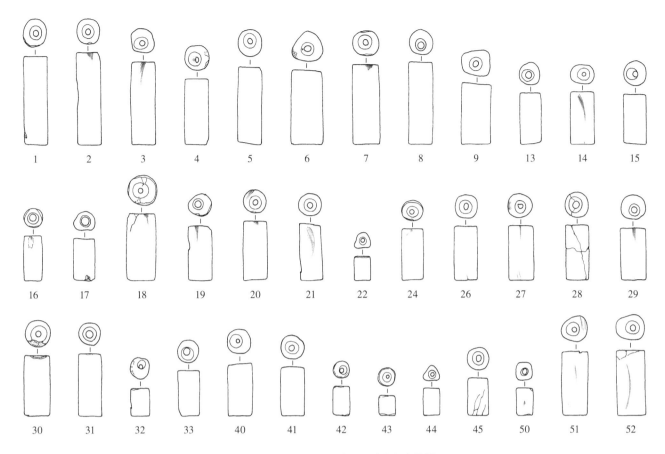

**Fig. 222.** Jade tubes in tomb M14 (2/3)

M14:14, it is cylindrical and has a hole drilled from both sides. It is 2.15 cm in length, 0.95 cm in diameter (Fig. 222; Picture 552).

M14:15, it is cylindrical and has a hole drilled from both sides. It is 1.95 cm in length, 0.95 cm in diameter (Fig. 222; Picture 552).

M14:16, it is cylindrical and has a hole drilled from both sides. It is 1.8 cm in length, 0.85 cm in diameter (Fig. 222; Picture 553).

M14:17, it is cylindrical and has a hole drilled from both sides, and the cross-section is irregular. It is 1.75 cm in length, 0.9 cm in diameter (Fig. 222; Picture 553).

M14:18: It had brown spots. It is cylindrical and has a hole drilled from both sides. Both ends are a little broken. It is 2.75 cm in length, 1.2 cm in diameter (Fig. 222; Picture 552).

M14:19, it is triangular prism and has a hole drilled from both sides. It is 2.2 cm in length, 0.95 cm in diameter (Fig. 222; Picture 552).

M14:20, it is cylindrical and has a hole drilled from both sides, and the cross-section is irregular. It is 2.4 cm in length, 0.95 cm in diameter (Fig. 222; Picture 552).

M14:21, it is cylindrical and has a hole drilled from both sides, and the cross-section is irregular. It is 2.2 cm in length, 1 cm in diameter (Fig. 222; Picture 554).

M14:22, it is triangular prism and has a hole drilled from both sides. It is 1 cm in length, 0.7 cm in diameter (Fig. 222; Picture 553).

M14:24, it is cylindrical and has a hole drilled from both sides. It is 2.15 cm in length is 0.9 cm, 0.9 cm in diameter (Fig. 222; Picture 554).

M14:26, it is cylindrical and has a hole drilled from both sides. It is 2.2 cm in length, 0.95 cm in diameter (Fig. 222; Picture 554).

M14:27, it is cylindrical and has a hole drilled from both sides. It is 2.2 cm in length, 1.05 cm in diameter (Fig. 222; Picture 554).

M14:28, it is cylindrical and has a hole drilled from both sides. It is 2.2 cm in length, 1 cm in diameter (Fig. 222; Picture 554).

M14:29, it has gray spots. It is cylindrical and has

a hole drilled from both sides. One side has a straight groove. It is 2.05 cm in length, 1.05 cm in diameter (Fig. 222; Picture 555).

M14:30, it is cylindrical and has a hole drilled from both sides, and one end is a little broken. It is 2.4 cm in length, 1.05 cm in diameter (Fig. 222; Picture 555).

M14:31, it is cylindrical and has a hole drilled from both sides. It is 2.5 cm in length, 0.95 cm in diameter (Fig. 222; Picture 555).

M14:32, it is cylindrical and has a hole drilled from both sides. It is 1.1 cm in length, 0.8 cm in diameter (Fig. 222; Picture 553).

M14:33, it has caesious spots. It is irregularly cylindrical and has a hole drilled from both sides. It is 1.8 cm in length, 0.8 cm in diameter (Fig. 222; Picture 553).

M14:40, it has grayish-brown spots. It is cylindrical and has a hole drilled from both sides. It is 2.2 cm in length, 1.05 cm in diameter (Fig. 222; Picture 555).

M14:41, it is irregularly cylindrical and has a hole drilled from both sides. It is 2 cm in length, 1.05 cm in diameter (Fig. 222; Picture 556).

M14:42, it has gray spots. It is cylindrical and has a hole drilled from both sides. It is 1.2 cm in length, 0.75 cm in diameter (Fig. 222; Picture 557).

M14:43, it is cylindrical and has a hole drilled from both sides. It is 0.84 cm in length, 0.75 cm in diameter (Fig. 222; Picture 557).

M14:44, it is triangular prism and has a hole drilled from both sides. It is 1.15 cm in length, 0.7 cm in diameter (Fig. 222; Picture 557).

M14:45, it is cylindrical and has a hole drilled from both sides. It is 1.5 cm in length, 0.9 cm in diameter (Fig. 222; Picture 557).

M14:50, it is cylindrical and the cross-section is slightly round and square, and has a hole drilled from both sides. It is 1.1 cm in length, 0.75 cm in diameter (Fig. 222; Picture 557).

M14:51, it has gray spots It is cylindrical and the cross-section is triangle and has a hole drilled from both sides. One side has cambered string-cutting marks. It is 2.6 cm in length, 1.1 cm in diameter (Fig. 222; Picture 556).

M14:52, it is shaped in irregularly square cylinder and has a hole drilled from both sides. There are two lines of cutting marks on the surface. It is 2.6 cm in length, 1.2 cm in diameter (Fig. 222; Picture 556).

(2) Pottery vessels

Four pieces.

The pottery vessels excavated are poor in texture and could not be restored. Their shapes could only be roughly identified according to the fragments.

**Ding** tripod: one piece (M14:47). It is fine sand-tempered pottery and has a reddish-brown surface that was left with scratching marks. Star-like quartz and mica substances are visible. It has a flared mouth, folded rim, shallow abdomen, approximately flat round bottom and fin-shaped legs.

**Dou**: one piece (M14:46). It is gray clay pottery. It has shallow plate and folded abdomen, whose shape of ring foot is unclear.

**Ring-foot jar**: one piece (M14:48). It is fine sand-tempered pottery, gray in the core and brown in the surface. It has a curled rim, bulging abdomen and short ring foot.

**Gang** vat: one piece (M14:49). It is dark brown sand-tempered pottery. It has a flared mouth, deep abdomen and a round pointed bottom.

# Chapter IV

# Artifacts Collected and Unearthed from the Stratum

Since May 1987 when Yaoshan site was robbed, Yuhang Cultural Relics Administrative Department has seized 344 pieces of artifacts which were said to be unearthed all from the area between tomb M7 and tomb M2. At that time, the remaining tomb were also revealed. Therefore, we took them as a group of burial objects numbered tomb M12 in following excavation brief report. The the Yuhang Committee of Cultural Relics Management also published a brief report.[1] In August 1987, Liangzhu culture artifacts including jade artifacts and stone artifacts were unearthed from the west of the excavation area.

Now it is Yuhang Cultural Relics Management Committee that houses these two groups of Liangzhu culture artifacts. By courtesy of the Committee, in late 2000, Rui Guoyao and Fang Xiangming from Zhejiang Provincial Institute of Cultural Relics and Archaeology made a comprehensive collation of these artifacts. This chapter will mainly introduce these artifacts. What should be mentioned is that since their ownership is fixed in accordance with the brief report of the Committee and the time when they entered the museum, the judgements may be somewhat inaccurate.

Besides, in the excavations from 1996 to 1998, there were also artifacts found from the top soil and Liangzhu cultural stratums. All these will be discussed in this chapter.

## Section 1 Tomb M12

Tomb M12 is located in the middle part of the south line of the tombs, with tomb M7 to the west and tomb M2 to the east. Judging from the revealed remaining tomb pit, tomb M12 disturbs the southern edge of the square red earth deposits at the center of the site. There are various kinds of unearthed jade artifacts, up to 344 individual pieces, including crown-shaped object, cylindrical object with cover, three-pronged object, semi-circular ornament, awl-shaped object, *cong*, *yue* axe, *cong*-stylistic tube, belt hook, cylindrical object and various tube, bead and particle. The main jade artifacts will be introduced as follows:

**Crown-shaped object:** one piece (2850[2]). It is white, flat and presented an upside-down trapezoid in shape, with two sides slightly concave. The upper two corners extend outward, the middle is slightly concave with a point in the center. The concave is formed by string-cutting, with cutting marks on it. Below the point there is an oval hole, with solid-drilling marks on the wall of the hole. There is a flat tenon at the bottom, with three holes drilled from both sides equidistantly. It is 3.8 cm in height, 5.95–7.2 cm in width and 0.4 cm in thickness (Fig. 223; Picture 558).

**Cylindrical object with cover:** one set (2853,

---

[1] Office of Yuhang Cultural Relics Heritage Committee, Archaeological Presentation of Yaoshan Tomb M12, Anxi, Yuhang County, Zhejiang Province, *Southeast Culture*, Issue 5, 1988.

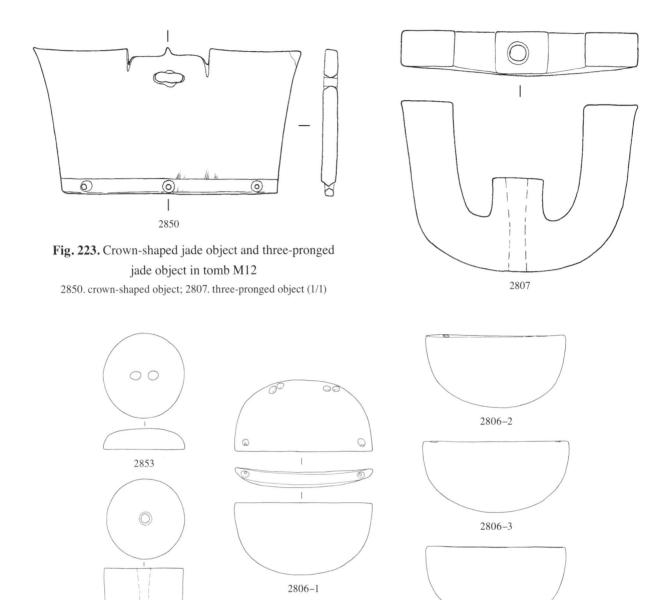

2850

**Fig. 223.** Crown-shaped jade object and three-pronged
jade object in tomb M12
2850. crown-shaped object; 2807. three-pronged object (1/1)

2807

2853

2854

2806-1

2806-2

2806-3

2806-4

**Fig. 224.** Cylindrical jade object with cover and semi-circular jade ornaments in tomb M12
2806-1–2806-4. semi-circular ornaments; 2853. the cover of cylindrical object; 2854. cylindrical object

2854). It consists of a cover and a cylindrical object.

2853, the cover. it is white and pie-shaped. One surface is convex, while the other one is straight, with a tunnel-shaped hole drilled from both sides. It is 4.45 cm in diameter and 1.1 cm in thickness (Fig. 224; Picture 559).

2854, the cylindrical object. It is white and cylindrical-shaped, it is drilled with a slightly slanting hole from both sides in the center. It is 2.7 cm in height, 4.3–4.4 cm in diameter and 0.6 cm in hole

diameter (Fig. 224; Picture 560).

**Three-pronged object:** one piece (2807). It is yellowish-white, with mixed color. The left and right prongs are at the same level, both of them spread out slightly while the middle one is lower. There is a hole in the center and the bottom end is arc-shaped. As for the whole object, one side is even while the other is slightly convex. One broken prong is repaired and at the cambered part of another prong's bottom, the slopes are left by cutting material but has been polished. On the inner side of the left and right prongs, up-down cambered string-cutting marks could be found. It is 4.4 cm in height, 6.42 cm in width an 1.13 cm in thickness (Fig. 223; Picture 561).

**Semicircular ornament:** one set of four pieces (2806), with the same shape. It is white with many gray spots, in semi-circular shape, with straight bottom and cambered top. One side is convex and the other is concave, with two pairs of tunnel-shaped holes on the bottom of the concave side. One pair of tunnel-shaped holes is drilled on two sides of the top end as well as the concave side. It is 3.76–3.89 cm in height, 7.5–7.92 cm in width and 0.76–0.87 cm in thickness. According to the unearthed objects from tomb M20 of Fanshan Cemetery, it could be inferred that such object is the tomb occupant's headdress[1] (Fig. 224; Pictures 562–565).

**Set of awl-shaped objects:** a set of nine pieces.

2816, it is white and square-cylinder shaped, with one end pointed and sharp and the other end with broken tenon. Only half a hole drilled from both sides was left. The lower part of the object is carved with sacred animal motifs that were separated by a vertical shallow groove and divided into two parts by a crosswise groove. The motifs spread out with the corner as axis. There are two stripes of bow string patterns on the upper part. It has single-circled and round eyes and a protruding nose. The lower part of the motifs is step-like by reducing background technique. It is 8.1 cm in residual length (Fig. 225; Picture 566).

2817, it is white and square-cylinder shaped, it is broken into two pieces. Its cross section has arc edges. One end is pointed and sharp and the other is with a tenon. There is a hole drilled from both sides on the tenon. The lower part of the object forms a convexity by reducing background technique, on which the sacred animal motif are carved. The motif are divided into two parts, with the same patterns. The top part is decorated with two belts of bow string patterns which

---

[1] Zhejiang Provincial Institute of Cultural Relics and Archaeology, Excavation of Liangzhu Tombs, Fanshan, Yuhang, Zhejiang Province, *Cultural Relics*, Issue 1, 1988. *See* Fig. 6 on Page 4. Besides, its locations and functions were described on Page 22.

are not straight. It has single-circled and round eyes, while one eye is shared by two motifs, and a convex nose at the corner. It is 10.9 cm in length (Fig. 225; Picture 567).

2818, it is white and square-cylinder shaped, broken into two parts. Its tail end has a broken tenon, with an incomplete hole drilled from both sides. On the lower part of the object forms a convexity, which is carved with sacred animal motifs with the corner as its central axis. The motif are divided by a crosswise shallow groove into two parts, upper and lower separately. There is sacred human motif on the upper part. Top end are decorated with two belts of bow string patterns. There are single-circled eyes, with thin-line canthi on both sides, a flat and protruding nose with intaglioed patterns. On the lower part is the animal face motif with bas-relief oval eyes and cambered eyepits. There are intaglioed rolling cloud patterns under the eyes. Between the two eyes there is an intaglioed nose whose form is partly same to that of sacred human motif. It is 10.4 cm in residual length (Fig. 225; Picture 568).

2819, it is white and broken. Its shape is similar to that of Sample 2817. It is 8.9 cm in residual length (Fig. 225; Picture 569).

2820, it is white and square-cylinder shaped, broken into three parts. One end is sharp and pointed, and the other has a slightly round and broken tenon. An incomplete hole drilled from both sides remained. On the lower part there forms a convexity. The surface is carved with sacred animal motif with corner as central axis. The motif is divided by a crosswise shallow groove into two parts, upper and lower separately. There is the sacred human motif on the upper part. Top end are decorated with two belts of bow string patterns. There are single-circled eyes, with canthi on two sides, and a flat and protruding nose with intaglioed patterns. At the lower part there is the animal face motif with bas-relief oval eyes and cambered eyepits. The intaglioed lines between the two eyes represent the nose bridge. The flat and protruding nose is carved with rolling cloud patterns (Fig. 225; Picture 570).

2821, it is white and square-shaped, it is broken. One end is sharp and pointed, and the other end and the middle part are broken. So the shape remains

2816

2817

2818

Expansion figure of patterns
(enlarged drawing)

2819

2820

Expansion figure of
patterns
(enlarged drawing)

2821

2822

2823

2824

**Fig. 225.** Awl-shaped jade objects in tomb M12 (1/1)

unknown. The half lower object is carved with sacred animal motifs which are separated by a vertical shallow groove. Broken eyes and flat and straight protruding nose are carved with rolling cloud patterns. The parts above and below the patterns were decorated with two belts of bow string patterns (Fig. 225; Picture 571).

2822, it is white, has a broken pointed end and tail end. The half lower object is carved with sacred animal motifs by bas-relief, with four corners as central axis. It is separated by a crosswise shallow groove. Another crosswise groove divides the pattern into the upper and lower part, up to 8 groups of same motifs are found. The upper part is decorated with two belts of bow string patterns. Below them there are intaglioed single-line and olivary eyes and a flat and protruding nose carved with the rolling cloud patterns. It is 6.9 cm in residual length (Fig. 225; Picture 572).

2823, it is white. The tenon is broken but the hole could be seen. The half lower object is carved with sacred animal motifs, with four corners as central axis. It is separated by a vertical shallow groove. Two crosswise shallow grooves divids the motifs into three parts, upper, middle and lower ones, up to 12 groups of almost the same motifs are found. Upper end is decorated with two belts of bow string patterns and below them there are single-circled eyes and a protruding nose. The nose is carved with rolling cloud patterns. It is 6.6 cm in residual length (Fig. 225; Picture 573).

2824, it is white and square-cylinder shaped. The pointed end and tail end are broken. Sacred animal motifs are carved around its half lower part. Upper end is decorated with two belts of bow string patterns below which every surface is carved with single-circle and round eyes, the eyes are shared by two motifs. The flat and horizontal protruding nose is at the corner. It is 3.95 cm in residual length (Fig. 225; Picture 574).

**Cong**: seven pieces.

2784, it is yellowish-white. There are large reddish-brown spots at the bottom end. It is in the shape of arc-edged square cylinder whose cross section is rounded square. The square had four protruding blocks whose intersection angle is larger than 90°. The object is

drilled with a hole whose walls had been polished and are slightly convex. Each protruding block is carved with the same sacred animal motif with corners as axis. There is a vertical straight groove between two nearby protruding blocks. The motifs are divided into the upper and lower part by a crosswise shallow groove. The top of upper part was decorated two belts of bow string patterns. Below which are double-circled eyes, whose inner circle are tubular-drilled. On both sides of eyes there are sharp-pointed canthi. The nose is flat and protruding. At the top end remained irregular slope forming by cutting of raw material, but polished, the concave and convex surfaces become smooth and clean. It is 6.05 cm in height, 12.7 cm in collar diameter and 5.7 cm in hole diameter (Figs. 226, 227; Picture 575).

2785, it is yellowish-white. It is in the shape of arc-edged square cylinder whose cross section is rounded square, with a hole drilled in the middle part. The square has four protruding blocks whose intersection angle is larger than 90°. Each protruding block is carved with the same sacred animal motif with corners as axis. There is a vertical straight groove between two nearby protruding blocks. The motifs are divided into the upper and lower part by a crosswise shallow wide groove. The top of upper part is decorated two belts of bow string patterns. Below which are double-circled eyes, whose inner circle were tubular-drilled. On both sides of eyes there are sharp-pointed canthi. The nose is flat and protruding. The shallow groove in the middle was formed by string-cutting. The whole object has a slight peeling loss, the bottom end has a concave surface due to cutting of jade raw material, but had been ground. It was 7.9 cm in height, 8.8–8.85 cm in collar diameter and 6.5–6.6 cm in hole diameter (Fig. 228; Picture 576).

2786, it is white, but more yellow in color. With the shape of arc-edged square cylinder, it has a round hole in the center. Its cross section is round-square shaped, with 4 protruding blocks whose intersection angle is larger than 90°. Every protruding block is carved with same sacred animal motif with corners as the axis. There is a vertical straight groove between two nearby protruding blocks. The motifs are divided into the

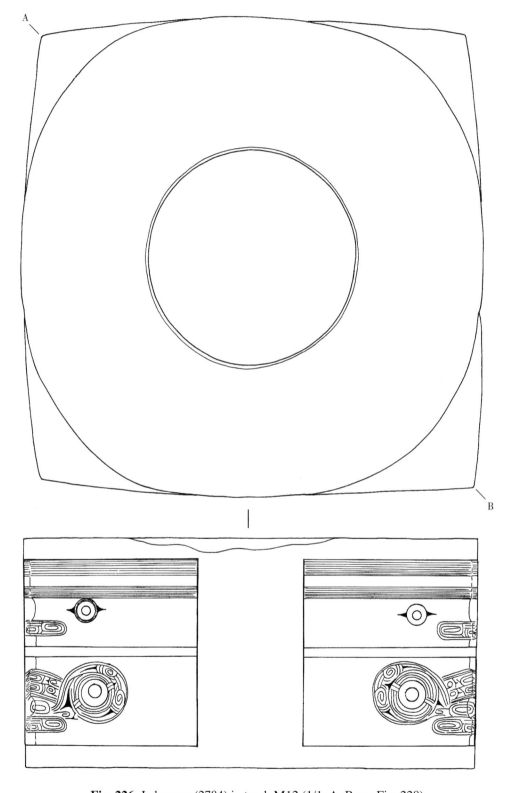

**Fig. 226.** Jade *cong* (2784) in tomb M12 (1/1; A, B *see* Fig. 228)

A: Expansion figure of patterns

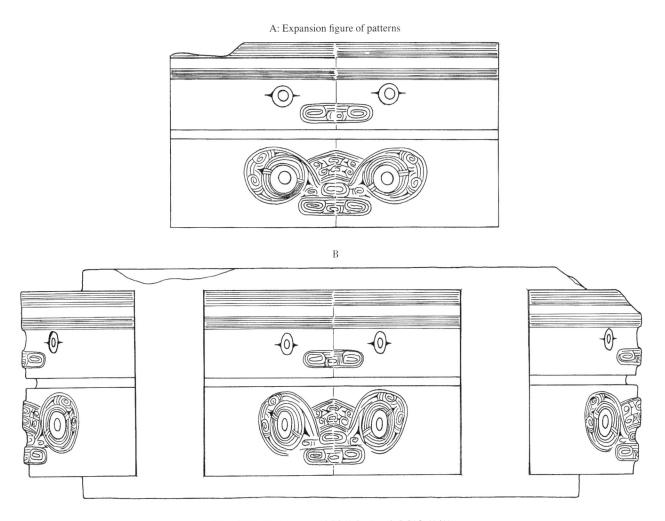

B

**Fig. 227.** Jade *cong* (2784) in tomb M12 (1/1)

upper and lower parts by a crosswise shallow groove. There is the sacred human motif on the upper part. Upper end is decorated with two belts of bow string patterns. Below which are double-line round eyes, on both sides of which there are sharp-pointed canthi. The nose is flat and protruding, with rolling cloud patterns and straight line patterns carved on. On the lower part is the sacred animal face with double-circled round eyes forming by tubular drilling, outside of which there are oval and bas-relief eyepits. Between the two eyes is a protruding nose bridge, below which there is a flat and protruding nose. The two lower corners of the animal face are carved with cambered lines representing face. The rolling cloud patterns, straight line patterns and cambered lines are carved between eyes and eyepit, between nose bridge and nose and on the nose. It is 6.95–7 cm in height, 7.95–7.98 cm in collar diameter and 6.15 cm in hole diameter (Fig. 229;

Picture 577).

2787, it is white with many yellow spots. With the shape of arc-edged square cylinder, it has a round hole in the center. Its cross section is round-square shaped, with 4 protruding blocks whose intersection angle is larger than 90°. Every protruding block is carved with the same sacred animal motif, with the corner as the axis. There is a vertical straight groove between two nearby protruding blocks. The motifs are divided into the upper and lower part by a crosswise shallow groove. There is the sacred human face motif on the upper part. The upper end is decorated with two belts of bow string patterns. Below there are double-circled round eyes. The inner-circle eyes are made by tubular drilling. The nose is flat and protruding, on which rolling cloud patterns and straight line patterns are carved. There is the sacred animal face motif with double-circled round eyes on the lower part. The inner-

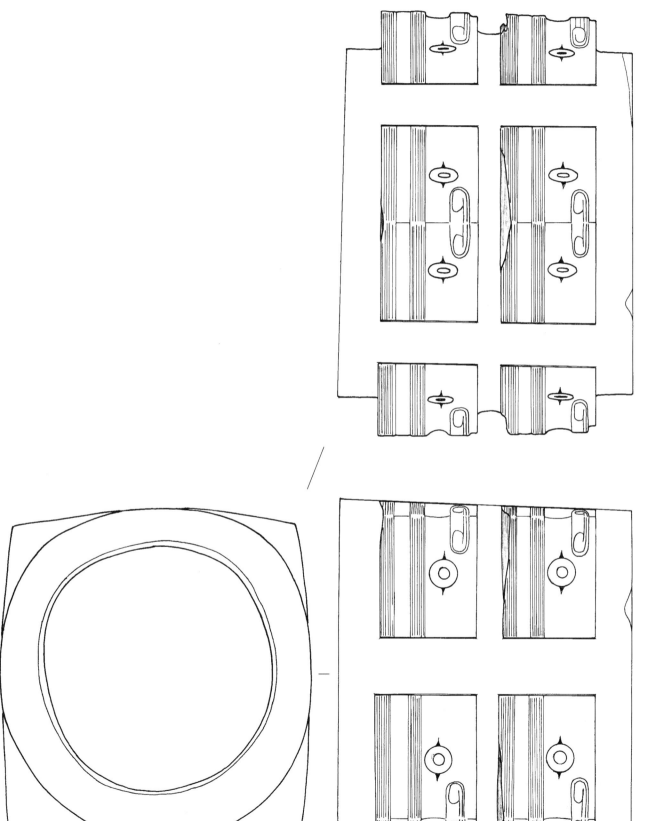

**Fig. 228.** Jade *cong* (2785) in tomb M12 (1/1)

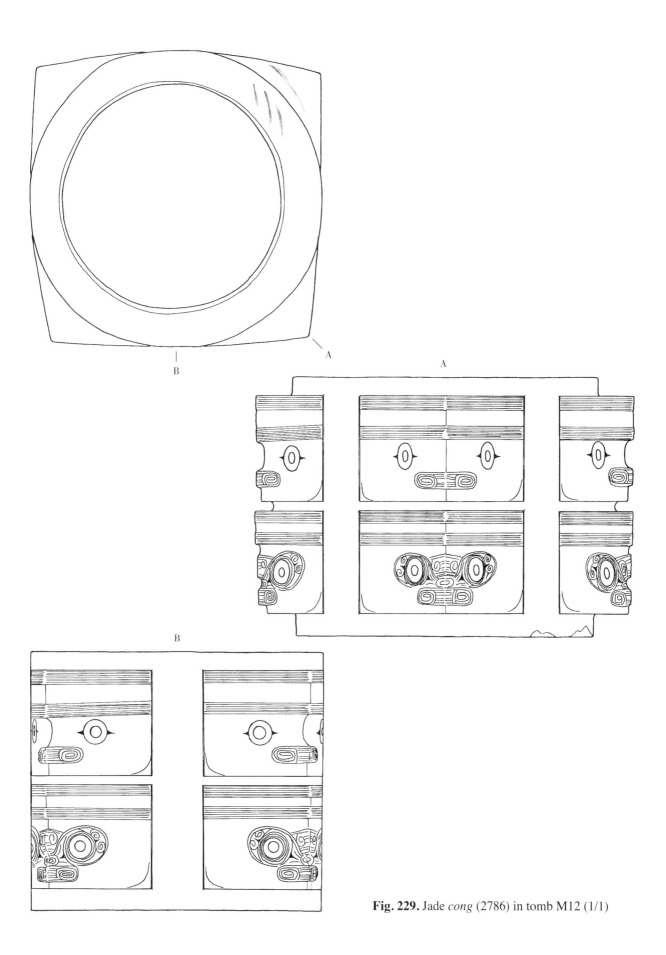

**Fig. 229.** Jade *cong* (2786) in tomb M12 (1/1)

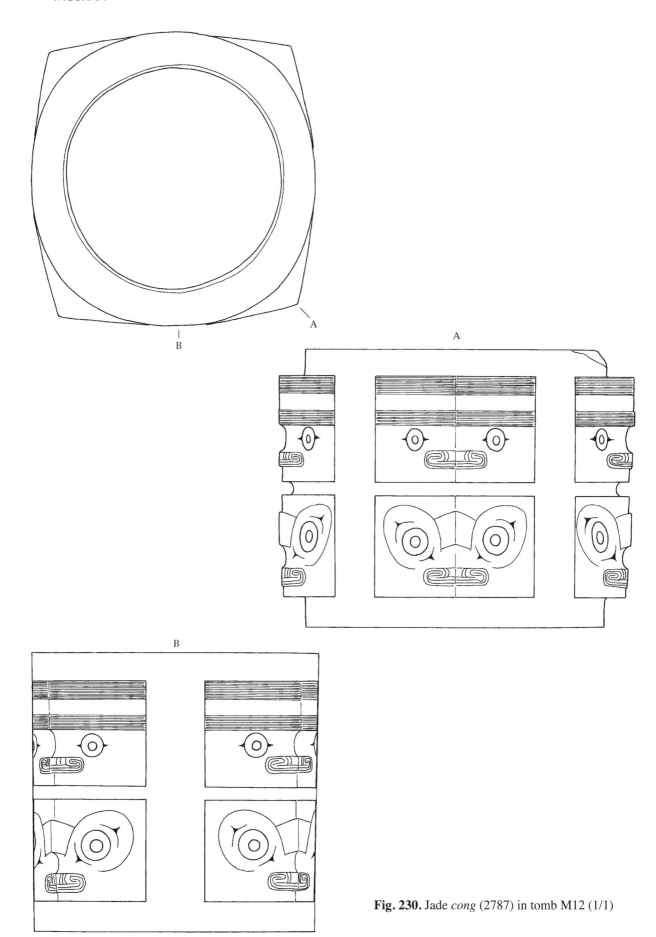

**Fig. 230.** Jade *cong* (2787) in tomb M12 (1/1)

circles were made by tubular drilled. Outside of the eyes there are oval and bas-relief eyepit. There are two intaglioed oblique pointed corners between eyes and eyepit. Between the two eyes is the nose bridge, below which there is a flat and protruding nose, with rolling cloud patterns and straight line patterns carved. At the top end are concave and convex surface and slopes left due to cutting of raw material, but polished. It is 7.4 cm in height, 7.95 cm in collar diameter and 6.3 cm in hole diameter (Fig. 230; Picture 578).

2788, it is white. With a shape of arc-edged square cylinder, it has a round hole in the center. Its cross section is round-square shaped, with 4 protruding blocks whose intersection angle is larger than 90°. Every protruding block is carved with same sacred

animal motifs, with corners as axis. There is a vertical straight groove between two nearby protruding blocks. The motifs are divided into the upper and lower part by the crosswise shallow groove. There is the sacred human motif on the upper part. The upper end is decorated with two belts of bow string patterns. Below which are double-circled round eyes, on both sides of which there are sharp-pointed canthi. The nose is flat and protruding, with rolling cloud patterns and straight line patterns are carved. On the lower part there is the sacred animal face motif, with double-circled round eyes which are tubular drilled, outside of which there are oval and bas-relief eyepits. Between the two eyes is the convex nose bridge, below which there is a flat and protruding nose. There are pointed-corner patterns on both sides of the nose. The rolling cloud patterns, straight line patterns and cambered lines are carved

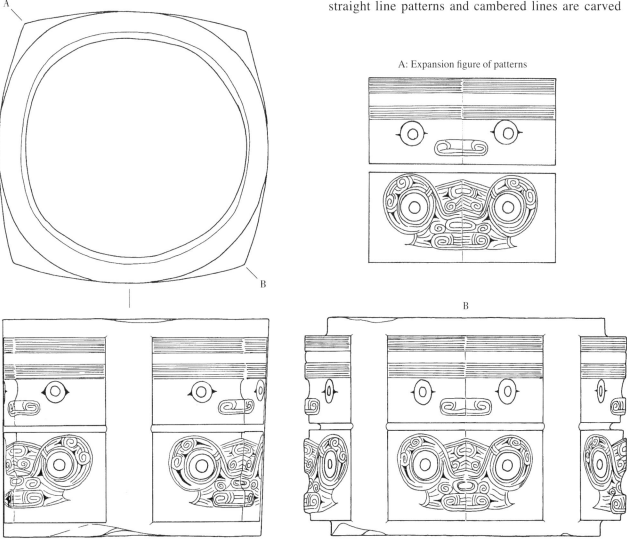

A: Expansion figure of patterns

**Fig. 231.** Jade *cong* (2788) in tomb M12 (1/1)

between eyes and eyepits, between nose bridge and nose and on the nose. On top and bottom ends there are concave and convex surfaces and slopes due to cutting of raw material, but they has been carefully polished. It is 5.8 cm in height, 7.2–7.3 cm in collar diameter and 6.2 cm in hole diameter (Fig. 231; Picture 579).

2789, it is white. There are brown spots at the top end and some other parts. With a shape of arc-edged square cylinder, it has a round hole in the center. Its cross section is round-square shaped, with 4 protruding blocks whose intersection angle is larger than 90°. Every protruding block is carved with the same sacred animal motif, with corners as axis. There is a vertical straight groove between two nearby protruding blocks. The motifs are divided into the upper and lower part

by the crosswise shallow groove. On the upper part there is the sacred human face motif whose both sides are respectively decorated with a belt of bow string patterns, between which the double-line rolling cloud patterns were carved. In the middle part of the lower belt (that is the corner), there is an up-side trapezoidal sacred human face motif. On the head upward and outward feather patterns are carved. On the lower part is the sacred animal face motif with double-circled and round eyes. The eyes are formed by tubular drilling. Oval eyepits in bas-relief are beside the eyes. There are arc patterns intaglioed between eyes and eyepits. A slightly protruding nose bridge are between two eyes, with rolling cloud patterns carved on it. The nose with wide nosewing is flat and protruding. Below the nose carved four pointed teeth, the inner two sticking upward and the outside two sticking downward. Rolling cloud patterns are intaglioed around the main

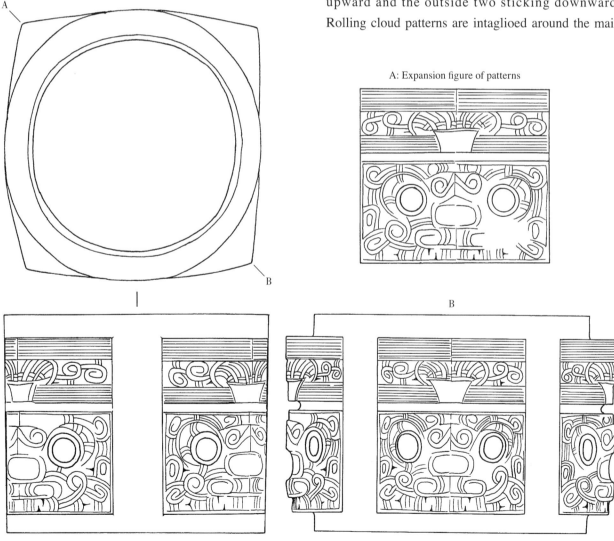

A: Expansion figure of patterns

B

**Fig. 232.** Jade *cong* (2789) in tomb M12 (1/1)

pattern as ground-tint. Cutting marks could be seen in shallow groove. It is 5.75 cm in height, 7.15 cm in collar diameter and 5.75 cm in hole diameter (Fig. 232; Picture 580).

2790, it is white, but more yellow in color. With a shape of arc-edged square cylinder, it is broken into pieces and has a round hole in the center. It has 4 protruding blocks, every protruding block is carved with the sacred animal motif with corners as the central axis. There is a vertical straight groove between two nearby protruding blocks. The motifs are divided into the upper, middle and lower part by the crosswise shallow groove. On the upper and lower parts are sacred human. End part of the sacred human motif are two belts of bow string patterns, with rolling cloud patterns between the belts. The motif had double-circled and round eyes, with pointed canthi on both sides of eyes. The nose is flat and protruding, with rolling cloud patterns and straight line patterns intaglioed. On the middle part is the sacred animal face motif, with double-circled round eyes which were tubular drilled, outside of which there are oval and bas-relief eyepits. Between the two eyes is the raised nose bridge, below which there is a flat and protruding nose. The rolling cloud patterns, straight line patterns and cambered lines are intaglioed between eyes and eyepits, between nose bridge and nose and on the nose. It is 5.5 cm in height, 7.7 cm in top collar diameter, 7.6 cm in bottom collar diameter and 5.8 cm in hole diameter. It was displayed in the National Museum of China.

**Yue axe:** one piece (2792). It is white with brown spots. It is in the shape of trapezoid with cambered blade. There is a hole drilled from both sides on the upper part. There are fine striations facing to two top corners at the hole's two sides. Above the hole there are horizontal fine striations. The whole object seems a little heavy whose cross section is thick in the center part and thin in the edges. The fracture surface after cutting could be seen on the top end, a section of which has been polished smooth after cutting. There are two stripes of cambered string-cutting marks on the surface of the object. It is 14.8 cm in height, 8.7 cm in top width, 11.2 cm in blade width, 1.1 cm in thickness and 1.35 cm in hole diameter (Fig. 233; Picture 581).

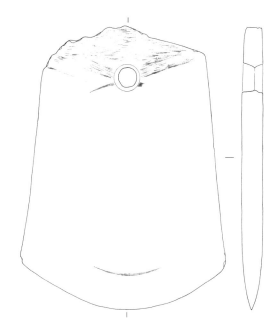

**Fig. 233.** Jade *yue* axe (2792) in tomb M12 (1/2)

**Cong-stylistic tube:** one piece (2825). It is white with gray spots. With a shape of arc-edged square cylinder, it has a hole drilled from both sides in the center. The inner wall's bottom end is a concave slope. Corners serving as the center shaft, every protruding block is carved with sacred animal motifs. There is a vertical straight groove between two nearby protruding blocks. The patterns are divided into five parts with same motifs by four circles of crosswise shallow grooves. There are 20 groups of motif for the whole object. Upper end has two belts of bow string patterns, below which single-circle eyes are intaglioed, with canthi beside eyes, and flat and protruding nose on which there are carved rolling cloud patterns. It is 4.5 cm in height, 1.4–1.5 cm in collar diameter and 0.7 cm in hole diameter (Fig. 234; Picture 582).

**Awl-shaped object:** one piece (3050). With a shape of short square, It is white. One end is sharp and pointed, and the other had a broken tenon. But the marks of a hole drilled from both sides could be seen. The lower half part is carved with a circle of simplified sacred animal motif. Upper end has two belts of bow string patterns. At the underneath corner there is a flat and protruding nose. It was 2.65 cm in residual length (Fig. 234; Picture 583).

**End ornaments:** three pieces.

2794, it is white with gray spots. It is cylinder-shaped with concave outer wall and slightly convex inner wall. The top end is tenon-shaped, the bottom end is trumpet-shaped. It is 3.1 cm in height and 2.9–3.85 cm in diameter (Fig. 234; Picture 584).

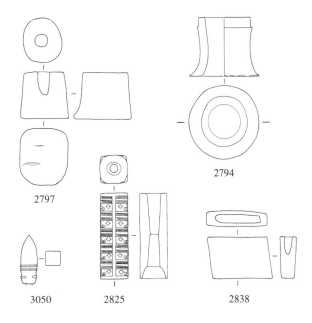

**Fig. 234.** Jade end ornaments, *cong*-stylistic jade tube and awl-shaped jade object in tomb M12

2794, 2797, 2838. end ornaments; 2825. *cong*-stylistic tube; 3050. awl-shaped object

2797, it is white with mixed colors. It is cylinder-shaped. The bottom end is rounded square and the top end is round. An oval mortise is drilled in the center. It is 2.6 cm in height and 2.3 cm in round end's diameter (Fig. 234; Picture 585).

2838, it is white. It is in a parallelogram shape and flat. One end is drilled with oblate mortises which are made by many solid drilled holes. The whole figure could not be recognized because of its damaged opening of the hole . It is 2.15 cm in height, 3.6 cm in width and 0.85 cm in thickness (Fig. 234; Pictures 586, 587).

**Cylindrical object:** nine pieces.

2798, it is white with gray dot-shaped spots. It is cylinder-shaped. There is a hole drilled from both sides in the center. One end is broken but polished. It is 2.4 cm in height, 4.6 cm in diameter and 0.6 cm in hole diameter (Fig. 235; Picture 588).

2799, two pieces shars the same reference number. They are white.

2799-1, its one end has gray-brown spots. It is cylinder-shaped. In the center there is a hole drilled from both sides. It is 2.6 cm in height, 3.1–3.2 cm in diameter and 0.6 cm in hole diameter (Fig. 235; Picture 589).

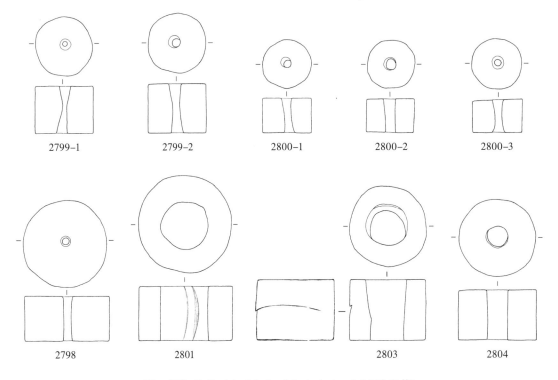

**Fig. 235.** Cylindrical jade objects in tomb M12 (1/2)

2799-2, its one end has gray-brown spots. It is cylinder-shaped. In the center there is a hole drilled from both sides. It is 2.7 cm in height, 3.25 cm in diameter and 0.65 cm in hole diameter (Fig. 235; Picture 590).

2800, three pieces shars the same reference number.

2800-1, it is white with gray spots. Cylinder-shaped, it has a hole drilled from both sides. It is 1.8 cm in height, 2.6 cm in diameter and 0.6 cm in hole diameter (Fig. 235; Picture 591).

2800-2, it is white with gray spots. Cylinder-shaped, it has a hole drilled from both sides. It is 1.8 cm in height, 2.6 cm in diameter and 0.7 cm in hole diameter (Fig. 235; Picture 592).

2800-3, it is white with gray-brown spots. Cylinder-shaped, it has a hole drilled from both sides. It is 1.75 cm in height, 2.7 cm in diameter and 0.7 cm in hole diameter (Fig. 235; Picture 593).

2801, it is white. One end has gray-brown spots. It is cylindrical shaped, on the inner wall of the hole, there are vertical cambered string-cutting marks which slightly cut into the internal face. It has a hole in the center. It is 2.85 cm in height, 5.2 cm in diameter and 2.6 cm in hole diameter (Fig. 235; Picture 594).

2803, it is white with gray spots. Cylinder-shaped, it has a hole drilled from both sides. There remains some step-shaped marks of the drilling and spiral marks on the hole's wall. It could be known that the object was remade by drilling core of *cong* for there is half a circle of tubular drilling marks. It is 3.4 cm in height, 4.3 cm in diameter and 1.85–2.15 cm in hole diameter (Fig. 235; Picture 595).

2804, it is white with brown spots. Cylinder-shaped, it has a hole in the middle. It is 2.7 cm in height, 4 cm in diameter and 1.1 cm in hole diameter (Fig. 235; Picture 596).

**Carved tubes:** 37 pieces, sharing the same reference number (2826), five of which were so broken that the patterns could not be recognized. The rest are cylinder-shaped, with a hole in the center. The object is carved with sacred animal motif by the bas-relief and intaglio carving technique, which is divided into two parts by straight shallow groove, four groups in total. It has double-circled and round eyes with oval eyepit.

There are line patterns and rolling cloud patterns between two eyes. The flat and protruding nose was carved with rolling cloud patterns. The line patterns and rolling cloud patterns are filled between the main parts' patterns. The patterns of these 32 pieces of jade tubes are similar, but not completely the same. What will be described respectively as follows:

2826-1, an upward sharp tusk was carved at the bottom of the nose. It is 2.68 cm in height, 1.13–1.2 cm in diameter and 0.55 cm in hole diameter (Fig. 236; Pictures 597, 599).

2826-2, it is yellowish in color. The upper half part was broken and only a circle of patterns could be seen. There is an outward sharp corner on both sides of the nose. It is 1.5 cm in residual length, 1.18 cm in diameter and 0.55 cm in hole diameter (Fig. 236; Picture 597).

2826-3, it is green with gray spots. The surface is so greatly polished that the patterns are not so clear, but sacred animal motif could be dimly seen. It is 2.56 cm in length, 1.05–1.1 cm in diameter and 0.5–0.6 cm in hole diameter (Fig. 236; Picture 597).

2826-4, it is 2.65 cm in length, 1.11–1.18 cm in diameter and 0.5 cm in hole diameter (Fig. 236; Picture 597).

2826-5, it is 2.7 cm in length, 1.2 cm in diameter and 0.5 cm in hole diameter (Fig. 236; Picture 598).

2826-6, the lower half part is slightly broken. It is 2.92 cm in length, 1.19–1.22 cm in diameter and 0.6 cm in hole diameter (Fig. 236; Picture 598).

2826-7, the upper half part remains. It is 1.08–1.12 cm in diameter (Fig. 236; Picture 598).

2826-8, it is 2.89 cm in length, 1.3 cm in diameter and 0.55–0.7 cm in hole diameter (Fig. 236; Picture 598).

2826-9, the nose is not so clear. It is 2.45 cm in length, 1.14 cm in diameter and 0.45–0.5 cm in hole diameter (Fig. 236; Picture 602).

2826-10, the top end is slightly broken. It is 2.75 cm in length, 1.18 cm in diameter and 0.5 cm in hole diameter (Fig. 236; Picture 602).

2826-11, the bottom end is broken. It is 3.08 cm in length, 1.1–1.15 cm in diameter and 0.5 cm in hole diameter (Fig. 236; Picture 602).

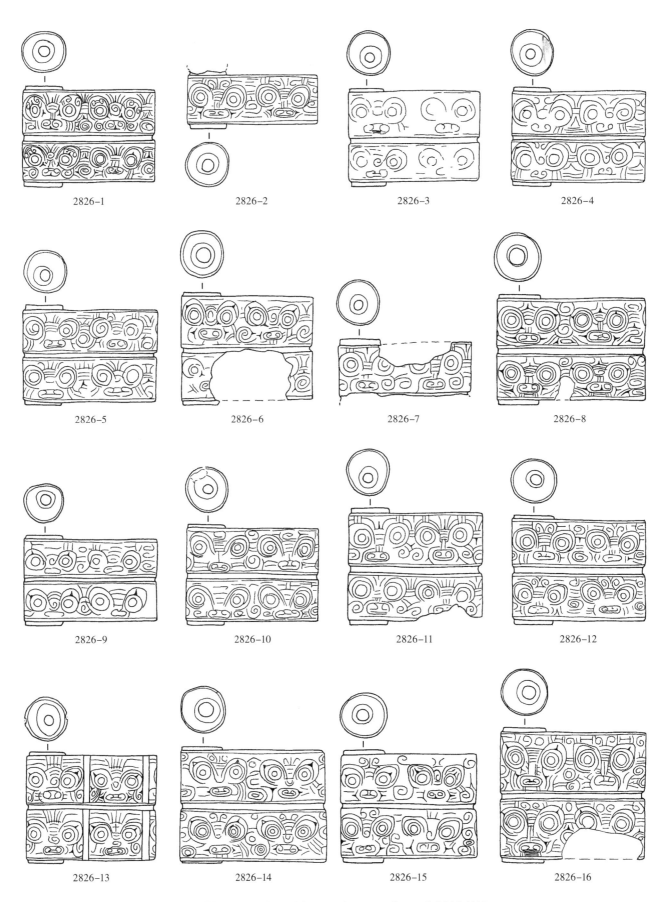

2826-1

2826-2

2826-3

2826-4

2826-5

2826-6

2826-7

2826-8

2826-9

2826-10

2826-11

2826-12

2826-13

2826-14

2826-15

2826-16

**Fig. 236.** Jade tubes with carved patterns in tomb M12 (1/1)

2826-12, more yellow in color, it was broken into two parts. It is 2.88 cm in length, 1.2 cm in diameter and 0.4–0.5 cm in hole diameter (Fig. 236; Picture 602).

2826-13, the hole in the center is slightly off-center. It is 2.93 cm in length, 1.1–1.15 cm in diameter and 0.6 cm in hole diameter (Fig. 236; Picture 603).

2826-14, the hole in the center is slightly off-center. It is 3.05 cm in length, 1.24 cm in diameter and 0.6 cm in hole diameter (Fig. 236; Picture 603).

2826-15, it is 2.95 cm in length, 1.14 cm in diameter and 0.5 cm in hole diameter (Fig. 236; Picture 603).

2826-16, the bottom end is slightly broken. It is 3.57 cm in length, 1.25–1.3 cm in diameter and 0.6 cm in hole diameter (Fig. 237; Pictures 601, 603).

2826-17, it is 2.68 cm in length, 1.1 cm in diameter and 0.6 cm in hole diameter (Fig. 237; Pictures 604, 606).

2826-18, it is 3.17 cm in length, 1.19 cm in diameter and 0.6 cm in hole diameter (Fig. 237; Picture 604).

2826-19, it is 3.33 cm in length, 1.23 cm in diameter and 0.6 cm in hole diameter (Fig. 237; Picture 604).

2826-20, the pattern is not so clear. It is 2.42 cm in length, 1.09–1.18 cm in diameter and 0.5–0.6 cm in hole diameter (Fig. 237; Picture 604).

2826-21, it is 2.56 cm in length, 1.15 cm in diameter and 0.5 cm in hole diameter (Fig. 237; Picture 605).

2826-22, the lower half part remains. It is 1.04–1.12 cm in diameter and 0.6 cm in hole diameter (Fig. 237; Picture 605).

2826-23, it is 2.85 cm in length, 1.05 cm in diameter and 0.5 cm in hole diameter (Fig. 237; Picture 605).

2826-24, it is 3.55 cm in length, 1.15 cm in diameter and 0.5 cm in hole diameter (Fig. 237; Pictures 605, 607).

2826-25, it is broken into two parts. The cross section is of slightly flat rounded square. It is 2.75 cm in length, 0.95–1.05 cm in diameter and 0.4–0.5 cm in hole diameter (Fig. 237; Picture 608).

2826-26, it is 3 cm in length, 1.15 cm in diameter and 0.6–0.75 cm in hole diameter (Fig. 237; Picture 608).

2826-27, the upper half part remains. It is 1.5 cm in length, 1.15 cm in diameter and 0.5 cm in hole diameter (Fig. 237; Picture 608).

2826-28, it is 2.83 cm in length, 1.2 cm in diameter and 0.4–0.5 cm in hole diameter (Fig. 237; Picture 608).

2826-29, it is 2.6 cm in length, 1.1 cm in diameter and 0.4 cm in hole diameter (Fig. 237; Picture 611).

2826-30, it is 2.9 cm in length, 1.2 cm in diameter and 0.5 cm in hole diameter (Fig. 237; Pictures 609, 611).

2826-31, it is 2.55 cm in length, 1.08 cm in diameter and 0.6 cm in hole diameter (Fig. 237; Pictures 610, 611).

2826-32, it is 2.5 cm in length, 1.1 cm in diameter and 0.45 cm in hole diameter (Fig. 237; Picture 611).

**Spoon-shaped object:** one piece (2837). It is white, broken into three pieces, with one end broken and some edges damaged. It is of flat and wide strip shape. It is arc-shaped from the side view. There is an oval hole at the handle. Square frames were carved in the handle's inner concave surface, with rolling cloud patterns. The convex surface near the object's end is drilled with an oval hole. One side of the object's end is carved with a notch, which is similar in appearance of half of that at the top end of a trapezoidal plaque. It is 2.55–3.15 cm in width and 0.5–0.63 cm in thickness (Fig. 238; Pictures 612, 613).

**Spoon:** one piece (2836). It is white and only the handle and the edges of the spoon are left. It is flat and wide, but slightly concave from the side. The handle is slightly-trapezoidal, on which there is an oval hole. The concave is intaglioed with sacred animal motifs. The motifs are divided into two parts. On the lower part, rolling cloud patterns are intaglioed around the hole. The motifs of the upper part are damaged. One oval eye could be seen but the other is damaged. The nose is made up of rolling cloud patterns. The nose bridge is upright and the nosewing is wide. Four tusks reach out of the flat mouth, two inner side ones upward and two outer side ones downward. Between the two inner side ones, there is a downward tusk. It is 1.84–3.52 cm in width and 0.47 cm in thickness (Fig. 238; Pictures 614, 615).

**Long tubes:** two pieces.

2795, it is white jade, half of the object has brown spots, cylindrical, with holes drilled from both sides in

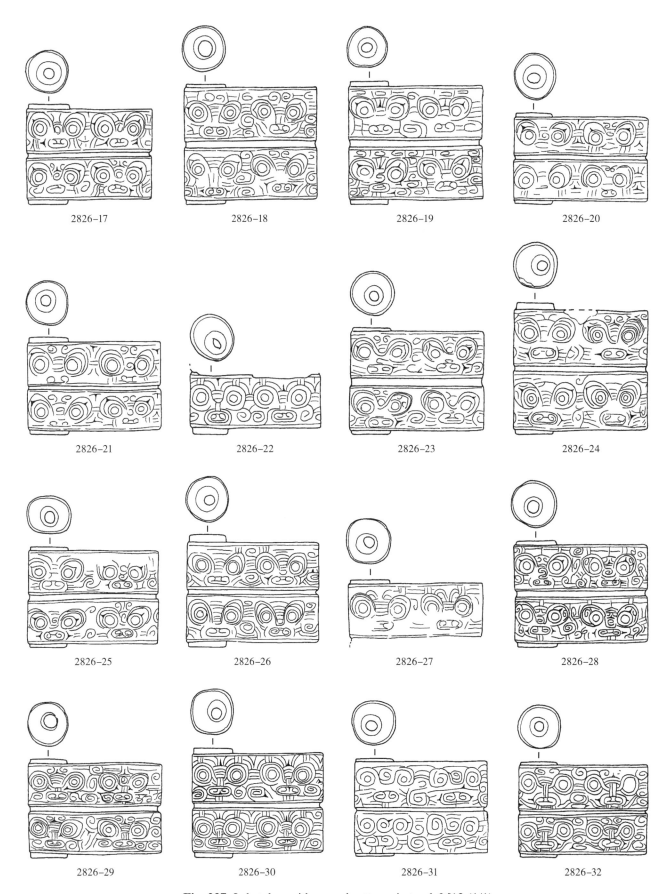

2826–17          2826–18          2826–19          2826–20

2826–21          2826–22          2826–23          2826–24

2826–25          2826–26          2826–27          2826–28

2826–29          2826–30          2826–31          2826–32

**Fig. 237.** Jade tubes with carved patterns in tomb M12 (1/1)

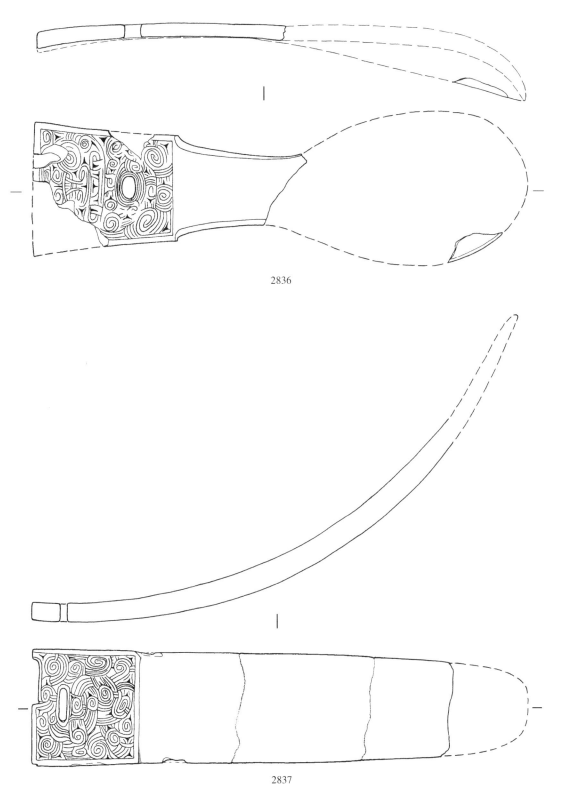

2836

2837

**Fig. 238.** Jade spoon and spoon-shaped jade object in tomb M12
2836. spoon; 2837. spoon-shaped object (1/1)

the middle. It is 8.55 cm in length, 2.13 cm in diameter and 0.84–1.05 cm in hole diameter (Fig. 239; Picture 616).

2808[1], it is white, cylindrical, with a hole in the middle, slightly thin on the wall, square cylinder on the base. It is carved with sacred animal motifs, with two belts of bow string patterns on the upper part using the two symmetrical corners as the axis, all carved with patterns. The double-line round eyes, oval eyepits, with outside canthi, as well as line patterns intaglioed between eyes. The nose is flat and protruding, with rolling cloud patterns on it, intaglioed with wide mouth and ponited tusks under the nose. Above the sacred animal motifs there is a belt of rolling cloud pattern, with sharp carved patterns. It is 8.23 cm in length, 1.02 cm in upper diameter, 1.18–1.22 cm in lower diameter and

0.7–1.05 cm in hole diameter (Fig. 239; Picture 618).

**Stand:** one piece (2793), it is white jade, slightly yellow, cylindrical trumpet-shaped, with an outward stretching bottom. It is 4.6 cm in height, and 9.8–12.6 cm in diameter (Fig. 240; Picture 617).

In addition, there are hemispherical jade beads, spherical jade beads, cylindrical jade tubes and jade particles.

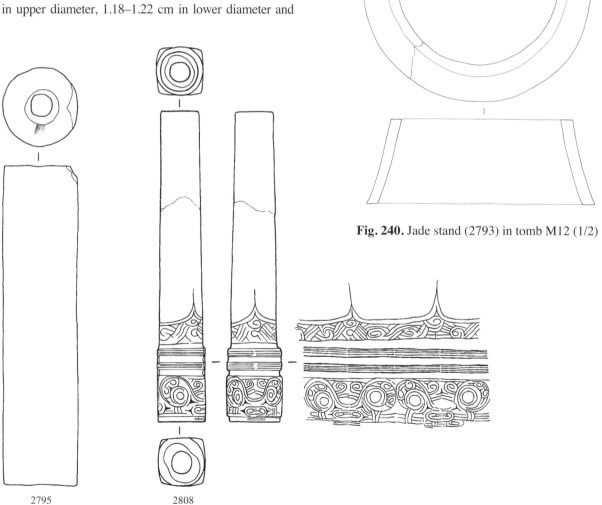

**Fig. 240.** Jade stand (2793) in tomb M12 (1/2)

2795                2808

**Fig. 239.** Long jade tubes in tomb M12 (1/1)

---

[1] This object maybe the long tube matching with the middle prong of the three-pronged object.

# Section 2 Artifacts Unearthed from the Western Area

In August 1987, a number of cultural artifacts were unearthed from the western part of the original excavation area (within the scope of T303 unearthed in the first half year of 1997), including jade artifacts and stone artifacts. At that time, the staff members of the Yuhang Committee of Cultural Relics Management decided on-site that all those artifacts unearthed in the western part were burial artifacts. Brief introductions are as follows:

(1) Jade artifacts

**Crown-shaped object:** one piece (3048), it is white jade with gray spots, it is flat and presented an upside-down trapezoid in shape. The top end is flat and straight, the middle is concave with a point in the middle. Under the point there is an oval hole made by solid drilling. At the bottom there is a flat tenon, with three small holes drilled from both sides equidistantly. It is 4.3 cm in height, 6.8 cm in width and 0.6 cm in thickness (Fig. 241; Picture 619).

**Cover of cylindrical object:** one piece (2805), it is white jade with brown spots. Its is round-pie shaped, which one side is flat, and the other is convex, with tunnel-shaped holes drilled from both sides. There are damages on the surface caused by robbery. It is 4.85 cm in diameter and 1.55 cm in thickness (Fig. 242; Picture 620).

**Set of awl-shaped objects:** seven in a set, all white jade, strip in shape, and generally round in cross sections.

2863-1, the pointed end is broken, and the other end is slightly flat, with the holes drilled from both sides. It is 6.6 cm in residual length (Fig. 243; Picture 621).

2863-2, one end is sharp and pointed, and the other end is slightly flat and straight, with holes drilled from both sides. The object has vertical cutting marks, which are cut into the object. It is 8.2 cm in length (Fig. 243; Picture 621).

2863-3, its middle part is slightly larger in diameter than the two ends. Its pointed end is broken, and the other end is slightly flat, with the holes drilled from both sides. It is 7.2 cm in residual length (Fig. 243;

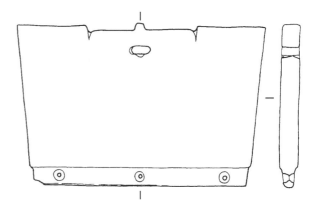

**Fig. 241.** Crown-shaped jade object (3048) unearthed from the western area (1/1)

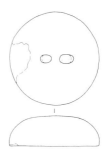

**Fig. 242.** Jade cover of cylindrical object (2805) unearthed from the western area (1/2)

Picture 621).

2863-4, it is broken on one tip, and the other tip is broken but then is processed into a flat plane, with the holes drilled from both sides, and the residual length is 7.5 cm (Fig. 243; Picture 621).

2863-5, it is broken into two pieces, one end is sharp and pointed, and the other end is falt, with a hole drilled from both sides. There is a straight cutting mark on the object, which is cut into the object. It is 6.9 cm in length (Fig. 243; Picture 621).

2863-7, this object is broken into eight pieces. The pointed end is broken, and the other end is slightly flat, with small hole drilled from both sides. There are straight cutting marks on the object. It is 9.5 cm in residual length (Fig. 243; Picture 621).

2863-8, both ends are broken, and has a straight cutting mark on the object. It is 5.5 cm in residual

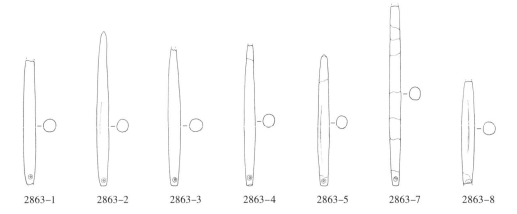

2863-1  2863-2  2863-3  2863-4  2863-5  2863-7  2863-8

**Fig. 243.** Awl-shaped jade objects unearthed from the western area (2/3)

length (Fig. 243; Picture 621).

**Three-pronged object:** one piece (2851), it is white with yellowish brown spots. The left and right prongs are at the same level, and the middle prong is lower, with a hole drilled from both sides. It has a round cambered bottom, and folded corners on both sides. The front side is convex, and the back side is even. There are cambered string-cutting marks on the object, and up-down cambered string-cutting marks on two outer prongs' inner sides. It is 4.5 cm in height, 4.9 cm in width and 1 cm in thickness (Fig. 244; Picture 622).

***Cong:*** four pieces.

2841, it is white, damaged. It is a square-cylinder shaped, with arc edges, and its cross section was square with round corners. It has four protruding blocks whose intersection angle larger than 90°. There is a round hole in the middle, whose inner wall is slightly convex, and each protruding block took the corner as the axis, and is carved with the same sacred animal motifs. There is a vertical straight groove between two nearby protruding blocks. The motifs are divided into the upper and lower part by a crosswise shallow groove. The upper part is carved with the sacred human motif, with two belts of bow string patterns on the upper part. Below which there are two double-circled round eyes, with sharp conical canthi at both sides. The nose is flat, wide and protruding, with intaglioed rolling cloud patterns on it. The lower part was carved with the sacred animal face motif, with oval eyepits, and double-circled round eyes, between

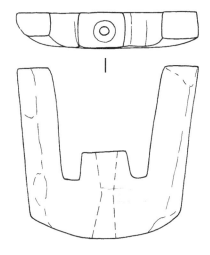

**Fig. 244.** Three-pronged jade object (2851)
unearthed from the western area (1/1)

which there is a nose bridge. The nose is flat, wide and protruding, intaglioed with rolling cloud patterns on. There are concave and convex surface left after cutting at the top of this object, which are carefully polished. It is 5.1 cm in height, 7.45 cm in collar diameter and 6.1 cm in hole diameter (Fig. 245; Picture 624).

2842, it is white, a short square cylindrical-shaped object with arc edge. Its cross section is square with round corners, with four protruding blocks whose angle is larger than 90°. There is a round hole in the middle, and the corner is used as the axis for each protruding block, which is carved with sacred animal motifs. There is a vertical straight groove between neighboring protruding blocks. The motifs are divided by the two belts of crosswise shallow groove into the upper, middle and lower part, with the upper

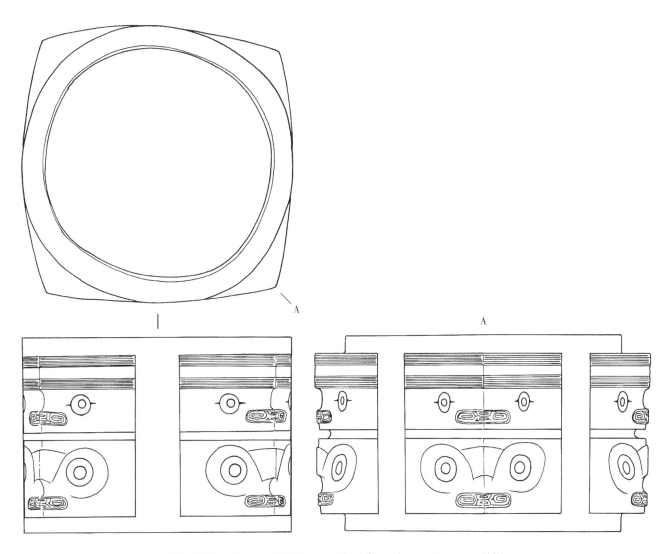

**Fig. 245.** Jade *cong* (2841) unearthed from the western area (1/1)

and lower parts carved the same sacred human motif. The top is decorated with two belts of bow string patterns, below which are two double-line round eyes, with sharp conical canthi on both sides, and a horizontal, flat and protruding nose with rolling cloud patterns on it. The middle part is carved with sacred animal motif, with double-line round eyes, and bas-relief oval eyepits at the outer side, and there is a nose bridge between eyes. The nose is flat, horizontal and protruding with rolling cloud patterns carved on it. The upper and middle parts of this object could form a complete sacred animal motif, and the lower part is a half of it. It is 5.85 cm in height, 6.6 cm in collar diameter and 5.9 cm in hole diameter (Fig. 246; Picture 623).

2844, it is white, a short square cylindrical-shaped

with arc edges. Its cross section is square with round corners, with four protruding blocks whose angle is larger than 90°. There is a round hole in the middle, and the corner is used as axis for each protruding block, which is carved with sacred animal motifs. There are two belts of bow string patterns at the top, double-line round eye, sharp conical canthi on both sides, and a flat, wide and protruding nose with rolling cloud patterns intaglioed on it. The end surface has an inclined surface left after string-cutting, which is then careful polished. It is 2.93–3.45 cm in height, 7.97–8.03 cm in collar diameter and 5.82 cm in hole diameter (Fig. 247; Picture 625).

2845, it is white, a short square cylindrical-shaped object with arced edges. Its cross section is a square with round corners, with four protruding blocks whose

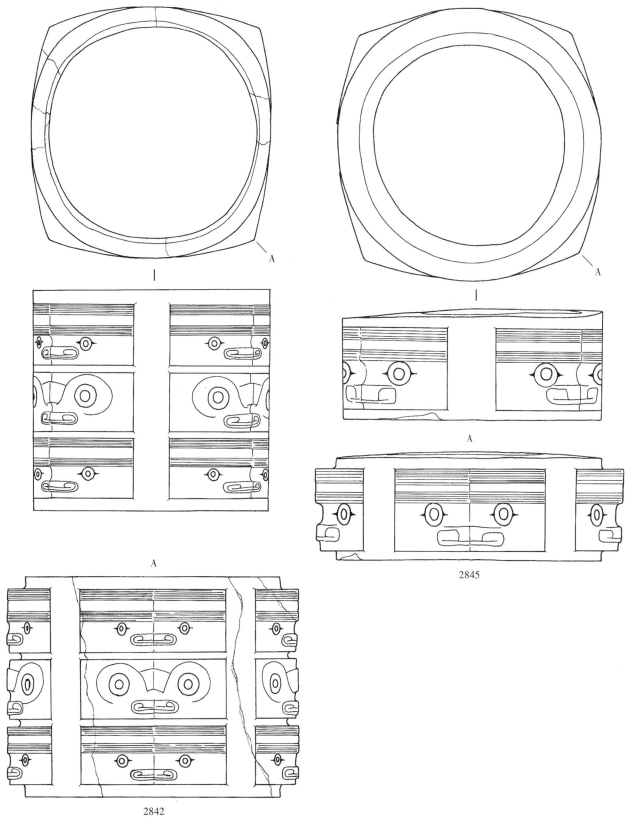

2845

2842

**Fig. 246.** Jade *cong* unearthed from the western area (1/1)

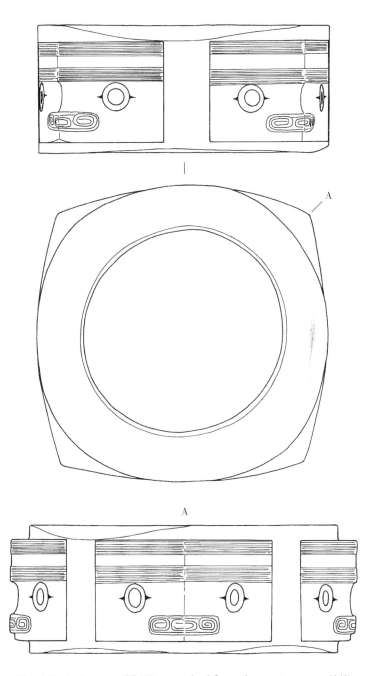

**Fig. 247.** Jade *cong* (2844) unearthed from the western area (1/1)

angle is larger than 90°. There is a round hole in the middle, and the corner is used as the axis for each protruding block, which is carved with sacred animal motifs. The top is decorated with two belts of bow string patterns, below which are two double-circled eyes, with sharp canthi on both sides, and a horizontal and flat protruding nose with rolling cloud patterns intaglioed on it. It has a flat top end and oblique bottom end, with concave and convex surfaces left after string-cutting, which are polished. It is 2.65–

2.95 cm in height, 7.1–7.2 cm in collar diameter and 5.85 cm in hole diameter (Fig. 246; Picture 626).

**Yue axe:** two pieces.

2840, it is white with gray spots and in a rectangle plane. The top end is flat, with cambered blade. There is a hole drilled from both sides in the upper part, with step-shaped marks remained (Picture 627).[1]

[1] This jade *yue* axe was borrowed from the National Museum of China and the photo was provided by the museum.

3047, it is white with gray spots and in a nearly rectangle plane. The top end is flat, with cambered blade. One blade corner is slightly broken and another is incomplete. There is a hole drilled from both sides in the upper part with step-shaped marks remained. On the top end there are blade-cutting and cutting marks, but polished. It is 12.8 cm in height, 11.1 m in top width and 2.5 cm in hole diameter (Fig. 248; Picture 628).

**Cong-stylistic tubes:** four pieces.

2846, it is white, square cylindrical-shaped, and its cross section is rounded square. At the center there is a hole drilled from both sides. It had four protruding blocks whose angle is larger than 90°. Each protruding block is divided by a straight shallow grooves, and is carved with sacred animal motifs with the corner as the axis. The motifs are divided into six groups by five crosswise shallow grooves, up to 24 groups in total, generally the same for each motif. The upper part is decorated with two belts of bow string patterns. For the lower part, there are double-line round eyes intaglioed on it, with canthi at both sides of eye, and there is also a flat, wide and protruding nose, intaglioed with rolling cloud patterns. The surface of the other end has cambered string-cutting marks. It is 10.2 cm in height, 2.25 cm in collar diameter and of 1–1.1 cm in hole diameter (Fig. 249; Picture 629).

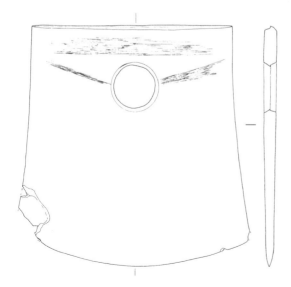

**Fig. 248.** Jade *yue* axe (3047) unearthed from the western area (1/2)

2847, it is white, with top end damaged. It is square cylindrical-shaped with arced edges. Its cross section is rounded square. At the center there is a hole drilled from both sides. It has four protruding blocks, each carved with the sacred animal motif, with the corner as the axis. The neighboring protruding blocks are separated by a vertical shallow groove, and the whole object is divided into upper and lower parts by a crosswise shallow groove, taking the corner as the axis, both carved with sacred animal motifs, up to eight groups in total, which consists of upper and lower parts. The upper part is carved with sacred human motif. The top end is decorated with two belts of bow string patterns, below which is single-circle eyes, with canthi at both sides, having a horizontal and flat protruding nose intaglioed with rolling cloud patterns on it. The lower part was carved sacred animal motifs with double-circled eyes and oval bas-relief eyepit at the outer side. Between eyes there was a protruding nose bridge, a horizontal, flat and protruding nose, intaglioed with rolling cloud patterns on it. It is 5.65 cm in height, 1.55 cm in collar diameter and 0.8 cm in hole diameter (Fig. 249; Picture 630).

2848, it is white, square cylindrical-shaped with arced edges, has a hole drilled from both sides in the middle. Each protruding block takes the corner as the axis, and are carved with simplified sacred animal motifs. The middle part is divided into upper and lower parts by a crosswise shallow groove. Specially, the motifs of the upper and lower parts are opposite to each other. It is 4.05 cm high, 1.5 cm in diameter and 0.6 cm in hole diameter (Fig. 249; Picture 631).

2849, it is white, square cylindrical-shaped with arced edges. The four protruding blocks takes the corner as axis, and are carved with sacred animal motifs. It is divided into upper and lower parts by a crosswise shallow groove. The whole object consists of eight groups, with generally the same motif for each group. The top is decorated with bow string pattern and below it there are irregular single-line round eyes, which are obscure in some part, and seems to be worn during the polishing. It is 2.5 cm in height, 1.4 cm in collar diameter and 0.6 cm in hole diameter (Fig. 249; Picture 632).

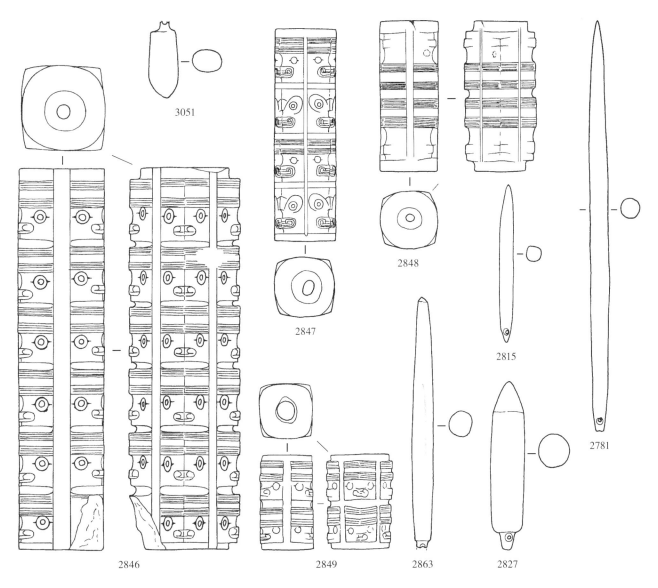

**Fig. 249.** *Cong*-stylistic jade tubes, awl-shaped jade objects and jade pendant unearthed from the western area
2846–2849. *cong*-stylistic tubes; 2781, 2815, 2827, 2863. awl-shaped objects; 3051. pendant (1/1)

**Awl-shaped objects:** four pieces.

2781, it is mainly yellow, with some brown-green and white color. It is strip-shaped and broken into two parts, with round cross section. One end is round and pointed, and the other end is relatively flat and round, with a small round hole drilled from both sides. It is 10.9 cm in length (Fig. 249).

2815, it is gray-green, with a round cross section. One end is pointed and slightly flat, and the other end is slightly flat, with a small hole drilled from both sides. It is 4.15 cm in length (Fig. 249; Picture 633).

2827, it is white, short strip-shaped and has a round cross section. One end is sharp and pointed, and the other end had a round tenon, with a small hole drilled from both sides. It is 4.4 cm in length (Fig. 249; Picture 634).

2863, it is white, and broken into two parts. One end is sharp and pointed, and the other end has a broken round tenon, with traces of drilling from both sides. There is a straight cutting mark on the surface of this object. It is 6.7 cm in residual length (Fig. 249; Picture 635).

**Pendant:** one piece (3051), it is white, in a water drop shape, and is oblate in cross section. It has a small broken tenon on the top, with traces of drilling from both sides. The other end is sharp and pointed. It is 2.1 cm in esidual length (Fig. 249; Picture 636).

**Cylindrical object:** one piece.

2855, it is white, has a round-platform shape. Its bottom is larger than the top. It has a hole in the middle, and its outer wall is oblique and straight. It is 3.2 cm in height, 3.9–4.4 cm in diameter and 1 cm in hole diameter (Fig. 250; Picture 637).

**End ornaments:** two pieces.

2780, it is green in color, and truncated cone-shaped, has a slightly concave outer wall and convex bottom surface. It has a hole in the middle, and a relatively larger top opening. It is 1.95 cm in height, 2.4–2.75 cm in diameter and 1 cm in hole diameter (Fig. 250; Picture 638).

2856, it is white, has many gray spots. It is cylinder shaped, with a hole in the middle. Its bottom is slightly larger than the top and had a slightly convex bottom surface. It is 1.8 cm in height, 2.78–2.83 cm in diameter and 0.8 cm in hole diameter (Fig. 250;

Picture 639).

**Bracelet:** one piece (2779), it is white, with some gray spots, cylinder shaped, its outer wall is slightly concave, and the inner wall is slightly convex. It is 3.4 cm in height, 6.75 cm in diameter and 5.5 cm in hole diameter (Fig. 250; Picture 640).

**Long tubes:** two pieces.

2852, it is white that is a little bit yellowish, cylinder shaped, the hole drilled at the middle is slightly inclined to one side. Its surface is irregular, has cutting faces and straight cutting marks. It is 6.6 cm in length (Fig. 250; Picture 641).

2858, it is white, has gray spots. It is long cylinder shaped, has a hole drilled at the middle. It is 6.65 cm in length, 1.65–1.72 cm in diameter, and 0.9–1 cm in hole diameter (Fig. 250; Picture 642).

(2) Stone artifacts: three pieces.

There is only one kind of stone artifact – stone *yue* axe.

2868, it is black brown in color, in a rectangle plane. Its top end has a slightly transverse inclination, and it has an cambered blade. There is a hole drilled from both sides at the upper part, with step-shaped marks left on the hole's inner wall. It is 13 cm in height, 10.1 cm in top width, 11.8 cm in blade width and 3.7 cm in hole diameter (Fig. 252; Picture 643).

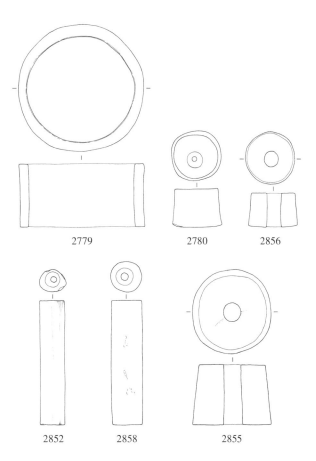

**Fig. 250.** Jade artifacts unearthed from the western area
2779. bracelet; 2780, 2856. end ornaments; 2852, 2858. long tubes; 2855. cylindrical object (1/1)

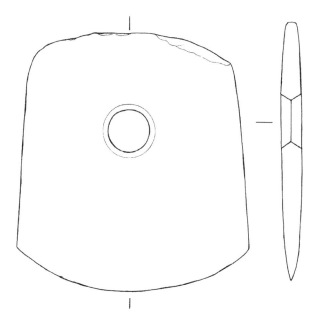

**Fig. 251.** Stone *yue* axe (3046) unearthed from the western area (1/2)

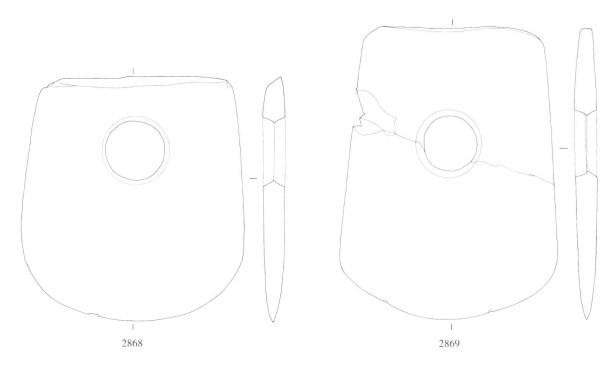

2868                                    2869

**Fig. 252.** Stone *yue* axes unearthed from the western area (1/2)

2869, it is black brown in color, broken into two parts. It is in a rectangle plane, the blade is wider than the top end. There is a round hole drilled from both sides at the middle and upper part, with step-shaped marks left. It is 15.6 cm in height, 9.9 cm in top width, 12 cm in blade width and 3.6 cm in hole diameter (Fig. 252; Picture 644).

3046, it is black brown in color, has a fracture surface at the top end without being polished. It is in a generally rectangle plane, with cambered blade. There is a hole drilled from both sides at the middle and upper part, with marks left on the inner wall of the hole. It is 13.6 cm in height, 10.9 cm in top width, 12.8 cm in blade width and 2.8 cm in hole diameter

(Fig. 251; Picture 645).

(3) Corollary

This group of artifacts include important artifacts of the Liangzhu culture such as crown-shaped jade object (one piece), jade *cong* (four pieces), jade *yue* axe (two pieces), three-pronged jade object (one piece) and so on. Since the scene had already been damaged at the excavation site, their original location could not be identified. In tombs of Liangzhu culture at south line of Yaoshan, only one piece of crown-shaped jade object, three-pronged jade object and jade *yue* axe were unearthed respectively for each tomb, but in this group, two jade *yue* axes were unearthed, so they may belong to two tombs.

## Section 3 Artifacts Unearthed from the Stratum

During the excavation from 1996 to 1998, many Liangzhu culture artifacts were unearthed from the top soil. In addition, in test trenches of different areas, many artifacts were found also in the Liangzhu culture stratums. A brief introduction is as follows:

(1) Jade artifacts

Three pieces.

**Tube:** one piece (T0111①:1), it is deep brown in color, it does not belong to nephrite judging from its surface. It is cylinder shaped, with a hole at the center. It is 0.6 cm in length and 0.8 cm in diameter (Fig. 253: 5).

**Awl-shaped object:** one piece (97 collection:1), only the sharp and pointed end is left. It is white with a round cross section. It is 1.9 cm in residual length and 0.5 cm in diameter (Fig. 253: 6).

**Ring:** one piece (97 collection:2), it is broken and only a quarter of it is left. It is white and flat, its inner side is thicker than the outer side (Fig. 253: 7).

(2) Stone artifacts

Fifteen pieces.

**Short adzs:** eleven pieces.

South trench T204④:1, it is flat and rectangle shaped. Its blade is single, flat and straight with a slightly convex back. It is 5.6 cm in length, 2.6 cm in width and 1.3 cm in thickness (Fig. 253: 2).

Middle trench T204①:1, it is damaged and has oblate rectangle shaped. Its blade is single, flat and straight, with a slightly convex back. It is 4.5 cm in length, 2.5 cm in width and 1 cm in thickness (Fig. 253: 8).

T206①:1, it is oblate rectangle shaped. Its body is thick, with a sloping single blade and a slightly convex back. It is 3.1 cm in length, 4.1 cm in width and 1.2 cm in thickness (Fig. 253: 4).

T206①:2, it is damaged, with only the upper part

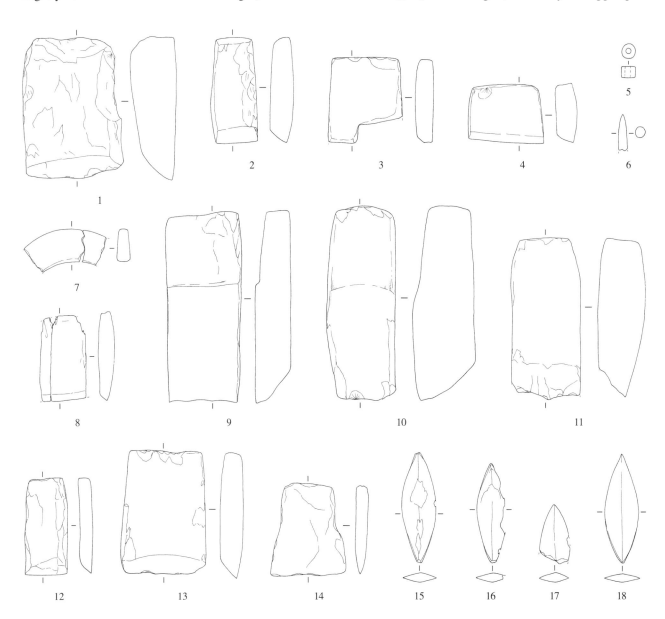

**Fig. 253.** Jade and stone artifacts unearthed from stratum

1–4. stone adzes (T311①:1, T204 south trench④:1, T206①:2, T206①:1) ; 5. jade tube (T0111①:1) ; 6. jade awl-shaped object (97 collection:1) ; 7. jade ring (97 collection:2) ; 8–14. stone adzes (T204 middle trench①:1, T0705①:1. T0502 ①:1, T311①:2, T0705①:2, T0210①:1, T0511②:1) ; 15–18. stone arrowheads (T204 south trench②:1, T204 south trench②:2, T204 north trench②:1, T0513:1) (1/2)

left. It is oblate. It is 4 cm in width and 0.9 cm in thickness (Fig. 253: 3).

T311①:1, it is slightly damaged and rectangle shaped. Its body is thick, its blade is single, with using cracks on the it, rough surface. It is 7.4 cm in length, 5.4 cm wide and 2.5 cm thick (Fig. 253: 1).

T311①:2, it is rectangle planed and its body is thick. Its blade is broken and it has an convex back. It is 8.6 cm in residual length, 3.8 cm in width and 2.6 cm in thickness (Fig. 253: 11).

T0210①:1, it is rectangle planed, and its body is oblate. It has a single blade, which is relatively straight and flat, the same as the back. It is 6.5 cm in length, 4.7 cm in width and 1.4 cm in thickness (Fig. 253: 13).

T0502①:1, it is strip-shaped, its cross section is square-shaped. It is slightly stepped, and its blade is broken. It is 10.5 cm in length, 3.7 cm in width, and 3.4 cm in thickness (Fig. 253: 10).

T0511②:1, it is trapezoid planed, its body is oblate. It has a flat blade and sloping back. It is 4.9 cm in length, 2.8–4.2 cm in width and 0.7 cm in thickness (Fig. 253: 14).

T0705①:1, it is long-strip shaped and step-shaped, with a square cross section. It has a single blade with a straight and flat blade back. It is 10.2 cm long, 4.1 cm wide and 2 cm thick (Fig. 253: 9).

T0705①:2, its body is oblate and it is in rectangle plane. It is 5.2 cm in length, 2.3 cm in width, and 0.8 cm in thickness (Fig. 253: 12).

**Arrowheads:** four pieces.

South Trench T204②:1, it is intact, and willow-leaf shaped, its cross section is rhombus-shaped. It is 5.8 cm in length, 1.9 cm in width and 0.5 cm in thickness (Fig. 253: 15).

South Trench T204②:2, it is broken, and willow-leaf shaped. Its cross section is rhombus-shaped. It is 5.3 cm in length, 1.6 cm in width and 0.5 cm in thickness (Fig. 253: 16).

North Trench T204②:1, it is broken, and only the sharp end is left. The body is oblate and it is willow-leaf shaped, and its cross section is rhombus-shaped. It is 3.1 cm in length, 1.7 cm in width and 0.6 cm in thickness (Fig. 253: 17).

T0513:1, it is willow-leaf shaped, with a rhombus-shaped cross section. It is 5.8 cm in length, 1.9 cm in width and 0.4 cm in thickness (Fig. 253: 18).

# Chapter V
# Research and Knowledge

## Section 1 The Assemblage of Burial Artifacts and Their Relative Ages

The unearthed burial objects in Yaoshan were mainly pottery vessels, stone artifacts and jade artifacts, whose assemblage will be discussed as follows.

### 1. Pottery Vessel Assemblage

Pottery vessels were found in 12 excavated tombs in Yaoshan.7 pieces were excavated from tomb M4 and tomb M11 respectively, ranking first in terms of quantity. Only 3 pieces were unearthed from tomb M5, making it the least, and all the other tombs had four pieces of unearthed pottery vessels respectively. 53 pottery vessels in total were unearthed from all the tombs, including 13 sand-tempered pottery *ding* tripods, among which two from tomb M11 and one from each of the other tombs respectively; 13 clay pottery *dou*, among which two from tomb M2 and one from each of the other tombs respectively; 9 sand-tempered pottery ring-foot jars, one was found in every tomb except tomb M1, tomb M4 and tomb M5; and 9 sand-tempered pottery *gang* vats, one came from every tomb except tomb M2, tomb M5 and tomb M6. The above-mentioned four kinds of pottery vessels unearthed had a total number of 44 pieces, accounting for 85% of all the pottery vessels unearthed. Therefore, it was obvious that, *ding* tripod, *dou*, ring-foot jar and *gang* vat were the main types of funeral pottery vessels of Yaoshan tombs. In addition, all the 12 tombs had at least three kinds of the these four main types. By inference, we could see that, the pottery vessel assemblage of Yaoshan was a combination of sand-tempered pottery *ding* tripod, clay pottery *dou*, sand-tempered pottery ring-foot jar and sand-tempered pottery *gang* vat. In the southern tombs, unearthed pottery vessels of tomb M3, and from tomb M7 to

**Table 2.** Table of pottery vessel assemblage unearthed from Yaoshan tombs

| Tomb \ Artifacts | *Ding* tripod | *Dou* | Ring-foot jar | *Gang* vat | Others |
|---|---|---|---|---|---|
| Tomb M1 | 1 | 1 | | 1 | 1 |
| Tomb M2 | 1 | 2 | 1 | | |
| Tomb M3 | 1 | 1 | 1 | 1 | |
| Tomb M4 | 1 | 1 | | 1 | 4 |
| Tomb M5 | 1 | 1 | | | 1 |
| Tomb M6 | 1 | 1 | 1 | | 1 |
| Tomb M7 | 1 | 1 | 1 | 1 | |
| Tomb M8 | 1 | 1 | 1 | 1 | |
| Tomb M9 | 1 | 1 | 1 | 1 | |
| Tomb M10 | 1 | 1 | 1 | 1 | |
| Tomb M11 | 2 | 1 | 1 | 1 | 2 |
| Tomb M14 | 1 | 1 | 1 | 1 | |

tomb M10 all fall into the foregoing assemblage and each tomb just had one piece of it for each kind, with the exception that only tomb M2 didn't have the sand-tempered pottery *gang* vat. For the details, please refer to the Table 2.

### 2. Stone Artifact Assemblage

The unearthed burial stone objects in Yaoshan included *yue* axe, cylindrical object with cover, narrow waist-shaped ornament and cylindrical object. The last three kinds were all from tomb M8, and therefore, stone *yue* axe was the main stone artifact of Yaoshan tombs. The stone *yue* axe was mainly made of ferro-actinolite. According to modern mineralogy, the ferro-actinolite was also a kind of nephrite, but in this report, we still adopted its original name for the custom of the excavations and researches related to the Liangzhu culture and regard stone *yue* axe as a kind of "stone artifact". In the Yaoshan tombs, 10 stone *yue* axes were unearthed, from tomb M2, tomb M3, tombs M7–M10 respectively, among which three from tomb M7, two from tomb M2 and tomb M10 respectively, and one from each of the other three tombs. All the unearthed *yue* axes were from tombs in the south line of Yaoshan. So, we could see, stone *yue* axes were unique burial objects to the south line.

### 3. Jade Artifact Assemblage

Jade artifact was main burial objects of Yaoshan. According to statistics by single piece, it accounted for over 97% of all the unearthed artifacts there. Apart from a large amount of tubes, beads, particles and other small jade ornaments, the jade artifacts could be classified into crown-shaped jade object, cylindrical object with cover, three-pronged object, set of awl-shaped objects, *yue* axe, *cong*, *cong*-stylistic tube, *huang* semi-circular pendant, round plaque, bracelet, cylindrical object, awl-shaped object, belt hook, plaque object, spindle whorl, bird and so on. We will introduce the unearthing situation of those jade artifacts in these tombs.

Only crown-shaped object was unearthed in every tomb among the unearthed jade artifacts, and only one piece for each tomb, which was a common characteristic for all the tombs. It also revealed the significance of crown-shaped jade object in the artifacts unearthed in the Yaoshan tombs.

Three-pronged object, set of awl-shaped objects, *yue* axe, *cong* and *cong*-stylistic tube were only discovered from tombs in the south line (tombs M2, M3, M7–M10), where just one three-pronged object and *yue* and one set of awl-shaped objects were discovered in each tomb. The triangular plaques were unearthed from each of tomb M7, tomb M9 and tomb M10 respectively. Eight jade *cong* were unearthed from tomb M2, tomb M7, tomb M9 and tomb M10. *Cong*-stylistic tubes were also just from tombs in the south line.

Cylindrical objects with cover were mainly from

tombs in the south line too. Except that the one from tomb M8 was made of stone, other tombs were all unearthed with only one piece of jade cylindrical object. However, in the tombs of north line, only one piece of cylindrical object with cover was unearthed from tomb M11.

The jade artifacts only unearthed in the north line tombs (tomb M1, tombs M4–M6, tomb M11 and tomb M14) were jade *huang* semi-circular pendants. 1–4 pieces of jade *huang* semi-circular pendants were unearthed from all tombs except tomb M5. For tombs from which more than two jade *huang* semi-circular pendants were unearthed, they all had one piece of jade *huang* semi-circular pendant forming an assemblage with a string of round jade plaques, which showed a close connection between the jade *huang* semi-circular pendants and the round jade plaques.

For the north line of tombs, 1–13 pieces of round jade plaques were unearthed from the tombs except tomb M6. Interestingly, one round jade plaque with carved patterns was also unearthed from tomb M2 in the south line. One spindle whorl was also unearthed respectively from tomb M6 and tomb M11 in the north line.

In addition to the set of awl-shaped objects, individual piece of awl-shaped objects were also unearthed from some particular tombs of both the north and south lines. Other artifacts commonly unearthed from both the north and south lines of tombs include jade bracelets and cylindrical objects.

Only one jade belt hook and one jade bird were unearthed from the whole tomb area, respectively from tomb M7 and tomb M2. For more information about the assemblage of unearthed jade artifacts, please refer to the Table 3.

### 4. Artifact Assemblage

The assemblage of Yaoshan's burial objects could be categorized into two groups:

Group A: this group includes crown-shaped jade object, cylindrical object with cover, set of awl-shaped objects, *yue* axe, *cong*-stylistic tube, stone *yue* axe, pottery *ding* tripod, pottery *dou*, pottery ring-foot jar, and pottery *gang* vat. Group B: this group includes crown-shaped jade object, *huang* semi-

**Table 3.** Table of major jade artifact assemblage unearthed from Yaoshan tombs

| Type | Tomb M1 | Tomb M2 | Tomb M3 | Tomb M4 | Tomb M5 | Tomb M6 | Tomb M7 | Tomb M8 | Tomb M9 | Tomb M10 | Tomb M11 | Tomb M14 |
|---|---|---|---|---|---|---|---|---|---|---|---|---|
| Crown-shaped object | 1 | 1 | 1 | 1 | 1 | 1 | 1 | 1 | 1 | 1 | 1 | 1 |
| Cylindrical object with cover | | 1 | 1 | | | | 1 | | 1 | 1 | 1 | |
| Three-pronged object | | 1 | 1 | | | | 1 | 1 | 1 | 1 | | |
| Set of awl-shaped objects | | 1 | 1 | | | | 1 | 1 | 1 | 1 | | |
| *Yue* axe | | 1 | 1 | | | | 1 | 1 | 1 | 1 | | |
| *Cong* | | 2 | | | | | 2 | | 1 | 3 | | |
| *Cong*-stylistic tube | | 2 | 2 | | | | 10 | | 5 | | | |
| *Huang* semi-circular pendant | 2 | | | 2 | | 1 | | | | | 4 | 1 |
| Round plaque | 6 | 1 | | 8 | 3 | | | | | | 13 | 1 |
| Bracelet | 1 | 1 | 3 | 3 | | 2 | 12 | 1 | 1 | 7 | 9 | 2 |
| Cylindrical object | | 3 | | 1 | | 1 | 2 | 1 | 2 | 8 | 4 | |
| Awl-shaped object | 1 | 2 | 1 | 1 | | 1 | 1 | 2 | 1 | | 2 | 1 |
| Belt hook | | | | | | | 1 | | | | | |
| Plaque object | | | | | | | 1 | | 1 | 1 | | |
| Spindle whorl | | | | | | 1 | | | | | 1 | |
| Bird | | 1 | | | | | | | | | | |

circular pendant, round plaque, spindle whorl, pottery *ding* tripod, pottery *dou*, pottery ring-foot jar, and pottery *gang* vat, but no stone artifacts. The tombs with Group A's burial objects are tomb M2, tomb M3, tomb M7, tomb M8, tomb M9 and tomb M10, all belonging to the tombs in south line; and the tombs with Group B's burial objects were tomb M1, tomb M4, tomb M5, tomb M6, tomb M11 and tomb M14, all belonging to the tombs in north line. So it could be seen that the assemblage of burial artifacts and the tomb arrangement were somewhat consistent.

## 5. Relative Ages of the Tombs

For the relative dates of Yaoshan tombs, we can refer to the unearthed pottery vessels. The tombs' pottery vessel assemblage included the sand-tempered pottery *ding* tripod, clay pottery *dou*, sand-tempered pottery ring-foot jar and sand-tempered pottery *gang* vat was also the main assemblage of the Liangzhu tombs in the Liangzhu Site Cluster. The pottery vessels were generally similar, which suggested that they belonged to the same period. The sand-tempered pottery *ding* tripods were mostly red-brown pottery vessels containing fine sand with mortar on the surface and therefore smooth in appearance, and had a straight or slightly concave rim and a flat round bottom. The *ding* tripods had fin-shaped legs with circular cambered inner edge, the cross sections were flat, with the outer side slightly thicker than the inner side. Pottery *dou* were made of clay pottery in gray color, and some of them were black-coating pottery decorated with vermilion patterns. Most pottery *dou* had wide, short and trumpet-like ring feet, a relatively open mouth, a shallow abdomen with folded walls, a relatively flat bottom. Some of them had combination pattern of triangular and round openwork holes on the outer wall of the *dou*, but the holes were not cut through. The ring-foot jars were made of red sand-tempered pottery, having a open mouth, concave rim, bulging abdomen, short trumpet-shaped ring-foot. The pottery *gang* vats were made of sand-tempered red pottery, mostly having a straight mouth and sharp tip and their surfaces were carved with basket patterns.

Through observations of above pottery vessels

and consideration of the periodization results of the Liangzhu culture[1], we could deduced that Yaoshan's tomb pottery vessel assemblage belonged to the third stage of the Liangzhu culture and the date of the Yaoshan's tomb is at the early period of middle stage of the Liangzhu culture.

# Section 2 Researches on Jade Artifacts

## 1. Carved Patterns on Jade Artifacts

The patterns' theme of the Liangzhu culture jade artifacts was the sacred human and animal face motif which was represented by the motifs on the large jade *cong* unearthed from Fanshan tomb M12.[2] This jade *cong*'s straight groove had shown a complete and nearly true-life combination of sacred human and animal face by bas-relief and intaglio carving techniques, laying emphasis on graphic visual effect. The use of the special shapes of large *cong* showed the significance of the sacred human and animal face motif to jade artifacts of the Liangzhu culture.

The patterns on jade artifacts unearthed from Yaoshan were also mainly the sacred animal motifs, including relatively complete shapes and simplified shapes. The jade artifacts carved with such patterns included *cong*, three-pronged object, crown-shaped object, awl-shaped object, *cong*-stylistic tube, *huang* semi-circular pendant, cylindrical object, and lower end ornaments of *yue* axe.

On the M10:20 triangular plaque object, the front side was carved with three-dimensional sacred animal motifs with bas-relief and intaglio carving techniques, with the upper part of rectangle feather-like crown in bas-relief and the sacred human motif in intaglio in the middle. The sacred human's faces were the same as the one on Fanshan tomb M12 large *cong*, with just the difference of hollowed-out holes on the two sides of the heads, which represented the long neck of the sacred human motif. And the lower part was the sacred animal motif in bas-relief. A wide mouth was carved on the lower edge of the object, which was straight and flat on the back side with oblique four pairs of small tunnel-shaped holes for the convenience of being stitched on something else.

The crown-shaped object (M2:1) unearthed from tomb M2 had fully displayed the sacred human and animal face motif on a flat surface. The object was slightly concave but generally flat, with sacred animal motif intaglioed on the concave side. The upper part of the motif was the sacred human wearing a feather-like crown with the same facial features as those in above plaque object, having stretched arms – it was the only jade object that had a sacred animal motif with arms. The lower half of the motif was the sacred animal face motif in intaglio. Both corners of this object's upper part were carved with bird motifs standing on clouds and watching back, which showed the special relation between the sacred animal motif and the bird motif.

Most jade objects' sacred animal motifs were simplified from above mentioned relatively complete motifs. The sacred human motif had its face and feather-like crown omitted, leaving only feather patterns to present the feather-like crown of the sacred human, such as the lower end ornament of *yue* axe unearthed from tomb M7 (M7:31) and the bracelet-shaped *cong* unearthed from tomb M9 (M9:4). A simpler way was to show the sacred human with crosswise bow string patterns, mainly found in *cong*, *cong*-stylistic tubes and awl-shaped objects.

The completeness, abstraction and complexity of the sacred animal motif were not associated with its date, but rather the individual object as its carrier. For example, the top of the M10:6 three-pronged object had used straight feather pattern to represent the sacred human, while M7:26 three-pronged object had used the half of relatively complete sacred human with feather-like crown on the top of its left and right prong.

[1] Rui Guoyao, Space-time Analysis of the Liangzhu Culture, The *Illumination of Civilization – Liangzhu Culture*, Zhejiang People's Publishing House, 1996.

[2] Zhejiang Provincial Institute of Cultural Relics and Archaeology, Fanshan Archaeological Team, Excavation of Liangzhu Tombs at Fanshan, Yuhang County, Zhejiang Province, *Cultural Relics*, 1988, Issue 1.

Besides carved sacred animal motifs, the unearthed jade objects from Yaoshan also had "dragon-head motif", which was represented by the jade bracelet M1:30. The M1:30 was in wide ring shape and showed the front image of a dragon's head on its wide and flat surface, and extended the motif to upper and lower end in bas-relief to form a three dimensional dragon head motif, with wide and flat mouth on the bottom. On the front side, there was also a pair of protruding and round eyeballs, with a round eyepit on the outer part. Above the two eyes was a pair of short horns carved in intaglio, and above which a pair of nearly square ears in bas-relief. A double-line rhombus-shaped pattern was intaglioed between the eyes and the nose. The profiles of the wide and flat mouth, as well as the nose and the head on the motif were presented in bas-relief and intaglio.

In the past, we called such object "*Chi You Ring*", which had a pair of protruding eyes and a circle of intaglioed rings, totally different from those sacred animal motifs using single-circle or double-circle in tubular drilling or intaglio to represent two-dimensional eyes. The double-line rhombus-shaped pattern intaglioed between the eyes and the nose, which was scarcely discovered in sacred animal motifs. All these showed that the rhombus-shaped patterns and round protruding eyes were main representation of dragon-head motifs.

The jade objects with dragon-head motifs include jade bracelets, round plaques, and *huang* semi-circular pendants. The jade *huang* semi-circular pendants had both sacred animal motifs and the dragon-head motifs. Though these two kinds of motifs were carved on the same kind of objects, their representations were totally different. For example, sacred animal motifs all appeared on the plane of *huang* semi-circular pendants, but the dragon-head motifs were all carved on the sides of *huang* semi-circular pendants vertically arranged. Round plaques also had their dragon-head motifs carved on the outside edges. In the tombs of Yaoshan, no dragon-head motifs were found carved on the surface of oblate jade artifacts.

According to our initial judgment of the gender of the occupants in the north and south lines of Yaoshan tombs, we could see that *huang* semi-circular pendants and round plaques were the main burial objects for female occupants in the north line of Yaoshan tombs. Therefore, the dragon-head motifs may had a close connection with the female occupants.

If round protruding eyes and double-line rhombus patterns were treated as the main characteristics of dragon-head motifs, then we could see some simplified patterns of them on some jade tubes. For example, the surface patterns of M10:21 long jade tube could be divided into the upper, middle and lower part by vertical grooves, and each part had four round protruding eyes, which were connected with each other by using round cambered lines. Between eyes there was a double-line rhombus-shaped pattern carved in intaglio. Then the whole pattern could be treated as four dragon heads with shared eyes. It also could be found on some other jade tubes.

In all, the themes of Yaoshan jade artifacts included sacred animal motifs and the dragon head motifs. In all jade artifacts with patterns, those with dragon head motifs accounted for about 12.5%, so it was obvious that the sacred animal motifs dominated the patterns carved on Yaoshan jade artifacts.

## 2. Production Techniques of Jade Artifacts

Surfaces of most jade artifacts had been carefully polished and so we could just discuss the production techniques of the unearthed jade artifacts of Yaoshan through observations of processing traces.

There were two methods of cutting the unearthed jade artifacts of Yaoshan, i.e. string-cutting and blade-cutting.

For the string-cutting method, the soft strings were adopted to cut the jade through abrasive, leaving the plane with oval or cambered lines. Such continuous cambered lines were not arranged in parallel (Picture 646). Through observations from the sides, the surface cut by this method could not be very flat and smooth and any surfaces without further processing were uneven. For bigger jade artifacts such as *huang* semi-circular pendants, there were many cutting marks in arc shape on the surface. On the gap surfaces of round *jue*-shaped jade plaque, if not processed carefully, there would also have many cutting marks (Picture 647). On some jade bracelets' inner walls, there were vertical cambered cutting marks. From these marks, we could see that the central holes of these jade artifacts were cut and processed by using the string cutting method.

Blade-cutting means cutting jade materials with a hard and thin object in a straight movement through abrasive. Blade-cutting was usually used for cutting the materials of slender and long jade artifacts such as awl-shaped objects and tubes.

For jade tubes, the materials were mainly cut into slender and long shapes through the blade-cutting method, which then be polished. Many jade tubes' surfaces had vertical planes, and presented a prismatic shape, which mean they were polished vertically to form an round surface. The end surface of jade tube often found the cambered string-cutting marks, which showed that they were mainly cut by the string cutting method (Picture 648). The top ends of *yue* axe often have blade-cutting marks (Picture 649). In addition, among the simplified sacred animal motifs carved on jade *cong*, the parallel string patterns representing feather-like crowns at the top, the intaglioed lines separating the upper and lower patterns and the vertical grooves were also made by using the blade-cutting method.

Tubular drilling was mainly used for drilling holes on jade artifacts; sometimes solid drilling would also be used. The holes were generally drilled from both sides, with similar depth. What should be noted here was that many solid drill specimens were cut after drilling from both sides, and the cutting place were usually placed at junctions of drilling. Due to the inaccurate alignment for most drilling holes, there were different level's mismatch traces at the junctions. The tubular drilling method could also be adopted to make eyes of sacred animal motifs on the jade *cong*. On some jade end decorations, there were also small square or flat square mortise holes, which were caused by intensive solid drilliing.

The fracture surface or concaves on jade artifacts due to material cutting were all polished, with some surfaces different in heights formed during cutting. Therefore, we presumed that the object for polishing

should be a soft one.

Except *cong*, bracelet and cylindrical objects, most other jade artifacts were used with other artifacts, such as string of jade tubes, string of jade beads and jade *yue* axe, to form a assemblage by adopting concatenation method or mortise and tenon structure. Some jade artifacts had small mortises carved on the tenon to form a compound structure. Such a compound structure of course represented an extremely high level of technique at that time.

Many jade particles were unearthed from those tombs. Those jade particles were convex and polished on one side, relatively even on the other side and was hardly polished. Many of them have cambered string-cutting marks. Those particles should be embedded in surfaces of certain artifacts for decoration. Such an embedding technique showed the advancement of the embedded technology at that time.

## 3. Research on Main Artifacts

1. The crown-shaped jade object was once known as the "inverted trapezoidal object". In the excavation of Fanshan and Yaoshan, due to its shape similar to that of the sacred animal motifs, we called it crown-shaped jade object. In the Yaoshan tombs, regardless of the tombs' sizes and burial objects' numbers, each of the tombs had only one piece of crown-shaped object. It was the same with Fanshan. So we could see the significance of crown-shaped object in the Liangzhu culture, and to some extent, the crown-shaped objects had a higher status than other artifacts.

The plane of a crown-shaped jade object was mainly in trapezoid with a wide upper part, at the middle of which there was a point, which were different in shapes, some were straight in top with a point in the middle, and the other were concave in the top with a point in the middle. Though different in shapes, they were all used to represent the feather-like crowns of sacred human motif, to show some connection between the crown-shaped jade object and sacred humans' feather-like crowns. Under the protruding part, there were mainly oval holes, which allowed the crown-shaped jade object to be seen and appreciated from both the front and the back sides.

The crown-shaped objects were usually thin and therefore they emphasized the visual effect of the front view. In Yaoshan, each tomb was unearthed with one crown-shaped object, and generally without patterns except those from tomb M2 and tomb M11. Obviously, by observing the shape of objects, one could not judge their front and back sides. The side with patterns of crown-shaped object from tomb M2 was a little concave, facing upward when unearthed, and the other side had no patterns. It was assumed that the crown-shaped object just presented one side. Crown-shaped jade object unearthed from Fanshan all had patterns on just one side, so it could be seen that presenting on just one side was the main feature of crown-shaped objects. But the crown-shaped object from tomb M11 had double-face sacred animal motifs in intaglio with the same style and graphs, which seemed to show that the crown-shaped objects also had visual effects for both sides. However, through careful observations, we found that the two sides' motifs were imperceptibly different, with the main difference in the complexity of lines. Among the objects with visual effect for both sides, one side was still emphasized. Therefore, the more complex side should be taken as the front and the simple one should be the back.

All crown-shaped objects had flat and thin protruding tenons, with 3–5 small holes for being embedded onto other objects and the holes probably being for fastening. When the M2:1 crown-shaped object was unearthed, the protruding tenon on the bottom had vermilion coating at the front and back side, extending outward about 10 cm and having the same width of the protruding tenon. Wood fiber traces were found but could not be took out; therefore, it was a pity that the original form could not be determined. When the crown-shaped object was unearthed in tomb M30, Zhoujiabang site of Haiyan, Zhejiang, its bottom was found to be embedded on an ivory comb, which was the only object with complete form for crown-shaped object unearthed.[1] The bottoms of the crown-shaped object unearthed from Yaoshan all had drilling holes, mainly 3 holes. The M1:3 crown-shaped object had no protruding tenon and the holes were drilled at the bottom edge. The M8:3 crown-shaped object had the holes at the junctions of the protruding tenon and the object body. It thus could be seen that the embedded object's thickness may be not exactly the same with the thickness of a crown-shaped object. Among the crown-shaped objects unearthed from Yaoshan, five crown-shaped objects had their bottom and protruding tenon in same width. Therefore, it was more possible that the width of the embedded objects was different from the width of the crown-shaped objects.

2. Jade *yue* axe were unearthed from six tombs in the south line tombs, and each tomb was unearthed with only one piece.

The top ends of the jade *yue* axe were all relatively rough, and some even had fracture surface without any polishing, some had traces due to broken after cutting at the top ends. However, other parts of the jade *yue* axe had all been carefully polished. Therefore, it showed that there was no requirement for the visual effect of the top end, which assumed to be embedded into other objects.

It had been known now that when buried, all the jade *yue* axes had elegant handles. The Yaoshan M7:32 jade *yue* axe was relatively complete, but the handle was lost due to decay. However, there were two jade end ornaments of *yue* axe with different shapes unearthed on the southern-northern extending lines. The southern one was close to the jade *yue* axe, flat and nearly square in shape, just 1.5 cm in thickness; from a side view, there were two step-like protruding parts on the top. The bottom was flat and straight, and there were rectangle-protruding parts in the middle, a straight notch and horizontal round pinhole piercing the protruding tenon, and one oval hole on the both sides of protruding tenon. The other one had an olive shaped cross section, 3.4 cm in thickness, and step-shaped bottom. The end correlated to the south end had an oval tenon head and horizontal notches, in which there were rectangle holes for installation. The two end ornaments had the similar width, and would have been riveted to the two ends of the handle of jade *yue* axe.

[1] Zhejiang Provincial Institute of Cultural Relics and Archaeology, *Essence of Archaeological Results*, P184, Cultural Relics Press, 1999.

The southern one was thin and flat and therefore could be matched for the jade *yue* axe's shape, and the other was thicker. The handle of *yue* axe for connection should be oblate, which was convenience for handling. By combining the two end ornaments with the decayed *yue* axe handle, a complete mortise and tenon joint structure was formed.

3. Three-pronged object. This object was named after the shape of its upper part. It was the major type of artifacts unearthed from the south line tombs of Yaoshan, each tomb had just unearthed only with one piece of them, six in total, with four of them having sacred animal motifs. Among the four objects, three had motifs carved on just one side. Therefore, it was obvious that the three-pronged objects were for representing single-side visual effect, which matched the fact that some three-pronged objects had tunnel-shaped holes at one side. The M9:2 three-pronged object had sacred animal motifs carved on both sides, which was an exception. In Fanshan, it was nearly the same. It could be seen that for three-pronged object, representation of front side was also emphasized.

For most three-pronged objects, the middle prong was lower than the left and right ones. For the tomb M8 and tomb M9 three-pronged objects, there were several pairs of tunnel-shaped holes with different directions on the left and right prongs, which could be used for being attached on some other objects. When the three-pronged objects were unearthed, there usually had a long jade tube unearthed nearby. When the three-pronged object M7:26 was unearthed, its middle prong was found closely connected with a long jade tube (M7:25), which showed the complete form of combinational use of three-pronged objects and long tubes. Through observations, we had found that the middle prongs of some three-pronged objects had holes with not straight wall, and the wall of holes of the connected long tube were also not straight. It seemed that the three-pronged object and long jade tube could not be interpenetrated up and down.

## Section 3 Altar and Cemetery

The revealed Yaoshan relics were mainly built along the northwestern slope of Yaoshan Hill. The cemetery's central area was generally even and the tombs were set rationally at the highest place of the relic site. The site was adjacent to the Yaoshan Hill in the eastern edge. Due to later damage by farming, there was no clear boundary between the cemetery and the mountain. The site's northern and southern edges had apparently steep slopes, with meters' height difference from the central area, which emphasized the center area's prominence. The site's west edge was located between the slopes of the Yaoshan Hill and the Fenghuangshan Hill, also without a clear boundary. Generally, the plane form of the site was not very regular.

There were many sloped stone revetment constructed with gravels in the building process of the whole site. Except the western No. 1 stone revetment and the northern No. 1 stone revetment that formed the central part, the remaining stone revetments were mostly built along the mountain to form a gentle-sloped terrace, especially for the southern No. 1 stone revetment, which formed a relatively flat and spacious platform to the south of the center area. According to the stratigraphic excavation of the yellow mottled earth piled on the outer side of the southern No. 1 stone revetment, we can confirm that the stratum of earth had not been fully covered stone revetments at the time of building. At the middle section of the southern No. 1 stone revetment, there was a breach due to destruction in the later stage. The gravels it used were scattered on the nearby yellow mottled earth stratum, with the volume generally the same as that of the breach. From here we can see that the yellow earth stratum had kept its original form and we can further infer that the whole site had generally maintained its initially gentle-sloped form except the center area.

In successive explorations and excavation through the years, we once tried to find the construction trace on the surface of the site yet no discovery was obtained. Except the piled stone revetments, there was no related trace of relics that had special significance. Therefore, relying on the archaeological achievements so far, we can not conclude any other purpose of the Yaoshan relics except its function as a cemetery. Of course, given the relatively even center and the spacious slow-sloped platform at its southern part, we could not rule out the possibilities that there had been some sacrificial activities after the site was established or the cemetery was built. However it now could not be confirmed by us with our current discoveries.

It was a cemetery site for elites in the Liangzhu culture with careful arrangements. From current discoveries in excavation, we can see that the tombs were all built at the highest place and were built regularly in the center area, which constituted the northern and southern tomb lines. The pottery vessels unearthed from the tombs were uniform in assemblages and shapes, which showed they were in the same period. In the tomb area, the "red earthen mound" at the central part was damaged by some tombs, but it still basically kept its original shape. It was obvious to us that there was a certain connection between the tomb and the "red earthen mound".

The tomb occupant's gender could not be identified because only in the tomb M7 did we discover some rotten human head traces and teeth. No other human remains were found in other tombs in the whole cemetery. We could just make some initial deductions according to the assemblages of artifacts unearthed from these. In the six south line's tombs of Yaoshan, each was unearthed with one jade *yue* axe and some stone *yue* axe. Tomb M12 belonging to the south line also was unearthed with one jade *yue* axe. *Yue*

axe could be regarded as an evolved product of the axe. Therefore it was often used as burial objects for male, especially in the pre-historical period of China. Therefore, we estimate that the south line's tombs belonged to male, which was probably right. In the six tombs of the north line tombs, there was no jade or stone *yue* axe but mainly jade artifacts assemblages such as *huang* semi-circular pendants and round plaques, also spindle whorls. Therefore it was reasonable for us to infer that the owner of the six tombs may be female.

The scope of tombs currently revealed had not gone beyond the scope of the "yellow earthen mound" (that had been piled at the third stage in center area, as mentioned in the Chapter II). But from the top soil of the western part of T3 excavated in 1986, jade artifacts including damaged crown-shaped object, complete jade tubes and jade beads, were unearthed. Then, important Liangzhu jade artifacts such as jade *cong*, jade *yue* axe, crown-shaped jade objects were also discovered in the "west part". Judging from this, we can know that several tombs of Yaoshan Cemetery Site had been damaged and the original tomb area were significantly larger than the currently discovered, the tombs were more than the currently discovered.

Liangzhu Site Cluster was the most important area of the Liangzhu culture and Yaoshan was one of the highest-level cemeteries of Liangzhu Site Cluster, even of the whole Liangzhu culture. Therefore, its discovery will undoubtedly promote the researches on the origin of Chinese Civilization.

# Postscript

Yaoshan, first excavated in 1987, was awarded along with Fanshan as one of Top 10 Archaeological Discoveries in China during the Seventh Five-Year Plan period. The excavation of Fanshan and Yaoshan deepens the research of Liangzhu culture and also advances the study on the origin of Chinese civilization. The sorting of data and compiling of excavation reports of these two sites were listed as projects supported by National Social Science Foundation during the Seventh Five-Year Plan period. In the following years, preliminary sorting was conducted by research team members based on the excavation findings with results successively published in related research works. From 1996 to 1998, the Institute conducted several excavations on Yaoshan relics and obtained important findings. After the retirement of Mr. Mu Yongkang, who presided over the first excavation, Rui Guoyao and Fang Xiangming conducted a complete sorting of all excavation data. They also sorted out the artifacts from Yaoshan that were collected and kept by relevant departments in Yuhang District, incorporating them into the Report. The Report was written by Rui Guoyao, the drawing and arrangement of diagrams was in charge by Fang Xiangming, and photos were taken by Li Yongjia.

A mineralogical detection report on unearthed jade artifacts was planned as appendix for the Report. Experts were invited to do mineralogical detection for the jade artifacts with conclusions dispersedly published in related works. However, official detection report has not yet been received, so it cannot be included into the Report. As the interdisciplinary study on the Liangzhu culture jade artifacts is believed to be a very important task, the Institute intends to make it a key subject and to conduct a comprehensive research on the Liangzhu culture jade artifacts in the Institute together with relevant departments. Meanwhile, the jade artifacts detection report is to be published as soon as possible in order to complement the Report.

Thanks for Mr. Mu Yongkang's scrupulous advice during our data sorting and report preparation. The title of the Report was carved by Mr. Bao Xianlun, deputy director of Zhejiang Provincial Department of Culture. The abstract was translated by Ms. Qin Ling from the School of Archaeology and Museology, Peking University. The jade artifacts' rubbings in the Report were made by Mr. Wan Yuren and Mr. Xu Yongxiang from Shanghai Museum after the completion of the first excavation. Sincere thanks to their contridgeutions.

*Zhejiang Provincial Institute of Cultural Relics and Archaeology*
November 28, 2011

# YAOSHAN

ISBN 978-7-5010-7441-9

First Edition: October 2022

Price: 480.00RMB


## Compiler

Zhejiang Provincial Institute of Cultural Relics and Archaeology


## Publishing Office

Cultural Relics Press

100007, Building 2, Beixiaojie, Dongzhimennei, Dongcheng District, Beijing, China

Tel: 86-10- 64010048

Web: www.wenwu.com


## Printer

Beijing Artron Graphic Art Co., Ltd.

101399, No.3 Dasheng Road, Jinma Industrial Zone, Shunyi District, Beijing, China

Tel: 86-10-80451188

# Pictures

DSM (Digital Surface Model) of the altar of Yaoshan Site

Drawing by Shaanxi October Cultural Relics Protection Co., LTD

Picture 1. Yaoshan in excavation of 1987

Picture 2. Yaoshan in excavation of 1997

Picture 3. Full view of the site revealed in 1987 (from south to north)

Picture 4. Western No. 1 stone revetment

Picture 5. Part of western No. 2 stone revetment

Picture 6. Part of southern No. 1 stone revetment

Picture 7. Southern No. 1 stone revetment

Picture 8. Northern No. 1 stone revetment

Picture 9. Tomb M1

Picture 10.
Jade *huang* semi-circular pendant in
tomb M1 when unearthed

M1

Picture 11. Crown-shaped jade object (M1:3)

Picture 12. Jade bracelet (M1:30)

M1

Picture 13. Jade bracelet (M1:30)

Picture 14. Jade bracelet (M1:30)

Picture 15. Jade *huang* semi-circular pendant (M1:5)

Picture 18. Round jade plaque (M1:13-1)

Picture 16. Jade *huang* semi-circular pendant (M1:12)

Picture 19. Round jade plaque (M1:13-2)

Picture 17. String of jade tubes (M1:4)

Picture 20. Round jade plaque (M1:13-3)

M1

Picture 21. Round jade plaque (M1:13-4)

Picture 22. Round jade plaque (M1:13-5)

Picture 23. Jade beads and tubes (M1:1, 2, 14, 19, 20)

Picture 24. Jade tubes (M1:6, 10, 11, 16–18)

M1

Picture 25. Jade tubes
(M1:21–23, 28, 29)

Picture 26. Awl-shaped jade
object (M1:15)

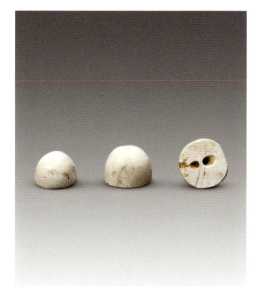

Picture 27. Jade beads (M1:7–9)

Picture 28. Tomb M2

Picture 29.
Jade *cong*, jade *yue* axe and
stone *yue* axe in tomb M2
when unearthed

M2

Picture 30. Crown-shaped jade object (M2:1)

Picture 31. Three-pronged jade object (M2:6)

Picture 32. Cylindrical jade object with cover (cover) (M2:2)

Picture 33. Cylindrical jade object with cover (cylindrical object) (M2:3)

M2

Picture 34. Long jade tube (M2:7)

Picture 35. Long jade tube (M2:18)

Picture 36. Awl-shaped jade object (M2:8-1)

Picture 37. Awl-shaped jade object (M2:8-2)

M2

Picture 38. Awl-shaped jade object (M2:9-1)

Picture 39. Awl-shaped jade object (M2:9-2)

Picture 40. Awl-shaped jade object (M2:10)

Picture 41. Awl-shaped jade object (M2:11)

Picture 42. Awl-shaped jade object (M2:12)

Picture 43. Jade *cong* (M2:22)

Picture 44. Jade *cong* (M2:23)

Picture 45. Jade *yue* axe (M2:14)

Picture 46. *Cong*-stylistic jade tube (M2:20)

Picture 47. *Cong*-stylistic jade tube (M2:21)

Picture 48. Cylindrical jade object (M2:4)

Picture 49. Cylindrical jade object (M2:5)

M2

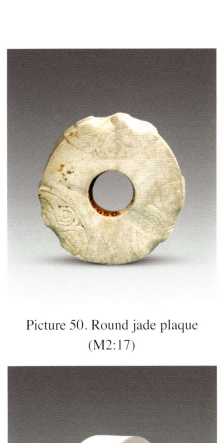

Picture 50. Round jade plaque
(M2:17)

Picture 51. Round jade plaque
(M2:17)

Picture 52. Cylindrical jade object
(M2:16)

Picture 53. Jade bracelet
(M2:24)

Picture 54. Jade end ornament
(M2:15)

Picture 55. Awl-shaped jade object
(M2:25)

Picture 56. Awl-shaped jade object
(M2:28)

Picture 57. Bar-shaped jade
ornament (M2:51)

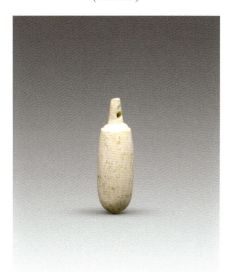

Picture 58. Jade pendant
(M2:26)

M2

Picture 59. Jade end ornament
(M2:44)

Picture 60. Jade end ornament
(M2:46)

Picture 61. Jade end ornament
(M2:54)

Picture 62. Jade bird (M2:50) (Front side)

Picture 63. Jade bird (M2:50) (Back side)

M2

Picture 64. Jade handle (M2:55)

Picture 65. Jade handle (M2:55) (details)

Picture 66. String of jade tubes (M2:37)

Picture 67. String of jade tubes (M2:40)

Picture 68. String of jade tubes (M2:57)

Picture 69. String of jade tubes (M2:58)

Picture 70. String of jade tubes (M2:19)

Picture 71. Jade tubes (M2:39, 48, 43-1, 43-2 )

Picture 72. Jade tubes (M2:29, 47, 52, 53)

Picture 73. String of jade tubes (M2:38)

M2

Picture 74. String of jade tubes (M2:59)

Picture 75. Jade beads (M2:13)

Picture 76. Jade beads (M2:42, 60, 41)

Picture 77. Jade particles (M2:30–33, 45, 49)

M2

Picture 78. Stone *yue* axe (M2:27)

Picture 79. Stone *yue* axe (M2:61)

Picture 80. Tomb M3

Picture 81. Cylindrical jade object
with cover (cover) (M3:1)

Picture 82. Cylindrical jade object
with cover (cylindrical object) (M3:2)

M3

Picture 83. Crown-shaped jade object (M3:5)

M3

Picture 84. Three-pronged jade object (M3:3)

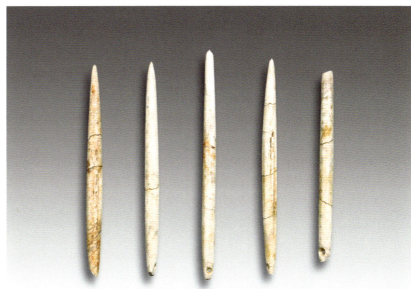

Picture 85. Long jade tube (M3:9)　　　　Picture 86. Awl-shaped jade objects (M3:4-1–4-5)

Picture 88. *Cong*-stylistic　　Picture 89. *Cong*-stylistic
　jade tube (M3:38)　　　　jade tube (M3:39)

M3

Picture 87. Jade *yue* axe (M3:12)　　　　Picture 90. *Cong*-stylistic jade tubes (M3:38, 39)

Picture 91. Jade bracelet (M3:14)

Picture 92. Jade bracelet (M3:15)

Picture 93. Jade bracelet (M3:16)

Picture 94. Awl-shaped jade object (M3:23)

Picture 95. Jade pendant (M3:44)

M3

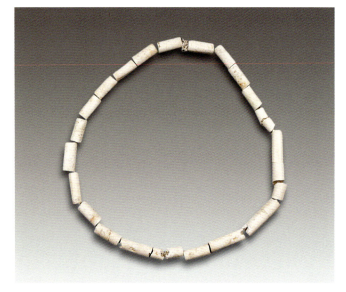

Picture 96. String of jade tubes (M3:29)

Picture 97. String of jade tubes (M3:31)

Picture 98. Jade tubes (M3:42)

Picture 99. Jade tubes (M3:6, 7, 21, 27, 37, 46)

Picture 100. Jade tube (M3:10)

Picture 101. Jade tubes (M3:11, 48)

Picture 102. Jade tubes (M3:17, 24, 26, 28, 35)

M3

Picture 103. Jade tube (M3:18)

Picture 104. Jade tubes (M3:19, 25)

Picture 105. Jade tube (M3:22)

Picture 106. Jade tubes (M3:30, 33, 34, 36)

Picture 107. Jade tube
(M3:47)

Picture 108. Jade beads
(M3:8)

M3

Picture 109. String of jade tubes (M3:41)

Picture 110. Stone *yue* axe (M3:13)

Picture 111. Tomb M4

Picture 112. Jade *huang* semi-circular
pendant, crown-shaped jade object and string
of jade tubes in tomb M4 when unearthed

Picture 113. Jade *huang* semi-circular
pendant and string of round jade plaques
in tomb M4 when unearthed

M4

Picture 114. Crown-shaped jade object (M4:28)

Picture 115. Jade *huang* semi-circular pendant (M4:6)

Picture 116. Jade *huang* semi-circular pendant (M4:34)

M4

Picture 117. Round jade plaque (M4:7)

Picture 118. Round jade plaque (M4:13)

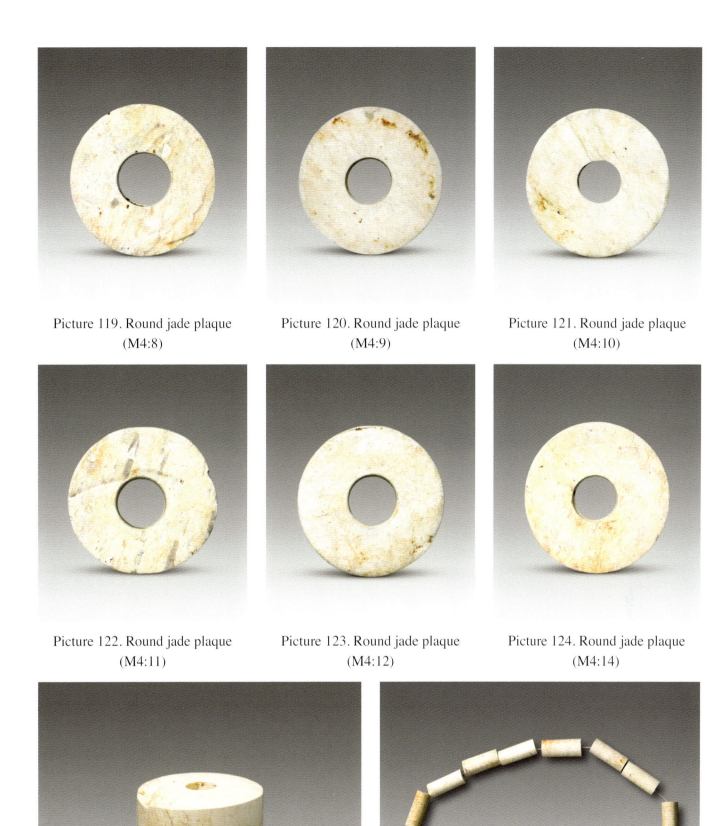

Picture 119. Round jade plaque
(M4:8)

Picture 120. Round jade plaque
(M4:9)

Picture 121. Round jade plaque
(M4:10)

Picture 122. Round jade plaque
(M4:11)

Picture 123. Round jade plaque
(M4:12)

Picture 124. Round jade plaque
(M4:14)

M4

Picture 125. Cylindrical jade object (M4:3)

Picture 126. String of jade tubes (M4:35)

Picture 127. Jade bracelet (M4:15)

Picture 128. Jade bracelet (M4:16)

Picture 129. Jade bracelet
(M4:17)

Picture 130. Awl-shaped
jade object (M4:18)

Picture 131. Jade tubes
(M4:2, 5)

M4

Picture 132. Jade tubes (M4:1, 24–26, 36)

Picture 133. Jade tubes (M4:19–22)

Picture 134. Jade tubes (M4:23, 27, 29)

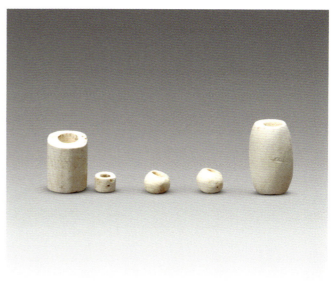

Picture 135. Jade tubes and beads (M4:44, 33, 31, 37)

Picture 136. Jade bead (M4:4)

Picture 137. Jade beads (M4:30, 32)

Picture 138. Pottery *dou* (M4:38)

Picture 139. Pottery dish (M4:45)

M4

Picture 140. Tomb M5

M5

Picture 141.
Crown-shaped jade object (M5:3)

Picture 142. Round jade plaque (M5:2)

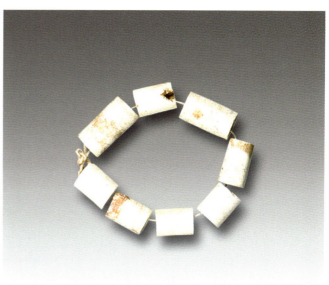

Picture 145. String of jade tubes (M5:5)

Picture 143. Round jade plaque (M5:8-2)

Picture 146. Jade tubes (M5:4)

Picture 144. Round jade plaque (M5:8-1)

Picture 147. Jade beads (M5:6, 1, 7)

M5

Picture 148. Tomb M6

M6

Picture 149. Crown-shaped jade object (M6:1)

Picture 150. Jade *huang* semi-circular pendant (M6:2)

Picture 151. Jade bracelet (M6:3)

Picture 152. Jade bracelet (M6:4)

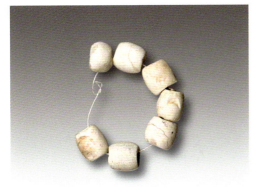

Picture 153. String of jade beads
(M6:8)

Picture 154. Jade ornament
(M6:9)

Picture 155. Awl-shaped jade
object (M6:14)

Picture 156. Jade spindle whorl (M6:5)

Picture 157. Jade tubes (M6:10, 16, 11, 12)

Picture 158. Cylindrical jade object (M6:6)

Picture 159. Jade beads (M6:7, 13, 15)

M7

Picture 160. Tomb M7

Picture 161.
Crown-shaped jade object
and string of jade tubes in
tomb M7 when unearthed

Picture 162. String of jade tubes in tomb M7 when unearthed

Picture 163.
Jade *cong* and part of jade artifacts in tomb M7 when unearthed

Picture 164. Jade inlaid lacquer in tomb M7 when unearthed

Picture 165. Jade plaque in tomb M7 when unearthed

Picture 166.
Three-pronged jade object in tomb M7 when unearthed

Picture 167. Three-pronged jade object (M7:26) (Front side)

Picture 168. Three-pronged jade object (M7:26)
(Back side)

Picture 169. Crown-shaped jade object (M7:63-27)

M7

Picture 170. Cylindrical jade object with cover (cover)
(M7:8-1)

Picture 173. Awl-shaped
jade object (M7:22)

Picture 174. Awl-shaped
jade object (M7:23)

Picture 171. Cylindrical jade object with cover (cover)
(M7:8-1)

Picture 175. Long jade
tube (M7:25)

Picture 176. Long jade
tube (M7:84)

M7

Picture 172. Cylindrical jade object with cover
(cylindrical object) (M7:8-2)

Picture 177. Long jade tube (M7:145)

Picture 178. Awl-shaped
jade object (M7:24-1)

Picture 179. Awl-shaped
jade object (M7:24-2)

Picture 180. Awl-shaped
jade object (M7:24-3)

Picture 181. Awl-shaped
jade object (M7:24-4)

Picture 182. Awl-shaped
jade object (M7:24-5)

Picture 183. Awl-shaped
jade object (M7:24-6)

Picture 184. Awl-shaped
jade object (M7:24-7)

Picture 185. Awl-shaped
jade object (M7:24-8 )

Picture 186. *Cong*-stylistic jade tube
(M7:43)

Picture 187. *Cong*-stylistic jade tube
(M7:44)

Picture 188. *Cong*-stylistic jade tube
(M7:45)

M7

Picture 189. Jade *cong* (M7:34)

Picture 190. Jade *cong* (M7:50)

Picture 191. Jade *yue* axe (M7:32)　　　　Picture 192. Jade *mao* end ornament (M7:31) of *yue* axe

M7

Picture 193. Jade *dui* end ornament (M7:33) of *yue* axe　　　　Picture 194. Jade *dui* end ornament (M7:33) of *yue* axe

Picture 195. *Cong*-stylistic jade tube (M7:46)

Picture 196. *Cong*-stylistic jade tube (M7:47)

Picture 197. *Cong*-stylistic jade tubes (M7:47, 46)

Picture 198. *Cong*-stylistic jade tube (M7:49)

Picture 199. *Cong*-stylistic jade tube (M7:51)

Picture 200. *Cong*-stylistic jade tube (M7:52)

Picture 201. *Cong*-stylistic jade tube (M7:54)

M7

Picture 202. *Cong*-stylistic jade tube (M7:147)

Picture 203. Awl-shaped jade object (M7:42)

Picture 204. Jade bracelet (M7:6)

Picture 205. Jade bracelet (M7:20)

Picture 206. Jade bracelet (M7:35)

Picture 207. Jade bracelet (M7:36)

Picture 208. Jade bracelet (M7:37)

Picture 209. Jade bracelet (M7:38)

Picture 210. Jade bracelet (M7:39)

Picture 211. Jade bracelet
(M7:40)

Picture 212. Cylindrical jade object
(M7:27)

Picture 213. Cylindrical jade object
(M7:98)

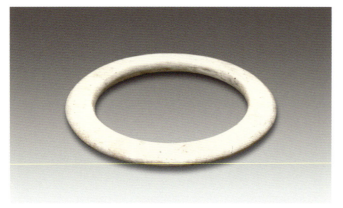

Picture 214. Jade bracelet (M7:30)

Picture 215. Jade bracelet (M7:41)

Picture 216. Jade bracelet (M7:57)

Picture 217. Jade bracelet (M7:58)

Picture 218. Jade end ornament (M7:18)

Picture 219. Jade end ornament (M7:29)

M7

Picture 220. Jade belt hook (M7:53)

Picture 221. Jade belt hook (M7:53)

Picture 222. Jade plaque (M7:55)

Picture 223. Jade pendant (M7:56)

Picture 224. Pie-shaped jade ornament (M7:11)

Picture 225. Semi-circular jade ornament (M7:101)

Picture 226. Semi-circular jade ornament (M7:133)

Picture 227. Semi-circular jade ornament (M7:134)

M7

Picture 228. Semi-circular jade ornament (M7:135)

Picture 231. String of jade tubes (M7:70)

Picture 229. String of jade tubes (M7:5)

Picture 232. String of jade tubes (M7:72)

M7

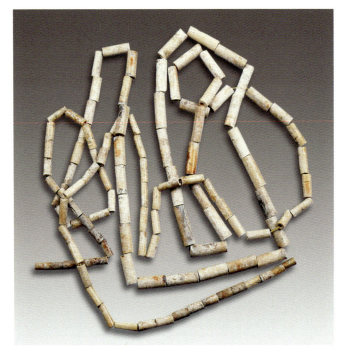

Picture 230. String of jade tubes (M7:28)

Picture 233. Jade tubes (M7:72)

Picture 234. String of jade tubes (M7:73)

Picture 235. Jade tubes (M7:80, 81)

Picture 236. String of jade tubes (M7:82)

Picture 237. Jade tubes (M7:102)

Picture 238. String of jade tubes (M7:104)

Picture 239. String of jade tubes (M7:114)

M7

Picture 240. Jade tubes (M7:115)

Picture 241. String of jade tubes (M7:116)

Picture 242. Jade tubes (M7:132)

Picture 243. String of jade tubes (M7:141)

M7

Picture 244. String of jade tubes (M7:148)

Picture 245. String of jade beads (M7:60)

Picture 246. String of jade beads (M7:61)

Picture 247. String of jade beads (M7:69)

Picture 248. String of jade beads (M7:136)

Picture 249. Jade tube (M7:10)

M7

Picture 250. String of jade beads (M7:59, 62, 64–68)

Picture 251. Jade tube (M7:9)

Picture 252. Jade tubes (M7:1–4)

Picture 253. Jade tubes (M7:12, 13, 15, 86, 88)

Picture 254. Jade tubes (M7:14, 21, 75, 96)

Picture 255. Jade tubes (M7:16, 87, 110, 111, 118)

Picture 256. Jade tubes (M7:48, 91, 100, 124, 128)

Picture 257. Jade tube (M7:77)

M7

Picture 258. Jade tubes (M7:85)

Picture 259. Jade tubes (M7:89, 92, 95, 107, 108)

Picture 260. Jade tubes (M7:90, 103, 120)

Picture 261. Jade tubes (M7:94, 122, 142)

Picture 262. Jade tubes (M7:97, 99, 106, 129)

Picture 263. Jade tubes (M7:105)

Picture 264. Jade tubes (M7:109, 117, 119, 125)

Picture 265. Jade tubes (M7:121, 123, 130, 131, 149, 161)

M7

Picture 266. Jade tubes (M7:126, 127, 146, 151)

Picture 267. Jade beads (M7:74, 93)

Picture 268. Jade bead (M7:78)

Picture 269. Jade bead (M7:79)

Picture 270. Jade beads (M7:112, 113)

Picture 271. Jade bead (M7:150)

Picture 272. Jade particles (M7:17)

Picture 273. Jade particles (M7:19)

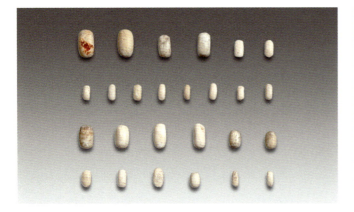
Picture 274. Jade particles (M7:63-1–63-26)

Picture 275. Jade particles (M7:143)

M7

Picture 276. Jade particles (M7:144)

Picture 277. Jade particles (M7:152)

Picture 278. Stone *yue* axe (M7:76)

Picture 279. Stone *yue* axe (M7:83)

Picture 280. Stone *yue* axe (M7:157)

Picture 281. Shark tooth (M7:137)

Picture 282. Shark tooth (M7:137)

M8

Picture 283. Tomb M8

Picture 284. Crown-shaped jade object (M8:3)

M8

Picture 285. Three-pronged jade object (M8:8)
(Front side)

Picture 286. Three-pronged jade object (M8:8)
(Back side)

Picture 287. Jade *yue* axe (M8:14)

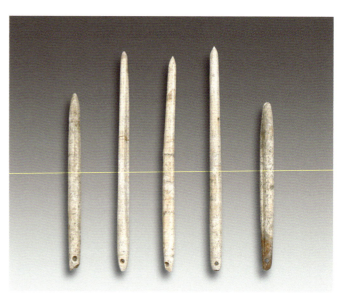

Picture 288. Awl-shaped jade objects (M8:10-1–10-5)

Picture 289. Awl-shaped jade object (M8:30)

Picture 290. Awl-shaped jade object (M8:31)

M8

Picture 291. Long jade tube (M8:27)

Picture 292. Cylindrical jade object (M8:28)

Picture 293. Jade bracelet (M8:29)

Picture 294. Jade pendant (M8:34)　　　Picture 295. String of jade tubes (M8:33)　　　Picture 296. String of jade tubes (M8:32)

Picture 297. Jade tubes (M8:1, 9, 11, 17, 25)　　　Picture 298. Jade tubes (M8:18, 24, 37)

Picture 299. Jade tubes (M8:22)　　　Picture 300. Jade tube (M8:26)　　　Picture 301. Jade bead (M8:35)

 M8

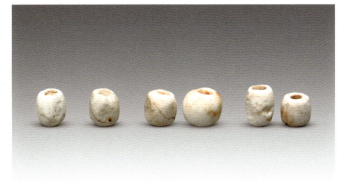

Picture 302. Jade beads (M8:12, 16, 20, 38)　　　Picture 303. Jade beads (M8:15, 19)

Picture 304. Jade particles (M8:13)

Picture 308. Cylindrical stone object
with cover (M8:2-1)

Picture 309. Cylindrical stone object
with cover (M8:2)

Picture 305. Jade particles (M8:36)

Picture 306. Stone tube with narrow
middle part (M8:4)

M8

Picture 307. Stone tube with narrow
middle part (M8:5)

Picture 310. Stone *yue* axe (M8:21)

M9

Picture 311. Tomb M9

Picture 312.
Crown-shaped jade object (M9:6)

Picture 313.
Cylindrical jade object with cover
(M9:1)

M9

Picture 314. Cylindrical jade object with cover (cover)
(M9:1-1)

Picture 315. Cylindrical jade object with cover
(cylindrical object) (M9:1-2)

Picture 316. Three-pronged jade object (M9:2)

Picture 317. Three-pronged jade object (M9:2)

Picture 318. Long jade tube (M9:3)

Picture 319. Long jade tube (M9:28)

Picture 320. Long jade tube (M9:29)

M9

Picture 321. Jade tube with carved
patterns (M9:5)

Picture 322. Jade *yue* axe (M9:14)

Picture 323. Awl-shaped jade object (M9:7)

Picture 324. Awl-shaped jade object (M9:8)

Picture 325. Awl-shaped jade object (M9:9)

M9

Picture 326. Awl-shaped jade object (M9:10)

Picture 327. Awl-shaped jade objects (M9:17–19)

Picture 328. Jade *cong* (M9:4)

Picture 329. The details of jade *cong* (M9:4)

Picture 330. *Cong*-stylistic jade tube (M9:11)

Picture 331. *Cong*-stylistic jade tube (M9:12)

Picture 332. *Cong*-stylistic jade tube (M9:49)

Picture 333. *Cong*-stylistic jade tube (M9:11, 12)

Picture 334. *Cong*-stylistic jade tube (M9:72)

Picture 335. *Cong*-stylistic jade tube (M9:50)

Picture 336. Jade bracelet (M9:41)

M9

Picture 337. Cylindrical jade object (M9:35)

Picture 338. Cylindrical jade object (M9:36)

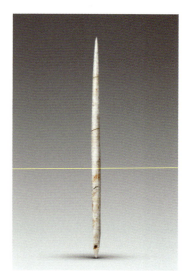

Picture 339. Awl-shaped jade object (M9:40)

Picture 340. Jade plaque object (M9:68)

Picture 341. Jade plaque object (M9:68)

Picture 342. Bar-shaped jade ornament (M9:57)

M9

Picture 343. String of jade tubes (M9:48)

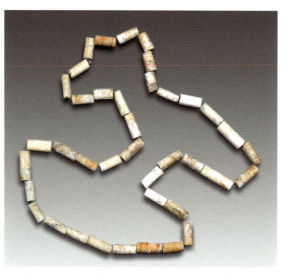

Picture 344. String of jade tubes (M9:31)

Picture 345. String of jade tubes (M9:66)

Picture 346. String of jade tubes (M9:70)

Picture 349. Jade tubes (M9:15, 65)

Picture 350. Jade tubes (M9:22, 23, 25, 27, 39, 56)

Picture 347. String of jade tubes (M9:71)

Picture 351. Jade tubes (M9:37, 38, 44, 45, 52)

M9

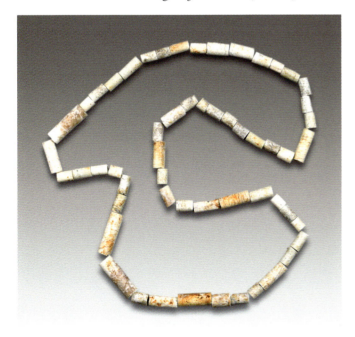

Picture 348. String of jade tubes (M9:77)

Picture 352. Jade tubes (M9:53–55, 63, 76)

Picture 353. Jade tubes (M9:58–61, 64)

Picture 354. Jade tubes (M9:67, 69, 73, 16, 21)

Picture 355. Jade tube (M9:74)

Picture 356. Jade beads (M9:24, 26)

Picture 357. Jade tube (M9:75)

Picture 358. Jade beads (M9:42, 43)

Picture 360. Jade particles (M9:30)

M9

Picture 359. Jade particles (M9:20)

Picture 361. Jade particles (M9:30)

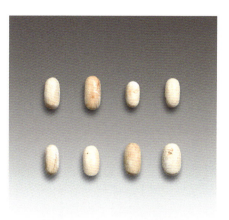

Picture 362. Jade particles (M9:32, 34)

Picture 363. Jade particle (M9:33)

Picture 364. Jade particles (M9:46)

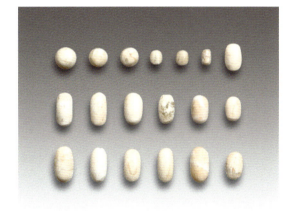

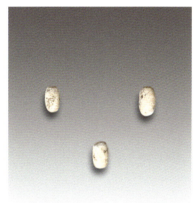

Picture 365. Jade particles (M9:47)

Picture 366. Jade particles (M9:51)

Picture 367. Jade particles (M9:62)

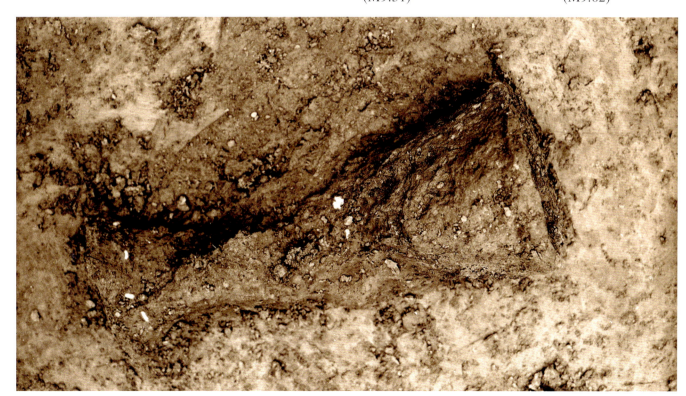

M9

Picture 368. Jade inlaid lacquer cup (M9:78) when unearthed

Picture 369. Stone *yue* axe (M9:13)

Picture 370. Pottery *ding* (M9:79)

M9

Picture 371. Pottery *dou* (M9:80)

Picture 372. Pottery *gang* (M9:82)

M10

Picture 373. Tomb M10

Picture 374. Burial objects in central part of tomb M10 when unearthed

M10

Picture 375. Three-pronged jade object and set of awl-shaped objects in tomb M10 when unearthed

Picture 376. Crown-shaped jade object (M10:4)

M10

Picture 377. Cylindrical jade object with cover (cover) (M10:2-1)

Picture 378. Cylindrical jade object with cover (cylindrical object) (M10:2-2)

Picture 379. Three-pronged jade object (M10:6)

M10

Picture 380. Three-pronged jade object (M10:6) (details)

Picture 381. Set of awl-shaped jade objects (M10:5-1–5-11)

M10

Picture 382. Jade *cong* (M10:15)

Picture 383. Jade *yue* axe (M10:14)

M10

Picture 384. Cylindrical jade object (M10:1)

Picture 385. Jade *cong* (M10:16)

Picture 386. Jade *cong* (M10:19)

Picture 387. Cylindrical jade object (M10:17)　　　　Picture 388. Cylindrical jade object (M10:34)

Picture 389. Cylindrical jade
object (M10:23)

Picture 390. Cylindrical jade object
(M10:32)

Picture 391. Cylindrical jade
object (M10:33)

M10

Picture 392. Cylindrical jade object (M10:38)　　　　Picture 393. Cylindrical jade object (M10:90)

Picture 395. Long jade tube (M10:37)

Picture 396. Long jade tube (M10:53)

Picture 397. Jade bracelet (M10:3)

Picture 394. Long jade tube (M10:21)

Picture 398. Jade bracelet (M10:28)

Picture 399. Jade bracelet (M10:26)

M10

Picture 400. Jade bracelet (M10:27)

Picture 401. Jade bracelet (M10:29)

Picture 402. Jade bracelet (M10:30)

Picture 406. Jade end ornament (M10:24)

Picture 403. Jade bracelet (M10:31)

Picture 407. Semi-circular jade ornament (M10:42)

M10

Picture 404. Jade end ornament (M10:18)

Picture 408. Semi-circular jade ornament (M10:42)

Picture 405. Jade end ornament (M10:18)

Picture 409. Semi-circular jade ornament (M10:43)

Picture 410. Semi-circular jade ornament (M10:44)

Picture 414. Semi-circular jade ornament (M10:99)

Picture 411. Semi-circular jade ornament (M10:44)

Picture 415. Crescent jade ornament (M10:46)

Picture 412. Semi-circular jade ornament (M10:45)

Picture 416. Crescent jade ornament (M10:46)

M10

Picture 413. Semi-circular jade ornament (M10:48)

Picture 417. Crescent jade ornament (M10:47)

Picture 418. Jade plaque (M10:20) (front side)

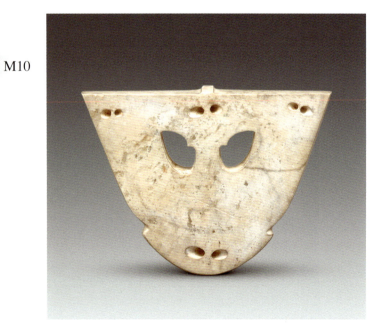

Picture 419. Jade plaque (M10:20) (back side)

Picture 420. Jade plaque (M10:20)

Picture 421. Ring-shaped jade ornament (M10:22)

Picture 422. String of jade tubes (M10:61)

Picture 423. Bar-shaped jade ornament (M10:25)

Picture 424. Bullet-shaped jade ornament (M10:67)

Picture 425. Bullet-shaped jade ornament (M10:70)

M10

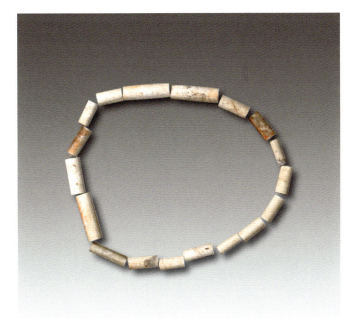

Picture 426. String of jade tubes (M10:49)

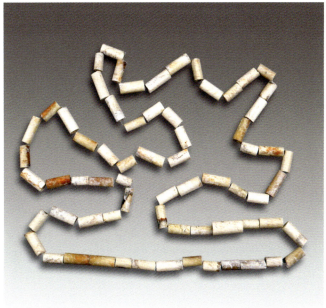

Picture 427. String of jade tubes (M10:63)

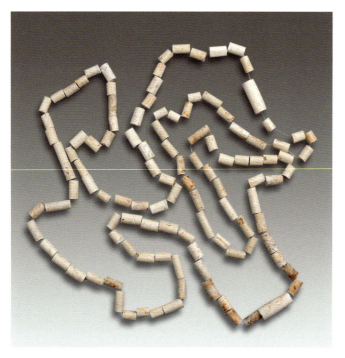

Picture 428. String of jade tubes (M10:65)

Picture 429. String of jade tubes (M10:97)

Picture 430. Jade tube (M10:36)

Picture 431. Jade tubes (M10:39, 40, 57, 60, 66)

M10

Picture 432. Jade tubes (M10:51)

Picture 433. Jade tubes (M10:101, 102, 59, 41, 74, 93)

Picture 434. Jade tube (M10:52)

Picture 435. Jade tubes (M10:54, 56, 58)

Picture 436. Jade tube (M10:55)

Picture 437. Jade tubes (M10:62)

Picture 438. Jade tubes (M10:68, 69, 71, 72, 75)

Picture 439. Jade tubes (M10:76–79)

M10

Picture 440. Jade tubes (M10:80, 81, 86, 87, 91)

Picture 441. Jade tube (M10:88)

Picture 442. Jade tubes (M10:104)

Picture 443. Jade tubes (M10:85, 106)

Picture 444. Jade
bead (M10:12)

Picture 445. Jade
bead (M10:10)

Picture 446. Jade
bead (M10:105)

Picture 447. Jade beads (M10:11, 9)

Picture 449. Jade beads (M10:35, 64)

M10

Picture 448. Stone *yue* axe (M10:8)

Picture 450. Jade bead (M10:50)

Picture 451. Jade beads (M10:94, 100, 103)

Picture 452. Pottery *dou* (M10:82)

Picture 454. Jade particles (M10:7)

Picture 455. Jade particles (M10:95)

Picture 456. Jade particles (M10:96)

Picture 453. Stone *yue* axe (M10:13)

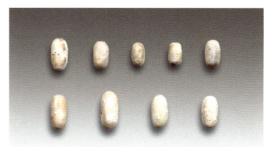

Picture 457. Jade particles (M10:98)

M10

Picture 458. Jade particles (M10:107)

M11

Picture 459. Tomb M11

Picture 460.
Burial objects in central part of tomb M11 when unearthed

Picture 461. Jade bracelet in tomb M11 when unearthed

Picture 462. Jade *huang* semi-circular pendant and string of tubes in tomb M11 when unearthed

Picture 463. Jade spindle whorl in tomb M11 when unearthed

Picture 464. Jade *huang* semi-circular pendant (M11:84)

Picture 465. Jade *huang* semi-circular pendant (M11:83)

Picture 466. Crown-shaped jade object (M11:86)

Picture 467. Crown-shaped jade object (M11:86)

Picture 468. Cylindrical jade object with cover (cover) (M11:89-1)

Picture 469. Cylindrical jade object with cover (cylindrical object) (M11:89-2)

Picture 470. Jade *huang* semi-circular pendant (M11:94)

Picture 471. Jade *huang* semi-circular pendant (M11:94)

M11

Picture 472. Jade *huang* semi-circular pendant (M11:54)

Picture 473. Round jade plaque (M11:53-1)

Picture 474. Round jade plaque (M11:53-2)

Picture 475. Round jade plaque (M11:53-3)

Picture 476. Round jade plaque (M11:53-4)

Picture 477. Round jade plaque (M11:56)

M11

Picture 478. Round jade plaque (M11:55)

Picture 479. Round jade plaque (M11:55)

Picture 480. Round jade plaque (M11:57)

Picture 481. Round jade plaque (M11:58)

Picture 482. Round jade plaque (M11:59)　　　Picture 483. Round jade plaque (M11:59)

Picture 484. Round jade plaque
(M11:62)

Picture 485. Round jade plaque
(M11:60)

Picture 486. Round jade plaque
(M11:61)

M11

Picture 487. Round jade plaque
(M11:43)

Picture 488. Jade bracelet
(M11:52)

Picture 489. Jade bracelet
(M11:66)

Picture 490. Jade bracelet (M11:42)

Picture 491. Jade bracelet (M11:65)

Picture 492. Jade bracelet (M11:67)

Picture 493. Jade bracelet (M11:68)

Picture 494. Jade bracelet (M11:69)

Picture 495. Jade bracelet (M11:70)

M11

Picture 496. Jade bracelet (M11:71)

Picture 497. Cylindrical jade object (M11:63)

Picture 498. Cylindrical jade object (M11:64)

Picture 499. Cylindrical jade object (M11:85)

Picture 500. Cylindrical jade object (M11:88)

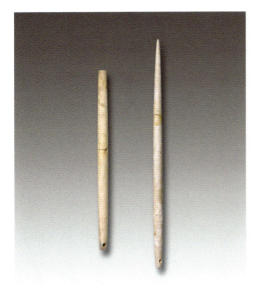

Picture 501. Awl-shaped jade objects
(M11:44, 75)

Picture 502. Long jade tube
(M11:20)

Picture 503. Jade handle
(M11:72)

Picture 504. Jade handle (M11:15)

Picture 505. Jade handle (M11:72)

M11

Picture 506. Jade spindle whorl and shaft (M11:16)

Picture 507. Bullet-shaped jade ornaments (M11:30)

Picture 508. Jade tube with carved
patterns (M11:73-1)

Picture 509. Jade tube with carved
patterns (M11:73-2)

Picture 510. Jade pendant
(M11:24)

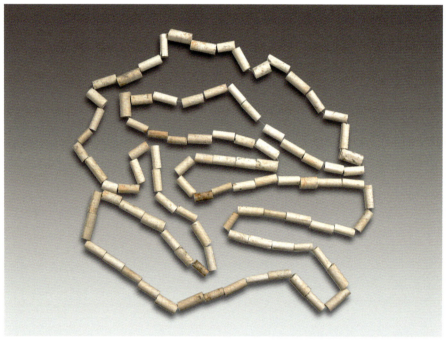

Picture 511.
String of jade tubes (M11:76)

M11

Picture 512.
String of jade tubes (M11:77)

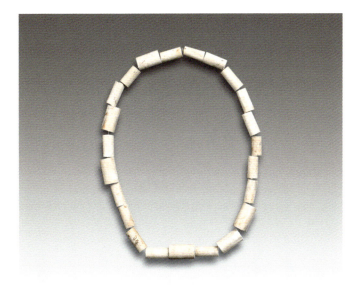

Picture 513. String of jade tubes (M11:95)

Picture 516. Petal-shaped jade ornaments (M11:81)

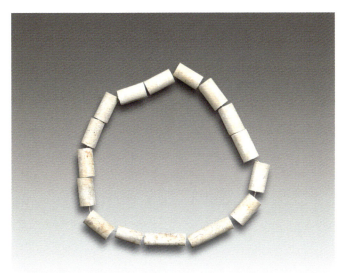

Picture 514. String of jade tubes (M11:96)

Picture 517. Petal-shaped jade ornaments (M11:82)

Picture 515. String of jade beads (M11:78)

Picture 518. Petal-shaped jade ornament (M11:82)
(back side )

Picture 519. Jade end ornament
(M11:3)

Picture 520. Jade end ornament
(M11:3)

Picture 521. Jade tubes
(M11:79, 1)

Picture 522. Jade tubes (M11:2, 5, 8, 12, 14, 4, 6, 21, 26)

M11

Picture 523. Jade tubes (M11:27, 11)

Picture 524. Jade tubes (M11:29, 31–33)

Picture 525. Jade tubes (M11:34, 37, 38, 40)

Picture 526. Jade tubes (M11:41, 90–92)

Picture 527. Jade tubes (M11:74)

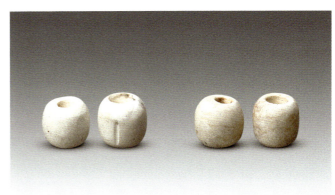

Picture 528. Jade beads (M11:7, 46)

Picture 529. Jade beads (M11:28, 87)

Picture 530. Jade particle (M11:23)

Picture 531. Jade beads (M11:35, 39, 93)

Picture 532. Jade particles (M11:17)

M11

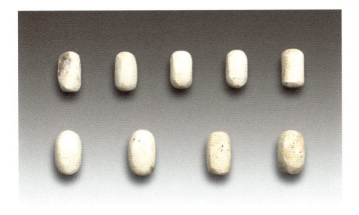

Picture 533. Jade particles (M11:18)

Picture 534. Jade particles (M11:25)

Picture 535. Jade particles (M11:80)

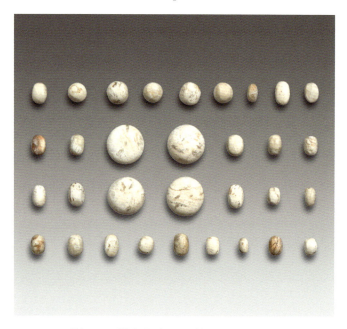

M11

Picture 536. Jade particles (M11:36)

Picture 537. Turquoise beads (M11:19, 22)

Picture 538. Pottery *zeng* (M11:47)

Picture 539. Pottery *ding* (M11:48)

Picture 540. Pottery *ding* (M11:10)

M14

Picture 541. Tomb M14

Picture 542. Crown-shaped jade object (M14:10)

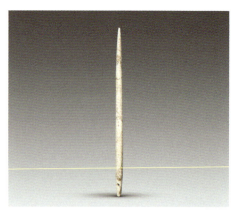

Picture 543. Awl-shaped jade object (M14:37)

Picture 544. Jade *huang* semi-circular pendant (M14:25)

Picture 545. Jade bracelet (M14:36)

M14

Picture 546. Jade bracelet (M14:39)

Picture 547. Round jade plaque (M14:23)

Picture 548. Petal-shaped jade ornaments (M14:34, 35, 38)

Picture 549. Jade beads (M14:11, 12)

Picture 550. Jade tubes (M14:1–5)

Picture 551. Jade tubes (M14:6–9, 13)

Picture 552. Jade tubes (M14:14, 15, 18–20)

Picture 553. Jade tubes (M14:16, 17, 22, 32, 33)

M14

Picture 554. Jade tubes (M14:21, 24, 26–28)

Picture 555. Jade tubes (M14:29–31, 40)

Picture 556. Jade tubes (M14:41, 51, 52)

Picture 557. Jade tubes (M14:42–45, 50)

Picture 558. Crown-shaped jade object (2850)

Picture 559. Cylindrical jade object with cover (cover) (2853)

Picture 560. Cylindrical jade object with cover (cylindrical object) (2854)

Picture 561. Three-pronged jade object (2807)

Collected artifacts

Picture 562. Semi-circular jade ornament (2806-1)

Picture 563. Semi-circular jade ornament (2806-2)

Picture 564. Semi-circular jade ornament (2806-3)

Picture 565. Semi-circular jade ornament (2806-4)

Picture 566. Awl-shaped jade object (2816)

Picture 567. Awl-shaped jade object (2817)

Picture 568. Awl-shaped jade object (2818)

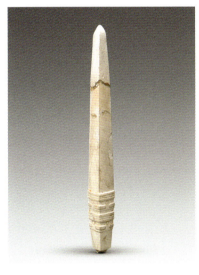

Picture 569. Awl-shaped jade object (2819)

Picture 570. Awl-shaped jade object (2820) and details

Collected artifacts

Picture 571. Awl-shaped jade object (2821)

Picture 572. Awl-shaped jade object (2822)

Picture 573. Awl-shaped jade object (2823)

Picture 574. Awl-shaped jade object (2824)

Picture 575. Jade *cong* (2784)

Picture 576. Jade *cong* (2785)

Picture 577. Jade *cong* (2786)

Picture 578. Jade *cong* (2787)

Picture 579. Jade *cong* (2788)

Picture 580. Jade *cong* (2789)

Picture 581. Jade *yue* axe (2792)

Picture 582. *Cong*-stylistic jade tube (2825)

Picture 583. Awl-shaped jade object (3050)

Picture 584. Jade end ornament (2794)

Picture 585. Jade end ornament (2797)

Picture 586. Jade end ornament (2838)

Picture 587. Jade end ornament (2838)

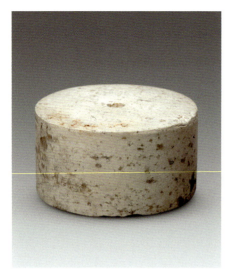

Picture 588. Cylindrical jade object
(2798)

Picture 589. Cylindrical jade object
(2799-1)

Picture 590. Cylindrical jade object
(2799-2)

Picture 591. Cylindrical jade object
(2800-1)

Picture 592. Cylindrical jade object
(2800-2)

Picture 593. Cylindrical jade object
(2800-3)

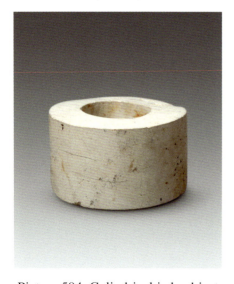

Picture 594. Cylindrical jade object
(2801)

Picture 595. Cylindrical jade object
(2803)

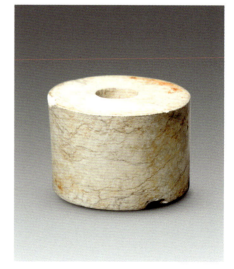

Picture 596. Cylindrical jade object
(2804)

Collected
artifacts

Picture 597. Jade tubes with carved patterns
(2826-1–2826-4)

Picture 598. Jade tubes with carved patterns
(2826-5–2826-8)

Picture 599. Jade tube with carved
patterns (2826-1)

Picture 600. Jade tube with carved
patterns (2826-14)

Picture 601. Jade tube with carved
patterns (2826-16)

Picture 602. Jade tubes with carved patterns
(2826-9–2826-12)

Picture 603. Jade tubes with carved patterns
(2826-13–2826-16)

Picture 604. Jade tubes with carved patterns
(2826-17–2826-20)

Picture 605. Jade tubes with carved patterns
(2826-21–2826-24)

Picture 606. Jade tube with
carved patterns (2826-17)

Picture 607. Jade tube with
carved patterns (2826-24)

Picture 608. Jade tubes with carved patterns
(2826-25–2826-28)

Picture 609. Jade tube with
carved patterns (2826-30)

Picture 610. Jade tube with
carved patterns (2826-31)

Picture 611. Jade tubes with carved patterns
(2826-29–2826-32)

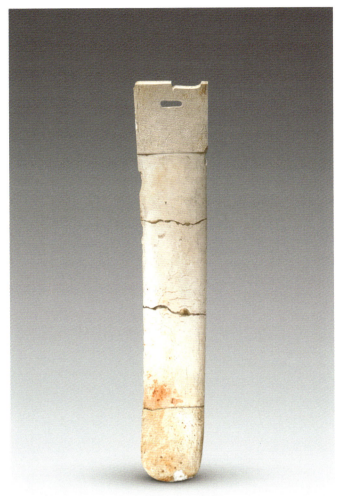

Picture 612. Dagger-shaped jade artifact (2837)

Picture 614. Jade spoon (2836)

Picture 613. Patterns on dagger-shaped jade artifact
(2837)

Picture 615. Patterns on jade spoon (2836)

Picture 616. Long jade tube (2795)

Picture 617. Jade stand (2793)

Collected artifacts

Picture 618. Long jade tube (2808)

Picture 619. Crown-shaped jade object (3048)

Picture 620. Cylindrical jade object with cover (cover) (2805)

Picture 621. Set of awl-shaped jade objects (2863-1–2863-5, 2863-7, 2863-8)

Picture 622. Three-pronged jade object (2851)

Picture 623. Jade *cong* (2842)

Picture 624. Jade *cong* (2841)

Picture 625. Jade *cong* (2844)

Picture 626. Jade *cong* (2845)

Picture 627. Jade *yue* axe (2840)

Picture 628. Jade *yue* axe (3047)

Picture 629. *Cong*-stylistic jade tube (2846)

Picture 630. *Cong*-stylistic jade tube (2847)

Picture 631. *Cong*-stylistic jade tube (2848)

Picture 632. *Cong*-stylistic jade tube (2849)

Collected
artifacts

Picture 633. Awl-shaped jade object (2815)

Picture 634. Awl-shaped jade object (2827)

Picture 635. Awl-shaped jade object (2863)

Picture 636. Jade pendant (3051)

Picture 637. Cylindrical jade object (2855)

Picture 638. Jade end ornament (2780)

Picture 639. Jade end ornament (2856)

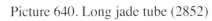

Picture 640. Long jade tube (2852)

Picture 641. Jade Bracelet (2779)

Picture 642. Long jade tube (2858)

Collected
artifacts

Picture 643. Stone *yue* axe (2868)

Picture 644. Stone *yue* axe (2869)

Picture 645. Stone *yue* axe (3046)

Collected
artifacts

Picture 646. Round jade plaque (M11:60) and
the string-cutting marks on it

Picture 647. The notch on the round jade plaque (M5:8)
and the string-cutting marks on it

Picture 648. The end surface of jade tube (M3:11) and
the string-cutting marks on it

Picture 649. Jade *yue* axe (M11:12) and
the blade-cutting marks on the top